JOURNAL FOR THE STUDY OF THE NEW TESTAMENT
SUPPLEMENT SERIES
189

Executive Editor
Stanley E. Porter

Sheffield Academic Press

The Old Testament in the New Testament

Essays in Honour of J.L. North

edited by
Steve Moyise

Journal for the Study of the New Testament
Supplement Series 189

Copyright © 2000 Sheffield Academic Press

Published by
Sheffield Academic Press Ltd
Mansion House
19 Kingfield Road
Sheffield S11 9AS
England

Typeset by Sheffield Academic Press
and
Printed on acid-free paper in Great Britain
by Biddles Ltd
Guildford, Surrey

British Library Cataloguing in Publication Data

A catalogue record for this book is available
from the British Library

ISBN 1-84127-061-X

CONTENTS

This collection of essays marks the retirement of Lionel North from his position as New Testament lecturer at Hull University (1980–99) and his seventeen-year chairmanship of 'The Use of the Old Testament in the New Testament' seminar, held latterly in Hawarden, North Wales. Its production involved a little subterfuge, as Lionel was under the impression that we were producing a set of essays in celebration of the seminar. It was on that basis that he agreed to write a short history of it, which appears as an epilogue to this volume. In that piece, Lionel charts the origins of the seminar, first as an interest group of the Studiorum Novi Testamenti Societas (SNTS), and then as a separate annual meeting under the leadership of Anthony Hanson and Max Wilcox. The contributors to this volume are all or have been members of the seminar and wish to register their thanks for the friendly and stimulating way that Lionel has led it. In lexical and text-critical matters, Lionel's expertise is formidable. As chair of the seminar, he ensured that rigorous debate was always constructive and conducted with courtesy. Many of us can point to articles and monographs that were first given an airing at the seminar and emerged in published form all the better for it. Unfortunately, not all who would have liked to contribute to this volume were able to do so. In particular, Max Wilcox joins us in wishing Lionel (and Wendy) a happy retirement.

Steve Moyise

AB	Anchor Bible
ABD	David Noel Freedman (ed.), *The Anchor Bible Dictionary* (New York: Doubleday, 1992)
AnBib	Analecta biblica
ANRW	Hidegard Temporini and Wolfgang Haase (eds.), *Aufstieg und Niedergang der römischen Welt: Geschichte und Kultur Roms im Spiegel der neueren Forschung* (Berlin: W. de Gruyter, 1972–)
AUSS	*Andrews University Seminary Studies*
BAGD	Walter Bauer, William F. Arndt, F. William Gingrich and Frederick W. Danker, *A Greek–English Lexicon of the New Testament and Other Early Christian Literature* (Chicago: University of Chicago Press, 2nd edn, 1958)
BDF	Friedrich Blass, A. Debrunner and Robert W. Funk, *A Greek Grammar of the New Testament and Other Early Christian Literature* (Cambridge: Cambridge University Press, 1961)
BETL	Bibliotheca ephemeridum theologicarum lovaniensium
BFCT	Beiträge zur Förderung christlicher Theologie
Bib	*Biblica*
BibRes	*Biblical Research*
BJRL	*Bulletin of the John Rylands University Library of Manchester*
BKAT	Biblischer Kommentar: Altes Testament
BNTC	Black's New Testament Commentaries
BSac	*Bibliotheca Sacra*
BWANT	Beiträge zur Wissenschaft vom Alten und Neuen Testament
BZ	*Biblische Zeitschrift*
BZAW	Beihefte zur *ZAW*
BZNW	Beihefte zur *ZNW*
CBQ	*Catholic Biblical Quarterly*
ConBNT	Coniectanea biblica, New Testament
CRBS	*Currents in Research: Biblical Studies*
EBib	Etudes bibliques
EKKNT	Evangelisch-Katholischer Kommentar zum Neuen Testament
EstBíb	*Estudios bíblicos*
ETL	*Ephemerides theologicae lovanienses*
EvQ	*Evangelical Quarterly*

ExpTim	*Expository Times*
FRLANT	Forschungen zur Religion und Literatur des Alten und Neuen Testaments
FzB	Forschung zur Bibel
GKC	*Gesenius' Hebrew Grammar* (ed. E. Kautzsch, revised and trans. A.E. Cowley; Oxford: Clarendon Press, 1910)
HDR	Harvard Dissertations in Religion
HKNT	Handkommentar zum Neuen Testament
HTKNT	Herders theologischer Kommentar zum Neuen Testament
HTR	*Harvard Theological Review*
IBS	*Irish Biblical Studies*
ICC	International Critical Commentary
Int	*Interpretation*
JAAR	*Journal of the American Academy of Religion*
JBL	*Journal of Biblical Literature*
JETS	*Journal of the Evangelical Theological Society*
JJS	*Journal of Jewish Studies*
JSNT	*Journal for the Study of the New Testament*
JSNTSup	*Journal for the Study of the New Testament*, Supplement Series
JSOTSup	*Journal for the Study of the Old Testament*, Supplement Series
JTS	*Journal of Theological Studies*
KNT	Kommentar zum Neuen Testament
LSJ	H.G. Liddell, Robert Scott and H. Stuart Jones, *Greek–English Lexicon* (Oxford: Clarendon Press, 9th edn, 1968)
MHT	J.H. Moulton, W.F. Howard and M. Turner, *A Grammar of New Testament Greek* (4 vols.; Edinburgh: T. & T. Clark, 1906–76)
MNTC	Moffatt NT Commentary
NCB	New Century Bible
Neot	*Neotestamentica*
NICNT	New International Commentary on the New Testament
NIGTC	The New International Greek Testament Commentary
NovT	*Novum Testamentum*
NovTSup	*Novum Testamentum*, Supplements
NRT	*La nouvelle revue théologique*
NTAbh	Neutestamentliche Abhandlungen
NTS	*New Testament Studies*
OBO	Orbis biblicus et orientalis
OTP	James Charlesworth (ed.), *Old Testament Pseudepigrapha*
RB	*Revue biblique*
RevQ	*Revue de Qumran*
RivB	*Rivista biblica*
SBLSCS	SBL Septuagint and Cognate Studies
SBLSP	SBL Seminar Papers

SBT	Studies in Biblical Theology
SJT	*Scottish Journal of Theology*
SNT	Studien zum Neuen Testament
SNTSMS	Society for New Testament Studies Monograph Series
Str-B	[Hermann L. Strack and] Paul Billerbeck, *Kommentar zum Neuen Testament aus Talmud und Midrasch* (7 vols.; Munich: Beck, 1922–61)
SVTP	Studia in Veteris Testamenti pseudepigrapha
TDNT	Gerhard Kittel and Gerhard Friedrich (eds.), *Theological Dictionary of the New Testament* (trans. Geoffrey W. Bromiley; 10 vols.; Grand Rapids: Eerdmans, 1964–)
TDOT	G.J. Botterweck and H. Ringgren (eds.), *Theological Dictionary of the Old Testament*
TLG	*Thesaurus Linguae Graecae*
TSAJ	Texte und Studien zum Antiken Judentum
TU	Texte und Untersuchungen
TynBul	*Tyndale Bulletin*
TZ	*Theologische Zeitschrift*
UBSGNT	United Bible Societies' *Greek New Testament*
VT	*Vetus Testamentum*
VTSup	*Vetus Testamentum*, Supplements
WBC	Word Biblical Commentary
WTJ	*Westminster Theological Journal*
WUNT	Wissenschaftliche Untersuchungen zum Neuen Testament
ZNW	*Zeitschrift für die neutestamentliche Wissenschaft*

LIST OF CONTRIBUTORS

David Instone Brewer, Research Fellow, Tyndale House, Cambridge

Maurice Casey, Professor of New Testament Languages and Literature, University of Nottingham

Peter Doble, Department of Theology and Religious Studies, University of Leeds

Crispin H.T. Fletcher-Louis, Durham University

Michael Goulder, Emeritus Professor of Biblical Studies at the University of Birmingham

Morna D. Hooker, Lady Margaret's Professor Emerita in the University of Cambridge and Fellow of Robinson College Cambridge

Ivor H. Jones, Formerly Principal of Wesley House, Cambridge, now a retired Methodist Minister in Lincoln

Judith Lieu, Department of Theology and Religious Studies, Kings College, London

Maarten J.J. Menken, Professor of New Testament, Catholic Theological University, Utrecht, The Netherlands

Steve Moyise, Senior Lecturer in Theology, University College, Chichester

J. Lionel North, formerly Barmby Senior Lecturer in New Testament Studies, Department of Theology, University of Hull

Wendy E. Sproston North, formerly Department of Theology, University of Hull

J.C. O'Neill, Professor Emeritus of New Testament Language, Literature and Theology, New College, University of Edinburgh

Ian Paul, Curate at St Mary's Longfleet, Poole in the Anglican Diocese of Salisbury and Managing Editor of Grove Books

INTRODUCTION

INTERTEXTUALITY AND THE STUDY OF
THE OLD TESTAMENT IN THE NEW TESTAMENT

Steve Moyise

Introduction

Julia Kristeva is generally credited as the first to introduce the term 'intertextualité' into literary discussion in 1969. Drawing on the work of Bakhtin, Kristeva suggests a dialogical relationship between 'texts', broadly understood as a system of codes or signs. Moving away from traditional notions of agency and influence, she suggests that such relationships are more like an *'intersection of textual surfaces* rather than a *point* (a fixed meaning)'.[1] Even the specific act of embedding one text inside another (the theme of this volume) does not result in a single resolution—the two shall become one—but a range of interpretative possibilities. The embedded text might be a faint echo, which barely disturbs the primary text, or a clanging cymbal which demands attention. It is the task of the reader, in his or her pursuit of meaning and coherence, to somehow configure these different 'voices'. And that involves choice, vested interests, and hence ideology.

The term was brought to the attention of biblical scholars by two books published in 1989. The first was a collection of essays entitled *Intertextuality in Biblical Writings*, which contains both theoretical discussions and examples of biblical intertextuality. For Vorster, intertextuality differs from *Redaktionsgeschichte* in three significant ways:

---

1. 'Word, Dialogue and Novel' was written in 1966 and appeared in *Sémé-iotiké: Recherches pour une sémanalyse* (Paris: Le Sevil, 1969) in 1969. It was translated in L.S. Roudiez (ed.), *Desire and Language: A Semiotic Approach to Literature and Art* (New York: Columbia University Press, 1980), and is now found conveniently in T. Moi (ed.), *The Kristeva Reader* (New York: Columbia University Press, 1986). The quotation is taken from Moi (ed.), *Kristeva Reader*, p. 36 (emphasis original).

> First of all it is clear that the phenomenon text has been redefined. It has become a network of references to other texts (intertexts). Secondly it appears that more attention is to be given to text as a process of production and not to the sources and their influences. And thirdly it is apparent that the role of the reader is not to be neglected in this approach to the phenomenon of text.[2]

The other book was *Echoes of Scripture in the Letters of Paul*, by Richard Hays. Hays does not mention Kristeva but draws on Hollander's work, *The Figure of Echo: A Mode of Allusion in Milton and After*.[3] Hays is impressed by the subtlety of Hollander's analysis and asks why this has not always been the case with biblical scholars. He attempts to put this right in a number of highly regarded studies on Paul, claiming that 'the most significant elements of intertextual correspondence between old context and new can be implicit rather than voiced, perceptible only within the silent space framed by the juncture of two texts'.[4]

Ten years on, the word 'intertextuality' has become common coinage among biblical scholars. Critics who once spoke of 'sources' now speak of an author's intertextual use of traditions. In George Buchanan's *Introduction to Intertextuality*,[5] the word covers traditional source criticism, Jewish midrash, typology and what Fishbane called 'inner biblical exegesis'. Literary critics describing the complex texture of a work speak of its deep intertextuality (the words 'tapestry' or 'mosaic' are sometimes used). Reader-response critics use it to show that a text does not simply disclose its meaning. What the reader brings to the text (the reader's own intertexts) has an effect on the reading process. Thus first century Christians reading the LXX were bound to import new meanings into old texts. Imagine what it must have been like to find χριστός and εὐαγγελίζω appearing in the ancient texts.

All this is good in the sense that scholars now realise that a text cannot be studied in isolation. It belongs to a web of texts which are

---

2. W. Vorster, 'Intertextuality and Redaktionsgeschichte', in S. Draisma (ed.), *Intertextuality in Biblical Writings* (Festschrift B. van Iersel; Kampen: Kok, 1989), p. 21.

3. J. Hollander, *The Figure of Echo: A Mode of Allusion in Milton and After* (Berkeley: University of California Press, 1981).

4. R.B. Hays, *Echoes of Scripture in the Letters of Paul* (New Haven: Yale University Press, 1989), p. 155.

5. G.W. Buchanan, *Introduction to Intertextuality* (Lewiston, NY: Edwin Mellen Press, 1994).

(partially) present whenever it is read or studied. And the way that a text has been interpreted down the ages is not irrelevant. It reveals something of the *potentiality* of the text, even if it cannot be shown that a particular interpretation was present in the mind of the author (can it ever?). These are positive gains from the use of the term intertextuality. But there is a down-side. The frequent use of the term is threatening to blunt the scholarly enterprise by lumping together a whole variety of approaches and calling them intertextuality. Even worse, it can sometimes be used to make vague and tenuous 'echoes' sound more credible. As a result, Porter suggests that the term is unhelpful and is best dropped from scholarly discussion.[6] However, the same criticisms can be levelled at terms like 'midrash', 'typology' and 'exegesis', all of which have been used to defend 'uses' of the Old Testament which might otherwise appear arbitrary. Indeed, the title of this volume of essays is quite deliberate. I chose *The Old Testament in the New Testament* to avoid the implication that our only interest is in an author's 'use' of the Old Testament. As Bruns says, 'We need to get out from under the model of methodical solipsism that pictures a solitary reader exercising strategic power over a text'.[7] The relationship between texts is never just one way. As Miscall notes, the

> relationship between two texts is equivocal. It includes, at the same time, both acceptance and rejection, recognition and denial, understanding and misunderstanding... To recognize that a text is related to another text is both to affirm and to deny the earlier text. It is affirmed as a type of model and source, while it is denied by being made secondary to the later text, precisely by being regarded as a model and a source that has been superseded.[8]

6.   S.E. Porter, 'The Use of the Old Testament in the New Testament: A Brief Comment on Method and Terminology', in Craig A. Evans and James A. Sanders (eds.), *Early Christian Interpretation of the Scriptures of Israel: Investigations and Proposals* (JSNTSup, 148; Studies in Scripture in Early Judaism and Christianity, 5; Sheffield: Sheffield Academic Press, 1997), pp. 79-96. Vernon Robbins says that the 'current terminology of "intertextuality" collapses three arenas of analysis and interpretation together in a manner that is confusing' (*The Tapestry of Early Christian Discourse: Rhetoric, Society and Ideology* [London: Routledge, 1996], p. 33). I discuss his proposals in the final section of this essay.

7.   G.L. Bruns, 'The Hermeneutics of Midrash', in R. Schwartz (ed.), *The Book and the Text* (Oxford: Basil Blackwell, 1990), p. 192.

8.   P.D. Miscall, 'Isaiah: New Heavens, New Earth, New Book', in D.N. Fewell

The value of the term 'intertextuality' is that it evokes such complexity and openness.[9] However, if intertextuality is best used as an 'umbrella' term, then it requires subcategories to indicate the individual scholar's particular interest or focus. In this essay, I suggest three such categories. The first I call *Intertextual Echo*. It is the bread and butter of many 'Old Testament in the New' studies and aims to show that a particular allusion or echo can sometimes be more important than its 'volume' might suggest. As I have said elsewhere, it is not just the loudest instruments in the orchestra that give a piece its particular character. Sometimes, subtle allusions or echoes, especially if they are frequent and pervasive, can be more influential than explicit quotations.[10]

The second category I have called *Dialogical Intertextuality*. This is where the interaction between text and subtext is seen to operate in both directions. As Davidson says of Eliot's *The Waste Land*, 'The work alluded to reflects upon the present context even as the present context absorbs and changes the allusion'.[11] One of the frequently debated topics in 'Old Testament in the New' studies is whether the new authors show respect for the original context of their citations.[12] The issue arises because on the one hand, the early church wants to claim that Jesus' life and death is a fulfilment of Scripture (1 Cor. 15.3-4). On the other hand, it wants to claim that it is only in Christ that Scripture finds its true meaning (2 Cor. 3.15). Dialogical Intertextuality tries to do justice to both of these claims.

The third I have called *Postmodern Intertextuality*. Both of the above are aiming to secure meaning by defining (controlling) how a text interacts with a subtext. Dialogical Intertextuality acknowledges that this is

(ed.), *Reading between Texts: Intertextuality and the Hebrew Bible* (Louisville, KY: Westminster/John Knox Press, 1992), p. 44.

9. Miscall, 'Isaiah', p. 44: ' "Intertextuality" is a covering term for all the possible relations that can be established between texts'.

10. S. Moyise, *The Old Testament in the Book of Revelation* (JSNTSup, 115; Sheffield: Sheffield Academic Press, 1995), p. 18, and endorsed by R.M. Royalty, *The Streets of Heaven: The Ideology of Wealth in the Apocalypse of John* (Macon: Mercer University Press, 1998), p. 125 n. 1.

11. H. Davidson, *T.S. Eliot and Hermeneutics: Absence and Interpretation in the Waste Land* (Baton Rouge: Louisiana State University Press, 1985), p. 117.

12. S. Moyise, 'Does the New Testament Quote the Old Testament Out of Context?', *Anvil* 11 (1994), pp. 133-43; G.K. Beale (ed), *The Right Doctrine from the Wrong Texts? Essays on the Use of the Old Testament in the New* (Grand Rapids: Baker Book House, 1994).

not straightforward but nevertheless endeavours to find ways of describing the result of such interactions. Postmodern Intertextuality turns this on its head and shows how the process is inherently unstable. The fact that a text always points to other texts and a reader always brings texts they know to every reading, means that there is never *only* one way of interpreting a text. Postmodern Intertextuality aims to show that 'meaning' is always bought at a price and explores what that price is. In other words, meaning can only result if some interactions are privileged and others are silenced.

It is not the aim of this study to argue that one of these categories is the correct one. The postmodern variety is closer to what Kristeva had in mind but as stated above, the term is now used in biblical studies in a variety of ways. But it is hoped that this analysis might help authors clarify what sort of intertextuality they have in mind, so that readers can know what is being claimed and how best to respond to it.

Intertextual Echo

In his ground-breaking book, Hays speaks of intertextual echo in order to suggest that echoes can be quite loud if they reverberate in an echo chamber. Previous studies on the Old Testament in the New have often divided references into quotations, allusions and echoes. There is no agreed definitions but generally, a quotation involves a self-conscious break from the author's style to introduce words from another context. There is frequently an introductory formula like καθὼς γέγραπται or Μωϋσῆς λέγει, or some grammatical clue such as the use of ὅτι. Next comes allusion, usually woven into the text rather than 'quoted', and often rather less precise in terms of wording. Naturally, there is considerable debate as to how much verbal agreement is necessary to establish the presence of an allusion.[13] Lastly comes echo, faint traces of texts

---

13. Hays proposes seven tests: availability, volume, recurrence, thematic coherence, historical plausibility, history of interpretation and satisfaction. These are useful guidelines to bear in mind but it would be wrong to think that they act as 'objective' criteria. Rigorous historical enquiry might clarify 'availability' (could it have been known?) and 'historical interpretation' (has it been seen before?) but most of the others are subjective judgments. Indeed, Hays recognizes this: 'Although the foregoing text are serviceable rules of thumb to guide our interpretive work, we must acknowledge that there will be exceptional occasions when the tests fail to

that are probably quite unconscious but emerge from minds soaked in the scriptural heritage of Israel.

It is not difficult to see why studies on the 'Old Testament in the New' have often focused on quotations. There is not usually much controversy as to the source text and the author is clearly 'intending' the reader to acknowledge the citation by drawing attention to it. However, if a subtext is well known, the slightest of allusions is sometimes sufficient to evoke its presence. A popular game show on television required contestants to guess the title of a piece of a music from its opening bars. Sometimes, the winner managed this from just two notes. Similarly, not many words are necessary to evoke Israel's Passover or Exile. The themes are so well known (and repeated liturgically) that a seemingly innocuous mention of 'doorposts' (in the appropriate language, of course) might well be sufficient. As Hays says of Paul's letters,

> Echoes linger in the air and lure the reader of Paul's letters back into the symbolic world of Scripture. Paul's allusions gesture toward precursors whose words are already heavy with tacit implication.[14]

Romans 8.20 and Ecclesiastes

In Paul's description of human depravity in Romans 1, those who did not acknowledge God 'became futile in their thinking' (v. 21). The Greek word is μάταιος, which Liddell and Scott define as 'vain, empty, idle, trifling, frivolous, thoughtless, rash, irreverent, profane, impious'.[15] Paul continues, 'Claiming to be wise, they became fools'. The same thought is found in 1 Cor. 3.20, where Paul quotes Ps. 94.11 in the form, 'The Lord knows the thoughts of the wise, that they are futile' (μάταιος). The wisdom of the world has not led to people believing in Christ and so from Paul's point of view, it is 'futile' (NRSV, NIV), 'worthless' (GNB), 'useless' (JB). Such contrasts between wise and foolish are of course frequent in the wisdom literature and appear in some of Jesus' parables. However, Paul goes further than this in Rom.

account for the spontaneous power of particular intertextual conjunctions. Despite all the careful hedges that we plant around texts, meaning has a way of leaping over, like sparks' (*Echoes of Scripture*, pp. 32-33).

14. Hays, *Echoes of Scripture*, p. 155.

15. H.G. Liddell and Robert Scott, *An Intermediate Greek–English Lexicon* (Oxford: Oxford University Press, 1987), p. 489.

8.20, where he claims that 'creation was subjected to futility' (ματαιότης). Lietzmann[16] thinks this is referring to cosmic powers but the
majority of commentators take ὑπετάγη to be a divine passive: Creation
was subjected to futility *by God*. Where did Paul get such a negative
idea from? If we are looking for a text, the most likely is the book of
Ecclesiastes, where the author says:

> I, the Teacher, when king over Israel in Jerusalem, applied my mind to
> seek and to search out by wisdom all that is done under heaven; it is an
> unhappy business that God has given to human beings to be busy with. I
> saw all the deeds that are done under the sun; and see, all is vanity and a
> chasing after wind (1.12-14).

The Hebrew word often translated as 'vanity', is הבל, frequently used
for the 'futility' or 'worthlessness' of idols (Deut. 32.21; 1 Kgs 16.13;
Ps. 31.6). Significantly, the LXX of Ecclesiastes renders this with
ματαιότης, the same word used by Paul in Rom. 8.20. And this is not
an isolated instance. The book of Ecclesiastes continues to survey the
activities of humankind and declares them all to be הבל. Not even
wisdom and righteousness escape his biting analysis. Thus in 2.15-16,
he concludes that 'there is no enduring remembrance of the wise or of
fools... So I hated life, because what is done under the sun was grievous
to me; for all is vanity and a chasing after wind.' And righteousness
fares no better. Grieved that 'there are righteous people who perish in
their righteousness, and there are wicked people who prolong their life
in their evildoing' (7.15), the author offers the following advice: 'Do
not be too righteous, and do not act too wise; why should you destroy
yourself?' (7.16).

Jerome was aware of rabbinic opposition to the book 'for the reason
that it affirms that the creatures of God are "vain", and considers the
whole (universe) to be as nothing'. Why then, he asks, was it 'included
in the number of divine volumes'? Because the last few verses proclaim
that the duty of everyone is to 'fear God, and keep his commandments'.
Thus 'it has from this one chapter acquired the merit of being received
as authoritative'.[17] In rabbinic terms, it was a dispute over whether the
book defiled the hands (that is, regarded as sacred). Thus Rabbi Simeon

16. Quoted in J.A. Fitzmyer, *Romans: A New Translation with Introduction and
Commentary* (AB, 33; London: Geoffrey Chapman, 1993), p. 507.
17. Quoted in A.P. Hayman 'Qohelet, the Rabbis and the Wisdom Text from the
Cairo Geniza', in A.G. Auld (ed.), *Understanding Poets and Prophets* (JSOTSup,
152; Sheffield: JSOT Press, 1994), p. 161.

b. Menasia said, 'The Song of Songs defiles the hands because it was composed under divine inspiration. Ecclesiastes does not defile the hands because it is only the wisdom of Solomon' (*Yad.* 2.14). The midrash on the book is a late composition but is testimony to the fact that the debate was not easily settled, observing that the 'sages sought to suppress the Book of Qohelet because they discovered therein words which savour of heresy' (*Qoh. R.* 1.3).

Few today would deny its canonical status but opinion about its fundamental message remains sharply divided. Crenshaw represents the critical strand when he declares that the author 'examines experience and discovers nothing that will survive death's arbitrary blow. He then proceeds to report this discovery of life's absurdity and to advise young men on the best option in the light of stark reality.'[18] On the other hand, there has recently been a concerted attempt to rescue Ecclesiastes from this negative image. Scholars such as Ogden[19] and Fredericks[20] claim that interpreters have been unduly influenced by the LXX's use of ματαιότης to render the Hebrew חבל and have largely ignored the positive statements in the book. For example, in 2.24 the claim is made that there is 'nothing better for mortals than to eat and drink, and find enjoyment in their toil. This also, I saw, is from the hand of God'. True, life is short and holds many surprises, but that is all the more reason to make the most of it. Thus 5.18 says, 'This is what I have seen to be good: it is fitting to eat and drink and find enjoyment in all the toil with which one toils under the sun the few days of the life God gives us; for this is our lot.'

Taking this as their point of departure, Ogden and Fredericks argue that חבל should not be rendered by words like 'futility' or 'vanity' but something like 'transitory'. As the epistle of James puts it, life is like a 'mist that appears for a little while and then vanishes' (4.14) but few have taken this to imply that life is futile. Likewise with Ecclesiastes. They acknowledge that outside the book, חבל is often associated with idols and hence 'futility' or 'vanity' is a suitable translation. But the positive commands to enjoyment in Ecclesiastes (2.24; 3.12; 3.22; 5.18; 8.15; 9.7; 11.9) make it unsuitable here. Thus Ogden claims that

18. J.L. Crenshaw, *Ecclesiastes* (OTL; London: SCM Press, 1988), p. 28.
19. G. Ogden, *Qoheleth* (Readings: A New Biblical Commentary; Sheffield: JSOT Press, 1993).
20. D.C. Fredericks, *Coping with Transience: Ecclesiastes on Brevity of Life* (The Biblical Seminar, 18; Sheffield: JSOT Press, 1993).

the term *hebel* in Qoheleth has a distinctive function and meaning: it conveys the notion that life is enigmatic, and mysterious; that there are many unanswered and unanswerable questions. The person of faith recognizes this fact but moves forward positively to claim and enjoy the life and the work which God apportions.[21]

Returning to Rom. 8.20, it is interesting that Paul's claim that 'creation was subjected to futility' has not met the resistance with which Ecclesiastes has had to face. For example, Barrett claims that, 'Paul would doubtless agree that the creation apart from Christ could have only an unreal existence'.[22] Nygren glosses over the word 'futility' and says that because of the curse of Gen. 3.17, the 'whole existence in which we are involved stands in bondage to corruption.'[23] Dodd draws a contrast to the state of humanity, which is our own fault, and the state of creation, which is 'by the will of God'. He adds that 'we cannot give any further answer to the question, Why?'[24] Dunn topically illustrates the meaning of ματαιότης as 'like an expensive satellite which has malfunctioned and now spins uselessly in space...or, more precisely, which has been given a role for which it was not designed and which is unreal or illusory'.[25]

Two factors seem to have led to this acquiescence. The first is that while there might be some doubt over the meaning of הבל, there is no such doubt about ματαιότης. Elsewhere in the New Testament, the word occurs in Eph. 4.17 ('you must no longer live as the Gentiles live, in the futility of their minds') and 2 Pet. 2.18 ('uttering loud boasts of folly' [RSV]). The verb occurs only once in the New Testament and that is Paul's statement in Rom. 1.21, that those who ignored God 'became futile in their thinking, and there senseless minds were darkened.' It is hard to decide whether Paul has been directly influenced by the ματαιότης of Ecclesiastes for it is generally recognised that the LXX text is post-Christian. But there is no doubt about his meaning; creation was subjected to futility (by God).

21. Ogden, *Qoheleth*, p. 22.

22. C.K. Barrett, *The Epistle to the Romans* (BNTC; London: A. & C. Black, 1962), p. 166.

23. A. Nygren, *Commentary on Romans* (Philadelphia: Fortress Press, 1949), p. 331.

24. C.H. Dodd, *The Epistle of Paul to the Romans* (London: Fontana Books, 1959), p. 149.

25. J.D.G. Dunn, *Romans 1–8* (WBC, 38; Dallas: Word Books, 1988), p. 470.

The second factor is that the context of Romans 8 is so overwhelmingly positive that the negative verdict has been completely swallowed up by 'the glory about to be revealed to us' (8.18). Indeed, the salvation that Paul is describing is enhanced by his negative verdict on creation. Creation was not subjected to futility as an end in itself but so that it might also 'obtain the freedom of the glory of the children of God' (8.21). The catena of Rom. 3.10-18 has a similar role before the momentous 3.21-26.

Quotation, Allusion or Echo?

There is clearly no question of Paul quoting Ecclesiastes in Rom. 8.20. Indeed, according to the tables in the back of *UBSGNT*, there is not a single quotation of Ecclesiastes in the whole of the New Testament (though see below). Is it then an allusion? Does Paul's use of ματαιότης 'activate' the ματαιότης of Ecclesiastes (LXX), to use Ben-Porat's expression?[26] And if so, with what result? Traditionally, this question would be asked in terms of the author's intention. Was Paul consciously directing the reader to the book of Ecclesiastes? The article on ματαιότης in *TDNT* says that, 'R.8:20 is a valid commentary on Qoh.'. It goes on to say that while the 'passage does not solve the metaphysical and logical problems raised by *vanitas*...it tells us plainly that the state of ματαιότης ("vanity") exists, and also that this has a beginning and end... Paul could speak of ἐλπίς and δόξα with an authority not found in Qoh.'[27] However, most commentators would want to see more evidence than Romans 8 can provide before agreeing that it was a *deliberate* allusion on Paul's part.

Is it then an echo or an unconscious allusion? Sanday and Headlam note that ματαιότης is the constant refrain of Ecclesiastes and therefore Paul's use of the word is 'appropriately used of the *disappointing* character of present existence, which nowhere reaches the perfection of which it is capable.'[28] The implication of this appears to be that while Paul is not consciously alluding to Ecclesiastes, he has nevertheless chosen a word that is thoroughly appropriate, given its particular usage

26. Cited in a useful glossary at the beginning of Fewell (ed.), *Reading between Texts*, p. 21.

27. *TDNT*, IV, p. 523.

28. W. Sanday and A.C. Headlam, *The Epistle to the Romans* (ICC; Edinburgh: T. & T. Clark, 5th edn, 1902), p. 208. Emphasis original.

in that book. In terms of a theory of echo, we might say that Ecclesiastes is the 'cave of resonant signification', to use one of Hollander's terms. The reader is not specifically directed to the book of Ecclesiastes but the haunting prose of that book *accompanies* a reading of Romans 8 as 'shading of voice'. Or, as Hays puts it, it 'places the reader within a field of whispered or unstated correspondences.'[29] At any rate, Barrett says that the reader of Rom. 8.20 'recalls at once passages such as Eccles.i.2'.[30]

A further piece of evidence can be added. In the catena of Rom. 3.10-18, Paul strings together a number of quotations (ostensibly) to show the wickedness of all humankind.[31] Since Rom. 3.11-12 is drawn from Ps. 13.2-3 (LXX), most scholars have concluded that Rom. 3.10 must be a paraphrase of Ps. 13.1. But as Dunn observes, Paul's words are closer to the LXX of Eccl. 7.20 than to Ps. 13.1, and we know from *Sanh.* 101a that Rabbi Eliezer ben Hyrcanus (late first century) used Eccl. 7.20 to demonstrate the sinfulness of humankind.

> οὐκ ἔστιν δίκαιος οὐδὲ εἷς (Rom. 3.10b)
> ὅτι ἄνθρωπος οὐκ ἔστιν δίκαιος ἐν τῇ γῇ (Eccl. 7.20)
> οὐκ ἔστιν ποιῶν χρηστότητα, οὐκ ἔστιν ἕως ἑνός (Ps. 13.1)

On the assumption that Paul does not quote from the book of Ecclesiastes, most scholars opt for Ps. 13.1 as the source of Rom. 3.10b, even though it lacks the key word δίκαιος. Stanley, for example, says that the 'introduction here of a word from the δικ- group could hardly be more Pauline'.[32] But if Rom. 8.20 can plausibly be seen as an allusion to the ματαιότης of Ecclesiastes, then it adds weight to the possibility that Rom. 3.10 is drawing on Eccl. 7.20 (indeed, a quotation according to Nestle-Aland), especially as it actually contains the phrase οὐκ ἔστιν δίκαιος. Thus what began as an investigation of a minor echo, could have a significant impact on a reading of Romans. The idea that 'no one is righteous' is hardly a common theme in the Old Testament. Nor is the idea that 'creation is subject to futility'. It could be that

---

29. Hays, *Echoes of Scripture*, p. 20.

30. Barrett, *The Epistle to the Romans*, p. 166.

31. S. Moyise, 'The Catena of Romans 3:10-18', *ExpTim* 106 (1995), pp. 367-70.

32. C.D. Stanley, *Paul and the Language of Scripture: Citation Technique in the Pauline Epistles and Contemporary Literature* (SNTSMS, 74; Cambridge: Cambridge University Press, 1992), p. 90.

the book of Ecclesiastes has been far more influential on Paul's thinking than the lack of explicit quotations would suggest.

One further point reinforces this. In Rom. 8.21, Paul says that creation is in 'bondage to decay'. Most commentators take this as an allusion to Gen. 3.17: 'cursed is the ground because of you; in *toil* you shall
eat of it all the days of your life'. But in Eccl. 1.3, the first example of
ματαιότης is *toil* ('What do people gain from all the *toil* at which they
toil under the sun?') Caution is needed since Ecclesiastes uses a
different word for 'toil' than Genesis. But the link between 'toil' and
'futility' in Ecclesiastes might be the 'transumed text' (Hollander) that
lies behind Rom. 8.20-21. Paul is never explicit about this and so
certainty is impossible. But is there a better explanation of Rom. 8.20-
21 than a background text which says οὐκ ἔστιν δίκαιος, which says
life is ματαιότης and which links ματαιότης with the story of the Fall?

Dialogical Intertextuality

The previous case study illustrates how a relatively minor echo could
have a big effect on how a text is read. But its parameters are one
dimensional. There is an argument being pursued in Romans and a
decision has to be made as to how much the context in Ecclesiastes (if
at all) is allowed to influence it. But it is often more complicated than
that. As Hays says:

> Allusive echo functions to suggest to the reader that text B should be
> understood in light of a broad interplay with text A, encompassing
> aspects of A beyond those explicitly echoed...(it)...places the reader
> within a field of whispered or unstated correspondences.[33]

His own exposition of 2 Corinthians 3 offers a good example. Firstly,
Paul introduces the figure of Moses as a 'foil against which to com-
mend the candor and boldness of his own ministry.'[34] The reader is led
to expect a completely negative verdict of religion under the old
covenant but v. 16 introduces a turn as dramatic as the one mentioned
in that verse ('but when one turns to the Lord, the veil is removed').
Initially, the implication seems clear. The generation of Moses was
unable to see clearly but those who have responded to Paul's preaching
(that is, the readers) have had the veil removed. However, the mention

33. Hays, *Echoes of Scripture*, p. 20.
34. Hays, *Echoes of Scripture*, p. 147.

of 'veil' reminds Paul that Moses did in fact remove his veil when he entered God's presence. Thus Moses is both a contrast to ministry under the new covenant and a witness to it:

> The rhetorical effect of this ambiguous presentation is an unsettling one, because it simultaneously posits and undercuts the glory of Moses' ministry... Since Paul is arguing that the ministry of the new covenant outshines the ministry of the old in glory, it serves his purpose to exalt the glory of Moses; at the same time, the grand claims that he wants to make for his own ministry require that the old be denigrated...by distancing his ministry from Moses, Paul paradoxically appropriates attributes similar to those that he insistently rejects; connotations bleed over from the denied images to the entity with which they are discompared.[35]

According to Hays, this is achieved by Paul's allusive use of Scripture, which 'leaves enough silence for the voice of Scripture to answer back'. Paul does not fill in all the 'intertextual space with explanations' but 'encourages the reader to listen to more of Scripture's message than he himself voices. The word that Scripture speaks where Paul falls silent is a word that still has the power to contend against him.'[36]

Revelation 5.5-6 and Genesis 49.9/Isaiah 11.1, 10

> Then one of the elders said to me, 'Do not weep. See, the Lion of the tribe of Judah, the Root of David, has conquered, so that he can open the scroll and its seven seals.' Then I saw between the throne and the four living creatures and among the elders a Lamb standing as if it had been slaughtered, having seven horns and seven eyes, which are the seven spirits of God sent out into all the earth.

There is little dispute that the image of Jesus as the 'Lion of the tribe of Judah, the Root of David' is an allusion to Gen. 49.9 and Isa. 11.1, 10. Both texts have a significant interpretative history. A messianic interpretation of Gen. 49.9 is found in both the Targumic literature and in the Dead Sea Scrolls.[37] Isaiah 11.10 says, 'On that day the root of Jesse shall stand as a signal to the peoples; the nations shall inquire of him, and his dwelling shall be righteous.' The prophecy was important to the Qumran community, who took it to be about the one who 'shall

---

35. Hays, *Echoes of Scripture*, pp. 132-33, 142.
36. Hays, *Echoes of Scripture*, p. 177.
37. *Targ. Neof.* and *Targ. Ps.-J.* of Gen. 49.9-12; *Tanḥ.* Gen. 12.12; *Gen. R.* 97; 1QSb 5.21-29.

arise at the end [of days]... God will uphold him with [the spirit of might, and will give him] a throne of glory and a crown of [holiness] and many-coloured garments...and he shall rule over all the [nations].' (4Q161). However, in Rev. 5.5-6, juxtaposed with these images of power is the image of a 'Lamb standing as if it had been slaughtered'. Aune notes that lambs or sheep are mentioned in the Old Testament with reference to the burnt offering (Exod. 29.38-46), the Passover (Exod. 12.1-20), rites of purification (Lev. 12.6), consecration (Num. 7), expiation of unintentional sins (Lev. 4.1–5.13), celebration of first fruits (Lev. 23.12), Nazirite vows (Num. 6.12) and as a metaphor for the Servant of God (Isa. 53.10).[38] Beale thinks that it basically boils down to two backgrounds, the Passover lamb and the Servant of God, and both are intended. As to the purpose of this juxtaposition, Caird's view has been extremely influential,

> 'Wherever the Old Testament says "Lion", read "Lamb".' Wherever the Old Testament speaks of the victory of the Messiah or the overthrow of the enemies of God, we are to remember that the gospel recognizes no other way of achieving these ends than the way of the Cross.[39]

Thus Sweet says:

> We may agree, then, with Caird that what John *hears*, the traditional OT expectation of military deliverance, is reinterpreted by what he *sees*, the historical fact of a sacrificial death, and that the resulting paradox is the key to all his use of the OT, 'as if John were saying to us... "Wherever the Old Testament says *Lion*, read *Lamb*" '.[40]

In his own words, the 'Lion of Judah, the traditional messianic expectation, is reinterpreted by the slain Lamb: God's power and victory lie in self-sacrifice'.[41] Boring says: 'It is as though John had adopted the familiar synagogue practice of "perpetual Kethib/Qere," whereby a word or phrase that appears in the traditional text is read as another word or phrase'.[42] He then quotes Caird: 'Wherever the tradition says

---

38. D. Aune, *Revelation 1–5* (WBC, 52A; Dallas: Word Books, 1997), pp. 372-73.

39. G.B. Caird, *The Revelation of St. John the Divine* (London: A. & C. Black, 2nd edn, 1984), p. 75.

40. J.P.M. Sweet, *Revelation* (London: SCM Press, 1990), p. 125.

41. Sweet, *Revelation*, p. 125.

42. M.E. Boring, *Revelation* (Louisville, KY: Westminster/John Knox Press, 1989), p. 110.

"lion," read "Lamb" '. The implication for both Sweet and Boring is that the apocalyptic violence of chs. 6–19 must be seen in the light of the slain Lamb, and definitely not vice versa. Bauckham is more nuanced and recognizes that the 'hopes embodied in the messianic titles of Revelation 5:5 are not dismissed by the vision of the Lamb.'[43] Nevertheless, he also quotes Caird and states that 'by juxtaposing these contrasting images, John forges a symbol of conquest by sacrificial death, which is essentially a new symbol'.[44] Finally, Beale says that 'John is attempting to emphasize that it was in an ironic manner that Jesus began to fulfill the OT prophecies' and then paraphrases Caird, 'Wherever the OT predicts the Messiah's final victory and reign, John's readers are to realize that these goals can begin to be achieved only by the suffering of the cross.'[45]

On the other hand, there is a line of interpretation that draws a contrast between the all-powerful Lamb of Revelation and the Lamb 'who takes away the sin of the world' (Jn 1.29). Thus Dodd cites *1 En.* 90 and *T. Jos.* 19.8 and concludes that 'we have here a prototype of the militant seven-horned "Lamb" of the Apocalypse of John'.[46] Barrett looks to passages like Exodus 12, Isaiah 53 and Leviticus 16 as possible backgrounds for the Lamb of Jn 1.29 but discounts *T. Jos.* 19.8 since it 'recalls the conquering lamb of Revelation…rather than the present passage'.[47] And Brown concludes his discussion of Jn 1.29 with the words, 'Thus we suggest that John the Baptist hailed Jesus as the lamb of Jewish apocalyptic expectation who was to be raised up by God to destroy evil in the world, a picture not too far from that of Rev xvii 14'.[48] This line of interpretation reaches its climax in Ford's commentary, who considers the book of Revelation to derive (largely) from followers of John the Baptist. Lion and Lamb, she says, are not contrasting symbols, as if one represented raw power while the other is about

43. R. Bauckham, *The Climax of Prophecy* (Edinburgh: T. & T. Clark, 1993), p. 183.

44. Bauckham, *The Climax of Prophecy*, p. 183.

45. G.K. Beale, *The Book of Revelation* (NIGTC; Grand Rapids: Eerdmans, 1999), p. 353.

46. C.H. Dodd, *The Interpretation of the Fourth Gospel* (Cambridge: Cambridge University Press, 1968), p. 232.

47. C.K. Barrett, *The Gospel According to St John* (London: SPCK, 1978), p. 147.

48. R. Brown, *The Gospel According to John* (2 vols.; AB, 29; Garden City, NY: Doubleday, 1966), I, p. 60.

sacrifice and vulnerability. Jewish apocalyptic texts predicted a conquering Lamb who will appear in the last days and destroy evil, as *T. Jos.* 19.8 makes clear:

> And I saw that a virgin was born from Judah, wearing a linen stole; and from her was born a spotless lamb. At his left there was something like a lion, and all the wild animals rushed against him, but the lamb conquered them, and destroyed them, trampling them underfoot.[49]

Ford maintains that there is nothing in the book of Revelation which compels us to depart from this picture. The Lamb of Revelation 5 has seven horns, indicating power, and seven eyes, a symbol of omniscience. In the very next chapter of Revelation (6.16-17), those who suffer the calamities set loose by the Lamb cry out:

> Fall on us and hide us from the face of the one seated on the throne and from the wrath of the Lamb; for the great day of their wrath has come, and who is able to stand?

And the picture does not change when the confederacy of kings in Rev. 17.14 confront the Lamb:

> they will make war on the Lamb, and the Lamb will conquer them, for he is Lord of lords and King of kings, and those with him are called and chosen and faithful.

Ford thus concludes that John's use of the title 'Lamb' is thoroughly consonant with the 'apocalyptic, victorious, and destroying lamb' known to tradition.[50] Few Revelation scholars have agreed with this but it does highlight the difficulty of accepting the 'Caird position'. If John's intention was to offer the hermeneutic, 'wherever you see images of power, replace them with images of self-sacrifice', why does he continue to use images of power so extensively? As Aune notes, while it may be a plausible explanation of Revelation 5, it is a 'marginal conception elsewhere in the book'.[51] Indeed, Revelation comes to an end with the description of Christ as the 'root and the descendant of

---

49. Though Bauckham thinks this verse 'has so evidently been rewritten—if not entirely composed—by a Christian editor, that it is no longer possible to tell whether the victorious lamb was already present in a Jewish version' (*Climax of Prophecy*, pp. 83-84).

50. J.M. Ford, *Revelation* (AB, 38, Garden City, NY: Doubleday, 1975), pp. 87-95.

51. Aune, *Revelation 1–5*, p. 352.

David, the bright morning star' (22.16). There is no suggestion that this needs replacing or even reinterpreting. Images of sacrifice or 'victory through suffering' are not even in the vicinity.

My suggestion in *The Old Testament in the Book of Revelation* is that John does not want his readers to simply replace one set of images with another. Rather, he wishes to encourage their mutual interpretation. The images of power inform our understanding of the Lamb and the image of a 'Lamb standing as if it had been slaughtered' provides a new context for the Old Testament messianic texts. I support this by noting that John uses this technique on other occasions. For example, in the opening vision, Jesus says to the seer, 'Do not be afraid; I am the first and the last, and the living one. I was dead, and see, I am alive for ever and ever' (Rev. 1.17-18). Images of eternal existence from Isa. 44.6, 48.12 are juxtaposed with the stark, 'I was dead', from Christian tradition. We are not told how the eternal God could die or how the crucified Jesus can be the eternal being of Isa. 44.6; 48.12. The ideas are simply juxtaposed and the reader is left to mutually interpret them.

In Rev. 7.4, John hears the number of those sealed, 12,000 from each of the twelve tribes of Israel. But in Rev. 7.9, he sees 'a great multitude that no one could count, from every nation, from all tribes and peoples and languages, standing before the throne'. Some scholars think that this refers to two different groups (Jews and Gentiles, martyrs and ordinary Christians) but the majority believe it is two ways of referring to the same thing. It does not appear to be John's intention to replace the image of the 144,000 by the image of the countless multitude. Nor does it seem to be his intention to reinterpret it, for he uses it again in ch. 14, this time without any corresponding reference to a great multitude. And if the image of the 144,000 is not replaced or reinterpreted, the only other option is that it is allowed to coexist in creative tension with the image of the countless multitude. As Resseguie says, 'Although he heard 144,000, he saw a great multitude. The two are not separate, but mutually interpret each other'.[52]

This does not mean that the reader can make these images mean whatever he or she likes. It is rather that the combination of Lion and Lamb points to a dynamic reality rather than a static one. Beale seems to accept this point when he says that

---

52. J.L. Resseguie, *Revelation Unsealed: A Narrative-Critical Approach to John's Apocalypse* (Leiden: E.J. Brill, 1998), p. 8.

the place of the Old Testament in the formation of thought in the Apocalypse is both that of a servant and a guide: for John the Christ event is
the key to understanding the Old Testament, and yet reflection back upon
the Old Testament context leads the way to further comprehension of
this event and provides the redemptive-historical background against
which the apocalyptic visions are better understood; the New Testament
interprets the Old and the Old interprets the New.[53]

However, his worry over intertextuality (and my approach, in particular) is the suggestion that readers *create* meaning. For him, the juxtaposition of images is (1) simply an aspect of John's overall Semitic
style; and (2) does not result in ambiguity but finds a single resolution,
which ultimately resides in John's intention:

> The notion that readers create meaning is likely due in part to a
> hermeneutical flaw of confusing original 'meaning' with 'significance'...
> By way of illustration, we can compare an author's original, unchanging
> meaning to an apple in its original context of an apple tree. When some-
> one removes the apple and puts it into another setting (say, in a basket of
> various fruits in a dining room for decorative purposes), the apple does
> not lose its original identity as an apple, the fruit of a particular kind of
> tree, but the apple must now be understood not in and of itself but *in
> relation to the new context* in which it has been placed... The new con-
> text does not annihilate the original identity of the apple, but now the
> apple must be understood in its relation to its new setting.[54]

The point of the analogy is that though the apple might now be
viewed in a different way, it never becomes a pear. Readers cannot
make a text mean whatever they like. Old Testament allusions certainly
gain new 'significance' by being placed in a new setting but this does
not result in new 'meaning'. The distinction comes from Hirsch.[55] The
meaning of an Old Testament text is what the original author intended
and that never changes. It is only the text's 'significance' that changes.
But does this really do justice to the Lion and Lamb of Revelation 5?
Calling Christ 'the Lion of the tribe of Judah' suggests a powerful military leader because that was the meaning of the phrase in Gen. 49.9 and
the tradition that stems from it. But Beale now wishes to understand the

---

53. G.K. Beale, *John's Use of the Old Testament in Revelation* (JSNTSup, 166;
Sheffield: Sheffield Academic Press, 1998), p. 127. Emphasis original.

54. Beale, *John's Use of the Old Testament*, pp. 51-52. For a reply, see my 'The
Old Testament in the New: A Reply to Greg Beale', *IBS* 21 (1999), pp. 54-58.

55. E.D. Hirsch, *The Aims of Interpretation* (Chicago: University of Chicago
Press, 1976).

phrase in the ironic sense of 'victory through self-sacrifice'. Thus Jesus is not a Lion in the Gen. 49.9 sense but only in the *new* sense of 'victory through self-sacrifice'. Indeed, Beale can speak of John 'offering new understandings of Old Testament texts and fulfilments of them which may have been surprising to an Old Testament audience'.[56] It seems to me quite arbitrary to call this a change of 'significance' but not a change of 'meaning'.

Dialogical Intertextuality would agree with Beale that the 'new context does not annihilate the original identity of the apple' but would want to make more of the following phrase, 'but the apple must now be understood not in and of itself but *in relation to the new context* in which it has been placed'. It seems to me that Beale wants to have his cake (or apple) and eat it. He wants to assert that John offers 'new understandings of Old Testament texts', while insisting that those texts remain perfectly intact (nice shiny apples). But a better analogy would be that of a fruit salad, where we no longer have nice shiny apples but *pieces* of apple, mixed up with *pieces* of pear and *pieces* of banana. There is a *connection* with the shiny apple that once hung on a tree but also dramatic differences: it is no longer round, the skin has been removed and it has been severed from its core.[57] But the real problem with this type of analogy is its corporeality. Texts do not have hard surfaces that protect them from change of context. They are more like ripples on a pond, which spread out, intersect with other ripples and form new patterns. Or even less corporeal, texts are like sound waves which 'interfere' with one another, producing a series of harmonics and distortions (hence the 'echo-chamber' analogy).

Dialogical Intertextuality suggests that not only is the powerful Lion reinterpreted by the image of the slain Lamb, but also that the image of Christ as a slaughtered Lamb also undergoes reinterpretation by being juxtaposed with the Lion. As Resseguie says,

> The Lion of the tribe of Judah interprets what John sees: death on the cross (the Lamb) is not defeat but is the way to power and victory (the Lion)...the Lamb, though not in nature a strong animal, is a being of incontrovertible might in this book.[58]

---

56. Beale, *John's Use of the Old Testament*, p. 128.

57. The fact that Rev. 5 goes on to allude to Ezekiel's scroll suggests another analogy—that John has taken bites from apples, pears and bananas and has chewed and digested them. I hardly like to continue the analogy but Rev. 3.16 is a clue!

58. Resseguie, *Revelation Unsealed*, pp. 34, 129. I find Beale's discussion of

Postmodern Intertextuality

In the 1989 book, *Intertextuality in Biblical Writings*, Ellen van Wolde describes the way a text is produced and read:

> The writer assigns meaning to [their] own context and in interaction with other texts...shapes and forms [a] text. The reader, in much the same way, assigns meaning to the generated text in interaction with other texts [they] know... A writer does not weave a web of meanings that the reader merely has to follow, but...presents them to the reader as a text. The reader reacts to the offer and enters into a dialogue with the possibilities the text has to offer.[59]

On this understanding, reading always has a subjective element for 'all interpretations must necessarily delimit a text's possible references in order to come up with a coherent meaning'.[60] And this involves choice and hence vested interests:

> Every text—as an intersection of other textual surfaces—suggests an indeterminate *surplus* of meaningful possibilities. Interpretation is always a *production* of meaning from that surplus.[61]

'respecting the original context' similarly inadequate. He acknowledges that John sometimes uses Scripture in ways that are very different (even diametrically opposite) to their Old Testament contexts. But this is explained by noting that 'these new interpretations are the result of John's new, presuppositional lenses through which he is now looking at the Old Testament... *Granted the legitimacy of these presuppositions*, John's interpretation of the Old Testament shows respect for Old Testament contexts' (*John's Use of the Old Testament*, p. 45). I would suggest that a better way of putting this is to say that John shows an 'awareness' of Old Testament contexts but his Christian presuppositions nevertheless allow him to change, modify and even (on occasions) invert them. If 'respect for context' simply means 'understandable given the author's presuppositions', then it surely becomes a truism. Even the most bizarre allegorical use of Scripture could be said to 'respect the context' if we accept the legitimacy of the author's presuppositions (such as substituting like-sounding words). R.M. Royalty concedes that John's use of Scripture 'shows conscious authorial intention' but argues that it is 'far-fetched to imagine that John's free recombination and rewriting of scriptural texts has anything at all to do with the purpose of the original passages' (*The Streets of Heaven*, p. 72 n. 95).

59. E. van Wolde, 'Trendy Intertextuality', in Draisma (ed.), *Intertextuality in Biblical Writings*, p. 47. The quotation has been altered so as to be inclusive.

60. T.K. Beal, 'Ideology and Intertextuality: Surplus of Meaning and Controlling the Means of Production', in Fewell (ed.), *Reading between Texts*, pp. 30-31.

61. Beal, 'Ideology and Intertextuality', p. 31. Emphasis original.

By exposing the bias of individual interpreters, Postmodern Intertextuality has much in common with feminist (some have played with the words intertextuality/intersexuality) and other liberation readings. And by focusing on the need for individual interpreters to 'produce meaning', it has much in common with those approaches broadly classed as deconstruction. For example, Seeley says of Matthew's Gospel, that its

> presumed univocity is undermined and cracked by the multiplicity of voices embedded within and speaking simultaneously through it. These voices cannot be silenced by appeals to overall redactional coherence, or to a hierarchy of plots. They are all there, like an unharmonious choir demanding to be heard.[62]

Boyarin has explored this with respect to Jewish midrash. He argues that the purpose of midrash was not to expose, once and for all, the true meaning of a text and thereby end all discussion. Rather, it is the 'laying bare of an intertextual connection between two signifiers which mutually read each other. It is not, nor can it be, decided which signifier is the interpreter and which the interpreted.'[63]

John 4.16-20

> Jesus said to her, 'Go, call your husband, and come back.' The woman answered him, 'I have no husband.' Jesus said to her, 'You are right in saying, "I have no husband"; for you have had five husbands, and the one you have now is not your husband. What you have said is true!' The woman said to him, 'Sir, I see that you are a prophet. Our ancestors worshipped on this mountain, but you say that the place where people must worship is in Jerusalem.'

The story of the 'woman at the well' has been the subject of a number of recent studies.[64] The 'traditional' reading sees Jesus (the male) in

---

62. D. Seeley, *Deconstructing the New Testament* (Leiden: E.J. Brill, 1994), p. 52.

63. D. Boyarin, 'The Song of Songs: Lock or Key? Intertextuality, Allegory and Midrash', in Schwartz (ed.), *The Book and the Text*, p. 223.

64. I.R. Kitzberger, 'Border Crossing and Meeting Jesus at the Well: An Autobiographical Re-Reading of the Samaritan Woman's Story in John 4:1-44', in I.R. Kitzberger (ed.), *The Personal Voice in Biblical Interpretation* (London: Routledge, 1999), pp. 111-27; G.A. Phillips, 'The Ethics of Reading Deconstructively, or Speaking Face-to-Face: The Samaritan Woman Meets Derrida at the Well', in E.S. Malbon and E.V. McKnight (eds.), *The New Literary Criticism and the New Testament* (JSNTSup, 109; Sheffield: Sheffield Academic Press, 1994), pp. 283-325;

conversation with the Samaritan (the female) but operating on a different (higher) plane. Her mind is set on earthly matters. She has come to the well for ordinary water (4.7). When Jesus speaks of 'living water', all she can think of is 'Sir, you have no bucket'. When he explains that 'Everyone who drinks of this water will be thirsty again, but those who drink of the water that I will give them will never be thirsty', her interest is aroused but only to save herself the daily journey (4.15). When Jesus exposes the fact that she has had five husbands, she tries to embroil him in a theological discussion about places of worship. But once again, Jesus is on a higher plane. Worship is not about place but spirit and truth (4.24). Lastly, she voices a basic tenet of her Samaritan beliefs: 'I know that Messiah is coming... When he comes, he will proclaim all things to us' (4.25). Jesus replies, 'I am he, the one who is speaking to you' (4.26). Schneiders calls this the typical male reading of the story which

> presents the woman as a disreputable (if interesting) miscreant who, failing in her attempt to distract Jesus from her sexually disgraceful past, surrenders to his overpowering preternatural knowledge of her, alerts her fellow townspeople to his presence, and then fades from the scene as they discover him for themselves and come to believe in him.[65]

A different reading is possible, however, for it is *Jesus* who asks for a drink. It is not that the woman can only think in earthly terms; it is Jesus who places the conversation in the temporal context. He is sitting by Jacob's great well and asks her for a (material) drink. But the woman looks beyond the material to ask why social taboos are being ignored for 'Jews do not share things in common with Samaritans' (4.9). Jesus replies that he can offer 'living water', which the woman (rightly) takes as a religious claim to be superior to Jacob and the patriarchs. Jesus then elaborates that the water he offers is such that those who drink of it will never again be thirsty, for it 'will become in them a spring of water gushing up to eternal life'. The woman is interested and replies using the same metaphor as Jesus used: 'Sir, give me this water, so that I may never be thirsty or have to keep coming here to draw water' (4.15). Thus it is possible to read the text as a serious theological

T. Okure, *The Johannine Approach to Mission: A Contextual Study of John 4:1-42* (Tübingen: J.C.B. Mohr, 1988); G.R. O'Day, *Revelation in the Fourth Gospel: Narrative Mode and Theological Claim* (Philadelphia: Fortress Press, 1986).

65. S. Schneiders, *The Revelatory Text: Interpreting the New Testament as Sacred Scripture* (San Francisco: HarperSanFrancisco, 1991), p. 194.

exchange and not a (foolish) woman continually misunderstanding the (superior) male. On this reading, she is far more astute than Nicodemus in the previous episode (3.1-21) and the disciples in this one (4.27).

However, it is problematic to this reading that Jesus says in 4.18: 'You are right in saying, "I have no husband"; for you have had five husbands, and the one you have now is not your husband. What you have said is true!' Is this not confirmation that the story is about her 'sexually disgraceful past', even if male scholars have exaggerated this aspect? But it has often been noted that (1) adultery is a common metaphor in the Old Testament for spiritual unfaithfulness, which is precisely what the Jews thought of the Samaritans; and (2) that the reference to five husbands is an allusion to the repopulation of Samaria in 2 Kings 17:

> The king of Assyria brought people from Babylon, Cuthah, Avva, Hamath, and Sepharvaim, and placed them in the cities of Samaria in place of the people of Israel; they took possession of Samaria, and settled in its cities…every nation still made gods of its own and put them in the shrines of the high places that the people of Samaria had made, every nation in the cities in which they lived; the people of Babylon made Succoth-benoth, the people of Cuth made Nergal, the people of Hamath made Ashima; the Avvites made Nibhaz and Tartak; the Sepharvites burned their children in the fire to Adrammelech and Anammelech, the gods of Sepharvaim (2 Kgs 17.24, 29-31).

This allegorical interpretation was once quite popular though the Enlightenment has made it difficult for moderns to accept (allegory was the enemy of rationalism). However, given the symbolic nature of much of John's Gospel, one has to admit with Brown and Schnackenburg that it is a *possibility*.[66] If the reader is supposed to know that 'Destroy this temple, and in three days I will raise it up' (Jn 2.19) is a reference to the 'temple of his body', it is certainly possible that a chapter which

---

66. 'The unusual life-story of the Samaritan has led many exegetes to suppose that she is a symbolic figure, representing the people of Samaria and the religious apostasy of this hybrid nation by the usual image of marital infidelity' (R. Schnackenburg, *The Gospel According to St John* [Tunbridge Wells: Burns & Oates, 1968], I, p. 433). However, he notes that the analogy is not exact for while 2 Kgs 17 mentions five nations, it actually lists seven gods. He therefore concludes that the 'symbolic interpretation, at least if given in isolation as the only one, is inacceptable'. Brown (*Gospel of John*, p. 171) says: 'Such an allegorical intent is possible; but John gives no evidence that it was intended, and we are not certain that such an allegory was a well-known jibe of the time which would have been recognized without explanation'.

discusses whether Jerusalem or Gerizim is the proper place for worship, assumes the reader is acquainted with Samaritan history. That being so, Moore notes that there is more at stake here than simply deciding between competing interpretations. For those who wish to condemn the woman for taking everything literally can do so only by insisting that 4.18 is taken literally. In other words:

> They can condemn her only if they participate in her error, can ascribe a history of immorality to her only by reading as "carnally" as she does—at which point the literal reading of 4:18 threatens to become a displaced reenactment of yet another Johannine episode, one in which an unnamed woman is similarly charged with sexual immorality by accusers who themselves stand accused (8:1-11).[67]

Postmodern Intertextuality draws attention to two aspects of reading. First, no text is an island.[68] Its words have all been used before, sometimes in very significant ways. In every reading of the primary text, other texts are present and this leads to multiple interpretations (polyvalency). There is never just one way of 'configuring' the interaction between text and subtexts. Second, in every reading of the primary text, the reader brings with them texts they know and in the case of biblical studies, quite often a whole history of interpretation. Thus Protestant scholars have only recently acknowledged the fact that their reading of Paul owed a great deal to significant 'intertexts', such as the writings of Luther and Calvin. They were aware, of course, that Paul's letters contain numerous references to the Jewish Scripture but were much less aware of the 'intertexts' that they themselves were bringing to the task.[69]

For some, Postmodern Intertextuality, like deconstruction, will seem a pointless exercise. The task of the interpreter is surely to grapple with a text until its meaning is disclosed, or, more realistically, to get as close to that meaning as possible. What possible benefit is it to show that all interpretations are inherently flawed? At least three answers can

---

67. S.D. Moore, *Poststructuralism and the New Testament: Derrida and Foucault at the Foot of the Cross* (Philadelphia: Fortress Press, 1994), p. 49.

68. Miscall, 'Isaiah', p. 45. More fully, but perhaps less elegantly, '*no text is an autonomous and self-sufficient entity*, but is always open, literarily and pragmatically' (I.H. Kitzberger, 'Introduction', in *idem*, [ed.], *The Personal Voice*, pp. 1-11 [6]).

69. As ruthlessly exposed by E.P. Sanders, *Paul and Palestinian Judaism: A Comparison of Patterns of Religion* (London: SCM Press, 1977), pp. 1-59.

be given to this. The first is that Postmodern Intertextuality is not saying that meaning is impossible. It is simply pointing out that a reader cannot derive meaning without 'touching' the text (Derrida). As Kitzberger says,

> Entering John's story-world from my own story-world and entering my own story-world from John's story-world, both have been informed and transformed intertextually. In this process a new story has emerged which is no longer one or the other, but both, a story of mixture and otherness.[70]

Meaning, in the sense of communication, is certainly possible, but always at a price. Reinterpreting the apocalyptic violence of Revelation in the light of Christ's self-sacrifice is certainly a *possible* way of reading the book. One might even say that it is ethically imperative that it is read in this way. But it cannot be said to be the only way or even the obvious way. In terms of the sheer quantity of material, the language of conquest and destruction in Revelation far outweighs the language of love and forgiveness. That is why Christian interpreters have to work so hard to persuade 'the public' to read it differently. It is the sheer quantity of violent and destructive language that people find so difficult.[71] The Christian interpreter 'chooses' to read the language of conquest and destruction in the light of the cross of Christ.

In order to prevent misunderstanding, I should point out that in using the word 'chooses', I am not suggesting that interpretation is arbitrary and merely the product of an author's whim. Interpreters adopt certain positions because they believe the evidence 'compels' them to see it that way. But the fact that equally sincere scholars feel 'compelled' to see things differently suggests that this process is not ideologically neutral. Robbins recognizes this in his attempt to describe intertextual-

---

70. Kitzberger, 'Border Crossing', p. 123. Male scholars have generally treated the Samaritan woman as the exploiter (eagerly moving from husband to husband) rather than the exploited (five husbands have married and divorced her and the present one refuses to marry). But the text is open on this point and it would be a naïve scholar that thought his/her gender and experience of life had no effect on their judgment.

71. 'Lurid and inhumane, its influence has been pernicious... Resentment and not love is the teaching of the Revelation of St. John... It is a book without wisdom, goodness, kindness, or affection of any kind' (H. Bloom, *The Revelation of St John the Divine* (Modern Critical Interpretations; New York: Chelsea House, 1988), pp. 4-5. Stephen Moore's contribution to Kitzberger (ed), *The Personal Voice* is called 'Revolting Revelations', pp. 183-200.

ity as an aspect of what he calls 'Socio-rhetorical Criticism'. He notes that most examples of biblical intertextuality have already made fundamental decisions, such as (1) giving priority to Jewish texts rather than Greek or Roman texts; (2) emphasizing the influence of texts over other expressions of culture; and (3) confining itself to historical and literary modes of discourse. But such choices already demonstrate the ideological nature of all interpretation:

> the ideological nature of all interpretation manifests itself in the interplay between the choice of a mode of interpretive discourse and the choice of dimensions of the text the interpreter reinscribes.[72]

For example, in choosing to read Rom. 8.20 in the light of Ecclesiastes, I made at least two assumptions. First, I assumed that it would be more profitable to look for a Jewish text rather than one from Greek or Roman literature. But given Paul's background and cultural context, it is quite possible that he has been influenced by discussions of 'futility' in Greek philosophy. Second, I assumed the influence was primarily from 'texts', rather than some other expression of cultural life. But it may have been an artifact 'to an unknown god' that weighed heavily on Paul's mind, or a discussion on the future of 'tent-making' after a series of cancelled orders. Robbins points out that words not only evoke other texts but also data from the wider 'cultural, social and historical world in which they participate and in which people live'.[73] In showing how complex it is to pin-down 'influence', Postmodern Intertextuality draws attention to the fact that choices have already been made:

> Different ideologies...establish different boundaries for intertextual analysis and these different boundaries encourage significantly different strategies of interpretation.[74]

Second, in showing how a text can point in a number of directions, one is actually saying something important about the text. I do not know for certain if Ecclesiastes was in Paul's mind when he wrote Rom. 8.20. But in drawing out what the text would mean *if* it were in his mind, I am revealing something about the *potentiality* of the text. To use an analogy from science, it is like shining a particular light on a substance and observing the resulting pattern. And then changing to

72. Robbins, *The Tapestry*, p. 213.
73. Robbins, *The Tapestry*, p. 238.
74. Robbins, *The Tapestry*, p. 101.

ultraviolet light and observing a different pattern. In neither case are we actually 'seeing' the substance as it is. But observing the different patterns is telling us something 'real' about the substance. A scientist would laugh at the suggestion that such a procedure is making the substance mean whatever we like. Similarly, using different interpretative strategies to examine a text is not making a text mean whatever we like. It really is saying something about the text, though not as directly as the hermeneutics of the Enlightenment would prefer.

> [S]ocio-rhetorical criticism uses a strategy of reading and rereading a text from different angles to produce a 'revalued' or 'revisited' rhetorical interpretation... The goal is to use the resources of other disciplines 'on their own terms' and to allow these resources to deconstruct and reconfigure the results of a particular focus and set of strategies in a particular discipline.[75]

Third, since it is clearly impossible for any one individual to perfectly grasp the meaning of a text, it seems to me inescapable that Postmodern Intertextuality is true *to some degree*. The critical question is whether this is significant or is simply an aspect of being human (finite). For example, every performance of a musical symphony is different. The conductor will never conduct in exactly the same way. Each of the violinists will differ depending on how they feel that day. The horns will differ. Sickness might mean that one or two players are making their debut. All of which means that there are literally thousands of interacting factors which determine the final performance.[76] Nevertheless, there will be no doubt that one is hearing Beethoven's fifth symphony and not his sixth (for example). The differences are real and worthy of study since they greatly affect one's pleasure (or annoyance) at the performance. But they should not be used to suggest that we can never know or say *anything* about a text.

Conclusion

Frequent use of the term 'intertextuality' is threatening to make it

---

75. Robbins, *The Tapestry*, pp. 40-41.

76. This seems to be A.C. Thiselton's concern when he writes, 'What is problematic about current notions of intertextuality is *not the huge scope* of the boundaries which have been enlarged, but the transposing of horizons of understanding into *matrices which generate an infinite chain of semiotic effects*' (*New Horizons in Hermeneutics* [London: HarperCollins, 1992], p. 506).

meaningless unless more attention is given to definitions. One option would be to focus on the meanings given to it by particular theorists (Kristeva, Barthes, Derrida, Eco, Riffaterre) and declare other uses invalid (or 'thin'). This is the stance taken by Aichele and Phillips in their introduction to the 1995 edition of *Semeia* devoted to biblical intertextuality. Compared with what Kristeva had in mind, they declare that most examples of biblical intertextuality are doing little more than traditional source criticism:

> Traditional 'banal' source critical ('intertextual') explanations of cita-
> tion, allusion, allegoresis and the like, which claim a concern for history,
> prove exceedingly thin by comparison because they fail to take into
> account the historical and cultural nature of textual productivity and the
> implicature of readers and readings in the production of culture...what
> they are really concerned with is agency and influence.[77]

On the other hand, the word 'intertextuality' has taken on a life of its own and now has to be interpreted (or abandoned) in the light of current practice rather than the originating moment (an irony not lost on Aichele and Phillips). My suggestion in this essay is that in the light of current usage, it is best used as an 'umbrella' term for the complex interactions that exist between 'texts' (in the broadest sense). It is an evocative word, like 'textuality', which reminds us that such interactions are rarely straightforward. However, the weakness of this suggestion is obvious; no one can tell what is being claimed when different scholars speak of intertextuality. It is hoped that the three categories described and illustrated in this essay will go some way towards meeting this need.

77. G. Aichele and G.A. Phillips, 'Introduction: Exegesis, Eisegesis, Intergesis', *Semeia* 69–70 (1995), p. 11.

CHRISTOLOGY AND THE LEGITIMATING USE OF THE OLD TESTAMENT IN THE NEW TESTAMENT

Maurice Casey

Christological exegesis of the Old Testament has been a fundamental aspect of western Christianity. It clearly distinguishes Christianity from Judaism. This difference is so marked that biblical interpretation was for centuries an important aspect of conflict between Christians and Jews. This was already so clear in the ancient world that western polemicists could describe the exegesis of their fellow Christians in Antioch and in the Syriac-speaking church as Jewish. For example, in the preface to his commentary on the Psalms, Theodoret expresses his determination to avoid the errors of two kinds of earlier commentaries. Some of these were too allegorical: 'others accommodated prophecy to some historical events, so that the interpretation supported the Jews rather than the children of the Faith' (PG 80, 869c-d). Theodoret goes on to declare that he would allow historical references where they were appropriate: 'but it is not appropriate to refer to any other events the predictions of Christ the Lord...as Jews love to do, for they live in wickedness and weave a defence of their unbelief'. It is clear from these general comments that Theodoret knew Jewish exegetes who put forward these interpretations—and he knew Christian exegetes who did the same. He himself regarded this as a serious Jewish mistake, which Christians should not repeat.

Jesus and the first disciples were Jewish, and they interpreted the Old Testament christologically too. The purpose of this article is to trace out the point at which Christological interpretation of the Old Testament first became seriously anti-Jewish. As with the development of Christology in general, we shall find that, despite some precedent in the Pauline churches, real trouble is first visible in the vicious dispute between the Johannine community and 'the Jews' reflected in the Fourth Gospel. This was, however, a relatively recent dispute when that document was written. We shall accordingly find one major peculiarity. Whereas many aspects of Johannine Christology are supported by Old Testament exegesis, the full deity of Jesus is not supported in this way. Old Testament support for Jesus' deity took more than a generation to develop, and it is accompanied by anti-Jewish polemic. I shall conclude that the underlying reason for this is that the deity of Jesus is profoundly unJewish.

Jesus and Stage 1

Jesus himself saw aspects of his ministry predicted in the Hebrew Bible. For example, at his final Passover with his disciples, Jesus used a general statement to predict his death and condemn the man who betrayed him:

> A/The (son of) man goes as it is written concerning him, and woe to that man by whose hand a/the (son of) man is betrayed/handed over. (It would be) good for him if that man had not been born (Mk 14.21).[1]

In addition to the general passages referred to here, Jesus also made more specific references to scriptural passages which referred to him alone. His interpretation of one of them can be reconstructed from the brief reference to it in v. 18.

> And they (were) reclining and eating and Jesus said, 'Amen I say to you, that one of you will hand me over, he who "eats" with "me".'

Here Mark's ὁ ἐσθίων μετ᾽ ἐμοῦ must reflect an underlying הוא דאכל עמי, or something very like this. It has the effect of singling out one person, yet by means of an activity which all those present were doing. The particular person referred to is the person of Ps. 41.10, 'the man of my peace, in whom I trusted, who eats my bread, he has made great his heel against me'. That is a reasonable description of one of the Twelve betraying Jesus: the reference to bread has been altered, because the unleavened bread had not yet been started. The betrayal of Jesus by Judah of Kerioth could be seen at Ps. 41.7: 'And if he comes to see me, his heart speaks falsehood, he gathers wickedness, he goes outside, he speaks of it'. This gets Judah to the chief priests and scribes, who may

---

1. I translate literally Mark's Aramaic source, which I have reconstructed and discussed in detail elsewhere: see my *Aramaic Sources of Mark's Gospel* (SNTSMS, 102; Cambridge: Cambridge University Press, 1998), Chapter 6.

be seen at v. 8, 'All those who hate me whisper together against me, they devise evil against me'. Their intention is given in v. 9, together with their denial of Jesus' predicted resurrection: 'A thing of Belial will constrain him, and when he lies down, he will not rise again'. Then Judah of Kerioth, as we have seen, at v. 10, 'Yes, a man of my peace, in whom I trusted, who eats my bread, has made great his heel against me'. There follows a plea for resurrection in v. 11, 'And you, Lord, be gracious and raise me up.'

All this is surely too simple, and too extensive, to be unintentional. We must infer that everyone knew Psalm 41, and that the betrayal of Jesus was written in Scripture. This extensive actualizing interpretation is perfectly Jewish. It emphasizes the great importance of Jesus in God's plans for Israel, in that the circumstances of his death and his plea for resurrection had been written centuries ago by David under the influence of the Holy Spirit. However much chief priests and scribes might disagree with this, it is completely within the confines of Judaism.

Similar remarks are appropriate in discussing the innovative exegesis employed by the first disciples after Jesus' death and resurrection, as reflected in the early speeches of Acts. For example, in a vigorous speech at Acts 2.14-36, Peter quotes Ps. 16.8-11. He boldly states that David was dead and buried, and his tomb was still known. This assumes a striking contrast to Jesus, who did not need his tomb to be known and venerated because he was with God in heaven. Peter takes David's known fate to mean that v. 10 of the Psalm cannot refer to David, but must be interpreted of Jesus. The original Hebrew is as follows:

כי לא־תעזב נפשי לשאול לא־תתן חסידך לראות שחת

Peter will have followed the Hebrew text when he spoke in Aramaic. He has interpreted the psalm to mean that Jesus did not go to the underworld, where David would be awaiting resurrection at the last day. Jesus went straight to heaven. Peter then declared that God raised Jesus up, 'of which we are all witnesses' (Acts 2.32), which refers to the original resurrection appearances, of which Peter himself had seen at least one. He has Jesus 'exalted to the right hand of God', and continuing the comparison with David by making the point that David did not ascend to heaven (he went to Sheol, so Ps. 16.10 could not refer to him), he applies Ps. 110.1 to Jesus:

נאם יהוה לאדני שב לימיני עד אשית איביך הדם לרגליך

Like Ps. 16.10, this does not imply bodily resurrection. In Greek, however, Ps. 16.10 says that 'your pious one' (τὸν ὅσιον σου) did not see
διαφθοράν. This could be interpreted to mean that Jesus' body cannot
have decayed, so that the speech entails the resurrection of the body.
This illustrates how easily a legitimating shift can take place, and it
may have been the interpretation of Luke, who will have had his own
resurrection narratives in mind. It is not however a reasonable interpretation of the original Hebrew, which will have been known to Peter
when he said something very similar in Aramaic. This cannot be coin-
cidental. The Scriptures used by the first disciples when they believed
in the resurrection of Jesus were interpreted to mean that Jesus was
raised by God and taken to sit at his right hand in heaven. There is no
indication at this stage of bodily resurrection or an empty tomb, because
this is not what the first disciples believed. This is especially important
in the early chapters of Acts. Acts has ample narrative space. If Jesus
had really been raised bodily from the dead, leaving a literally empty
tomb, this would have been a very remarkable event in itself. The site
of the tomb would surely not have been forgotten, and the narrative of
Acts would surely tell us of excited disciples visiting it. We must infer
that Jesus was buried in a common tomb for criminals. The earliest
form of belief in his resurrection was that God had vindicated him by
taking him up to heaven.

Like Jesus' exegesis of Psalm 41, Peter's exegesis of Psalms 16 and
110 was vigorous and original, and had Jesus at the centre of it. It
remains nonetheless quite within the parameters of Judaism. This situation continued throughout the first of the three stages into which it is
fruitful to divide Christological development in the New Testament
period, that in which all Christians were Jews.[2]

Stage 2

In the second stage of Christological development, Gentiles entered
the Christian communities in significant numbers, without becoming

2. For a discussion of Christological development in these three stages, see
P.M. Casey, *From Jewish Prophet to Gentile God: The Origins and Development
of New Testament Christology* (The Edward Cadbury Lectures at the University
of Birmingham, 1985–86; Louisville, KY: Westminster/John Knox Press, 1991),
Chapters 7–9.

Jewish. This was a major factor in the massive Christological development of this period. Developments which were not needed in Stage 1
included the grounding of Christian ethics in baptism into Jesus' death,
and in having life analogous to his resurrection (Rom. 6). In Judaism,
morals are grounded in the Torah. This particular Christological development was fruitful in Stage 2, because Gentile Christians did not generally take on observance of the Torah. Paul's argument enabled him to
take whatever ethical decisions the community needed, with reference
to the central figure of Christ.

At this stage, Christological development was sufficiently extensive
to raise the question as to whether Jewish monotheism was breached by
some developments. The so-called Philippians hymn is a good example
of how high Christology could go. Criteria for describing this as a
hymn, however, have never been satisfactorily determined.[3] Its only
obvious feature is that it is not in Greek verse, and a major feature of
scholarly attempts to portray it as a hymn has been the excision of
pieces, all of which have an excellent *Sitz im Leben* where they are.
Translating it into Aramaic has been a dubious enterprise altogether,
and it has an excellent *Sitz im Leben* where it is rather than in earlier
Jewish Christianity. At the same time, it does raise Jesus to an extraordinarily high position. He is pre-existent at the beginning, and after his
exaltation he is given the name of God. His position is indeed on the
verge of deity, sufficiently close for anyone involved in Jewish culture
to feel that it needed to be legitimated. For this purpose, the author has
used the standard Jewish source, Scripture.

In the first place, this means the Adam story.[4] This legitimates the
idea that Jesus was ἐν μορφῇ θεοῦ. Adam was created κατ᾽ εἰκόνα θεοῦ
(Gen. 1.27 LXX). The words μορφή and εἰκών overlap to a significant
extent, and there were two reasons why the author should not use εἰκών
at this point. First, many Jews believed that man did not lose the image
of God at the fall of Adam (cf. 1 Cor. 11.7). Second, μορφή is more
suitable for drawing the contrast with μορφὴν δούλου λαβών, when
Jesus began his earthly life (Phil. 2.7). Further, the form of God
included his glory, the visible radiance of light that could be seen at a
theophany. It is obvious that man does not possess this (cf. Rom. 3.23;

3. Detailed discussion of the secondary literature cannot be offered here.
4. I cannot discuss here the controversy over this in the massive secondary literature. See especially M.D. Hooker, 'Adam *Redivivus*: Philippians 2 Once More',
pp. 218-32 in this volume.

3 Bar. 4.16; *Apoc. Mos.* 21.6). The μορφή θεοῦ was therefore something that Adam could be thought to have lost, and Jesus could be thought to have laid aside μορφὴν δούλου λαβών. Accordingly, if Adam was created κατ᾽ εἰκόνα θεοῦ, Jewish monotheism could be thought not to be breached by presenting Jesus as ἐν μορφῇ θεοῦ before he was born.

Similarly, 'Being on a level with God' (ἴσα θεῷ) indicates high status, but not full deity. The term ἴσα overlaps in meaning with כ, 'like', used at Gen. 3.5, 22, where the serpent told Adam that he would become כאלהים, and God said that he had become כאחד ממנו, when he obtained knowledge of good and evil. Since the Genesis story did not breach Jewish monotheism, Paul could feel that he had not done so either. Whatever the precise meaning of ἁρπαγμόν, this also begins a series of contrasts between Jesus and Adam. Adam did consider being on a level with God something to be grasped, for he tried to obtain it by eating of the tree of life (Gen. 3.5, 22): he did not empty himself, but was punished by God for his sin, being made to work the ground and to be subject to death. It was also believed that God would exalt man with all the glory of Adam. This may be explicit (cf. CD 3.20; 1QS 4.23; 1QH 17.15), or it may take the form of the glorification of the righteous (see, for example, Dan. 12.3; Wis. 3.1-9; 4.16; 5.1, 15-16; *2 Bar.* 51). These contrasts are so basic and extensive that they can hardly have been absent from the mind of the author of this piece.

Jesus' final position has been legitimated by midrashic interpretation of Isa. 45.18-25. The words πᾶν γόνυ κάμψη and πᾶσα γλῶσσα ἐξομολογήσηται are from Isa. 45.23, with ἐξομολογήσηται being interpreted in terms of early Christian confession of Jesus. The text contains both the name of God, and a word for God, אלהים. Consequently, it can be interpreted of the two figures, Jesus and God. For example, the LXX of Isa. 45.25 reads: ἀπὸ κυρίου δικαιωθήσονται καὶ ἐν τῷ θεῷ ἐνδοξασθήσονται πᾶν τὸ σπέρμα τῶν υἱῶν Ισραηλ—'They shall be justified by the Lord, and in God all the seed of the sons of Israel will be glorified'. It is not difficult to interpret that of the Gentile mission, in which Gentiles were justified by faith in the Lord Jesus, and of the ultimate salvation of Israel in accordance with God the Father's overall plan for salvation (cf. Rom. 9–11).

Accordingly, Scripture has been used in such a way as to ensure that Paul felt himself remaining within the bounds of Jewish monotheism. Moreover, it has been used in two different ways. The Adam story provided an outline for similarities and contrasts: the use of Isaiah includes clear quotations. This makes no difference: either use of Scripture could be felt to legitimate the high position of Jesus. It is also of central importance that other people do not seem to have thought that Jewish monotheism was being breached either, since there is no dispute about it. The Pauline epistles are full of controversy over all kinds of matters, but at no point is there any suggestion that Paul's opponents considered his view of Jesus to be blasphemous. We must infer that this was not a matter of dispute.

The extraordinarily high Christology of the epistle to the Hebrews is legitimated at Heb. 1.5-14 with a whole series of direct quotations.[5] The quotations begin with Ps. 2.7, which provides the position of Jesus as the Son, in the strong sense in which this Christological title is used in this document. The fifth quotation applies Ps. 45.7 to Jesus: πρὸς δὲ τὸν υἱόν, Ὁ θρόνος σου, ὁ θεός, εἰς τὸν αἰῶνα τοῦ αἰῶνος. Again this might seem to us to indicate the full deity of Jesus, but again we must be careful. We will remember the application of Pss. 7.8-9 and 82.1 to Melchizedek in 11QMelchizedek, and the frequent use of אלהים and אלים with reference to the highest angels in 4Q400-405. It follows that we need direct information before we can tell whether the unique position of Jesus was believed to have breached Jewish monotheism. The next quotation applies part of Psalm 102 to the Son. This involves him in the creation of the universe, unlike which he is eternal. Finally, the quotation of Ps. 110.1 is introduced with a formula which asserts his superiority to the angels: πρὸς τίνα δὲ τῶν ἀγγέλων εἴρηκέν ποτε…

There is accordingly no doubt that this collection of direct quotations legitimates an extremely high Christology, which puts Jesus in a position greater than that of any purely Jewish messianic or intermediary figure. At the same time, however, this document, which does see a need to legitimate Jesus in a higher position than the angels or Moses, shows no sign of controversy over any breach of Jewish monotheism.

At this point, the Christologies of Paul, the deutero-Paulines, Hebrews and Revelation must be taken together, because all of them show features which are of central importance. The Christology has gone very high, and it is at times legitimated by the use of Scripture. All these documents provide evidence of very serious controversy. None of

5. For the place of the Christology of Hebrews in the development of New Testament Christology, see Casey, *From Jewish Prophet to Gentile God*, esp. pp. 143-46.

them, however, shows any sign of suggestions that the position of Jesus has breached Jewish monotheism, or has been considered to be blasphemous. We must accordingly infer that in Stage 2 of Christological development, the position of Jesus was believed by everyone to have remained within the confines of Jewish monotheism. The use of Scripture will have helped to ensure this.

Professor Larry Hurtado

The major attempt to argue that a serious change in Jewish monotheism took place much earlier than I have suggested is that of Professor Larry Hurtado, and it is of such importance that a detailed critique must be offered here. In several learned and ingenious works, Hurtado has argued that worship of Jesus altered Jewish monotheism, and was the major factor in Christological development. He has described this as a 'binitarian mutation'. By 'mutation' he means that it was a direct outgrowth from ancient Jewish tradition which, however, exhibited a sudden and significant difference in character from Jewish tradition. By 'binitarian' he means that this mutation may be seen as an unprecedented reshaping of monotheistic piety to include a second object of piety alongside God, a mutation carried through by people who remained committed to belief in one God.[6] Hurtado has also dated this cultic activity soon after Jesus' death, in the first of the three stages into which I divide Christological development, when the churches were still Jewish, let alone the second, when many Gentiles entered the churches.[7]

The evidence to which Hurtado has drawn attention is important, and must be subsumed in any fully explanatory theory. It is especially important that, when compared with purely Jewish figures, Jesus was developed in a partly unique manner. It seems to me that, like most

6. L. Hurtado, *One God One Lord: Early Christian Devotion and Ancient Jewish Monotheism* (London: SCM Press, 2nd edn, 1998 [1988]), pp. 99-100.

7. Hurtado, *One God One Lord*; *idem*, 'What Do We Mean by "First-Century Jewish Monotheism"?', in E.H. Lovering, Jr (ed), *Society of Biblical Literature 1993 Seminar Papers* (Atlanta: Scholars Press, 1993), pp. 348-68; *idem*, 'Christ-Devotion in the First Two Centuries: Reflections and a Proposal', *Toronto Journal of Theology* 12 (1996), pp. 17-33; *idem*, 'Pre-70 C.E. Jewish Opposition to Christ-Devotion', *JTS* 50 (1999), pp. 35-58. I am grateful to Professor Hurtado for sending me copies of these last two papers, and for discussing the major issues with me, both personally and in correspondence.

Christian scholars, Hurtado has exaggerated the degree of uniqueness. In particular, I am not convinced that early development may be properly described as a 'binitarian mutation', because our sources do not indicate that a serious departure from Jewish monotheism was perceived until what I describe as Stage 3, when the Johannine community had Gentile self-identification.

For example, Hurtado suggests that Paul's persecution of Jewish Christians was occasioned 'partly by the reverence they gave to Jesus', and that the 'devotion' of 'early Jewish Christians' 'to Jesus may have caused other Jews to regard them as having violated the uniqueness of God'.[8] This suggestion goes too far. After Jesus' death, it was the chief priests who took action against the earliest Jewish Christians (for example Acts 4.1, 6-7), sometimes at least with scribes and elders (for example Acts 4.5). When Paul set off for Damascus, he obtained letters authorising persecution from the High Priest (Acts 9.1-2). When Paul himself was finally arrested, it was the high priest Ananias and some elders who brought an orator to set out the case against Paul (Acts 24.1). Throughout all these proceedings, there is no charge which appears to be connected with violating the uniqueness of God. We must therefore infer that this was not a significant issue. That the persecution was occasioned partly by the reverence which Jewish Christians gave to Jesus is true. Indeed it is central, for Jesus was at that stage the only detectable identity factor marking off the Jesus movement from Judaism as a whole, and it is precisely his centrality to the Jesus movement which explains why it was he whom Paul saw on the Damascus road. Moreover, Jesus was central to a movement which claimed divine vindication through him: the claim that he was at the right hand of God, and had appeared to his disciples after his death, could mean nothing less than God's approval of the Jesus movement, and the guilt of chief priests, scribes and elders follows ineluctably (cf. Acts 5.28). Hence Luke portrays the Captain of the Temple, with priests and Sadducees, aggravated about the preaching of the resurrection of the dead through Jesus (Acts 4.2), not the violation of the uniqueness of God. We must infer that the central Jewish power group perceived a threat to themselves, not a violation of the uniqueness of God.

We must be equally careful about another important piece of evidence of early Christological development, the use of the Aramaic invocation

8.   Hurtado, *One God One Lord*, p. 2.

מרָאנָא אתָא, 'Come, Lord', written in Greek letters as μαραναθα at 1 Cor 16.22. Hurtado correctly argues that this is an invocation of the risen Christ, and that it comes from the Aramaic-speaking church.[9] This does mean that the veneration of Jesus went beyond that normal in the case of other figures, such as Michael and other angels, Moses and Enoch. Several such figures had a variety of functions attributed to them,[10] but none of them was addressed quite like this. Accordingly, the use of μαραναθα gives us valuable insight into the religious experience of early Christians. It is probable that it goes back well before the epistle to the Corinthians, to a stage when Christians spoke Aramaic and were to some considerable extent Jewish. It must have been preserved because Pauline churches shared the early faith in the risen Jesus, and in his second coming. It must have been said, sung or shouted at meetings for prayer and worship. It will therefore have reinforced faith in the reality of the resurrection and the second coming. It is evidence of the dialectical relationship between belief and experience which was an essential part of the development of New Testament Christology. We must not exaggerate, however. We cannot date it, it is a brief Aramaic prayer, not a fragment of a long one, and above all it occurs in one of a group of letters which show signs of much polemic, but not about monotheism. We must therefore infer that it was not felt to breach normal Jewish monotheism, which was flexible enough to allow these developments. Accordingly, 'binitarian mutation' is surely too strong a term.

Again, we have seen that Phil. 2.6-11. is an important passage in which Jesus is so highly exalted that only the exercise of sympathetic Gentile perception is required to turn him into a full deity. Hurtado takes from previous scholarship the notion that this is a hymn, and describes it as 'a "window" opening upon the faith and devotion of Jewish Christians from still earlier years'.[11] We have, however, noted that criteria for describing this piece as a hymn have never been satisfactorily

---

9. Hurtado, *One God One Lord*, pp. 106-107. I have discussed this in the light of the most recent research in an essay, 'Monotheism, Worship and Christological Development in the Pauline Churches', in C.C. Newman, J.R. Davila and G.S. Lewis (eds.), *The Jewish Roots of Christological Monotheism: Papers from the St Andrews Conference on the Historical Origins of the Worship of Jesus* (Leiden: E.J. Brill, 1999).

10. Casey, *From Jewish Prophet to Gentile God*, Chapter 6.

11. Hurtado, *One God One Lord*, p. 96.

determined, and we have traced out its legitimating use of Scripture, which appears designed precisely to keep it within the realms of Jewish monotheism. Even here, therefore, we must be careful. This piece shows exceptional development, but it was not necessarily anchored in cultic veneration, nor can it be shown to have been produced before the Gentile mission had been flourishing for years. We must therefore classify it where it is, as part of a letter by the outstanding known missionary to the Gentiles, at the limits of Jewish monotheism but not threatening enough to cause controversy. For such controversy we must move to the Johannine community, where the Jewish version of monotheism was abandoned in favour of a new Christian monotheism.

Hurtado's treatment of the evidence of the Synoptic Gospels should not be accepted either. He quotes Hare on persecution reflected in Matthew: 'The Christological titles applied to Jesus by Christians must have been early regarded as a challenge to Jewish monotheism, and Christian adoration of their risen Lord must have provoked cries of "Idolatry!" from many fellow Jews'.[12] This is exactly what is missing from the primary source material. Since there is no trace of this in Acts and the Epistles, which have ample evidence of Christological development and of controversy about other matters, we should not invent it behind the Gospels. There are two other reasons why it should not be produced from behind Matthew. First, this Gospel provides abundant evidence of dispute over other aspects of the observance of Jewish Law (for example, 5.17-48; 23.1-36, both noted by Hurtado). Second, it was possible to object vigorously to the position of Jesus before monotheism was perceived to have been breached. We have seen this in the early chapters of Acts, and might therefore reasonably conjecture it elsewhere.

Hurtado also goes further than Hare, as for example in pushing too hard Matthew's use of προσκυνῶ. He treats this as if it always means 'worship' in a very strong sense. He notes especially Mk 6.50//Mt. 14.27, where Jesus identifies himself with ἐγώ εἰμι, 'I am He', or 'It is I'. Hurtado suggests that this has epiphanic significance (noting LXX Isa. 43.10, where it is attributed to God), revealing Jesus' divine status. He finds this dramatically made explicit in the conclusion, where the disciples offer worship, complete with the acclamation, ἀληθῶς θεοῦ

12. Hurtado, 'Pre-70 C.E. Jewish Opposition', p. 5, quoting D.R.A. Hare, *The Theme of Jewish Persecution of Christians in the Gospel According to St Matthew* (SNTSMS, 6; Cambridge: Cambridge University Press, 1967), p. 17.

υἱὸς εἶ (Mt. 14.33).[13] What Hurtado has done, however, is to breach a boundary marker without showing that Matthew did the same. The Greek word προσκυνῶ, like related words in biblical text and versions, does not have to mean full worship. For example, LXX Ruth 2.10 uses προσεκύνησεν of Ruth bowing down before Boaz, representing the Hebrew וַתִּשְׁתַּחוּ, which is also translated with the Aramaic and Syriac סגד. All three words have a semantic area which covers this degree of submissiveness, as well as full-scale worship. Equally, ἐγώ εἰμι may simply identify Jesus as himself, meaning 'It is I'—it need have no connection with Isaiah. Son of God was what every faithful Jew was: Mt. 14.33 does not have the articles with Son of God, and should not be read against the backcloth of later Christology. Accordingly, all these three points were ideal for the rising Christology of Matthew, for all three are very flexible and need not be pushed beyond Jewish experience of the meaning of monotheism. Consequently, Jewish monotheism had no prohibition against such developments, and it is this which explains how a faithful if assimilating Jew like Matthew could accede to and/or produce them. Similar problems attend all Hurtado's comments on evidence from the Synoptic Gospels. In all cases he fastens on genuinely important evidence of rising Christology, but does not make out his case that Jewish monotheism has been breached.

All these points underline the fact that Hurtado never really offers us a definition of the cultic veneration of Jesus which is genuinely comparable to the cultic veneration of God in the Jewish world, or of significant gods and goddesses in the Graeco-Roman world. By these standards of judgment, the cultic veneration of Jesus was seriously lacking in the following ways. First, there was no sacrificial cultus devoted to him. This marks him off from all serious deities, including God himself. Second, no temple was built to him. Third, to make prayers and hymns to him a serious matter, we have to generalise from one prayer-like expression (μαραναθα), one or two expressions (calling upon his name), and a small number of passages which do not particularly have the structure of hymns, and which are never said to have been sung. There is no question of any serious liturgy to be used in worshipping him. This ought to make it clear that he was not the object of cultic veneration, as that was normally practised in the environment of the Jews among whom Jesus lived, nor among the Gentiles who were

13. Hurtado, 'Pre-70 C.E. Jewish Opposition', p. 7.

converted during the Gentile mission.

We can now see what Hurtado has done. He has isolated a few points in early Christian treatment of Jesus which are analogous to normal treatment of deities, and has fitted them into his own pattern, rather than into the cultural environment to which they originally belonged. It was partly to avoid this mistake that I devoted a whole chapter to messianic and intermediary figures in Second Temple Judaism.[14] I pointed out the very varied ways in which these figures were developed, and that the only detectable limitation was that of Jewish monotheism. In particular, there was no bar against taking over features of God. For example, at Wis. 10–11, the major events of Salvation History are attributed to Wisdom, rather than to God, while in the *Similitudes of Enoch* God's function as the eschatological judge has been taken over by Enoch. It is this massive flexibility within a framework of commitment to Jewish monotheism which explains how devotion to Jesus could be expressed with genuinely unique features, without the perception that Jewish monotheism has been breached. Moreover, Hurtado has mistaken the significance of unique features of Christological development by form-ing one of the hermeneutical circles which are such a major feature of New Testament scholarship. Worship of Jesus is extremely important to Professor Hurtado because he and his fellow Christians worship Jesus as the Son of God, the second person of the Trinity. He has conse-quently exaggerated the importance of worship of Jesus in the first century. In particular, the hermeneutical circle has caused him to adopt an incorrect standard of judgment when deciding whether worship of Jesus was perceived to breach Jewish monotheism. This is an obvious danger for anyone working with an apparently raw experiential cate-gory. No category is really that raw, and all undergo interpretation in the light of the life experiences of interpreters.

This does not mean that the evidence discussed by Hurtado is not important. On the contrary, it is of central importance to any possible explanation of Christological development that we should mark out points at which it is unique. It does mean that we must reject his con-tention that there was a perceived breach of Jewish monotheism in what I have labelled Stages 1 and 2 of Christological development. For this we must turn to Stage 3, when the Johannine community had Gentile self-identification.

14. Casey, *From Jewish Prophet to Gentile God*, Chapter 6.

The Johannine Community

The actual breach with the Jewish community came with the confession of Jesus' full deity in the Johannine community. The Fourth Gospel begins with a prologue in which Jesus' deity is openly declared. At the very beginning, θεὸς ἦν ὁ λόγος (Jn 1.1). At the climax of the prologue, ὁ λόγος σὰρξ ἐγένετο, and his name and title are given as Ἰησοῦς Χριστός (Jn 1.14, 17). This is clearly God incarnate, and the prologue ends with a summary which also makes Jesus' deity explicit: θεὸν οὐδεὶς ἑώρακεν πώποτε· μονογενὴς θεὸς ὁ ὢν εἰς τὸν κόλπον τοῦ πατρὸς ἐκεῖνος ἐξηγήσατο (Jn 1.18). Since the discovery of P[66] and P[75], it has been increasingly recognised that the more paradoxical reading, which refers to Jesus as μονογενὴς θεός, is the correct one.[15] There is an equally explicit declaration of Jesus' deity towards the end of the original Gospel, where Thomas addresses Jesus: ὁ κύριός μου καὶ ὁ θεός μου (Jn 20.28).

Throughout the Fourth Gospel, Jesus is portrayed as conscious of his position as the incarnate Son of God who is co-equal with the Father. One classic declaration is ἐγὼ καὶ ὁ πατὴρ ἕν ἐσμεν (10.30). On the one hand, this shows the Johannine community remaining within the traditional confession that God is one, rather than two. On the other hand, the text treats this declaration as so provocative that 'the Jews' immediately take up stones to throw at Jesus. At 10.33, they give their reasons: περὶ βλασφημίας, καὶ ὅτι σὺ ἄνθρωπος ὢν ποιεῖς σεαυτὸν θεόν. This reaction is of central importance, because it shows that non-Christian Jews[16] believed that Johannine Christology violated Jewish monotheism. Similar reactions are found elsewhere in this document (Jn 5.18; 8.59; 19.7), and this is exactly what is missing from the earlier New Testament material. Throughout this Gospel, Jesus refers to himself as ὁ υἱός, and to God as his Father. God is the Father of others as well, but this Gospel calls other people God's τέκνα, reserving the term

15. See B.L. Mastin, 'A Neglected Feature of the Christology of the Fourth Gospel', *NTS* 22 (1975–76), pp. 32-51; cf. also D.A. Fennema, 'John 1.18: "God the Only Son" ', *NTS* 31 (1985), pp. 124-35.

16. For a discussion of attempts to argue that the Johannine Ἰουδαῖοι are not really Jews, see P.M. Casey, *Is John's Gospel True?* (London: Routledge, 1996), pp. 116-27. Cf. further P.M. Casey, 'Some Anti-Semitic Assumptions in the *Theological Dictionary of the New Testament*', *Novum Testamentum* 41 (1999), pp. 280-91, with bibliography at pp. 285-86 n. 18.

υἱός for Jesus alone. This is another indication that the Johannine community saw an ontological rather than merely functional difference between Jesus and other people.

A major point of continuity with earlier New Testament documents lies in the use of the Old Testament in support of Johannine Christology.[17] We must review some main points before we approach the central concern of this article. Christological comments may be supported with a quotation introduced with a formula, as with the rather free quotation from Zech. 9.9, introduced with καθώς ἐστιν γεγραμμένον at Jn 12.14-15. Equally, the authors may quote enough of a particular passage for us to be certain that they have used it, without any such introduction. This is so at Jn 1.51: ὄψεσθε τὸν οὐρανὸν ἀνεῳγότα καὶ τοὺς ἀγγέλους τοῦ θεοῦ ἀναβαίνοντας καὶ καταβαίνοντας ἐπὶ τὸν υἱὸν τοῦ ἀνθρώπου. This certainly makes midrashic use of Gen. 28.12, a text which is visible enough for its use to be verifiable. This saying may also have been formed with the help of Zech. 12.10 (ὄψεσθε) and Dan. 7.13 (τὸν υἱὸν τοῦ ἀνθρώπου). This is of course more conjectural. Again, there may be a reference to a known incident in the Old Testament, without an actual quotation. For example, Jn 3.14 begins with an obvious reference to Num. 21.8-9: καὶ καθὼς Μωϋσῆς ὕψωσεν τὸν ὄφιν ἐν τῇ ἐρήμῳ. The origin of the second half is more difficult to determine: οὕτως ὑψωθῆναι δεῖ τὸν υἱὸν τοῦ ἀνθρώπου. Is this simply further development of Num. 21.8-9 in the light of Jesus' crucifixion? Or is it a result of a more complex midrashic process, in which ὑψωθῆναι has been drawn from Isa. 52.13, and τὸν υἱὸν τοῦ ἀνθρώπου

---

17. Here too a full discussion of the secondary literature is not possible. In addition to the commentators, see especially E.D. Freed, *Old Testament Quotations in the Gospel of John* (NovTSup; Leiden: E.J. Brill, 1965): G. Reim, *Studien zum alttestamentlichen Hintergrund des Johannesevangeliums* (SNTSMS, 24; Cambridge: Cambridge University Press, 1974); A.T. Hanson, *The Prophetic Gospel: A Study of John and the Old Testament* (Edinburgh: T. & T. Clark, 1991); B.G. Schuchard, *Scripture within Scripture: The Interrelationship of Form and Function in the Explicit Old Testament Citations in the Gospel of John* (SBLDS, 133; Atlanta: Scholars Press, 1992); M.J.J. Menken, *Old Testament Quotations in the Fourth Gospel: Studies in Textual Form* (Kampen: Kok, 1996); A. Obermann, *Die christologische Erfüllung der Schrift im Johannesevangelium. Eine Untersuchung zur johanneischen Hermeneutik anhand der Schriftzitate* (WUNT, 2.83; Tübingen: J.C.B. Mohr, 1996); M.J.J. Menken, 'The Use of the Septuagint in Three Quotations in John: Jn 10,34; 12,38; 19,24', in C.M. Tuckett (ed.), *The Scriptures in the Gospels* (BETL, 131; Leuven: Peeters, 1997), pp. 367-93.

has resulted from more prolonged meditation on Dan. 7.13? This is very difficult to determine.

There are also cases where a complex midrashic process may be uncovered, even though no single text is overtly referred to. Such a case is to be found at Jn 1.34: κἀγὼ ἑώρακα, καὶ μεμαρτύρηκα ὅτι οὗτός ἐστιν ὁ ἐκλεκτὸς τοῦ θεοῦ. In this verse, most mss read υἱός rather than ἐκλεκτός, but *difficilior lectio potior*. The minority reading ἐκλεκτός is attested by P[5vid] ℵ*, with some Latin and Syriac support. This is quite sufficient attestation, when transcriptional probability carries such great weight. Christian scribes did not think of Jesus as merely a chosen man, but as ὁ υἱὸς τοῦ θεοῦ, and the term υἱός is used of Jesus no less than 28 times in this very document. They would therefore be very strongly motivated to alter ἐκλεκτός to υἱός, and this explains the majority reading. The minority reading ἐκλεκτός, however, cannot be explained unless it is original. Moreover, whereas Jesus is hailed as ἀγαπητός by the heavenly voice at his baptism in the Synoptic Gospels (Mk 1.11//Mt. 3.17//Lk. 3.22), the Johannine ἐκλεκτός has resulted from meditation on scriptural passages which included Isa. 42.1. There are several points of contact with the Hebrew text:

הן עבדי אתמך־בו בחירי רצתה נפשי
נתתי רוחי עליו ומשפטו לגוים יוציא

Jesus has clearly been identified as the Servant of this passage. He is also described by God as 'my elect one' (LXX ὁ ἐκλεκτός μου), the text notes the putting of the Spirit on him, and the reference to the Gentiles at the end of the verse is especially suitable in the Johannine context which has referred to his taking away the sins of the world. The LXX has another interesting feature. It interpolates the definition Ἰακωβ before translating עבדי as ὁ παῖς μου, and it likewise inserts Ἰσραηλ before its translation of בחירי with ὁ ἐκλεκτός μου. Now we have already seen that in its midrashic use of Gen. 28.12, Jn 1.51 has the Son of Man in place of Jacob, who is of course also Israel. This suggests that all this midrashic exegesis belonged together as part of the vigorous use of Scripture in the Johannine community. They must surely have known LXX Isa. 42.1, and replaced Jacob and Israel with Jesus there, much as they did at Gen. 28.1.

Other scriptural passages may be in mind too. There is a mass of scriptural references to the place chosen by God for the people to go to sacrifice. This is so, for example, at Deut. 12.5-7, 11, 14, where LXX has ἐκλέξηται repeatedly, as well as the offering of πᾶν ἐκλεκτὸν τῶν δώρων ὑμῶν at Deut. 12.11. We do not naturally think of Jesus as a place, but in the Johannine narrative he has just replaced the sacrificial system (1.29), he will shortly replace the Temple (2.13-22), and he is the reason why Jerusalem is becoming redundant (4.20-24). We should therefore probably add intertextual echoes of these passages to our list of those used in the midrashic work of the Johannine community, whose replacement theology was so important to it.[18] The evangelist had therefore good reason to regard ὁ ἐκλεκτὸς τοῦ θεοῦ as a suitable term to close this stage of the revelation to Israel (cf. 1.31), before moving on to τὸν Μεσσίαν ὅ ἐστιν μεθερμηνευόμενον Χριστός at 1.41, and ὁ υἱὸς τοῦ θεοῦ at 1.49.

The Christological use of Scripture in the community also included the symbolic replacement of major feasts commanded in Scripture with Christological symbolism. The passage which we have just discussed also presents Jesus as ὁ ἀμνὸς τοῦ θεοῦ (Jn 1.29, 36). As such, he certainly replaces the Tamid and the Passover victim. Meditation on Isaiah 53 may also be relevant, as well as the ram sacrificed by Abraham in place of Isaac. The extensive Christological use in chs. 7–8 of the symbolism of water and light, which were central to the biblical feast of Tabernacles, is also well known.[19] The equally extensive use of the symbolism of Hanukkah in John 10 has not however been generally noted. It is clearly stated at Jn 10.22 that the occasion was in fact τὰ ἐγκαίνια ἐν τοῖς Ἱεροσολύμοις: cf., for example, αἱ ἡμέραι τοῦ ἐγκαινισμοῦ τοῦ θυσιαστηρίου at 1 Macc. 4.59. It is noted at 2 Macc. 10.6 that on the original occasion this feast was celebrated σκηνωμάτων τρόπον, and it is referred to as σκηνοπηγίας at 2 Macc. 1.18, and as τῆς σκηνοπηγίας τοῦ Χασελευ μηνός at 2 Macc. 1.9. It is this close connection between Tabernacles and Hanukkah which explains the continued use of the symbolism of light and the use of the pool of Siloam in John 9, and the lack of any indication of a major change of time or place right through Jn 7.10–10.39. The symbolism of these two closely connected feasts has overriden the more mundane aspects of a story line.

At the feast of Hanukkah, Jews celebrated their deliverance from the persecution of Antiochus IV Epiphanes. Antiochus' full title was 'Antiochus God Manifest' (Θεός Ἐπιφανής; he is simply Ἀντίοχος Ἐπιφανής at 1 Macc. 1.10, and similarly 2 Macc. 2.20; 4.7; 10.9, 13;

---

18. Casey, *Is John's Gospel True?*, pp. 134-36.
19. On all this, see briefly Casey, *Is John's Gospel True?*, pp. 71, 134-35.

4 Macc. 4.15). For Jews, his claim to deity was blasphemous, and he is duly described as βλάσφημος at 2 Macc. 9.28. Some people called him Antiochus Ἐπιμανής, 'Antiochus the Mad'. Some Jews also believed that the death of the righteous martyrs had enabled God to deliver Israel (cf. Dan. 11.35; 2 Macc. 7.37-38; *4 Macc.* 17.20-22). It was also believed that the martyrs themselves had gone to eternal life (cf. e.g. Dan. 12.2-3, 2 Macc. 7.9; *4 Macc.* 17.17-18). As soon as victory was won, the Temple, and especially a new altar, was once again made holy (1 Macc. 4.36-59, with τὰς αὐλὰς ἡγίασαν at 1 Macc. 4.48 and σκεύη ἅγια καινά at 4.49; 2 Macc. 10.1-8), and the martyrs themselves are described in scriptural terms as ἡγιασμένοι at *4 Macc.* 17.19 (LXX Deut. 33.3), and as ἁγιασθέντες at 4 Macc. 17.20.

In the Fourth Gospel, all these basic aspects of Hanukkah are reapplied to Jesus and the Jews. Jesus does not reject the accusation of 'the Jews' that he makes himself God (Jn 10.33), for he was God manifest. Many of 'the Jews' say of him, μαίνεται (10.20). 'The Jews' make to stone him for blasphemy (10.31-39), the accusation which Jewish people had correctly made against Antiochus Epiphanes. The Father sanctified him (ἡγίασεν, 10.36). Jesus achieves more than the Maccabean martyrs, for it is not only Israel whom he delivers: καὶ τὴν ψυχήν μου τίθημι ὑπὲρ τῶν προβάτων. καὶ ἄλλα πρόβατα ἔχω ἃ οὐκ ἔστιν ἐκ τῆς αὐλῆς ταύτης· κἀκεῖνα δεῖ με ἀγαγεῖν, καὶ τῆς φωνῆς μου ἀκούσουσιν, καὶ γενήσονται μία ποίμνη, εἷς ποιμήν (10.15-16). This is the reason for the very strong statement of 10.17, which also makes clear that Jesus is more than a martyr because he has control over laying down his life and taking it up again: διὰ τοῦτό με ὁ πατὴρ ἀγαπᾷ ὅτι ἐγὼ τίθημι τὴν ψυχήν μου, ἵνα πάλιν λάβω αὐτήν. Equally, he gives eternal life, he does not merely go to it (10.28). 'The Jews' ask him: ἕως πότε τὴν ψυχὴν ἡμῶν αἴρεις; (10.24). In his reply, Jesus tells them bluntly, ἀλλὰ ὑμεῖς οὐ πιστεύετε, ὅτι οὐκ ἐστὲ ἐκ τῶν προβάτων τῶν ἐμῶν (10.26). This is another clear exclusion of 'the Jews' from salvation.

There are two major points here. First, regardless of how sacred the first and second books of Maccabees were in Ephesus towards the end of the first century, the Christological use of Hanukkah has gone beyond the sacred text and has used features of the festival and of the story which it celebrated. This makes all the more remarkable the second point, that it has used this material Christologically against 'the

Jews', when it was originally a major Jewish feast celebrating triumph over heathen blasphemy.

This underlines the fact that the Christological use of the Scriptures in this Gospel is varied and extensive, and it separated the Johannine community from the Jewish community. This is stated bluntly at the end of the discourse of ch. 5, which is directed against οἱ Ἰουδαῖοι (5.16, 18): εἰ γὰρ ἐπιστεύετε Μωϋσεῖ, ἐπιστεύετε ἂν ἐμοί, περὶ γὰρ ἐμοῦ ἐκεῖνος ἔγραψεν (5.46). Thus the Jews are accused of not believing in Moses, on the grounds that they do not accept the Johannine community's Christological exegesis of Scripture.

The Deity of Jesus

We have seen that the most controversial aspect of Johannine Christology was the deity of Jesus. This, however, is not supported on the basis of Scripture. It has sometimes been thought to be supported in the difficult passage Jn 10.34-36, which uses Ps. 81.6 LXX, Ἐγὼ εἶπα, Θεοί ἐστε. However, this passage probably presupposes that the Psalm is addressed to the wilderness generation, who became Θεοί when they received the Law on Mount Sinai, and lost this status when they made the golden calf.[20] Accordingly, the description of them as πρὸς οὓς ὁ λόγος τοῦ θεοῦ ἐγένετο may mean simply that they received the Word of God from Moses. Alternatively, ὁ λόγος τοῦ θεοῦ may refer to Jesus as the pre-existent divine Word known to us especially from the prologue.[21] Even in this case, however, Jesus' deity is being asserted, not supported from Scripture. The description of him in Jn 10.36 is an assertion: ὃν ὁ πατὴρ ἡγίασεν καὶ ἀπέστειλεν εἰς τὸν κόσμον. This entitles Jesus to say Υἱὸς τοῦ θεοῦ εἰμι without blaspheming. The argument from Scripture is an analogy from lesser beings: it is not scriptural support for his deity, which is taken for granted.

We can also find intertextual echoes of Scriptures which are about God himself. Take, for example, Jn 14.15: Ἐὰν ἀγαπᾶτέ με, τὰς ἐντολὰς τὰς ἐμὰς τηρήσετε. The association between loving God and keeping his commandments is found abundantly in Scripture (for exam-

20. See especially J.H. Neyrey, ' "I Said: You Are Gods": Psalm 82:6 and John 10', *JBL* 108 (1989), pp. 647-63 (655-69).

21. So notably A.T. Hanson, 'John's Citation of Psalm LXXXII', *NTS* 11 (1964–65), pp. 158-62; *idem*, 'John's Citation of Psalm LXXXII Reconsidered', *NTS* 13 (1966–67), pp. 363-67; *idem*, *Prophetic Gospel*, pp. 144-49.

ple, Lev. 26.3, 11, 12; Deut. 6.4-6; 7.11-12). This however does not entail the deity of Jesus either, since there was no limit to the aspects of God which could be taken over by messianic and intermediary figures in the Judaism of this period.[22] It rather underlines the main point—why is there no support from Scripture for the deity of Jesus, when Christological use of Scripture is so pervasive and the deity of Jesus was a central point of controversy with the Jewish community?

The answer to this question is very simple. The deity of Jesus is completely unJewish. It violates Jewish monotheism. We have seen this reflected in the polemic of the Fourth Gospel, in which charges of blasphemy are called forth from 'the Jews'. We have seen also that in this document, as in its predecessors, the authors have taken care to remain within Jewish monotheism in their own eyes. This is however the document in which, for the first time, 'the Jews' say otherwise. From a cultural point of view, this is absolutely coherent. Jewish monotheism was very flexible, and consequently Paul and other early Christians could develop the figure of Jesus in significantly new ways without being held to have violated Jewish monotheism. However, in the Fourth Gospel the deity of Jesus is openly and repeatedly declared and referred to. This is the point at which 'the Jews' object, precisely because it is the point at which the Johannine community openly and deliberately stepped beyond the limits of the Jewish community. When the Fourth Gospel was written, this development was relatively recent. The deity of Jesus is too unJewish for the community to have found it in Scripture, involved as it was in the Christological interpretation of these Scriptures.

For this reason, it was some considerable time before Christian authors did support the deity of Jesus from the Scriptures, and when they do so, they patently interpret these texts in an unJewish manner. Ignatius was like the Fourth Gospel. He believed in the deity of Jesus, and states it openly. For example, the opening of Ignatius' *Letter to the Ephesians* has in its greeting Ἰησοῦ Χριστοῦ τοῦ θεοῦ ἡμῶν, and the body of the epistle refers to him as ἐν ἀνθρώπῳ θεός (Ignatius, *Eph.* 7). Ignatius does not, however, give any scriptural support for his conviction. The first extant document in which the deity of Jesus is given scriptural support is Justin's *Dialogue with Trypho*.

Justin's *Dialogue with Trypho* was written c. 160 CE. It purports to

22. Casey, *From Jewish Prophet to Gentile God*, Chapter 6.

give an account of a dialogue between the Christian Justin on the one hand, and the Jew Trypho and his companions on the other, some 25 years previously. Regardless of how literally accurate it is, it gives us firsthand evidence of how one Christian author in the middle of the second century believed that the deity of Jesus could be supported from the Jewish Scriptures. Justin begins to discuss the large set of scriptural texts which he uses in section 56. In the preceding section, he declares that God had hidden from 'you', so from the Jewish people, the ability to perceive the wisdom in his words, because of their wickedness. This declaration that the Jewish community could not see the deity of Jesus in Scripture because their wickedness had caused God to hide this from them is a baleful foretaste of the centuries of polemic and persecution which were to come. From a theological perspective, it is also as inaccurate as possible. The Jewish people regarded the deity of Jesus as a violation of Jewish monotheism because of their existing commitment to the oneness of God. From the perspective of Christological exegesis of the Old Testament, however, this was part of the same revelation to them as the rest of the Scriptures. What Justin has done is to attribute to God a series of culturally inappropriate distortions.

Justin begins with Gen. 18.1-3.[23] With the help of Gen. 18.14 and 21.9-12, Justin argues that the being 'God' at Gen. 18.1 is a God and Lord other than the maker of all things. This tradition of textual analysis could only begin when Christianity was quite separate from Judaism. When the separation had only just occurred, a tradition such as that adhered to in the first place by Trypho, that the three beings in Gen. 18.1-3 were all angels, would be too established to move. Moreover, there would always be such a tradition because in Judaism Scripture always was interpreted from within the parameters of Jewish monotheism. This is also the case with Justin's next three passages, Gen. 19.23-

---

23. On this series of texts, see especially O. Skarsaune, *The Proof from Prophecy: A Study in Justin Martyr's Proof-Text Tradition; Text-Type, Provenance, Theological Profile* (NovSup, 65; Leiden: E.J. Brill, 1987), pp. 206-13, 409-24. For recent general discussion of this document, see S.G. Wilson, *Related Strangers: Jews and Christians 70–170 C.E.* (Philadelphia: Fortress Press, 1995), pp. 258-85: J.M. Lieu, *Image and Reality: The Jews in the World of the Christians in the Second Century* (Edinburgh: T. & T. Clark, 1996), pp. 103-53; G.N. Stanton, 'Justin Martyr's Dialogue with Trypho: Group Boundaries, "Proselytes" and "God-Fearers"', in G.N. Stanton and G.G. Strousma (eds.), *Tolerance and Intolerance in Early Judaism and Christianity* (Cambridge: Cambridge University Press, 1998), pp. 263-78, all with recent bibliographical information.

25, Ps. 110.1 and Ps. 45.6-7, all of which are also adduced to help with the exegesis of Gen. 18.1-3. In each case, a reference to 'Lord' is taken to be a reference to the second of two fully divine beings. This interpretation would not occur within the Jewish tradition because it is controlled by Jewish monotheism. The figure of Prov. 8.22-23 is an interpretation of this divine figure too (*Dial. Try.* 61), where Jewish tradition correctly saw only the figure of Wisdom. This is then used to interpret the plural of Gen. 1.26-28 in terms of two divine beings (*Dial. Try.* 62), which is again contrary to Jewish tradition.

We can now see why it took so long for Christians to find the deity of Jesus in the Scriptures. To adopt exegesis of this kind, you have to be so far out of the Jewish community as to have dropped all its exegesis of such passages in favour of exegesis which could never occur within the parameters of Judaism. This is quite different from the novel Christological exegesis of Jesus, Peter and Paul. All this new exegesis set off from normal actualising exegesis and from normal references to messianic and intermediary figures, and it stayed within the parameters of the Judaism which Jesus and his first disciples sought to recreate. This is also the reason why the influence of Western Christological exegesis in the Syriac-speaking church was always relatively limited. Syriac-speaking Christians were generally more in touch with the Jewish community. They consequently continued with a great deal more Jewish exegesis than did their Christian colleagues in the West. They were also not so influenced by the Roman Empire, which conquered only part of their area for intermittent periods. This reduced their need for actualising exegesis of a rather different kind. They therefore tended to maintain Jewish exegesis, with a second level at which they might see a mysterious reference to Christ and to other aspects of Christian existence.[24]

Conclusions

The following conclusions may therefore be drawn. Christological exegesis of the Old Testament began during the historic ministry of

---

24. In general, see B. de Margerie, *Introduction à l'histoire de l'exégèse*. I. *Les Pères grecs et orientaux* (Paris: Cerf, 1980); and for detailed discussion of a complex of Christological and other exegesis set in its original cultural context, P.M. Casey, 'The Fourth Kingdom in Cosmas Indicopleustes and the Syrian Tradition', *Rivista di Storia e Letteratura Religiosa* 25 (1989), pp. 385-403.

Jesus of Nazareth. It continued in the hands of Peter and the first disciples during Stage 1 of Christological development, when all the followers of Jesus were Jewish. At this stage, however creative and vigorous the new developments were, the interpretation of the Old Testament remained within the parameters of Judaism. In Stage 2 of the Christological development, when many Gentiles entered the churches without becoming Jewish, many new developments went ahead, some of which could not have occured in the Jewish community. At this second stage, some scholars have seen the development of the full deity of Jesus. We have however seen reason to believe that Jewish monotheism was not perceived to be breached at the time.

This situation changed in the Johannine community. Here the full deity of Jesus was openly declared. This was accompanied by charges of blasphemy, which is culturally appropriate, since it is precisely the open declaration of the full deity of Jesus which caused the Jewish community to perceive a breach of traditional Jewish monotheism. Christological exegesis of the Old Testament was also vigorously pursued in the Johannine community, and it was rightly perceived to be a major difference between the Johannine and Jewish communities. At this point, however, there was a hiccough in the development of Christological exegesis of the Old Testament. Scriptural support for the full deity of Jesus was not found there for more than a generation. The reason for this is that the deity of Jesus is so profoundly unJewish.

It is time that Christian scholars considered more carefully the problem which this poses. If the deity of Jesus cannot be found in the Old Testament because it is so radically unJewish; if its presentation has been accompanied for centuries by polemic and pogroms in which Christians have persecuted Jewish communities whose members could not accept the deity of a man; if this is because Jews have been conditioned by the revelation of God's oneness to them; in what sense can the doctrines of the Incarnation and the Trinity really be true? This question has traditionally been responded to with polemic and persecution—in the light of the Holocaust, it is currently being omitted. If, however, Christianity were in any sense true, such questions would not need to be avoided. It follows that Christian scholars with a genuine concern for truth should take them up, and see what modifications to traditional Christian doctrines, or to the mode in which they are held, might be made, with the integrity of Jewish as well as Christian communities in mind.

GOSPELS AND ACTS

THE ANOINTED[*]

Michael Goulder

Isaiah 61.1 is probably the most primitive and the most determinative text in the history of the Christian movement. It is likely that it formed Jesus' first conception of his vocation; that it provided a bridge to his later and more ambitious identity; that it gave shape to his own view of his message, and to that of both the principal wings of his movement; and that it led to a limitation which was the ruin of one of them.

'The Spirit of the Lord (Yahweh) is upon me'

MT: רוח אדני יהוה עלי

LXX: πνεῦμα κυρίου ἐπ' ἐμέ

Luke describes Jesus' opening sermon, in the Nazareth synagogue, as beginning with this text, which he has just read from the scroll. The Spirit has descended upon (ἐπί) him at his Baptism (Lk. 3.22); 'full of Holy Spirit' he has gone out to his temptations (4.1); he has returned to Galilee 'in the power of the Spirit', teaching (4.14-15). Matthew gives us a similar picture. At his Baptism Jesus sees the Spirit of God coming upon (ἐπί) him (Mt. 3.16); he is led up by the Spirit to be tempted by the devil (4.1); he settles in Galilee, preaching, healing and calling his first disciples. Then he goes up into the mountain and teaches his disciples, beginning 'Blessed are the poor in spirit (οἱ πτωχοὶ τῷ πνεύματι)... Blessed are those who mourn (οἱ πενθοῦντες...)': the very groups, the poor and the mourners, to whom the Isaianic prophet was to bring the good news. Matthew has of course glossed 'the poor' with 'in spirit', because he does not want to give the impression that

---

[*]   I am grateful to Lionel and Wendy North for their perseverance in organizing the annual conferences on 'The Old Testament in the New'. Lionel gave me the chance to try out a variety of ideas, and I took part in many lively discussions; it is a pleasure to have been asked to contribute to this *Festschrift*.

paupers will inherit the kingdom; but his gloss is probably related to Isaiah's πνεῦμα.

It is often noticed that Mark is not so distant. He also has the Spirit coming at Jesus' Baptism, though it comes into (εἰς) him (Mk 1.10); the Spirit at once drives him out for his temptation (1.12-13), and at 1.14 he comes to Galilee proclaiming τὸ εὐαγγέλιον τοῦ θεοῦ. The link with εὐαγγελίσασθαι of Isa. 61.1 LXX is often marked. It is less common to note that Mark's πεπλήρωται ὁ καιρός is also linked with Isaiah: the last verse of Isaiah 60 (60.22), immediately preceding 61.1, promises κατὰ καιρὸν συνάξω αὐτούς—καιρός, meaning a critical time, a rarity in Isaiah.[1]

The agreement of the three Synoptists on such a theme may lead to appeals to multiple attestation, and so to evidence for the historical Jesus; for here we have three independent sources, have we not?—L, Q and Mark. I should myself regard the multiple attestation argument as dubious, and the claim of three independent sources as naïve: for both Matthew and Luke have read Mark, and may be freely expanding his thin tale, not to speak of the likelihood of Luke's developing Matthew.[2] But scepsis over so simple a form of argument should not lead us to disillusion. Both the later Synoptists have developed Mark's account on a generous scale, and they have done so in quite different ways. Even if they have made the developments themselves, creatively, it is hard to think that they have done so without any support from tradition. They have surely heard that Jesus began his ministry under inspiration of the Spirit text of Isa. 61.1; they believed that Jesus found from his Baptism onwards that he could preach effectively, draw disciples and heal, and that he interpreted these gifts as the fulfilment of Isa. 61.1. The prophet says he was sent to carry the good news (לבשׂר//εὐαγγελίσασθαι) and to heal (להבשׂ [to bind up]//ἰάσασθαι).

Mark similarly opens his book with a series of fulfilments of the later chapters of Isaiah. It is ἀρχὴ τοῦ εὐαγγελίου, the εὐαγγέλιον which

---

1. It is found in this sense also in Isa. 49.8, 50.4 and 64.9. There is no mention of Isa. 60.22 as an influence on Mk 1.15 in J. Gnilka, *Das Evangelium nach Markus* (Zürich: Benzinger; Neukirchen–Vluyn: Neukirchener Verlag, 3rd edn, 1989), I, p. 66; R.A. Guelich, *Mark 1–8:26* (WBC, 34A; Dallas: Word Books, 1989), p. 45; M.D. Hooker, *The Gospel According to St Mark* (London: A. & C. Black, 1991), p. 54; R.A. Gundry, *Mark* (Grand Rapids: Eerdmans, 1992), p. 65. Gundry suggests a parallel from Lam. 4.18.

2. See my *Luke: A New Paradigm* (JSNTSup, 20; Sheffield: JSOT Press, 1989).

was to be proclaimed on the mountains in Isa. 40.9 and 52.7, and at 61.1. The 'voice of one crying in the wilderness' was taken from Isa. 40.3. The divine word to Jesus, ἐν σοὶ εὐδόκησα, is taken from Isa. 42.1. The good news that the kingdom of God has drawn near comes from Isa. 52.7, βασιλεύσει σου ὁ θεός. The verb ἤγγικεν comes from Isa. 56.1, ἤγγικεν τὸ σωτήριόν μου. So Mark sees the whole opening of Jesus' ministry as based on later Isaiah.

It is always hazardous to move from 'we have a strong multiple tradition' to 'Jesus is likely to have...'; but if we are to make any but the most general statements about him, this is the path we have, hesitantly, to tread. All our three Synoptists seem confident that Jesus' ministry was seen by him as a fulfilment of Isa. 61.1: so it is likely that Jesus himself saw events this way. He found himself a powerful preacher, able to draw crowds and to inspire men to leave all and follow him; and he could exorcise and heal. So the divine word was fulfilled: 'The Spirit of the Lord (Yahweh) is upon *me*'.

'Because he (Yahweh) has anointed me'

MT: יַעַן מָשַׁח יְהוָה אֹתִי

LXX: οὗ εἵνεκεν ἔχρισέν με

Traditional exposition interpreted Jesus' most regular title, Christ, with two comments. First, Jewish people had been waiting for centuries for a king, a descendant of David, who would deliver them from foreign oppression, and this king was spoken of as 'the Christ', the anointed one. Second, Jesus saw himself as this figure, but spiritualized its content: there should be no violence, and the kingdom of God was not of this world. Unfortunately neither of these glosses is certain.

(1) While it has been disputed whether the expression 'the Messiah'/ 'the Christ' was in current use at the turn of the era,[3] it is widely thought that it was; it is difficult to explain the centrality of the concept in the New Testament if it was not. William Horbury has argued impressively for its importance in Jewish thought, and for its potential as leading to the worship of Jesus the Christ.[4] But its roots lie in Jewish

---

3.   M. de Jonge, 'The Use of the Word "Anointed" in the Time of Jesus', *NovT* 8 (1966), pp. 132-48; *idem, Christology in Context* (Philadelphia: Fortress Press, 1988); M. Casey, *From Jewish Prophet to Gentile God* (Cambridge: James Clarke, 1991).

4.   *Jewish Messianism and the Cult of Christ* (London: SCM Press, 1998).

aspirations to political independence under a Davidic king (2 Sam. 7.13), and the hope of deliverance after the exile with such a leader (Isa. 11.1-10, and many texts[5]). The perseverance of such a political conception is implied in New Testament passages about false messiahs leading rebellions (see Mt. 24.23-26 and parallels). Jesus was executed by the Romans as 'the king of the Jews' (Mk 15.26), so it is likely that they saw him as a political threat.

E.P. Sanders says correctly that there may have been many ideas of Messiah in first-century Palestine.[6] The *Psalms of Solomon* speak of the Messiah as purging Jerusalem of Gentiles and of impious Jews, but it seems that the cleansing is done by God and not by his army (17.33-34); the Messiah's powerful word is sufficient (17.24-25). At the same time he is a military figure, with 'strength to destroy the unrighteous rulers' and to 'shatter all the substance of sinners with an iron rod' (17.22-23). The Qumran documents reveal two Messiahs, a priestly Messiah of Aaron and a royal Messiah of Israel; and we find a similar picture in the *Testaments of the Twelve Patriarchs*.[7] Such a duality had its place already in the prophecy of Zechariah, with Joshua and Zerubbabel, and as there, the royal figure takes a second place: the High Priest was the key person in post-exilic Israel. In the War Scroll from Qumran the Messiah of Aaron takes the lead, exhorting and empowering the sons of light, and the Messiah of Israel seems rather spare. But it is an exaggeration to think of him as playing no part in the war. The situation is envisaged after the pattern of 2 Chronicles 19, where the lead is taken by Jahaziel and his Levites, and God himself ambushes the enemy; Jehoshaphat the king plays a walk-on part, but he does not do nothing. So even if the Davidic Messiah is not always thought of as leading an army, he is generally associated with the expulsion of occupying powers and collaborators, and the enforcing of righteousness.

(2) Jesus rode into Jerusalem on an ass, in what looks like a deliberate fulfilment of Zech. 9.9; so it seems that he saw himself as a royal Messiah. The title on his cross makes the same self-understanding likely: he thought he was, in some sense, king of the Jews. Sanders glosses plausibly, '"king" yes, of a sort; (military conqueror no)'.[8] But

5. Psalm 89 takes up the promises to the anointed one of Pss. 2, 18 and 45, among others; Jer. 30.8-9; Ezek. 37.21-28; Zech. 9.9; 2 Esdras; Baruch.

6. *The Historical Figure of Jesus* (London: Penguin, 1993), pp. 89-90, 240-41.

7. *T. Reub.* 6.7-8; *T. Sim.* 7.2.

8. Sanders, *Historical Figure*, p. 242.

the problem remains how Jesus came to use such a term for himself, when it had military associations for many people, and when his own life had had no obvious suggestions of a Davidic-type calling.[9] Sanders himself defines Jesus' self-concept as being *'charismatic and autonomous prophet'*.[10] Gerd Theissen and Annette Merz set the historical Jesus out as a charismatic, a prophet, a healer and a poet.[11] N.T. Wright speaks of Jesus as primarily a prophet, though also as Christ and other titles.[12] So how did a charismatic prophet come to think of himself as Messiah?

The happy feature of Isa. 61.1 is that it forms a bridge.[13] Our traditions about Jesus' preaching and healing link them with the gift of the Spirit; and the Spirit's coming on him is spoken of as an anointing. It is a short step from 'the Lord anointed me' to 'I am the Lord's Anointed', from ἔχρισέν με to Ἰησοῦς Χριστός. We seem to see this step being taken in the speeches in Acts. Peter says at Acts 10.36 that God sent the word to Israel, preaching peace by Jesus Christ: εὐαγγελιζόμενος εἰρήνην draws on Isa. 52.7. But Ἰησοῦ Χριστοῦ is drawn from Isa. 61.1, for two verses later Peter continues: '...Jesus of Nazareth, how God anointed (ἔχρισεν) him with Holy Spirit and power, who went about doing good and healing (ἰώμενος)...' (10.38). This is a clear and emphatic echo of our text. In Luke's view, Peter saw Jesus' Christhood as being rooted in a prophetic Christology.

We may infer then that there were two stages in Jesus' idea of his vocation. He felt moved to proclaim the coming of God's kingdom, and found that he had gifts of exorcism and healing: and these successes led him to think that he had been anointed by God with the Spirit, to proclaim and to heal, in fulfilment of Isa. 61.1. With time, and success, a grander conception began to dawn: perhaps he was not just anointed

9. The problem is well set out by Ferdinand Hahn, *The Titles of Jesus in Christology* (trans. Harold Knight and Geolge Ogg; London: Lutterworth, 1969 [orig. German edn, 1963]), p. 148.

10. Sanders, *Historical Figure*, p. 238, Sanders' emphasis.

11. *The Historical Jesus* (London: SCM Press 1998 [orig. German edn, 1996]) devotes a section to each of the four headings.

12. *Jesus and the Victory of God* (London: SPCK, 1996), pp. 489-93, for the discussion of Jesus as Messiah, with the primary evidence from 'praxis', that is, the triumphal entry and the *titulus*.

13. This was first seen (to my knowledge) by Anthony Harvey in *Jesus and the Constraints of History* (London: Gerald Duckworth, 1982), pp. 140-42; though he has developed the idea rather differently from me.

as a prophet, but as the Anointed, the long-awaited Davidic Messiah. Why should it be thought that the two were different? Isaiah 11.1-10 speaks, just as Isaiah 61 does, of the Spirit of Yahweh coming on a man, only this time it is on a shoot from the stump of Jesse. It may be also that we have the same progression reflected in Mk 8.27-29. The first impression Jesus made was that he was a prophetic figure, Elijah returned, or one of the prophets; only at the end of his ministry did people begin to think that he was the Christ, and see his movement as 'the coming kingdom of our father David' (Mk 11.10).

'To bring good news to the poor has he sent me'

MT: לבשׂר ענוים שׁלחני

LXX: εὐαγγελίσασθαι πτωχοῖς ἀπέσταλκέ με

There is some evidence that Jesus spoke of his movement as 'the poor people'.[14] I have already mentioned Luke's and Matthew's accounts of his first preaching, Luke with the citation of Isa. 61.1-2 at 4.18-19, Matthew with the first two Beatitudes (5.3-4). Both Evangelists include reference to the πτωχοί; Matthew emphatically, since they are the first blessed. But Matthew knows that penury is not the qualification for possessing the kingdom, and he adds the ambiguous gloss τῷ πνεύματι. It is perhaps unclear what it means to be 'poor in spirit', but the mention of spirit suggests the further influence of Isa. 61.1.

Luke gives a second form of the Beatitude at 6.20, 'Blessed are the poor'—poor absolutely. It is often thought that Luke has the earlier (Q) version here,[15] and that Jesus directed his preaching to the poor of his district. But this seems both unnecessary and unlikely. Matthew is glossing Isaiah 61 (with its πενθοῦντες, 61.3, and its κληρονομήσουσιν τὴν γῆν, 61.7), spiritualizing it—we have no reason to posit a second

14. This was suggested by Karl Holl in an article, 'Der Kirchenbegriff bei Paulus in seinem Verhältnis zu der Urgemeinde', originally published in 1921 and available in his *Gesammelte Aufsätze zur Kirchengeschichte* (Tübingen: J.C.B. Mohr, 1933), II, pp. 44-67. The proposal was strongly criticised by Leander Keck in two articles, 'The Poor among the Saints in the New Testament', *ZNW* 56 (1965), pp. 100-29, and 'The Poor among the Saints in Jewish Christianity and Qumran', *ZNW* 57 (1966), pp. 54-78. I have expanded and defended Holl's arguments in 'A Poor Man's Christology', *NTS* 45 (1999), pp. 332-48.

15. See the dialogue between Christopher Tuckett and myself, 'The Beatitudes: A Source-Critical Study', in *NovT* 25 (1983), pp. 193-216.

source for him with μακάριοι οἱ πτωχοί. Nor is there any sign that Jesus was specially concerned with the submerged tenth. All the converts whose circumstances we know are *petits bourgeois*. Peter owned a house and a boat; James and John came from a family with hired labour; Levi/Matthew ran a tax business; there were women in the movement who could pay for the food for some twenty members over a considerable period; Mary Magdalene seems to have done quite well on the streets. These people are not poor: Luke understands the poverty, the hunger and the weeping to be the disciples' lot *after* their conversion, either from rejection (6.20-23), or from voluntary giving (12.33-34; 14.33). But it was real poverty, not Matthew's 'spiritual' variety; he goes back to Isaiah's plain πτωχοί.

Luke's stress on voluntary poverty marries well with his account of the shared purse policy of the first Christian community in Jerusalem (Acts 2–4). Such communal living might seem appropriate in the world's last days, but the history of other such groups suggests that real poverty is inevitable when the capital dries up. Such a situation seems to have been reached with Paul's visit to Jerusalem in 48 CE. The 'pillars' gave him the right hand of fellowship; they asked only τῶν πτωχῶν ἵνα μνημονεύωμεν (Gal. 2.10). These οἱ πτωχοί are not the indigent generally, but the Jerusalem Christians, who, after nearly two decades of communal living, are running out of funds. This may be seen from the fact that Paul's consequent collection is taken up 'for the saints' (1 Cor. 16.1; 2 Cor. 9.1; Rom. 15.25, 31). At Rom. 15.26 these are referred to as τοὺς πτωχοὺς τῶν ἁγίων τῶν ἐν Ἰερουσαλήμ: Paul is adapting the Jerusalem church's name for itself—'the poor people'—so as to emphasize that the money will be going only to the deserving—no rich Christian will benefit. Only now the movement is not just called 'the poor people' after Isaiah: they are *really* poor.

All Christians spoke of Jesus as anointed, but the term meant different things to different groups. For Paul Jesus was Messiah, with an existence before his birth, even in so early a letter as 1 Corinthians (8.6; 10.4). But for the Jerusalem church Luke testifies to a consistently prophetic Christology. In Acts 3.20 God will send his chosen anointed; but this is then identified with the prophet like Moses whom God would raise (3.22), with salvation dependent upon obedience to him. The same text is put in the mouth of Stephen at Acts 7.37. Both Peter and the early community more generally are represented as proclaiming a vague Christology, once more going back to Deutero-Isaiah with Jesus as God's παῖς. Of the four Servant passages, two (Isa. 42.1-4; 52.13-53.12) speak of ὁ παῖς μου in the third person, while Isa. 49.1-7 and 50.4-9 are in the first person, like 61.1. So we find Peter speaking of God glorifying his servant Jesus (Acts 3.13). At 4.24-30 the Church prays, citing Psalm 2 where the rulers gather against the Lord and his Christ; but Herod and Pilate are then said to have gathered 'against your holy servant Jesus, whom you anointed' (4.27), and the title is repeated at 4.30. Luke believed that the Jerusalem church had not proclaimed Jesus as Son of God, or even clearly as royal Messiah. It had aligned Isa. 61.1 with the Servant of Isaiah 42–53, and with the Prophet of Deut. 18.15, 18. It was in this sense that they had spoken of 'Christ', and had used terms like the Holy One, Leader, Saviour and Lord.

In the long run, the higher Pauline Christology triumphed and most Jewish Christians fell in with it—but not all. Thus we find two wings of the old Jerusalem view sticking to their guns from the second to the fourth century. Both of them retain the prophetic Christology. On the one hand there is a compromising wing, the Nazarenes, who have produced the Pseudo-Clementines with the doctrine of the True Prophet. But on the other, there is also a harder line, taken by the so-called Ebionites, who are already treated as a heresy by Irenaeus (*Adv. Haer.* 1.26.2). They believed that Jesus was the son of Joseph and Mary, conceived like everyone else; that 'Christ' was the name of a divine spirit who entered Jesus at his baptism and left him before his passion; and that this enabled Jesus to do miracles and reveal the unknown Father (I. 26.1). In other words, he was a prophet. 'Ebionites' is a Graecised form of the Hebrew , אביונים, the poor people.

So Isa. 61.1 was to have a lasting and varied effect on the Christian movement; indeed, it is difficult to think of any text which has been so influential. So far as our evidence goes, it had a primary impact on Jesus himself: as he found himself able to communicate *the good news* of the kingdom, and to *bind up/heal* the sick, it suggested to him that he had been *anointed* by God with *his Spirit* for this mission. It was then a short step to assimilating a prophetic to a royal anointing: in the last phase of his ministry he was able to see himself as *the Christ*, the long-promised royal Messiah. Every movement needs a name, and Isaiah suggested a suitable one, *the poor people*: God's faithful were often spoken of in the Psalms as עניים ואביונים, and a movement whose members gave up earning in order to proclaim the kingdom was bound to be poor. Jesus was right in this, and in time the Jerusalem church did indeed become poor. The LXX had rendered Isaiah's עֲנָוִים with πτωχοί, and that is the name by which James spoke of it to Paul in Gal. 2.10; but, אֶבְיוֹנִים was a more exact counterpart. So, in the long run, the more conservative Jewish-Christian wing became known to the Great Church as the Ebionites; and their simple prophetic Christology, the Christology of Jesus and Peter, was condemned as heresy.

JESUS' OLD TESTAMENT BASIS FOR MONOGAMY

David Instone Brewer

Polygamy in Judaism

Polygamy was undoubtedly part of life in first-century Judaism, but it is uncertain how widespread it was. Although it was sometimes thought that only the rich could afford more than one wife, it is now known that the middle classes also practiced polygamy.

Polygamy was allowed in Mosaic Law[1] though it was nowhere spoken of with approval. Although many Old Testament characters and heroes had more than one wife, there is no evidence that polygamy was widespread in Israel, except perhaps after times of war when the male population was diminished.[2] In the Old Testament, polygamy is almost always related to childlessness,[3] and is often associated with problems.[4]

---

1. See Exod. 21.10-11; Deut. 21.15-17. Polygamy may also be implied in the laws that a man who seduces an unbetrothed virgin (Exod. 22.16) or rapes her (Deut. 22.28-29) must marry her, because it does not state that the man must be unmarried.

2. See Isa. 3.25; 4.1. Nelly Stienstra points out that even when war made an imbalance of women–men ratio, polygamy was seen as a shameful response to it— N. Stienstra, *YHWH is the Husband of His People: Analysis of a Biblical Metaphor with Special Reference to Translation* (Kampen: Kok, 1993), p. 79

3. E.g. Sarah and Hagar (Gen. 16.1-4). Elkanah also had a second wife because his favourite (perhaps his first) could not conceive (1 Sam. 1). Jacob was a special case because of Laban's trick (Gen. 29.15-30). This mirrors the situation in other ancient Near Eastern countries; see G.P. Hugenberger, *Marriage as a Covenant: A Study of Biblical Law and Ethics Governing Marriage, Developed from the Perspective of Malachi* (VTSup, 52; Leiden: E.J. Brill, 1994), pp. 108-12 .

4. Stienstra lists Hagar and Sarah (Gen. 16.4-6), Rachel and Leah (Gen. 30.14-16), and Peninnah and Hannah (1 Sam. 1.6-8). She also lists laws which imply problems with polygamy: Lev. 18.18 prohibits against the marrying of two sisters, because this may cause rivalry (cf. the story of Rachel and Leah); Deut. 21.15-17 says the son of a favourite wife should not rob the firstborn of his rights (cf. the

Leaders and kings like Gideon, Samson, David and Solomon had many wives, probably to imitate leaders in other countries[5]. Although there is some criticism of the 'many wives' of the kings, some of whom were foreigners, there is little or no criticism of other polygamy.[6]

It is unlikely that there was any teaching against polygamy in the early history of Israel. The phrase 'they shall be one flesh' would probably have been interpreted to mean 'they shall be one family'.[7] In the Later Prophets monogamy was taught as an ideal,[8] but polygamy was never made illegal, and God was portrayed as married to both Israel and Judah, without any shame attached to this.[9]

In the first century CE, polygamy was still considered to be part of traditional Jewish teaching and practice[10] though, in practice, most men would have had only one wife for financial reasons. There is very little evidence of polygamy in this period, and it might be assumed that only

story of Joseph); Exod. 21.10-11 assumes there will be problems of neglect for the first wife. She also cites the Targum of Ruth 4.6 which has Ruth's kinsman redeemer say: 'On this ground I cannot redeem it, because I have a wife already, and I have no desire to take another, lest there should be contention in my house' (Stienstra, *YHWH is the Husband*, p. 82).

    5.   Cf. 1 Sam. 8.5 and 19-20, criticized in Deut. 17.17.

    6.   Louis Epstein summarized the biblical data in *Marriage Laws in the Bible and Talmud: A Study in the Status of the Woman in Jewish Law* (Repr. New York: Johnson Corp., 1968 [1942]), pp. 3-7. He points out that the Law assumed polygamy in Exod. 21.10, Deut. 21.15 and Lev. 18.18. He lists among the polygamists of the Old Testament, Lamech, Abraham, Nahor, Esau, Jacob, Simeon, Gideon, Elkanah, Saul, David, Solomon, Rehoboam, Jehoash, Abiah, Manasseh and Sheharaim.

    7.   Skinner pointed out that flesh, בשׂר, is synonymous with 'clan', 'family group' in both Hebrew and Arabic usage. Cf. Lev. 25.49, 'a near kinsman belonging to his flesh may redeem him', and see John Skinner, *Genesis* (ICC; Edinburgh: T. & T. Clark, 1930), p. 70.

    8.   E.g. Isa. 50.1; Jer. 2.2; Ezek. 16.8; Prov. 12.4; 18.22; 19.14; 31.10-31; Ps. 128.3.

    9.   See Jer. 3.7-20; Ezek. 23.

    10.   Safrai cites Josephus (*Ant.* 17.14; *War* 1.477). Justin Martyr (*Dialogue* 141) and some examples of polygamy in first-century rabbinic sources (*t. Yeb.* 1.10; *b. Suk.* 27a; *b. Yeb.* 15a); S. Safrai, 'Home and Family', in S. Safrai *et al.* (eds), *The Jewish People in the First Century: Historical Geography, Political History, Social, Cultural and Religious Life and Institutions* (2 vols.; Compendia Rerum Iudaicarum ad Novum Testamentum, 1; Assen: Van Gorcum, 1974 [vol. 1]; Philadelphia: Fortress Press, 1976 [vol. 2]), II, pp. 728-92 (749).

the very rich practiced polygamy. However, this may simply be due to the paucity of family records from that time, except for those of the rich.[11] The family documents of one middle-class family, the Babatha family of the late-first and second century, have survived almost intact. They show that when Babatha was widowed she became another man's second wife,[12] which might indicate that polygamy was much more widespread in the middle classes than previously thought. Polygamy among Jews is stated as normal practice by Josephus[13] and Justin Martyr,[14] and the early rabbinic writings contains much legislation concerning it, including regulations for middle-class families.[15]

Monogamy in Judaism

Many people were unhappy with the practice of polygamy. Even in Rabbinic Judaism, which was the last section of Judaism to register this unease, there are negative comments about it in the early centuries.[16]

---

11. Most first-century examples of bigamy occur among the rich. Epstein (*Marriage Laws*, p. 17) lists Herod Archelaus, Herod Antipas (*Ant.* 17.13.1); from priest's families, Alubai, Caiaphas, and Josephus (*t. Yeb.* 1.10; *b. Yeb.* 15b; *y. Yeb.* 3a; *Life* 75); from the rabbis, Abba b. Rn. Simeon b. Gamaliel I (*b. Yeb.* 15a), R. Tarphon (*t. Ket.* 5.1), Rab and R. Nahman (*b. Yom.* 18b; *b. Yeb.* 37b).

12. The documents of the Babatha family dating from 93–132 CE have been found in found in a cave at Naḥal Ḥever. These are edited in H.M. Cotton and A. Yardeni, *Aramaic, Hebrew and Greek Documentary Texts from Nahal Hever and Other Sites: With an Appendix Containing Alleged Qumran Texts* (Discoveries in the Judaean Desert, 27; Oxford: Clarendon Press, 1997).

13. *Antiquities* 17.14 'For it is our ancestral custom that a man may have several wives at the same time'; cf. also *War* 1.477

14. Justin Martyr says that Jews practiced polygamy (*Dialogue* 141)

15. Epstein (*Marriage Laws*, p. 18) lists teaching concerning the co-wife (Zareh) which is discussed frequently (e.g. *m. Yeb.* 1, among others); the interval between marriages (*b. Ket.* 93b—less than one day!); that wives should know each other, lest their children marry each other (*b. Yom.* 18b); compelling a second wife if the first is barren (*b. Yeb.* 21b; *b. Soṭ.* 24a). He does not list *m. Ket.* 10.5 which is important because it can be dated before 70 CE and because it refers to a case where the husband could not afford to pay the *ketuvoth* for all his wives, which suggests that he was not rich.

16. The rabbinic writings have many negative comments about it. Epstein (*Marriage Laws*, p. 19) lists: *m. Ab.* 2.5, 'He who multiplies wives multiplies witchcraft'; *b. Yeb.* 44a, polygamy creates strife in a house; *b. Yeb.* 44a, no more than four wives are permitted so that each gets their conjugal rights at least each month.

Polygamy was eventually prohibited in Judaism in the eleventh century,[17] though it had probably ceased to be practiced long before this.

Outside Israel the disquiet with polygamy can be seen in the marriage contracts in Elephantine. The large body of papyri unearthed at Elephantine in Egypt include several marriage contracts and documents relating to divorce. They are the documents of a few Jewish families living in this Greek society in the fifth century BCE. [18] The collection includes a betrothal contract,[19] seven marriage contracts (though four of these are very fragmentary),[20] two documents concerning payment of the divorce settlement[21] and many other commercial and family documents.

These are not typical Jewish contracts, and are affected more by Gentile customs than Jewish ones.[22] Nevertheless, they show the kinds of influences which Greek and Roman customs were beginning to have

---

17. The Herem of R. Gershom of Mayence (960–1040 CE) finally prohibited it (*Responsa 'Asheri'* 42.1), probably in 1030 CE at Worms (the document has not survived). Previously the marriage contract had prohibited polygamy without the wife's consent, but this Herem prohibits it even with wife's consent.

18. The marriage and divorce texts are published with useful commentary in A.E. Cowley, *Aramaic Papyri of the Fifth Century BC* (Oxford: Clarendon Press, 1923); Emil G. Kraeling, *The Brooklyn Museum Aramaic Papyri: New Documents of the Fifth Century B.C. from the Jewish Colony at Elephantine* (New Haven: Yale University Press, 1953). These and the other texts from Elephantine have been re-edited and translated in Bezalel Porten and Ada Yardeni, *Textbook of Aramaic Documents from Ancient Egypt. II. Contracts* (Jerusalem: Akedemon, 1989). The traditional numbering is based on the collections of Cowley (C1 and so on) and Kraeling (K1 and so on) but the later numbering used by Porten and Yardeni (B1.1 and so on) is more useful because it groups together texts which belong to the same family archive or the same type of document. The two main family archives belonged to Mibtahiah (B2.1-11, 471–410 BCE) and Anani (B3.1-13, 456–402 BCE). Marriage contracts which are not part of these archives are collected as B6.1-4.

19. C48 = B2.5, a very small fragment which includes the words 'your daughter to take her for wifehood'.

20. Three marriage contracts are mostly complete (C15 = B2.6, concerning a divorcee; K2 = B3.3, concerning a slave girl; K7 = B3.8, concerning a freedwoman) and four are fragmentary (K14 = B6.1; C36 = B6.2; C46 = B6.3; C18 = B6.4).

21. C14 = B2.8; C35 = B4.6.

22. If these are typical of fifth century BCE contracts, we must conclude that either the Jewish *ketuvah* changed a great deal during the next few centuries, or the Jews at Elephantine had lost most of their Jewish roots. Hillel, in the first century BCE, recognized that the marriage contracts of Egyptian Jews were different from those of Palestinian Jews (*t. Ket.* 4.9).

on Judaism. One of the most significant influences is the move towards monogamy.[23] Although a monogamy clause is found in some ancient Near Eastern marriage contracts,[24] the Graeco-Roman was a stronger influence because it held to a strict monogamy.[25]

Some of the marriage contracts state that the man must not marry more than one wife, and nor must the wife marry more than one husband. If they do, they are liable to be divorced.

> And <the wife> shall not be able to take another man beside <her husband>. And if she do thus, it is hatred. They shall do to her the law of hatred.[26] And <the husband> shall not be able to take another woman beside <his wife>. And if he do thus, it is hatred. He shall do to her the law of hatred.[27]

23. These contracts were also influenced by ancient Near Eastern contracts, but the move to monogamy and other aspects of sexual equality can perhaps be traced to early Semitic influences. E. Lipiński, 'The Wife's Right to Divorce in the Light of an Ancient Near Eastern Tradition', in B.S. Jackson (ed.), *The Jewish Law Annual* 4 (Leiden: E.J. Brill, 1981), pp. 9-26, collected a handful of early Semitic ancient Near Eastern marriage contracts which do show equality of divorce rights for men and women. He points out that the terminology of these contracts show such substantial similarities to the Elephantine contracts that they may be considered as their precursors. He said that they were not influenced by Egyptian divorce certificates, because Egyptian divorce documentation has survived from the nineteenth Dynasty (1320–1200 BCE) but there is no divorce on the wife's initiative. However, in the area of monogamy, the most likely influence is the Graeco-Roman world.

24. Of Roth's 45 marriage certificates, fifteen have a clause anticipating what will happen if the husband divorces his wife because he wants to marry another woman (numbers 1, 2, 4, 5, 6, 8, 15, 16, 17, 19, 20, 25, 26, 30, 34; M.T. Roth, *Babylonian Marriage Agreements: 7th–3rd Centuries B.C.* [Neukirchen–Vluyn: Neukirchener Verlag, 1989]).

25. See Deborah F. Sawyer, *Women and Religion in the First Christian Centuries* (London: Routledge, 1996), pp. 15-19. Other aspects of equality, as found at Elephantine did not develop this far in the Graeco-Roman world until about the third century.

26. It is 'hatred' was a standard ancient Near Eastern term for divorce. This passive 'they shall do to her the law of hatred' is probably what made I. Abrahams conclude that women at Elephantine could not truly declare a divorce, but they could claim one. (*Studies in Pharisaism and the Gospels* (London: Macmillan, 1917), p. 67). However, this passive occurs only in K7 = B3.8. The same passive is not used with regard to women divorcing husbands for neglecting their conjugal rights ('she shall do to him the law of hatred'; see the next paragraph), though it must be admitted that there is only one contract for those words too.

27. K7 = B3.8; C18 = B6.4; C15 = B2.6. C15 = B2.6 forbids polygamy only to

Many other sections of Judaism were also leaning towards monogamy. One indication of this is a gloss which is found in non-Massoretic versions of Gen. 2.24, which adds the word 'two' so that it reads, 'and they two shall become one flesh'. The word 'two' is not present in the Massoretic text, but it is found in almost every other ancient version—Syriac *Peshiṭta*, *Samaritan Pentateuch*, Vulgate, *Targum Pseudo-Jonathan*, *Targum Neofiti* and LXX, including the quotations of the text in the New Testament.[28] It is missing only from *Targum Onqelos*, but this is probably because this Targum was consciously corrected back to the Massoretic text. It is not found in any Hebrew text or any quotation of the Hebrew text. [29]

It appears that this gloss was a very common addition to the text. The gloss affirmed that a marriage is made between only two individuals, so that polygamy is an aberration of this.

Qumran Arguments against Polygamy

The documents preserved at Qumran shows that some sections of Judaism actually forbade polygamy. The sectarians at Qumran differed from the rest of Judaism over several matters concerning worship, cleanliness and other laws. They separated from the worship of other Jews because of differences of interpretation concerning the religious calendar. Many of them separated physically from other Jews, living apart in the desert, because of their concern over cleanliness. Many of them also lived celibate lives,[30] but they were still interested in matters

the husband, and speaks in the first person, using completely different language: 'And I shall not be able to say: I have another wife beside <name of wife> and other children besides the children whom <the wife> shall bear to me. If I say: I have other children and wife beside <name> and her children, I shall give to <the wife> silver, 20 karsh by the stone-weights of the king. And I shall not be able to release my goods and my property from <name of wife>. And should I remove them from her, I shall give to <the wife> silver, 20 karsh by the stone-weights of the king.' C18 = B6.4 also forbids polygamy to the husband only, but it uses the same wording as K7 = B3.8, and the fragmentary nature of this document means that it may also have included a prohibition to the wife.

28. See Mt. 19.5; Mk 10.8; 1 Cor. 6.16.

29. The Hebrew text is not found at Qumran, so we only have the witnesses of rabbinic literature, much of which is late, though is cited by Aqiva (*b. Sanh.* 58a, early second century) and Hananiah (*Gen. R.* 18.5, mid-second century), both without the word 'two'.

30. The Manual of Discipline found at Qumran suggests that the community

of marriage, and especially polygamy. These matters were discussed in their writings particularly when they were criticizing the practices of others.

In the Damascus Document,[31] the sectarians criticise the 'builders of the wall' (CD 4.19–5.5), which may be a reference to the Pharisees or non-Qumran Jews in general.[32] They accuse them of sexual sin and of polluting the Temple.[33] They presumably thought that they polluted the Temple by going there when they were themselves polluted. They were polluted by two other practices concerning sexual taboo—menstrual blood and marrying near relations.

One of the two main criticisms which the Damascus Document brought against the Pharisees concerned the practice of polygamy, which they regarded as a sexual sin.

> (20) They are caught by two (snares). By sexual sin [זנות], (namely) taking (21) two wives in their lives [בחייהם], while the foundation of creation is 'male and female he created them' [Gen. 1.27]. (5.1) And those who entered (Noah's) ark went in two by two into the ark [Gen. 7.9]. And of the prince [נשיא] it is written, (2) 'Let him not multiply [לא ירבה] wives for himself' [Deut. 17.17]. And David did not read the sealed book of the Torah which (3) was in the Ark (of the Covenant), for it was not opened in Israel since the day of the death of Eleazar (4) and Joshua and the elders. For (their successors) worshipped the Ashtoreth, and that which had been revealed was hidden (5) until Zadok arose, so David's works were accepted, with the exception of Uriah's blood, (6) and God forgave him for them (CD 4.20–5.6).[34]

was celibate, though an appendix to it (1QSa 1.8-11) and the Damascus Document (CD 7.7-8) suggest that at least some members were married.

31. The Damascus Document is named after its references to Damascus. It was first discovered in the Cairo Geniza, so it was called CD for Cairo: Damascus.

32. The 'wall' may be a reference to the 'fence' which the Pharisees put around the law (*m. Abot.* 1.1). The fence was the system of rabbinic laws which amplified and specified what the biblical law said and what it implied. By keeping all these rabbinic laws, one would be certain to fulfil all the biblical laws, so they were a 'fence' to protect one from trespassing a biblical law. Charlesworth suggests that the similar phrase at CD 8.12 may also refer to the Pharisees (J.H. Charlesworth, *The Dead Sea Scrolls: Hebrew, Aramaic and Greek Texts with English Translations* [Tübingen: J.C.B. Mohr, 1995]). In the same passage they are also called 'white-wash-daubers' which has interesting New Testament parallels (Mt. 23.27; Acts 23.3).

33. Two of the three sins are listed in CD 4.17, the other was probably arrogance or materialism, which was perhaps reserved for the Sadducees.

34. Charlesworth, *Dead Sea Scrolls*. This portion only exists in the Geniza MS

This passage contains three independent exegetical arguments for monogamy, which will be dealt with in turn. It is perhaps significant that the variant text of Gen. 2.24 with the word 'two' is not employed as one of the arguments. I have suggested elsewhere that this was omitted because the Palestinian rabbis, against whom this is a polemic, did not accept exegesis from variant texts. Therefore, on this occasion, they only used arguments with which these rabbis could find no fault.[35]

1. *'Taking two wives in their lives'—Based on Leviticus 18.18*

Taking two wives in their lives (Lev. 18.18). לקחת שתי נשים בחייהם

The phrase 'taking two wives in their lives' has a masculine suffix for 'their', so that it appears to criticize any man who takes two wives within his own lifetime. This would include those who practice polygamy, remarriage after divorce or remarriage after widowhood. This led some early commentators like Schechter to argue that this virtually prohibited divorce, because it did not allow divorcees to remarry.[36] Other early commentators like Rabin suggested that 'in their [masc.] lives' was an allusion to Lev. 18.18 so it should be read as 'in their [fem.] lives'[37]. This would mean that divorce and remarriage was possible but only after the former wife had died.

This suggestion caused a great deal of debate, but the publication of the Temple Scroll (11QT) convinced most scholars that this emendation was correct.[38] Temple Scroll Col. 57, which is an expansion of Deut.

A. CD has been found in Qumran fragments 6Q15 and 4Q226-273 but only a couple of words from this passage are found in these fragments.

35. D. Instone Brewer, 'Nomological Exegesis in Qumran "Divorce" Texts', *RevQ* 18 (1998), pp. 561-79.

36. Solomon Schechter, *Documents of Jewish Sectaries* (Cambridge: Cambridge University Press, 1910 [repr. New York: Ktav, 1970]). For a full bibliography and an analysis of the exegesis of this passage see my 'Nomological Exegesis'.

37. That is, בחייהן instead of בחייהם; for example Chaim Rabin, *The Zadokite Documents* (Oxford: Clarendon Press, 1954). It should be noted that Schechter probably realized this too, though he does not say so in his commentary, because in his introduction he concluded that CD prohibited 'marrying a second wife, as long as the first wife is alive though she had been divorced' (p. xvii). Yadin says 'most of the early scholars' read it this way (Yigael Yadin, *The Temple Scroll* [3 vols.; Jerusalem: Israel Exploration Society, 1983], I, p. 356).

38. According to Yadin, only J. Murphy-O'Conner still defends the masculine

17.14-20 concerning kings, also used Lev. 18.18 as a proof text for monogamy.

> (15) ...And he [the king] shall not take a wife from all (16) the daughters of the nations, but from his father's house he shall take unto himself a wife, (17) from the family of his father. And he shall not take upon her another wife, for (18) she alone shall be with him all the days of her life [כול ימי חייה]. But should she die, he may take (19) unto himself another (wife) from the house of his father, from his family (11QT 57.15-19).[39]

This section of the Temple Scroll concerns the king's wife and is an expansion of Deut. 17.17: 'And he shall not multiply wives for himself, lest his heart turn away'. The Temple Scroll interprets this as an injunction against polygamy, whereas the standard rabbinic interpretation is that one may not take more than 18 wives.[40] The Temple Scroll author seems to interpret the phrase 'lest his heart turn away' in the light of Deut. 7.3-4[41] and 1 Kgs 11.1-2 which says that their hearts will be turned away by foreign women, as Solomon's was. Therefore, the Temple Scroll says, the king may only marry an Israelite and may only take one wife. In order to justify the interpretation 'one wife' rather than 'few wives', the Temple Scroll alludes to Lev. 18.18 with the phrase 'all the days of her life'.[42] Leviticus 18.18 says that one may not marry the sister of one's wife (or former wife) while she is still alive. In order to apply this law to the king, the Temple Scroll emphasizes that the whole of Israel is one family: 'he shall not take a wife from all the daughters of the nations, but from his father's house'.[43]

It is impossible to know whether the Temple Scroll regarded monogamy as mandatory for all Jews, but they would at least have regarded

reading since the publication of the Temple Scroll. He has carried on a long debate with Yadin; see the references in Yadin, *The Temple Scroll*, I, p. 356.

39. Based on Yadin, *The Temple Scroll*, II, p. 258.

40. See R. Judah at *m. San.* 2.4; *Pal. Targ.* This is probably based on the tradition that David had 18 wives (*b. Sanh.* 21a; *y. Sanh.* 2.6 [20c]).

41. Cf. Lawrence H. Schiffman, 'Laws Pertaining to Women in the Temple Scroll', in D. Dimant and U. Rappaport (eds.), *The Dead Sea Scrolls: Forty Years of Research* (Leiden: E.J. Brill, 1992), pp. 210-28 (213).

42. Yadin (*The Temple Scroll*, I, p. 355, II, p. 300) suggests that Lev. 18.18 was cited at the top of col. 57, which is missing.

43. It was natural to regard God as the father of Israel (as at Isa. 63.16; Jer. 31.9) when the context concerned turning away to other gods. Schiffman ('Laws Pertaining to Women', pp. 214-15) says that the main emphasis was to make the king like a High Priest, who may not marry a non-Israelite.

the king as an example to look up to and probably to emulate. It is unfortunate that the section regarding Deut. 21.15-17 (which allows polygamy for the ordinary Israelite) is not preserved—it would have been at the start of col. 54 which is missing.

In the Damascus Document, the allusion to Lev. 18.18 is not accompanied by any elaboration. There is not even the briefest of explanations, as found in the Temple Scroll. The reader is assumed to understand the text and its importance.

In both the Damascus Document and the Temple Scroll, this exegesis of Lev. 18.18 is accompanied by other arguments for monogamy (see below). It now seems likely that the whole force of both passages was against polygamy, and there are no implications for divorce or remarriage. Rabin's emendation of the Damascus Document suggested that a man was forbidden to remarry during the lifetime of his former wife,[44] while Ginzburg suggested a way of reading this text without any emendation, and without any reference to divorce or remarriage.[45] Ginzberg's interpretation has been confirmed both by the Temple Scroll and by other more recent texts which show that divorce was accepted at Qumran.

Ginzberg argued that the Damascus Document read the word 'sister' (אחתה) in Lev. 18.18 as 'other', which is linguistically possible, so that this law forbade a man marrying 'another' woman besides his wife. This is confirmed by the way the Temple Scroll also reads אחתה as 'other'.

The law of Lev. 18.18 states:

> You shall not take a wife with her sister to be a rival, to uncover her nakedness beside her, during her life.

ואשה אל־אחתה לא תקח לצרר לגלות ערותה עליה בחייה

The Temple Scroll paraphrased Lev. 18.18 as follows (the shared vocabulary is underlined and other shared ideas are dotted):

> And he shall not take with her another wife, for she alone shall be with him all the days of her life.

ולוא יקח עליה אשה אחרת כי היאה לבדה תהיה עמו כול ימי חייה

44. C. Rabin, *The Zadokite Documents* (Oxford: Clarendon Press, 1954), pp. 16-17.

45. L. Ginzberg, *An Unknown Jewish Sect* (New York: Jewish Theological Seminary of America, 1978), pp. 19-20.

Unlike the Damascus Document, the Temple Scroll exegetes gave a new emphasis to the idea of אחתה as 'sister'. They understood 'sister' as 'fellow Israelite', so that the text not only prohibited polygamy but also assumed that one would only marry an Israelite. This is given great emphasis in the Temple Scroll passage: '...from his father's house... from the family of his father...another (wife) from the house of his father, from his family'. If the primary meaning of אחתה is regarded as 'other', then an exegete is entitled to point out that this is an unusual word and to look for a reason for it.[46] The reason they found is that a wife should only be taken from among one's 'sisters', so one should not marry a non-Israelite.

Ginzberg pointed out that the natural meaning of 'during their lives' now becomes 'you may not have another husband or another wife during the lives of your present husband or wife'. This does not, of course, preclude remarriage after divorce, because then you no longer have a husband or wife. The law of Lev. 18.18 (according to the Qumran exegetes) concerns a man who has a wife and wants to take another, which is prohibited unless the first wife has died. If a man is divorced from his first wife, he no longer has a wife, so this law does not apply to him. We can see that this interpretation was in the minds of the Qumran exegetes in the way they summarize the teaching of Lev. 18.18 with the words 'taking two wives during their lives'. This phrase reminds the reader that Lev. 18.18 is emphatically speaking about being married to two wives at once: 'You shall not take a wife *with* her sister *to be a rival*, to uncover her nakedness *beside* her, during her life.'

Ginzberg's explanation removes all references to divorce or remarriage from the Damascus Document. The Temple Scroll has a more stringent rule for the King, as it does for many other matters than divorce and remarriage. This explanation is confirmed considerably by the Qumran texts which show that divorce was permitted.[47] Therefore

---

46. This is an exegetical technique which is found in early rabbinic exegesis; see my *Techniques and Assumptions in Jewish Exegesis before 70 CE* (TSAJ, 30; Tübingen: J.C.B. Mohr [Paul Siebeck], 1992), pp. 20-21.

47. Divorce is assumed to be lawful in 11QT 54.4-5, 'But any vow of a widow or of a divorced woman...'; 11QT 66.8-11, 'If a man violates a young virgin...she will be his wife...and he cannot dismiss her all his life'; CD 13.15-17, 'the examiner who is (in charge of) the camp... A[ny]one who ma[rr]ies a wo[man], i[t] (must be)[with] (his) counsel. And thus (also) for one who divorces (his wife)'. The latter text is fragmentary. Lawrence H. Schiffman's reconstruction (*Reclaiming the*

this exegetical argument does not prohibit divorce or remarriage at Qumran, but is directed solely at the practice of polygamy which the Qumran exegetes considered to be unlawful.[48]

2. *'Male and female'—Based on Genesis 1.27 and 7.9*

| The foundation of creation is | ויסוד הבריאה |
| *male and female* he created them (Gen. 1.27). | זכר ונקבה ברא אותם |

| And those who entered (Noah's) ark | ובאי התבה |
| went in *two by two* into the ark (Gen. 7.9). | שנים שנים באו אל התבה |

Lövestam pointed out that these two passages, Gen. 1.27 and 7.9, are linked by the words 'male and female' (זכר ונקבה) which occurs immediately after the text cited from Gen. 7.9.[49] When the texts have been linked by a shared phrase, the definition or description of this phrase in one of the texts can be applied to the other text. This type of exegesis was later called *gezerah shahvah*, but it was already common in early rabbinic Judaism before 70 CE.[50]

The second text showed that the phrase 'male and female' meant a pair, because they went in 'two by two'. The first text showed that God himself was responsible for putting the male and female together. Taken together, these texts could be used to show that God put men and women together in pairs. Therefore God instituted marriage as one wife and one husband. Marriage is not actually mentioned in either text, but in the verse following 1.27 God tells them to multiply, so it could be argued that marriage is implied.

From the opening phrase 'beginning of creation' it might be supposed that the force of the argument lay in the fact that this is how it was done 'in the beginning'. However the emphasis was more likely to be on 'creation', which was an act of God. In other words, if God did

Dead Sea Scrolls: The History of Judaism, The Background of Christianity, The Lost Library of Qumran [Philadelphia: The Jewish Publication Society, 1994], p. 122) has been confirmed by the newly published 4Q266 (col. 8 ll. 6-7); see Tom Holmén, 'Divorce in CD 4.20–5.2 and in 11Q 57.17-18: Some Remarks on the Pertinence of the Question', *RevQ* 71 (1998), pp. 397-408 (403).

48. I have dealt with these matters in greater detail in my 'Nomological Exegesis'.

49. Evald Lövestam, 'Divorce and Remarriage in the New Testament', in B.S. Jackson (ed.), *The Jewish Law Annual* 4 (Leiden: E.J. Brill, 1981), pp. 47-65 (50).

50. See my *Techniques and Assumptions*, pp. 17-18.

something one way, we should follow his example. The same type of argument, based on an example given by God, is found in a Hillel-Shammai debate about how many children one has to have before one has fulfilled the command to 'increase and multiply' (Gen. 1.28). The Shammaites argued that 'two children' were sufficient, based on the example of Moses (Exod. 18.2-3). The Hillelites said 'a male and female' were sufficient, based on the example of God who created Adam and Eve. The Hillelites won the debate because they cited a higher example than Moses.[51]

3. *'Not multiply wives'—Based on Deuteronomy 17.17*

And of the prince it is written,	ועל הנשיא כתוב
'Let him not multiply wives for himself' (Deut. 17.17).	לא ירבה לו נשים

This text appears to apply only to kings in the context of Deut. 17.17. However, the text would have little value here if it was understood in this way. It seems that the Qumran exegetes intended to apply it to all Israelites but they do not state how they did this. Probably they used the same kind of argument as found a couple of generations later on the lips of Simeon b. Yohai. who said: 'all Israelites are children of kings' (*m. Šhab.* 14.4)[52]. Although he was a mid-second century Rabbi, it is likely that he was presenting a traditional interpretation.

Presumably the Qumran exegetes felt that this interpretation was too obvious to be spelled out. This same interpretation is found in the Well Midrash at CD 6.3-9, where the 'princes' (שרים) of Num. 21.18 are interpreted as 'the returned of Israel who went out from the land of Judah and sojourned in the land of Damascus'—that is, the members of the Qumran community, or the true Israel.

The phrase used here, 'of the prince [הנשיא] it is written' confirms a

---

51. See *t. Yeb.* 8.4; *m. Yeb.* 6.6; *y. Yeb.* 6.6; *b. Yeb.* 61b-62a. Different versions have different rulings for the Shammaites. The Mishnah and the Jerusalem Talmud have 'two sons'. The Babylonian Talmud has '2 males and 2 females' while the Tosephta has two opinions: Nathan said it was 'two children' and Jonathan said it was 'male and female' (while Hillelite was 'male or female').

52. כל ישראל בני מלכים, 'all Israel are princes' (lit: 'all sons of kings'), is cited frequently, usually attributed to Simeon (*m. Šab.* 14.4; *y. Šab.* 14.4; *b. Šab.* 67a; *b. B. Meṣ.* 113b; *b. Šab.* 128a; Rashi at *b. Šab.* 59b). There is no early exegetical basis for this, but the later Rabbi Levi derived it from 1 Chron. 24.5 'the princes of God' and Ps. 82.6 'you are gods...but you will fall like one of the princes' (*Shir. R.* 1.2.5).

link with this traditional interpretation. It would have been more natural to say 'of the king [מלך] it is written', because 'king' is used constantly in Deut. 17.14-20. It seems that 'prince' has been deliberately used here to point to the well-known equivalence of 'princes = all Israel'.

The Temple Scroll also cites Deut. 17.17 in 11QT 56.18, applying it to the ideal king. It is part of the long passage describing the ideal king (11QT 56.12–58.21), so it is difficult to know whether it was supposed to apply to all Israel. Some of the regulations for the king are higher than those for the normal Israelites, while others are those which apply to everyone. Baumgarten claims that the Temple Scroll allows polygamy, because 11QT 64 partially preserves a discussion of Deut. 21.15 concerning a man who has two wives. However the text is totally missing, and it is impossible to reconstruct how it was interpreted.[53]

An interesting exegesis of 'do not multiply' has been preserved by Simeon b. Yohai, the same rabbi who is normally associated with the equation 'all Israelites are children of kings'. He records a story that the book of Deuteronomy went up to heaven to charge Solomon with annulling a yod in the Law. Solomon had changed 'he shall not multiply [לא ירבה] wives to himself' to 'to a multitude [לארבה] of wives for himself'. This removal of a yod amounted to a cancellation of the entire Law. God assured him (the book of Deuteronomy) that 'Solomon and a thousand like him will perish, but a word of thee will not perish'.[54]

Although the exegesis is told in fanciful haggadic language which is normally associated with later traditions, it is possible that the core of the exegesis is early. Daube[55] pointed out that this is very similar to the gospel logion about the yod, and he suggested that Luke's juxtaposition of this logion next to the divorce logion may be particularly significant:

> But it is easier for heaven and earth to pass away, than for one *yod* of the law to become void. 'Every one who divorces his wife and marries another commits adultery, and he who marries a woman divorced from her husband commits adultery' (Lk. 16.17-18).

---

53. J.M. Baumgarten, 'The Qumran-Essene Restraints on Marriage', in L.H. Schiffman (ed.), *Archaeology and History in the Dead Sea Scrolls* (JSPSup, 8; Sheffield: JSOT Press, 1990), pp. 13-24 (14).

54. See *Exod. R.* 6.1, where it is attributed to 'our Sages', and *Lev. R.* 19.2 where it is attributed to Simeon b. Yohai. This was pointed out by David Daube (*The New Testament and Rabbinic Judaism* [London: Athlone Press, 1956], p. 298), though the rabbinic references there are incorrect.

55. Daube, *New Testament*, p. 299.

As will be seen below, Jesus' teaching on monogamy is found within a digression on his teaching about divorce.

The Qumran exegetes, therefore, used 'do not multiply wives' as one of their proof texts for monogamy among all 'princes', which included all true Israelites. They followed this with a long apology about why David did not obey this law, arguing that he was ignorant of the Law because it was hidden during his time.

These three arguments in the Damascus Document, with the similar arguments in the Temple Scroll, show that the authors of both documents were highly critical of polygamy. They regarded it as sexual immorality, as contrary to the ideals shown in the examples of God at creation, of Adam, and of Noah's Ark, and contrary to the commands in Torah at Lev. 18.18 and Deut. 17.17. One of these exegetical arguments is used by Jesus (discussed below), and another is possibly alluded to by Luke in his editorial arrangement of pericopae.

The Divorce Debate in the Gospels

Matthew portrayed Jesus as taking part in the Hillel-Shammai debate about the grounds for divorce. The same material is present in Mark, but the interaction with the rabbinic debate is less obvious in his version. I will not cover the divorce debate in any detail here, except as far as it concerns the structure of these pericopae, and the accompanying teaching about monogamy.[56]

> Mark 10.2:
> And Pharisees came up and in order to test him asked, 'Is it lawful for a man to divorce his wife?'
>
> Καὶ προσελθόντες Φαρισαῖοι[57] ἐπηρώτων αὐτὸν εἰ ἔξεστιν ἀνδρὶ γυναῖκα ἀπολῦσαι, πειράζοντες αὐτόν.

---

56. I am covering the whole topic of Jewish background of divorce and remarriage in a forthcoming monograph. In the meantime my work is available on the Web at: http://www.tyndale.cam.ac.uk/Brewer/divorce.htm.

57. MS D omits Καὶ προσελθόντες Φαρισαινοι and some editors of the UBS text think that the phrase was assimilated from Matthew (Bruce M. Metzger, *A Textual Commentary on the Greek New Testament: A Companion Volume to the United Bible Societies' Greek New Testament* [Stuttgart: Deutsche Bibelgesellschaft, 2nd edn, 1994]).

Matthew 19.3:

And Pharisees came up to him and tested him by asking, 'Is it lawful for a person to divorce his wife *for any matter?*'

Καὶ προσῆλθον αὐτῷ Φαρισαῖοι πειράζοντες αὐτὸν καὶ λέγοντες· εἰ ἔξεστιν ἀνθρώπω.[58] ἀπολῦσαι τὴν γυναῖκα αὐτοῦ κατὰ πᾶσαν αἰτίαν;

The main difference between the accounts in Mark and Matthew is the inclusion of the phrases 'for any matter' and 'except (for a matter of) indecency' in Matthew. Most commentators have concluded that these phrases have been added by Matthew, because the latter phrase is present in both the logion in Mt. 5.32 (while it is absent from Lk. 16.18) and in the debate in Mt. 19.9 (while it is absent in Mk 10.12). Although I will conclude that Matthew has probably added these phrases to the tradition which he received, I will also argue that he has correctly re-inserted something which was present in the original debate. These phrases (or their equivalent) were removed when the debate was summarized for oral or written transmission, because they were so obvious and well known to the original audience that they were superfluous. They would have been mentally inserted by any Jewish reader whether they were included or not.

The phrases 'any matter' and 'except indecency' were the phrases which encapsulated the positions of the Hillelites and Shammaites respectively in their debate about the meaning of עָרְוַת דָּבָר in Deut. 24.1.

> The School of Shammai says: A man should not divorce his wife except if he found indecency in her, since it says: *For he found in her an indecent matter* [Deut. 24.1].
>
> And the School of Hillel said: Even if she spoiled his dish, since it says: *[Any] matter.*
>
> (*Sifre* 269. See also *m. Giṭ.* 9.10; *y. Soṭ.* 1.2, 16b)

These phrases would be well known by a large proportion of the Jewish population, because they were the basis of divorce law. They would have been as well known as similar legal phrases today, such as

---

58. Some important MSS omit ἀνθρώπω, (א B L 579 700) and one minuscule imports ἀνδρὶ from Mark. Metzger points out these are mainly Alexandrian MSS, which might have preferred a more concise literary style, though he admits that scribes would be more likely to add the word than omit it.

'irreconcilable breakdown', 'joint custody', 'maintenance', and so on. The phrases 'any matter' and 'a matter of indecency' were very important for a lay person to understand *before* they went to see a legal expert, because their understanding of these would determine which legal expert they went to visit. If they wanted to punish an unfaithful partner by divorcing them, they would choose to go to a Shammaite court which would apply the interpretation 'for a matter of indecency'. If they wanted a divorce for a lesser matter or they did not want to go through the difficult and humiliating procedure of proving adultery or other faults, they would go to a Hillelite court which would apply the interpretation 'for any matter'. Therefore this debate between the Hillelites and Shammaites, and these phrases which summarize the debate, would be well known by anyone who had a divorce in their family or circle of friends.

A first-century Jewish reader would mentally insert the phrase 'for any matter' into the question which the Pharisees asked Jesus, whether or not it occurred in the text. They would do this, not only because they were familiar with the debate, but also because the question makes no sense without it. The question 'Is it lawful to divorce a wife' is a nonsensical question because it can only be answered by 'Yes—it says so in the Law'. This question would only make sense if there was a portion of the Jewish world which did not allow divorce under any circumstances, so that the question would mean 'Are you one of those who does not allow divorce?'. However, as far as we know, there was no such group.[59]

The progression of the debate in the gospels confirms that the opening question concerned the phrase 'for any matter' and the interpretation of Deut. 24.1. The Pharisees brought Jesus back to the interpretation of Deut. 24.1 when they spoke about Moses' divorce certificate, because Deut. 24.1-4 is the only text which deals with the divorce certificate. Before Jesus gave an answer to their question, he digressed into other matters concerning monogamy and lifelong marriage, which he felt were more important.

---

59. It had been thought in the past that the Qumran exegetes held this position. However, as I showed in 'Nomological Exegesis' and as summarized above, the so-called divorce texts at Qumran are actually concerned solely with polygamy.

Jesus' Digression on Monogamy

Jesus' digression is dealt with differently by Matthew and Mark. A certain amount of unraveling is necessary to understand the text, and some tentative judgments must be made about which version came first.

The Synoptic problem is still a problem. The recent revival of Matthean primacy may prove to be a passing fad, and consensus certainly lies with Markan priority. But good arguments come from both sides, and any conclusion in the overall argument may not provide a definitive solution about every passage. For that reason, we must examine this pericope on its own merits. I will conclude that both Matthew and Mark have edited the material for different purposes.

Matthew	*Mark*
The Question	*The Question*
And Pharisees came up to him and tested him by asking, 'Is it lawful to divorce one's wife **for any matter?'** (19.3)	And Pharisees came up and in order to test him asked, 'Is it lawful for a man to divorce his wife?' (10.2)
Digression	*Moses' Teaching*
He answered, 'Have you not read that **he who created them from the beginning** *"made them male and female"* [Gen. 1.27] and said, *"For this reason a man shall leave his father and mother and be joined to his wife, and the two shall become one flesh?"* [Gen. 2.24]. So they are no longer two but one flesh. What therefore God has joined together, let not man separate' (19.4-6).	**He answered them, 'What did Moses command you**?' They said, 'Moses allowed a man to write a certificate of divorce, and to put her away'. But Jesus said to them, 'For your hardness of heart **he wrote you this commandment**'' (10.3-5).
Moses' Teaching	*Digression*
They said to him, 'Why then did Moses command one to give a certificate of divorce, and to put her away?' He said to them, 'For your hardness of heart Moses allowed you to divorce your wives, **but from the beginning it was not so** (19.7-8).	'But **from the beginning of creation**, *"He made them male and female"* [Gen. 1.27]. *"For this reason a man shall leave his father and mother and be joined to his wife, and the two shall become one flesh"* [Gen. 2.24]. So they are no longer two but one flesh. What therefore God has joined together, let not man separate' (10.6-9).

Answering the Question
'**And I say to you:** whoever divorces his wife, **unless for indecency,** and marries another, commits adultery.'

Answering the Question
And in the house the disciples asked him again about this matter. And he said to them, 'Whoever divorces his wife and marries another, commits adultery against her; and if she divorces her husband and marries another, she commits adultery' (10.10-12)

Marriage is Optional
The disciples said to him, 'If such is the case of a man with his wife, it is not expedient to marry...' (19.10-12)

The differences between the two pericopae are highlighted in bold. The two accounts of Jesus' teaching on divorce in Matthew and Mark are clearly related, but they have been edited for two different purposes or situations. They both share an overall structure, of Question–Digression–Moses' Teaching–Jesus' Answer, though the middle two sections are reversed in the two versions, and Matthew has an additional section on optional marriage.

Mark's version is more suitable for use in a sermon. The question-and-answer session at the beginning (10.2-4) summarizes the position of the Jews and the latter three quarters (vv. 5-12) has the teaching of Jesus. The teaching of Jesus is directed first to the Jews (vv. 5-9) and then to the Church (vv. 10-12). The flow of the teaching is more natural than in Matthew. The question leads to the statement that Moses' command was necessitated by sin, which leads to teaching on monogamy based on the ideals of sinless Eden, which leads to the answer for a sinful society.

Matthew's version reflects a real rabbinic debate. The opening question (v. 3) frames the debate and leads into an exegesis concerning a related point (vv. 4-6). A second question brings Jesus back to the area of the original question (v. 7). The second question is answered (v. 8) and then finally the opening question is dealt with (v. 9). This is not a typical form for recording rabbinic debates. Normally a question would be followed by an answer, and then a further question from the original questioner, or a counter question from the person who was questioned. There was usually a degree of balance in the reporting of a debate, so that both sides are more-or-less equally represented. In this debate with Jesus, the Pharisees' point of view is very poorly represented, though

Matthew takes care to record a summary of the two main Pharisaic viewpoints in this debate.

From this structure, it could be argued that neither of these accounts was the original. It could be argued that Matthew reconstructed the teaching into the form of a rabbinic debate in order to interact with the debate which was still going on in the Jewish world. Equally, it could be argued that Mark transformed a rabbinic debate, which was becoming increasingly irrelevant to the church, into a form which lent itself to Christian teaching.

Further analysis provides no more support for the originality of either version. It has often been argued that Matthew's version is secondary because he has added the phrases summarizing the two schools of opinion, 'for any matter' and 'a matter of indecency'. It is likely that these have been added by Matthew rather than omitted by Mark, because both accounts in Matthew have such summaries, but neither account in Mark or Luke have them. It is also likely that Matthew has changed 'from the beginning of creation' in Mk 10.6 and witnessed to in CD 4.21, to 'who created them from the beginning'. On the other hand, it could equally be argued that Mark's version has lost the contrast where the Pharisees say 'Moses commanded divorce' and Jesus says 'Moses allowed divorce'. He has managed to retain the phrase 'Moses allowed', but his editing has put this into the mouth of a Pharisee, and he has had to repeat 'Moses commanded', once in the words of the Pharisees, and once in the words of Jesus.

Another structure which can also be discerned is Public Question–Public Answer–Private Question–Private Answer. This is a structure which occurs in a few rabbinic debates at about 70 CE.[60] In Matthew the private question concerns whether one should marry or not (19.10-12).

60. Five early debates of Yohannan b. Zakkai follow this form. In two debates with Angetos, a Gentile, he is asked a question and he first gives a public answer which is well reasoned and acceptable. Then his disciples say to him in private that *they* cannot be dismissed with such an easy answer, and so he gives them an answer which is more difficult for the uncommitted Gentile to accept. See *y. San.* 1.2, 19b; *Num. R.* 19.8—for a full analysis, see my *Techniques and Assumptions*, pp. 80-82. In his three debates with the Sadducees he uses a variant of this form, giving the same questioner first an obscure and clever reply and then a more closely argued reply. The second reply is prompted when the Sadducee, like his disciples, says that he cannot be dismissed with that answer. *See b. B. Bat.* 115b-116a; *b. Men.* 65ab; *Meg. Ta'an.* 338; for a full analysis and parallels, see my *Techniques and Assumptions*, pp. 96-100, 109-14.

In Mark the private question is a repeat of the original question ('And in the house the disciples asked him again about this matter', 10.10) and the private answer is Jesus' answer to the original question which is given in public in Matthew. Both Matthew and Mark have retained this form, though they have employed it in different ways. Again, it is difficult to decide which version was adapted from which.

It could be argued that Mark's version is closest to the rabbinic form, where the same question is always asked in both halves of the debate. Also it could be said that Matthew has clumsily added the teaching on optional marriage into the debate by transforming it into a private question and answer. On the other hand, the double question and answer in Matthew does conform very closely to the rabbinic form, and the extra question in private may simply be an extension of it.[61] Also it seems unlikely that the Pharisees in Mark's version would consider that their question had been answered. It is likely that, as in Matthew's version, they would have attempted to pin Jesus down to a definite answer.

It is unlikely that any definitive answer can be reached about which version developed from which. It is my personal view that both versions show signs of adaptation, though Matthew's version represents more aspects of the original version. It is likely that Matthew did add the summaries of the Hillelite and Shammaite position, but that these correctly represented ideas which had been omitted when the pericope had been abbreviated previously. He added them because he realized that his readers were not so easily able to supply them from their own knowledge of Jewish oral law. The debate form was probably original. If Matthew had wanted to reconstruct it into the form of a rabbinic debate, he would have given more balance to the two sides. Mark has also edited the original in order to make it more usable in sermons and other Christian teaching, and has removed much of the debate structure. Both writers have adapted the original debate in order to help their own readers.

---

61. Matthew may be regarded as an amalgamation of the two varieties of this form as seen in the debates of Yohannan b. Zakkai. The first public debate with the Pharisees is very similar to Yohannan's debates with the Sadducees, where the original answer is dismissed as irrelevant, and they are finally satisfied with a clearer answer. The second question and answer in private is like the second half of Yohannan's debates with the Gentile where he gives his disciples a more difficult teaching in private.

Jesus' Teaching on Monogamy

Mark 10.6-9:
'But from the beginning of creation, "He made them male and female"
[Gen. 1.27]. "For this reason a man shall leave his father and mother and
be joined to his wife, and the two shall become one flesh" [Gen. 2.24].
So they are no longer two but one flesh. What therefore God has joined
together, let not man separate.'

ἀπὸ δὲ ἀρχῆς κτίσεως ἄρσεν καὶ θῆλυ ἐποίησεν αὐτούς.[62] ἕνεκεν
τούτου καταλείψει ἄνθρωπος τὸν πατέρα **αὐτοῦ** καὶ τὴν μητέρα [καὶ
προσκολληθήσεται **πρὸς** τὴν γυναῖκα αὐτοῦ],[63] καὶ ἔσονται οἱ δύο
εἰς σάρκα μίαν· ὥστε οὐκέτι εἰσὶν δύο ἀλλὰ μία σάρξ. ὃ οὖν ὁ θεὸς
συνέζευξεν ἄνθρωπος μὴ χωριζέτω.

Matthew 19.4-6:
He answered, 'Have you not read that he who created them from the
beginning made them male and female' [Gen. 1.27], **and said,** "For this
reason a man shall leave his father and mother and be joined to his wife,
and the two shall become one flesh?" [Gen. 2.24]. So they are no longer
two but one flesh. What therefore God has joined together, let not man
separate.'

ὁ δὲ ἀποκριθεὶς εἶπεν· οὐκ ἀνέγνωτε ὅτι ὁ κτίσας[64] ἀπ' ἀρχῆς
ἄρσεν καὶ θῆλυ ἐποίησεν αὐτούς; **καὶ εἶπεν·** ἕνεκα τούτου
καταλείψει ἄνθρωπος τὸν πατέρα καὶ τὴν μητέρα καὶ κολληθήσεται[65]
τῇ γυναικὶ αὐτοῦ, καὶ ἔσονται οἱ δύο εἰς σάρκα μίαν. ὥστε οὐκέτι
εἰσὶν δύο ἀλλὰ σὰρξ μία. ὃ οὖν ὁ θεὸς συνέζευξεν ἄνθρωπος μὴ
χωριζέτω.

62. Several MSS read ὁ θεός instead of αὐτούς. Metzger (*Textual Commentary*)
suggests that a scribe wanted to make clear that 'he' is not a reference to Moses,
who was the last named subject.

63. Most MSS retain this phrase (only missing in ℵ B Ψ). Perhaps a scribe
missed it due to the two occurrences of και or perhaps it was assimilated from Mt.
19.5 or from Gen. 2.24.

64. Almost all MSS read ποιησας instead of κτίσας (which is only in B Θ 1 124
700). Metzger (*Textual Commentary*) thinks it more likely that a scribe would
change the text to ποιησας which conforms with the LXX, than change to the text to
κτίσας which fits better with the Hebrew 'create', ברא.

65. Many MSS read προσκολληθήσεται (ℵ C G K L M Y Δ Π f¹ 118 124 1071
33 565 579 700 1424 τ) which agrees with Mark.

Jesus does not appear at first to be interested in answering the question about the interpretation of Deut. 24.1. He is more concerned to remind the Pharisees that marriage was meant to be monogamous and lifelong. He used two exegetical arguments to prove that the Old Testament taught monogamy. He then combined them to produce the new conclusion, that married partners are joined together by God.

1. 'Male and female'—Based on Genesis 1.27 (and 7.9)

The first text used by Jesus has clear links with the Damascus Document proof texts. Not only is the same text used at Qumran, but the same introductory phrase is used.[66]

The foundation of creation (CD 4.21).	יסוד הבריאה
... from the beginning of creation (Mk 10.6).	ἀπὸ δὲ ἀρχῆς κτίσεως
... created them from the beginning (Mt. 19.4).	κτίσας ἀπ᾽ ἀρχῆς

As discussed above, this introductory phrase indicates that the importance of the exegesis lies in the fact that this is the example that the Creator set for everyone else. Matthew has a slightly different version, perhaps to indicate this even more clearly.

It is unlikely that Jesus was consciously or unconsciously referring to the Damascus Document. It is more likely that this was a standard proof for monogamy which was well known. For this reason both Jesus and the Qumran exegete start off with this proof.

The text used by Jesus, Gen. 1.27, would normally be linked with Gen. 7.9. By linking these two texts by *gezerah shahvah* the exegete

---

66. See F.F. Bruce, *Biblical Exegesis in the Qumran Texts* (London: Tyndale Press, 1959), p. 33. The phrases are not identical, and neither use the vocabulary of Genesis in Greek or Hebrew, but they are semantically equivalent. If this phrase in Mark was based on Genesis one might expect the use of ποιεω instead of κτίσμα for creation. However, κτίσμα is common in Wisdom Literature (it occurs with αρχη in Prov. 8.22; Sir. 24.9; 36.14; 39.25; Wis. 18.12) and phrases identical to ἀρχης κτισεως are found in Mk 13.19, 2 Pet. 3.4, and very similar in Rev. 3.14. If this phrase in the Damascus Document was based on Genesis, one might expect the use of ברא, 'to create', instead of יסד, 'to found'. The use of יסד may have been influenced by its use in Ezek. 13.14 which is alluded to in CD 8.12. In the latter text the 'builders of the wall' are also called the 'whitewash-daubers' (טחי התפל; cf. Ezek. 13.14 טחתי תפל, as well as the New Testament parallels in Mt. 23.27 and Acts 23.3), and these same 'builders of the wall' are being addressed in CD 4.19. Therefore both Mark and the Damascus Document had influences which moved them away from the obvious vocabulary of Gen. 1.1.

could infer that 'male and female' in 1.27 is defined as 'a pair' by the phrase 'two by two' in 7.9. This means that marriage involved only two people. The second half of this pair of proof texts, Gen. 7.9, has been lost in the abbreviation of the argument in the Gospels.

One might try to guess why the text from Gen. 7.9 was omitted. Perhaps this omission was deliberate, on the assumption that the audience would be able to mentally supply the missing text, but this supposes a very sophisticated audience. More likely the text was omitted in the mistaken belief that it was not necessary for the argument. A more generous conclusion would be that it was omitted knowing that any learned person would be able to mentally fill the gap, and that an unlearned person would not miss it.

Either way, the text of Gen. 7.9 is not necessary for the more significant argument which Jesus develops in Stage 3 below.

2. *'The two shall become one flesh'—Based on a Variant of Genesis 2.24*
The use of Genesis 2.24 to prove monogamy was very widespread by the time of the Gospels, as indicated by the addition of the variant 'two' in almost all the ancient versions except the Hebrew. It is possible that there was a Hebrew text which contained this variant, but the widespread use of this variant in ancient versions in contrast to the most influential Hebrew text, suggests that there was either a theological reason for including it or a contrary theological reason for the rabbis to exclude it. The actual situation was probably a mixture of these two.

This variant text is used very self-consciously in the Gospels. It is highlighted by the additional comment 'So they are no longer two but one', which emphasizes the presence of the word 'two'.

3. *'Whom God has joined'—Based on the Combined Proofs*
Jesus combined these two standard proofs for monogamy and produced an argument for lifelong marriage. He linked the two texts, Gen. 1.27 and 2.24, by *gezerah shahvah*, so that a single conclusion can be drawn from them. The two texts are linked by the phrases 'male and female' in 1.27 and 'the man and his wife' in 2.25 (immediately after the quoted text). This exegesis did not need to be explained, because it would have been obvious to any intelligent listener. This type of exegesis is not normally accompanied by any kind of explanation when it occurs in rabbinic literature or in the Targums.

In Gen. 2.24 the act of joining is not ascribed to anyone, though it might be inferred that the couple join themselves to each other. In Gen. 1.27 the first male and female are brought together by God. By combining both texts it can be concluded that a couple are joined together by God.

In Judaism it would generally be assumed that a couple were joined together by their promises to each other, as formalized in the marriage contract. Or it might be assumed that they were joined by a business transaction based on payment of the dowry and exchange of goods. Jesus wished to re-emphasize the role of God in the joining of marriage. This is probably based on the picture presented by Malachi, who pictures God as a witness to the marriage vows (Mal. 2.14-16).[67]

> The LORD was witness to the covenant between you and the wife of your youth, to whom you have been faithless, though she is your companion and your wife by covenant...let none be faithless to the wife of his youth for I hate divorce (2.14-16a, RSV translation).

This leads into Jesus' final and startling statement: 'Whom God has joined, let no man separate' (Mt. 19.6; Mk 10.9). The word 'separate' (χωριζω) is a standard term meaning 'to divorce', with almost exactly the same semantic field as the word ἀπολυω, divorce (lit. 'to release'), which was used in the Pharisee's question to Jesus. The word χωριζω was probably used because it formed a better antonym to 'join'. If ἀπολυω had been used, the saying would have to be something like: 'what therefore God has bound, let no-one release'. The picture of God's activity in Gen. 1.27 is much more that of someone who 'joins' than one who 'binds'.

In passing, it should be noted that Daube proposed a very different explanation of the word 'joined'. He suggested that this is a reference to the rabbinic *haggadah* about the androgynous Adam, who had both male and female organs before Eve was created. This was deduced from the mixing of singular and plural in Gen. 1.27, 'God created him; male and female he created them'.[68] This may possibly be an underlying

---

67. This passage is notoriously difficult to translate. Hugenberger (*Marriage as a Covenant*) has done more than others to solve the problems. However one might solve the various difficulties, there are two clear themes: God is a witness to the marriage vows, and he is against the one who ends the marriage by treacherously breaking the marriage vows.

68. This tradition was known to Philo and rabbis tell us that the LXX said 'a male with his female parts created he them' or 'male and female created he him'

theme, but it does not fit in with the overall theme of Jesus' exposition.

We could attempt to reconstruct the unabbreviated version of Jesus' teaching on monogamy. It would contain a reference to Gen. 7.9, and it might also have an extended quotation from Gen. 2.24, as suggested above. Therefore a fuller version of Jesus' argument for monogamy might be:

> From the beginning of creation, '*He made them male and female*' (Gen. 1.27), and those who entered (Noah's) ark '*went in two by two...into the ark, male and female*' (Gen. 7.9). When taken together, these texts, show that God created human males and females in pairs. Scripture also says: '*For this reason a man shall leave his father and mother and be joined to his wife, and they shall become one flesh, and the* two *were naked, the man and woman*' (Gen. 2.24-25). This shows that they have been joined by God. So they are no longer two but one flesh. What therefore God has joined together, let not man separate.

When the exegesis is restored in this way, the flow of the argument is smoother. The argument has three stages which flow naturally from one to the next. First he puts together the two texts Gen. 1.27 and 7.9 in a well established way, to show that human 'male and female' groups should be made up of two people, and not three or more in a polygamous marriage. He then moves to another standard proof text for monogamy based on 'two' in Gen. 2.24-25, which is linked to the previous verses by a phrase similar to 'male and female'. Combining these, Jesus shows that the couple are joined by God. He then makes the same plea as Malachi, that marriage should be lifelong, and one should not cause a separation by breaking one's marriage vows.[69]

Effects on the Early Church

It is difficult to know whether this teaching on monogamy would have had many practical consequences, because we do not know how widespread polygamy was among the Jews of the first century. As

---

(*Gen. R.* on Gen. 1.26-27; *Mek.* on Exod. 12.40). No surviving LXX manuscripts contain this wording. See Daube, *New Testament*, p. 73

69. This does not mean that divorce is impossible. If divorce was not possible, Jesus would have said: 'No one *can* separate'. Both Matthew and Mark have the imperative χωριζέτω which implies that it is possible for couples to separate. If it were not possible to divorce, it would be meaningless to command them not to do so.

stated above, it used to be assumed that it occurred only among the rich, but now it appears that it was also the practice of the middle classes. It is likely that there were few polygamous marriages outside Israel, because they would not be recognized in Roman law.

There would have been four consequences of this teaching for the early church, but only the latter two leave any evidence in the New Testament; these are found in Acts and the Epistles. The first two, which involve the subject of divorce and remarriage, cannot be explored in detail here.[70]

1. *Remarriage After an Invalid Divorce was Adulterous*

Jesus rejected most of the grounds which Jews used for divorce, and pointed out that remarriage after an invalid divorce was adulterous. This is presumably because the previous marriage was still valid, so that the new partner is committing adultery.

In first-century Judaism, a woman who remarried after an invalid divorce was treated exactly like an adulteress,[71] but a man did not face this problem because he could have more than one wife. Jesus taught that both the man and the woman would be guilty of adultery because a man could only have one wife.

2. *Women Gain the Right to Use Adultery as a Ground for Divorce*

In ancient Judaism, when polygamy was still permitted, a husband did not make a vow of sexual exclusiveness when he married. This meant that he could not be divorced for being sexually unfaithful. He could still be accused of adultery, but the offense was against the husband of the other woman, and not against his wife. However, if polygamy was no longer permitted, a husband must be assumed to owe sexual exclusivity to his wife, and therefore adultery becomes a ground for divorce which can be used equally by men and women. This was already the case in some contracts which had an additional monogamy clause, such as some of those at Elephantine, as seen above. When this clause was added, a man could be divorced if he was unfaithful.

Women already had the right to divorce their husbands in first-century Judaism. While they could not write out their own divorce

---

70. See n. 56.
71. This type of situation is dealt with at length in *m. Git.* 8.5; *m. Yeb.* 10.1. See the helpful analysis in Judith R. Wegner, *Chattel or Person? The Status of Women in the Mishnah* (Oxford: Oxford University Press, 1988), pp. 65-66.

certificate, they could take their case to a court of three rabbis or priests. If these agreed that she had sufficient grounds, they would force her husband to write the divorce certificate.[72] Although this was the correct procedure, it is likely that some Jewish women employed a scribe to write out a divorce. One such document has survived from the second century, though this is still under dispute.[73]

The permissible grounds for women to get a divorce from their husbands in first-century Judaism were infertility, or neglect of the physical and emotional support as defined in Exod. 21.10-11. However, as a result of Jesus' teaching, divorce would also be possible on the grounds of adultery.

3. *Widows Could Not Become a Second Wife*
As mentioned above, the family records of a middle-class second wife of the second century have survived. If she is typical, a second wife was often a widow. Marrying a widow was affordable even for the lower-middle classes, because the dowry was half, and she often came with money of her own from the previous marriage which would help the family finances. However, if polygamy was no longer permitted, a widow could only marry an unmarried man, of which there were far fewer. Therefore, one consequence of Jesus' teaching on monogamy for the early church would have been an increase in the number of unmarried widows.

The early church appears to have met this problem very soon. The widows of Acts 6.1 may simply have been the equivalent of the poor in any Jewish community, but by the time of the Pastoral Epistles, the widows were starting to pose problems.[74] Unmarried widows had more freedom than married women, and they were causing problems by going from house to house and gossiping.[75] Therefore the young widows were actively encouraged to marry,[76] and the older ones were

---

72. See my 'Jewish Women Divorcing their Husbands in Early Judaism: The Background to Papyrus Se'elim 13', *HTR* 92 (1999), pp. 349-57.

73. See the history of the dispute in my 'Jewish Women'.

74. The whole subject of widows in the New Testament and the early church is covered in superb detail by Gustav Stählin in 'χήρα', *TDNT*, IX, pp. 440-65.

75. See 1 Tim. 5.13; 2 Tim. 3.6. The letter text does not specifically mention widows, but the language used here normally refers to widows; see Stählin 'χήρα', p. 455 n. 140.

76. See 1 Tim. 5.11, 14. In the Roman world widows were expected to remarry

organized into a special order of widows.[77] They were supported by the church,[78] and they were given tasks such as teaching the younger women.[79]

In the early centuries, widows were a significant burden on the church. There were over 1500 widows and needy in the Roman church, and 3000 widows and virgins in Antioch who received daily support.[80] The orders of widows declined after a few hundred years, probably because they were replaced by convents.[81]

4. *Some Converts Had Too Many Wives*

Converts with more than one wife faced the problem of what to do with their extra wives. This is a problem which still causes great anguish in several African countries. The almost total silence of the Epistles on this matter suggests that the problem was not felt very keenly—perhaps because the number of people involved was small. Most men with more than one wife would have been relatively wealthy and would be very unlikely to live in the Diaspora where polygamy was unacceptable; in contrast, however, most early Christians were less wealthy and lived in the Diaspora.

It seems likely that polygamous converts were permitted to join the church without divorcing any of their wives. Jesus did not specifically teach that a second wife should be divorced. This is in contrast to marriages which took place after an invalid divorce, which he declared

---

if of child-bearing age—that is, under 50. Augustus even put this into law in 9 CE; B.W. Winter, 'Providentia for the Widows of 1 Timothy 5.3-16', *TynB* 39 (1988), pp. 83-99 (85).

77. See 1 Tim. 5.9-12. It is not certain whether this was a recognized order in New Testament times (Stählin, 'χήρα', p. 455 n. 144), but it became one soon after, and in some places the order came to hold a status almost akin to deaconesses; Stählin, 'χήρα', pp. 459-65.

78. Acts 6.1 is presumably the starting point for this. Tabatha supported the widows in her community, and Stählin suggested that she may have been doing this on behalf of the church (Acts 9.36-41; Stählin, 'χήρα', pp. 451-52). By the time of 1 Tim. 5.3-16, the church is beginning to restrict the women who qualify for support.

79. 1 Timothy 5 does not list any specific tasks, because it is dealing with entrance requirements. Perhaps they had tasks similar to deaconesses in Tit. 2.3-5, leading younger women to proper marriage and family life, and taking part in visitation of women.

80. Stählin, 'χήρα', p. 460.

81. Stählin, 'χήρα', p. 465.

to be adulterous. While the church would forbid a member to marry a second wife, if a convert had more than one wife when he joined, the teaching of Jesus did not have any consequences for him.

The restriction of leaders to those who were a 'husband of one wife'[82] implies a slight discrimination against polygamy. However, it also implies that a polygamous man was permitted into church membership.

The meaning of the phrase 'man of one wife' is not certain. It could refer to 'a man who has not remarried after divorce or death of his wife', or 'a man who is not a womanizer'. These alternative meanings have the advantage of working well with the similar phrase 'woman of one husband' at 1 Tim. 5.9. Craig Keener has made a very persuasive case for the latter meaning,[83] pointing out that funeral inscriptions and other honorary references use a similar phrase when speaking about men who were not necessarily married to the same woman throughout their life. However, even if the phrase did exclude those who were remarried, or those who were unfaithful, it would also undoubtedly exclude those who were married to more than one wife at the same time.

It would appear that the number of individuals in the church with more than one wife were few, and that they were allowed to keep their wives. The only restriction was that they could not serve in leadership positions. This is consistent with the teaching of Jesus who forbade a second marriage, but did not call a second wife an 'adulterer', in the way that a marriage after an invalid divorce was called 'adultery'.

Conclusions

Judaism allowed polygamy, but it was not widespread and it was already declining in the first century. There was already an established feeling that polygamy was inappropriate and some groups taught that it

82. See 1 Tim. 3.2, 12; Tit. 1.6.
83. The term 'wife-of-one-man' (Latin *univera*, Greek μόνανδρος) occurs commonly, and refers to a faithful wife. It is often on Jewish funeral inscriptions, written by the surviving husband—that is, it was not a term for a widow. It therefore fits in with the list of other attributes of a leader who should be 'above reproach'. See Craig S. Keener, *...And Marries Another: Divorce and Remarriage in the Teaching of the New Testament* (Peabody, MA: Hendrickson, 1991), pp. 81-103. See also the discussion in Stählin, 'χήρα', pp. 442-43, 457; W. Lock, *The Pastoral Epistles* (ICC; Edinburgh: T. & T. Clark, 1936), at 1 Tim. 3.2 and 5.10.

was not permitted by Scripture. Jesus' teaching on monogamy echoed that found at Qumran, even so far as using the same proof texts and an identical introductory phrase. Both sources probably reflected a widely accepted teaching, though rabbinic Judaism did not forbid polygamy for several centuries. This teaching was easily accepted by the church, especially in the Diaspora where monogamy was the norm. Within the early church there would have been a minority of converts with more than one wife. While polygamy was not permitted in the early church, it seems that the pre-existing polygamous marriages of converts were tolerated. The one restriction seems to have been that converts with more than one wife could not serve as leaders within the church. With the decline in the numbers of Jewish converts it seems that polygamy ceased to be a 'live issue' in the church. As a result, by the time the Gospels were written, the teaching on monogamy was recorded as an unimportant digression within Jesus' teaching on divorce.

THE QUOTATION FROM JEREMIAH 31(38).15 IN MATTHEW 2.18: A STUDY OF MATTHEW'S SCRIPTURAL TEXT

Maarten J.J. Menken

The first Evangelist concludes several episodes of his account of Jesus' origins with a fulfilment quotation. One of the scenes in which Matthew observes the realization of a prophecy is the massacre of the innocents in Bethlehem and its surrounding area (2.16-18). At the end of the episode, Matthew informs his readers that then a saying from Jeremiah (Jer. 31[38].15) was fulfilled. I give the Greek text, followed by a literal English translation:

> φωνὴ ἐν Ῥαμὰ ἠκούσθη,
> κλαυθμὸς καὶ ὀδυρμὸς πολύς·
> Ῥαχὴλ κλαίουσα τὰ τέκνα αὐτῆς,
> καὶ οὐκ ἤθελεν παρακληθῆναι,
> ὅτι οὐκ εἰσίν,

> A voice was heard in Ramah,
> weeping and much lamentation:
> Rachel weeping her children,
> and she would not be comforted,
> because they are no more.

There is a variant reading in which the words θρῆνος καί are added at the beginning of the second line (among others: C D L W[1]); the addition is an obvious effort to adapt the text of the quotation to the LXX version of the verse from Jeremiah, and for that reason it should be considered as secondary.[2]

The textual form in which Jer. 31(38).15 is presented in Matthew, shows both similarities with and differences from the MT and the LXX.

---

1. For a fuller list of witnesses, see the 4th edn of *UBSGNT*.

2. See B.M. Metzger, *A Textual Commentary on the Greek New Testament* (Stuttgart: Deutsche Bibelgesellschaft, 2nd edn, 1994), p. 8; M. Quesnel, 'Les citations de Jérémie dans l'évangile selon saint Matthieu', *EstBíb* 47 (1989), pp. 513-27 (516 n. 7).

Such a state of affairs can be considered as characteristic of Matthew's fulfilment quotations, and requires an explanation. For several fulfilment quotations (Mt. 2.15; 4.15-16; 8.17; 12.18-21; 13.35; 21.5), I have tried to give an explanation of the peculiar textual form in terms of a revised LXX used by Matthew (for he, as the final redactor of the Gospel, inserted them). It seems that the Evangelist has drawn from this translation, which he knew as a continuous text, without making many changes in its wording; his main contribution has been to determine the size of the quotation.[3] In this paper, I intend to scrutinize Matthew's quotation from Jer. 31(38).15, to see whether a similar explanation also holds true in this case.

In the MT, Jer. 31.15 reads as follows (the Hebrew text is followed by a literal English translation):

קול ברמה נשמע

נהי בכי תמרורים

רחל מבכה על־בניה

מאנה להנחם על־בניה

כי איננו:

> A voice is heard in Ramah,
> wailing and bitter weeping:
> Rachel weeping for her sons,
> refusing to be comforted for her sons,[4]
> because they are no more.

---

3. See M.J.J. Menken, 'The Quotations from Zech 9,9 in Mt 21,5 and in Jn 12,15', in A. Denaux (ed.), *John and the Synoptics* (BETL, 101; Leuven: Peeters, 1992), pp. 571-78 (573-74); *idem*, 'The Source of the Quotation from Isaiah 53:4 in Matthew 8:17', *NovT* 39 (1997), pp. 313-27; *idem*, 'The Textual Form of the Quotation from Isaiah 8:23–9:1 in Matthew 4:15-16', *RB* 105 (1998), pp. 526-45; *idem*, 'Isaiah and the "Hidden Things": The Quotation from Psalm 78:2 in Matthew 13:35', in L.V. Rutgers *et al.* (eds.), *The Use of Sacred Books in the Ancient World* (Contributions to Biblical Exegesis and Theology, 22; Leuven: Peeters, 1998), pp. 61-77; *idem*, 'The Quotation from Isaiah 42:1-4 in Matthew 12:18-21: Its Relation with the Matthean Context', *Bijdragen* 59 (1998), pp. 251-66; *idem*, 'The Quotation from Isaiah 42:1-4 in Matthew 12:18-21: Its Textual Form', *ETL* 75 (1999), pp. 32-52; *idem*, 'The Greek Translation of Hosea 11:1 in Matthew 2:15: Matthean or Pre-Matthean?', forthcoming in *Filología Neotestamentaria*.

4. As is normal in Biblical Hebrew, the participle מבכה is continued by the finite verb מאנה; see GKC, §116x; P. Joüon and T. Muraoka, *A Grammar of Biblical Hebrew* (Subsidia Biblica, 14; Rome: Pontifical Biblical Institute Press, 1991), §121j; cf. the English translations in, for example, J. Bright, *Jeremiah* (AB, 21;

The LXX reads in Jer. 38.15 as follows according to the editions of A. Rahlfs and J. Ziegler (again, I offer a literal translation):[5]

> φωνὴ ἐν Ραμὰ ἠκούσθη
> θρήνου καὶ κλαυθμοῦ καὶ ὀδυρμοῦ·
> Ραχὴλ ἀποκλαιομένη
> οὐκ ἤθελεν παύσασθαι ἐπὶ τοῖς υἱοῖς αὐτῆς,
> ὅτι οὐκ εἰσίν,

> A voice was heard in Ramah
> of wailing and weeping and lamentation:
> Rachel weeping
> would not cease for her sons,
> because they are no more.

This is, in fact, the text of LXX B. The important variant readings become immediately clear from a comparison with LXX A:

> φωνὴ ἐν τῇ ὑψηλῇ ἠκούσθη
> θρήνου καὶ κλαυθμοῦ καὶ ὀδυρμοῦ
> Ραχὴλ ἀποκλαιομένης ἐπὶ τῶν υἱῶν αὐτῆς,
> καὶ οὐκ ἤθελεν παρακληθῆναι,
> ὅτι οὐκ εἰσίν.

At this point, there is no need to discuss these variant readings or to choose between them; it is sufficient to establish that the LXX text has been transmitted in two main forms.

Divergent explanations of the textual form of Matthew's quotation have been presented. Most scholars seem to think that it is the Evangelist's abbreviated translation of the Hebrew text, possibly with some LXX influence, although the extent of LXX influence is weighed differently.[6] In the view of others, the quotation comes from a non-LXX

Garden City, NY: Doubleday, 1965), p. 275; W. McKane, *A Critical and Exegetical Commentary on Jeremiah*. II. *Commentary on Jeremiah XXVI–LII* (ICC; Edinburgh: T. & T. Clark, 1996), p. 796; *The Revised English Bible* (1989).

5.   Between the two editions, there is only an insignificant difference of spelling in the fourth line: Rahlfs has ἤθελεν, Ziegler ἤθελε.

6.   So (with various nuances, of course) Th. Zahn, *Das Evangelium des Matthäus* (KNT, 1; Leipzig: Deichert, 2nd edn, 1905), p. 108 n. 11; M.-J. Lagrange, *Evangile selon saint Matthieu* (EBib; Paris: Gabalda, 1923), pp. 35-36; S.E. Johnson, 'The Biblical Quotations in Matthew', *HTR* 36 (1943), pp. 135-53 (137); K. Stendahl, *The School of St Matthew and its Use of the Old Testament* (Philadelphia: Fortress Press, 2nd edn, 1968 [1954]), pp. 102-103; E. Lohmeyer, *Das Evangelium des Matthäus* (Meyer K.; ed. W. Schmauch; Göttingen: Vandenhoeck & Ruprecht,

Greek translation (maybe in oral form).[7] Some scholars assume that the quotation comes from a collection of testimonies.[8] Others again posit some relationship to the LXX.[9] The quotation from Jer. 31(38).15 in

1956, 4th edn, 1967), pp. 28-29; R.H. Gundry, *The Use of the Old Testament in St. Matthew's Gospel, with Special Reference to the Messianic Hope* (NovTSup, 18; Leiden: E.J. Brill, 1967, 2nd edn, 1975), pp. 95-97; R.S. McConnell, *Law and Prophecy in Matthew's Gospel: The Authority and Use of the Old Testament in the Gospel of St. Matthew* (Theologische Dissertationen, 2; Basel: Friedrich Reinhardt, 1969), p. 112; W. Rothfuchs, *Die Erfüllungszitate des Matthäus-Evangeliums: Eine biblisch-theologische Untersuchung* (BWANT, 88; Stuttgart: W. Kohlhammer, 1969), pp. 63-65; M.D. Goulder, *Midrash and Lection in Matthew* (London: SPCK, 1974), p. 240 n. 40; G.M. Soares Prabhu, *The Formula Quotations in the Infancy Narrative of Matthew: An Enquiry into the Tradition History of Mt 1–2* (AnBib, 63; Rome: Pontifical Biblical Institute Press, 1976), pp. 104-106, 253; J. Gnilka, *Das Matthäusevangelium*. I. *Kommentar zu Kap. 1,1–13,58* (HTKNT, 1.1; Freiburg: Herder, 1986), pp. 52-53; W.D. Davies and D.C. Allison, *A Critical and Exegetical Commentary on the Gospel According to Saint Matthew*. I. *Introduction and Commentary on Matthew I–VII* (ICC; Edinburgh: T. & T. Clark, 1988), pp. 267-70; M. Knowles, *Jeremiah in Matthew's Gospel: The Rejected-Prophet Motif in Matthaean Redaction* (JSNTSup, 68; Sheffield: JSOT Press, 1993), pp. 36-38; B. Becking, ' "A voice was heard in Ramah": Some Remarks on Structure and Meaning of Jeremiah 31,15-17', *BZ* NF 38 (1994), pp. 229-42 (230-32); G. Fischer, 'Zum Text des Jeremiabuches', *Bib* 78 (1997), pp. 305-28 (316).

7. So G.D. Kilpatrick, *The Origins of the Gospel According to St. Matthew* (Oxford: Clarendon Press, 1946), p. 57; C.H. Dodd, *According to the Scriptures: The Sub-Structure of New Testament Theology* (London: Nisbet, 1952), p. 85; C. Wolff, *Jeremia im Frühjudentum und Urchristentum* (TU, 118; Berlin: Akademie Verlag, 1976), pp. 157-58; U. Luz, *Das Evangelium nach Matthäus*. I. *Mt 1-7* (EKKNT, 1.1; Zürich: Benziger Verlag; Neukirchen–Vluyn: Neukirchener Verlag, 1985, 3rd edn, 1992), pp. 126-27, 137-39. Cf. also D.J. Harrington, *The Gospel of Matthew* (Sacra Pagina, 1; Collegeville, MN: Liturgical Press, 1991), pp. 45, 47.

8. So W.C. Allen, *A Critical and Exegetical Commentary on the Gospel According to St Matthew* (ICC; Edinburgh: T. & T. Clark, 3rd edn, 1912), p. lxii; A.H. McNeile, *The Gospel According to St. Matthew* (London: Macmillan, 1915), p. 20; G. Strecker, *Der Weg der Gerechtigkeit: Untersuchung zur Theologie des Matthäus* (FRLANT, 82; Göttingen: Vandenhoeck & Ruprecht, 1962, 2nd edn, 1966), pp. 58-59.

9. So Allen, *St Matthew*, p. 16 (the testimony [see n. 8] is a 'citation from memory of the LXX text'); B. Lindars, *New Testament Apologetic: The Doctrinal Significance of the Old Testament Quotations* (London: SCM Press, 1961), p. 217 with n. 4; D.S. New, *Old Testament Quotations in the Synoptic Gospels, and the Two-Document Hypothesis* (SBLSCS, 37; Atlanta: Scholars Press, 1993), pp. 112-13.

Justin's *Dialogue with Trypho* agrees completely with Matthew's quotation (*Dial. Try.* 78.8). The agreement is, however, unimportant for the purpose of explaining the textual form of Matthew's quotation, because Justin here depends on Matthew: in what precedes (78.7), he has paraphrased the story of the massacre of the innocents.[10]

In order to test the hypothesis of Matthew's use of a revised LXX in the form of a continuous text, three steps have to be taken:

(1)   An examination of the integration of the quotation in its context. The more tension there is between the quotation in its present size and wording and the Matthean context, the better chances there are that it comes from a collection of fixed testimonies.

(2)   A study of the quotation itself: how does it relate to the Hebrew text and the LXX?

(3)   The Matthean element in the wording of the quotation has to be investigated: what indications are there for either Matthean redaction or pre-Matthean material?

1. *The Quotation in Its Matthean Context*

Although the general theme of mourning for lost children makes Jer. 31(38).15 an appropriate fulfilment quotation for the massacre of the innocents, the connection between narrative and formula quotation seems to be less than perfect in some details. The massacre takes place in Bethlehem, 7 km south of Jerusalem, but Rachel's voice is heard in Ramah, 8 km north of Jerusalem. Bethlehem is situated in the territory of Judah, Ramah in Benjamin; Leah was Judah's mother, Rachel that of Benjamin.

Now the issue of Rachel's motherhood is not very problematic. According to Jer. 40.1, Ramah was a transit station for the exiles from Jerusalem and Judah to be deported in 587 BCE. In the light of that verse, Rachel's complaint at Ramah in Jer. 31.15 refers to the Babylonian Exile.[11] The Targum explicitly connects the two verses when it

---

10. See Stendahl, *School of St. Matthew*, p. 102; Wolff, *Jeremia*, p. 184; O. Skarsaune, *The Proof from Prophecy: A Study in Justin Martyr's Proof-Text Tradition: Text-Type, Provenance, Theological Profile* (NovTSup, 56; Leiden: E.J. Brill, 1987), p. 120.

11. So, for example, P.M. Arnold, 'Ramah', *ABD*, V, pp. 613-14 (614); Becking, '"Voice"', p. 238; cf. R.E. Brown, *The Birth of the Messiah: A Commentary*

gives the following paraphrase in Jer. 31.15: '…the house of Israel who weep and lament after Jeremiah the prophet, when Nebuzaradan, the chief of the killers, sent him from Ramah, with a dirge'.[12] Rachel is apparently thought to be the ancestress of those who were deported to Babylon as well. One may compare a rabbinic teaching: 'We find Israel [the nation] called after Rachel, as it says, Rachel weeping for her children [Jer. 31.15]' (*Gen. R.* 82.10; ascribed to R. Simeon b. Gamaliel, c. 140 CE).[13] Matthew very probably thought along the same lines, and saw Rachel as the mother of all Israel.[14]

The geographical problem is more serious, precisely because 'theological geography' is an important element of Matthew 2, including the four formula quotations, each of which contains a geographical name (vv. 6, 15, 18, 23). One of the things the Evangelist wishes to explain in this chapter is how Jesus, the Christ, born in Bethlehem, can come from Nazareth.[15] Within this framework, what is the sense of seeing a prophecy about mourning in Ramah realized in a massacre in Bethlehem?

Within the Old Testament, there are two traditions about the place where Rachel had been buried. According to 1 Sam. 10.2 and Jer. 31.15, Rachel's tomb is in the territory of Benjamin, in the vicinity of Ramah. According to Gen. 35.19-20 and 48.7 in their present form, however, she was buried 'on the way to Ephrath, that is, Bethlehem'

on the Infancy Narratives in the Gospels of Matthew and Luke (AB Reference Library; New York: Doubleday, 2nd edn, 1993 [1977]), pp. 205-206; Knowles, *Jeremiah in Matthew's Gospel*, pp. 46-47.

12. The translation comes from R. Hayward, *The Targum of Jeremiah* (The Aramaic Bible, 12; Edinburgh: T. & T. Clark, 1987), p. 131.

13. The same tradition is found in *Pes. K.* 141b (ascribed to R. Simeon b. Yochai); *Gen. R.* 71.2 (ascribed to R. Samuel b. Nachman); *Ruth R.* 7.13 (also ascribed to R. Simeon b. Yochai). The translation comes from H. Freedman and M. Simon, *The Midrash Rabbah.* I. *Genesis* (London: Soncino Press, 1977), p. 760.

14. See L. Hartman, 'Scriptural Exegesis in the Gospel of St. Matthew and the Problem of Communication', in M. Didier (ed.), *L'évangile selon Matthieu: Rédaction et théologie* (BETL, 29; Gembloux: Duculot, 1972), pp. 131-52 (140-41).

15. See K. Stendahl, '*Quis et unde?* An Analysis of Mt 1-2', in W. Eltester (ed.), *Judentum, Urchristentum, Kirche* (Festschrift J. Jeremias; BZNW, 26; Berlin: Alfred Töpelmann, 1960, 2nd edn, 1964), pp. 94-105; Brown, *Birth of the Messiah*, pp. 50-54; R.T. France, 'The Formula-Quotations of Matthew 2 and the Problem of Communication', *NTS* 27 (1981), pp. 233-51 (237-40); F.J. Moloney, 'Beginning the Gospel of Matthew: Reading Matthew 1:1–2:23', *Salesianum* 54 (1992), pp. 341-59.

(see also *Jub.* 32.34). The second tradition seems to be secondary: the words 'that is, Bethlehem' in the two Genesis passages are probably glosses, added with the intention to identify Ephrath in Benjamin (also mentioned in Gen. 35.16) with Bethlehem, also called Ephrathah, David's place of origin (Mic. 5.1; Ps. 132.6; Ruth 4.11).[16] Matthew has then simply confused the two traditions on Rachel's tomb, probably by reading Jer. 31(38).15 in the light of the glosses in Gen. 35.19 and 48.7; he then connected the Jeremiah passage with an event that took place at Bethlehem. It seems that he tried to solve the tension between Ramah and Bethlehem by inserting the words καὶ ἐν πᾶσι τοῖς ὁρίοις αὐτῆς, 'and in all that region', into v. 16 after 'in Bethlehem'.[17] The words are unnecessary after 2.5-6, where the scribes have given unequivocal information to Herod that the Christ will be born in Bethlehem. Matthew uses ὅρια six times: three times he borrowed the word from Mark (Mt. 8.34 // Mk 5.17; Mt. 15.22, cf. Mk 7.24; Mt. 19.1 // Mk 10.1);[18] two occurrences are clearly redactional (Mt. 4.13, cf. Mk 1.14; Mt. 15.39, cf. Mk 8.10); so it is quite possible that in 2.16 as well, the word is due to Matthean redaction. Redactional insertion of hyperbolic πᾶς is found in, for example, Mt. 8.32 // Mk 5.13; Mt. 8.34 // Mk 5.14; Mt. 21.12 // Mk 11.15; Mt. 24.8 // Mk 13.8. We do not know the quality of Matthew's geographical knowledge; in any case, it seems that he located Ramah not far from Bethlehem.[19]

We may say, then, that the quotation has been integrated sufficiently

16. See, for example, C. Westermann, *Genesis. II. Genesis 12–36* (BKAT, 1.2; Neukirchen–Vluyn: Neukirchener Verlag, 1981), pp. 675, 676.

17. So also Soares Prabhu, *Formula Quotations*, p. 259; G. Stanton, 'Matthew', in D.A. Carson and H.G.M. Williamson (eds.), *It is Written: Scripture Citing Scripture* (Festschrift B. Lindars; Cambridge: Cambridge University Press, 1988), pp. 205-19 (215) (reprinted in G. Stanton, *A Gospel for a New People: Studies in Matthew* [Edinburgh: T. & T. Clark, 1992], pp. 346-63).

18. Mark has the word twice in 7.31; in the Matthean parallel (15.29), Matthew has radically rewritten Mark's very confused geographical information, as a result of which the double ὅρια has disappeared. The only other New Testament occurrence is in Acts 13.50.

19. See McNeile, *St. Matthew*, p. 20; McConnell, *Law and Prophecy*, p. 113; Brown, *Birth of the Messiah*, p. 205; Luz, *Matthäus*, I, p. 130 n. 27; Davies and Allison, *Saint Matthew*, I, p. 268; M. Oberweis, 'Beobachtungen zum AT-Gebrauch in der matthäischen Kindheitsgeschichte', *NTS* 35 (1989), pp. 131-49 (135-36); Quesnel, 'Citations de Jérémie', pp. 517-18; Knowles, *Jeremiah in Matthew's Gospel*, pp. 45-46.

into its Matthean context. Matthew, presupposing that Rachel had been buried in the vicinity of Bethlehem, connected the episode of the massacre of young boys at Bethlehem with Rachel's complaint for her children at Ramah. He then tried to smoothe away, to the best of his knowledge and ability, the slight unevenness arising from 'Ramah' in the quotation by adding 'and in all that region' in the narrative. The measure of integration of the quotation makes a provenance from a collection of testimonies improbable—still apart from the question what function Jer. 31(38).15 would have had in such a collection.

2. *The Character of the Greek Translation in Matthew*

In the first line of the quotation, the agreement with the LXX in the use of φωνή and ἀκούειν is not very surprising: in both cases, we have to do with standard translations of the Hebrew equivalents. The translation of the Hebrew niphal participle נשמע by the Greek aorist passive indicative ἠκούσθη is, however, not an immediately obvious one.[20] When used as a predicate, the Hebrew participle mostly has the temporal value of a present,[21] and most modern translations render accordingly in Jer. 31.15 ('is heard'). The participle נשמע, used as a predicate, is translated elsewhere in the LXX either by a present indicative (Ps. 18[19].4; Eccl. 9.17) or by an aorist indicative (Jer. 3.21; Neh. 6.6). So the form of the verb in the first line of the quotation may well be a trace of the LXX.

The Hebrew ברמה is rendered in Matthew and LXX B by ἐν Ῥαμά, 'in Ramah', while LXX A reads ἐν τῇ ὑψηλῇ, 'in the height'. Aquila has (according to MS 86) ἐν ὑψηλῇ. Other ancient versions offer the same interpretation: the Targum has ברום עלמא, 'in the height of the world', and the Vulgate has *in excelso*, 'in the height'. 'Height' here indicates heaven (cf. Heb. 1.3).[22] The Hebrew רמה can be a geographical name; it is then mostly used with the article (הרמה), but not always (see Neh. 11.33). It can also be a substantivised feminine qal participle of רום, with the meaning 'high place', 'height'. So ברמה, whether vocalized with בְּ or with בָּ, allows both interpretations. As far as the LXX is concerned, ἐν Ῥαμά (LXX B) has the better chances to be the original

---

20. I presuppose that the Masoretic vocalization essentially reflects earlier practice of pronunciation.

21. See Joüon and Muraoka, *Grammar*, §121c.

22. See Lohmeyer, *Matthäus*, p. 30 n. 1.

translation: the reading ἐν τῇ ὑψηλῇ (LXX A) may well be a hexaplaric one, and it reflects a more developed theological understanding. Moreover, it can be the result of the conviction, based on Gen. 35.19 and 48.7, that Rachel had been buried near Bethlehem.[23] That the text of LXX B was influenced by the quotation in Matthew, is not very probable, because in the rest of the quotation LXX B and Matthew's text differ considerably. At this stage of the investigation we can only conclude that the words ἐν Ῥαμά in the quotation may come from the LXX but can also have their origin in independent translation of the Hebrew.

In Matthew's text, the words κλαυθμὸς καὶ ὀδυρμός in the second line function as an apposition to φωνή in the first line, while the LXX has a series of genitives which depend on φωνή. Matthew's text is here obviously a better translation of the Hebrew than the LXX.[24]

In this line, Hebrew text and LXX have three substantives, while Matthew's text has two substantives and the adjective πολύς at the end. The two substantives in Matthew, κλαυθμός and ὀδυρμός, are the second and third of the series of the LXX; θρῆνος is there the first one. There can hardly be any doubt that not only in the LXX but also in Matthew's quotation κλαυθμός is the translation of בכי: the Greek word is an obvious equivalent of the Hebrew one, and it is in the LXX and in what remains of the other ancient Greek translations of the Old Testament more or less its standard equivalent, just as the Greek verb κλαίειν is the standard equivalent of the Hebrew verb בכה. In both the LXX and the quotation in Matthew, κλαυθμός is followed by ὀδυρμός as a translation of תמרורים. From a semantic point of view, the translation leaves to be desired: 'lamentation' is not the same as 'bitterness'. From a syntactic point of view, the translation is incorrect: in Hebrew, תמרורים is a genitive to בכי, so that the two words together mean: 'weeping of bitterness', 'bitter weeping'. Aquila and Symmachus have translated here more correctly, and have, in addition, also made the second substantive into a genitive to the first one: μέλος κλαυθμοῦ πικραμμῶν, 'a song of bitter weeping'. In the LXX and in Matthew's text, however, the substantives are coordinated by means of καί. Both the translation ὀδυρμός and the coordination by καί are, in the quotation, clear signs of dependence on the LXX.

The disappearance of the first of the three substantives can be

23. Cf. Lohmeyer, *Matthäus*, p. 30 n. 1.
24. See Gundry, *Use of the Old Testament*, p. 95; Brown, *Birth of the Messiah*, p. 222.

plausibly explained if it is considered together with the addition of πολύς. The Greek words θρῆνος (or another good equivalent of the Hebrew word נהי)[25] and ὀδυρμός are virtually synonymous; I translated them above by 'wailing' and 'lamentation' respectively.[26] The circumstance that they are virtually synonymous was probably the reason to omit one of them, and the adjective πολύς was then added to make up for the omission. The question of the level at which these two cohering changes took place, will be discussed later. In any case, it is clear that they are possible only on the basis of the Greek translation of תמרורים into ὀδυρμός.

Some scholars, who assume that in the second line of the quotation Matthew himself translated from the Hebrew, think that the Evangelist changed the sequence of the two Hebrew nouns נהי and בכי, and then translated (influenced by the LXX) בכי into κλαυθμός, נהי into ὀδυρμός and תמרורים into πολύς.[27] W. Rothfuchs, on the basis of the same assumption, thinks that Matthew (influenced by the LXX) translated נהי into κλαυθμός, בכי into ὀδυρμός and תמרורים into πολύς.[28] There are, however, improbable elements in these hypotheses. In the former one, there is an unexplained change of sequence. In both, there are instances of unusual translation. The translations of נהי into ὀδυρμός or κλαυθ-μός, or of בכי into ὀδυρμός are semantically defensible, but they have, as far as we know, no parallels in the ancient Greek translations of the Old Testament; besides, as I have already observed, κλαυθμός is the normal equivalent of בכי. The translation of תמרורים into πολύς would be highly free and unusual. The LXX translates the Hebrew word in Jer. 6.26 by οἰκτρός, 'lamentable', and in Hos. 12.15, it renders by means of the verb παροργίζειν, 'to provoke to anger'. So in all three cases (including Jer. 31[38].15), the LXX offers a translation in which the semantic component 'bitter' is present. Aquila and Symmachus give in

25. In the Hebrew Bible, נהי occurs seven times; four times, it has been translated in the LXX by θρῆνος.

26. Cf. LSJ, θρῆνος I; ὀδυρμός.

27. Gundry, *Use of the Old Testament*, p. 95 with n. 2; *idem, Matthew: A Commentary on His Handbook for a Mixed Church under Persecution* (Grand Rapids: Eerdmans, 2nd edn, 1994), p. 36; Soares Prabhu, *Formula Quotations*, p. 253; Brown, *Birth of the Messiah*, p. 222; Davies and Allison, *Saint Matthew*, I, p. 269. Cf. also Goulder, *Midrash and Lection*, p. 240 n. 40; Knowles, *Jeremiah in Matthew's Gospel*, p. 36; Becking, '"Voice"', p. 231.

28. Rothfuchs, *Erfüllungszitate*, pp. 63-64.

Jer. 6.26; 31.15 the correct translation πικραμμοί (or πικρασμοί), 'bitterness'.[29] The translation πολύς would lack the semantic component 'bitter'. To my mind, the wording of the second line of the quotation (including καί) is much better explained by assuming dependence on the LXX. Such a view precludes that one has to resort to the implausible assumption that Matthew translated the Hebrew text but drew his vocabulary from the LXX.

In the third line of the quotation, we find for the Hebrew piel participle מבכה the Greek participle κλαίουσα, while the LXX has ἀποκλαιομένη.[30] As I have already noted, κλαίειν is in the ancient Greek Old Testament translations a standard rendering of בכה. This Hebrew verb occurs mostly in the qal, twice only in the piel (Jer. 31.15; Ezek. 8.14; in the latter case, the LXX translates into θρηνεῖν); there is no difference of meaning between the two conjugations.[31] The compound ἀποκλαίεσθαι, which may have a slightly stronger meaning than simple κλαίειν,[32] is also used in Jer. 31(48).32 LXX for בכה qal. So in Matthew's quotation, the usual translation has been preferred, either as a direct translation of the Hebrew or as a correction of the LXX.[33] Below, we shall discuss another possible incentive for this change.

The object of Rachel's weeping is in Matthew's text τὰ τέκνα αὐτῆς. The Hebrew text has here על־בניה, and these words return in the next line of the Hebrew text: Rachel refuses to be comforted 'for her sons'. The Vulgate and Targum agree with the Hebrew text in having 'for her sons' twice. Matthew's text, however, has no counterpart of these words in the fourth line. The LXX is divided: LXX A has in the third line ἐπὶ τῶν υἱῶν αὐτῆς but nothing similar in the fourth line, LXX B has

29. They even translate the Hebrew plural by a Greek one. In Jer. 31.21, they wrongly translate תמרורים II, 'sign-post', also by πικραμμοί. The LXX has here— wrongly as well—τιμωρία, 'retribution' or 'help'.

30. In LXX A, καί has been added at the beginning of the next line, probably under the influence of Matthew's quotation (cf. the first apparatus in Ziegler's edition). This addition has then (together with the genitives of the second line) led to the genitive reading ἀποκλαιομένης: it is an effort to improve the Greek construction by avoiding an independent clause with a participle instead of a finite verb. Both variant readings are clearly secondary, even post-Matthean.

31. See W. Baumgartner *et al.*, *The Hebrew and Aramaic Lexicon of the Old Testament*, I (Leiden: E.J. Brill, 1994).

32. See LSJ, ἀποκλαίω, 'weep aloud'.

33. Cf. the quotation from Hos. 11.1 in Mt 2.15: Matthew's text has there ἐκάλεσα for קראתי, the LXX of Hos. 11.1 has μετεκάλεσα.

nothing in the third line but has in the fourth line ἐπὶ τοῖς υἱοῖς αὐτῆς. This state of affairs can be explained in various ways (for instance, by assuming corruption of the Hebrew text). For our purposes, it is sufficient to state that the quotation in Matthew seems to come from a text which had על־בניה or a Greek equivalent in the third line, but not in the fourth. A plausible explanation for this aspect of the textual form of the quotation will be offered below.

The Hebrew noun בן has been translated in the quotation not by υἱός (so the LXX), but by τέκνον. Now this translation is maybe not what one would expect, but it is certainly adequate: it occurs regularly in the ancient Greek Old Testament translations that the plural בנים, if it comprises both males and females, is rendered by τέκνα (see, for example, Gen. 3.16 LXX; Prov. 31.28 LXX Aq Symm Theod; Job 17.5 Symm Theod).[34] In the case of Jer. 31.15, we have not only an instance of 'sons' being used for both males and females, but the direct context of the verse also contains clear suggestions that females are part of the group. The Hebrew text of v. 8 mentions women who are pregnant and in labour among those who are brought back by the Lord (the LXX translates differently here). In v. 13, the prophet speaks of the future joy of girls and men, young and old. The gloomy picture of v. 15 is immediately followed by its reversal, the return from the exile (vv. 16-20). According to v. 17, the 'sons' will return to their country; although the LXX is here shorter than the MT, it is evident that בנים, comprising males and females, has been translated by τέκνα. All these pointers in the context of Jer. 31(38).15 may very well have incited a translator or reviser to prefer in this verse τέκνα to υἱοί.

Matthew's text stands out among the known ancient versions of Jer. 31(38).15 in connecting the verb 'to weep' with a direct object instead of with a prepositional object. The Greek verb κλαίειν can be used transitively (just as the Hebrew verb בכה), and there are in the LXX some instances of בכה with a prepositional object (ל, על) having been translated by κλαίειν with a direct object.[35] So we have here a possible but unusual translation. Is there any reason for it?

Before answering this question, we have to consider another peculiar trait of the quotation: its fourth line begins with καί. This conjunction

---

34. Of course, υἱοί can also comprise both sexes, but τέκνα is in this respect more unequivocal.

35. See Gen. 50.1 B; 2 Kgdms 3.34; Jer. 22.10 (twice).

has no equivalent in the Hebrew text, and is not found in LXX B.[36] In Matthew, it causes an unbalanced sentence structure: a participial statement is linked, by καί, to an independent clause with a finite verb.[37] It seems that the addition of a conjunction does not, in this case, improve the Greek translation. Why then has καί been added?

To my mind, the best explanation for this and some other traits of the quotation is to be found in the influence of an analogous Old Testament passage. Two Old Testament passages are analogous if they have at least one word in common; usually, they also have a similar content. In early-Jewish and early-Christian use and explanation of Scripture, the wording of a passage could be adapted to that of an analogous one.[38] Now there is, in Genesis 37, the story of Joseph being sold to merchants by his brothers. At the end of the story (vv. 29-36), we are told that Joseph's brothers dip his robe in the blood of a goat, and bring it to their father Jacob, who concludes that Joseph must have been devoured by a wild beast. Jacob then mourns for his son, and all his sons and daughters try to comfort him. Genesis 37.35 provides the words that are vital to the quotation in Matthew: וימאן להתנחם...ויבך אתו אביו, 'and he refused to be comforted ... and his father bewailed him'. The LXX translates: καὶ οὐκ ἤθελεν παρακαλεῖσθαι ... καὶ ἔκλαυσεν αὐτὸν ὁ πατὴρ αὐτοῦ, 'and he would not be comforted ... and his father bewailed him'. The analogy of Gen. 37.35 and Jer. 31(38).15 is obvious, on the points of both wording and content. The two verses share (in MT and LXX) the words ימאן/οὐ θέλειν, נחם/παρακαλεῖν (LXX A) and בכה/κλαίειν, ἀποκλαίεσθαι. In addition, the texts share common themes: Gen. 37.35 is about the mourning of Jacob, Rachel's husband, for their son Joseph; Jer. 31(38).15 is about the mourning of Rachel, Jacob's wife, on the tribe of Ephraim (see Jer. 31.6, 9, 18, 20), and Ephraim was Joseph's son.[39]

---

36. About καί in LXX A, see above, n. 30. Gundry (*Use of the Old Testament*, p. 95) assumes, without good reasons, a Hebrew text with ו behind the LXX and Matthew's text.

37. Even if one assumes, with BDR, §128.3, that a form of εἶναι has been omitted after κλαίουσα, the construction remains unbalanced.

38. See M.J.J. Menken, *Old Testament Quotations in the Fourth Gospel: Studies in Textual Form* (Contributions to Biblical Exegesis and Theology, 15; Kampen: Kok, 1996), pp. 52-53 (with the literature mentioned there).

39. The analogy of Jer. 31.15 and Gen. 37.35 has been noticed by E. Hühn, *Die messianischen Weissagungen des israelitisch-jüdischen Volkes bis zu den Targumim ... II. Die alttestamentlichen Citate und Reminiscenzen im Neuen Testamente*

Now the assumption of influence of Gen. 37.35 on Jer. 31(38).15 explains several features of Matthew's quotation. The words καὶ οὐκ ἤθελεν in the fourth line agree literally with Gen. 37.35 LXX, where they are a correct translation of the Hebrew, so that the odd καί in the quotation may very well come from the analogous passage. That in the third line of the quotation the verb 'to weep' has a direct object, finds a parallel in the Genesis verse, in both Hebrew and Greek; it seems that the influence of the Genesis text explains another curious detail of Matthew's text. The influence of Gen. 37.35 also explains why the text of Matthew has על־בניה or its Greek equivalent in the third line, and not in the fourth line or in both the third and fourth lines: if 'for her sons' was not yet present in the third line, the translator or reviser took care to combine it with Rachel's weeping only, and not with her refusal of comfort, to adapt the Jeremiah passage to that from Genesis. The use of κλαίειν instead of the compound ἀποκλαίεσθαι, though already plausibly explained by normal translation practice, may find an additional explanation in the influence of Gen. 37.35 LXX.

Continuing our examination of the fourth line, we observe that in Matthew מאנה has been translated as οὐκ ἤθελεν. This is a lexically adequate translation, also found in Jer. 38.15 LXX. Twenty more instances of translation of the root מאן into οὐ/μὴ θέλειν can be found in the LXX, among them Gen. 37.35 LXX. Alternative translations of the Hebrew are, however, possible: ἀνανεύειν, ἀπαναίνεσθαι, ἀπειθεῖν, and especially οὐ/μὴ βούλεσθαι can, combined with an infinitive (in some cases preceded by τοῦ), have the meaning 'to refuse to do something', and occur in this sense in the ancient Greek translations of the Old Testament as translations of מאן,[40] together more than twenty times. The translation by οὐ θέλειν can be a slight trace of the LXX.

Syntactically, οὐκ ἤθελεν is not quite correct: in Hebrew, the entire clause about Rachel ('Rachel weeping...refusing...') functions as an apposition to what precedes. The translation in Matthew and the LXX agree in translating מאנה as a finite verb. They also agree in verbal tense: both have the imperfect ἤθελεν, while, to judge from the LXX, an

---

(Tübingen: J.C.B. Mohr, 1900), p. 3; W. Dittmar, *Vetus Testamentum in Novo: Die alttestamentlichen Parallelen des Neuen Testaments* (Göttingen: Vandenhoeck & Ruprecht, 1903), pp. 290, 323.

40. See, for example, Exod. 4.23 LXX; 1 Kgdms 28.23 LXX; Neh. 9.17 LXX; Ps. 76(77).2 LXX and Aq; Prov. 21.7 LXX; Jer. 15.18 Aq; Zech. 7.11 LXX.

aorist would have been the more obvious choice.[41] So ἤθελεν in the quotation can, as far as its verbal vorm is concerned, be assessed as a trace of the LXX.[42]

At the end of the fourth line, we meet παρακληθῆναι as the equivalent of the Hebrew לִהִנָּחֵם. The same Greek translation is found in LXX A and in Aquila's translation; LXX B has παύσασθαι. The latter reading is probably the original LXX translation: the reading of LXX A may be due to influence of Matthew or to hexaplaric influence or to both at the same time, and is in any case (as will appear below) the easier one. The Hebrew verb נחם is translated in the LXX in various ways; in the majority of occurrences, however, παρακαλεῖν is the preferred translation (for all conjugations in which the verb occurs).[43] It is the usual Greek translation of the Hebrew verb in instances in which it means 'to find consolation' (niphal), 'to comfort' (piel), 'to become consoled' (pual), or 'to allow oneself to be comforted' (hithpael) (see, for example, Gen. 24.67; Isa. 66.13; Ps. 119[118].52).[44] In Jer. 31(38).15, παύεσθαι is a possible but not very obvious translation of נחם niphal.[45] In Matthew's quotation, then, the more usual translation is found, either as a correction of the LXX or as an independent translation from the Hebrew; in both cases, influence of Gen. 37.35 LXX may also have been at work.

In the final line, כִּי אֵינֶנּוּ has been rendered as ὅτι οὐκ εἰσίν. The same rendering is found in the LXX and Aquila, and it is a very obvious

41. The perfect מֵאֵן is translated by οὐ θέλειν in the aorist in LXX Hos. 11.5; Jer. 5.3 (twice); 8.5; 11.10; 27(50).33; in the imperfect in LXX Ps. 77(78).10; Jer. 9.5; 38(31).15.

42. In theory, οὐκ ἤθελεν could come from Gen. 37.35 LXX; in fact, however, there are no reasons to surmise that Matthew's biblical text had a different wording before it was influenced by the Genesis verse. On both accounts, the present wording agrees with the LXX.

43. See G. Bertram, in O. Schmitz and G. Stählin, 'παρακαλέω κτλ.', *TWNT*, V (1954), pp. 771-98 (775 n. 20).

44. See W. Baumgartner *et al.*, *The Hebrew and Aramaic Lexicon of the Old Testament*, II (Leiden: E.J. Brill, 1995), נחם; LSJ, παρακαλέω III.2; W. Bauer, *Griechisch-deutsches Wörterbuch zu den Schriften des Neuen Testaments und der frühchristlichen Literatur* (ed. K. and B. Aland; Berlin: W. de Gruyter, 1988), παρακαλέω 4.

45. In the LXX, (ἀνα)παύεσθαι occurs a few more times as translation of נחם niphal, mostly in instances where God is said to regret his earlier decision to punish Israel: Jer. 33(26).3, 13, 19; 49(42).10.

one, also in interpreting the singular suffix of the Hebrew text as a plural one (which occurs in almost all ancient and modern translations of the verse).[46] The translation in Matthew can be evaluated as being due to the LXX or as the result of fresh translation of the Hebrew.

From the above, the following conclusions may be drawn. A considerable part of the quotation agrees with the LXX. Some of the corresponding elements, being Greek standard translations of Hebrew terms, are not very telling, but in several instances the agreement can hardly be fortuitous and points to dependence on the LXX: the verbal form of ἠκούσθη in the first line; ὀδυρμός and the coordination by καί in the second line; οὐκ ἤθελεν in the fourth line. Next, there are cases where the translation in Matthew renders the Hebrew text better or more in standard fashion than the LXX does: the apposition constituted by the second line; κλαίουσα in the third line; παρακληθῆναι in the fourth line. On the basis of the dependence on the LXX, these cases are best assessed as corrections of the LXX. In the second line, there is a stylistic improvement in the combination of the omission of θρῆνος and the addition of πολύς; it also presupposes the LXX text. The use of τέκνα in the third line is due to attention to the Jeremian context of the quotation. Finally, several traits of the quotation find an explanation (in some instances an additional one) in the influence of the analogous Old Testament passage Gen. 37.35: κλαίουσα combined with a (direct) object in the third line; καί and παρακληθῆναι in the fourth line. We have here apparently a revised LXX text, influenced by Gen. 37.35.

3. *Matthean and Pre-Matthean Elements in the Quotation?*

Now that we have established that Matthew's quotation is best considered as coming from a revised LXX, we have to ask how far the Evangelist is responsible for its textual form. Can we find elements that have to be ascribed to the Evangelist? Can we identify features that must be pre-Matthean?

Because, as we have seen, several scholars think that Matthew translated the Hebrew text, we have to look here first at the points of agreement between quotation and LXX: is there any chance that elements which we ascribed to the LXX, actually come from the Evangelist? The instances of what I have called 'standard translation' are insignificant in

---

46. The singular suffix has been used distributively, referring to a plural; see GKC, §145m, where several examples are given.

this respect as well, even if the words used also belong to Matthew's preferred vocabulary (such as ἀκούειν, κλαυθμός):[47] any translator would very probably use them. Among the significant points of agreement with the LXX listed above there is none that betrays a special Matthean interest. The verb θέλειν belongs to Matthew's preferred vocabulary and is used several times by the Evangelist as editor (see, for example, 15.28, 32; 17.4),[48] but it is at the same time a good and fairly obvious translation, so that there is no need to ascribe it specifically to Matthew.

Next, we consider the points of revision of the LXX text that have been detected. In none of the three instances of correction of the LXX listed above is there any reason to ascribe the correction to Matthean redaction: it can be due to any reviser. The situation seems to be different for the stylistic improvement in the second line. When we look at Matthew's editing of Mark, we can observe that he frequently replaces redundant duplicate expressions of Mark by simple ones.[49] Among these are several cases where Mark has two synonymous nouns or verbs connected by καί or οὐδέ or οὔτε, and Matthew retains only one of them, sometimes not the first but the second one.[50] Especially interesting is the way in which Matthew edits Mk 6.4. According to Mark, Jesus says that a prophet does not lack honour εἰ μὴ ἐν τῇ πατρίδι αὐτοῦ καὶ ἐν τοῖς συγγενεῦσιν αὐτοῦ καὶ ἐν τῇ οἰκίᾳ αὐτοῦ, 'except in his home town and among his relatives and in his family'. Out of the three coordinated substantives, Matthew (13.57) has retained the first and third one: a prophet does not lack honour εἰ μὴ ἐν τῇ πατρίδι καὶ ἐν τῇ οἰκίᾳ αὐτοῦ. He apparently considered συγγενεῖς and οἰκία as

47. See Luz, *Matthäus*, I, pp. 36, 43.

48. See Luz, *Matthäus*, I, p. 42. Matthew has the verb 42 times, Mark 25 times, Luke 28 times.

49. See J.C. Hawkins, *Horae Synopticae: Contributions to the Study of the Synoptic Problem* (Oxford: Clarendon Press, 2nd edn, 1909), pp. 139-42; Allen, *St Matthew*, pp. xxiv-xxvi; F. Neirynck, with Th. Hansen and F. Van Segbroeck, *The Minor Agreements of Matthew and Luke against Mark, with a Cumulative List* (BETL, 37; Leuven: Leuven University Press, 1974), p. 287. Some examples: Mt. 8.16 // Mk 1.32; Mt. 9.15 // Mk 2.19; Mt. 17.1 // Mk 9.2; Mt. 26.10 // Mk 14.6.

50. See the following sets of parallel verses (italicization indicates that Matthew retains the second element): *Mt. 9.18* // Mk 5.23; *Mt. 12.3* // Mk 2.25; *Mt. 13.57* // Mk 6.4; *Mt. 14.15* // Mk 6.36; Mt. 16.9 // Mk 8.17; Mt. 17.12 // Mk 9.12; Mt. 26.2 // Mk 14.1; *Mt. 26.21* // Mk 14.18; Mt. 26.63 // Mk 14.61; Mt. 26.70 // Mk 14.68. Cf. also Mt. 9.23 // Mk 5.38.

more or less synonymous, omitted the former substantive, and so obtained a series of two. Something similar has happened in the quotation in 2.18. Of the three coordinated substantives θρῆνος, κλαυθμός and ὀδυρμός, the first and third are synonymous; the latter is retained, and so a series of two is obtained. The addition of πολύς in itself cannot be shown to be a feature of Matthew's redaction: he sometimes adds the word to his source, and sometimes he omits it.[51] Besides, addition of πολύς without equivalent in the Hebrew text also occurs in the LXX;[52] it could therefore represent here a pre-Matthean variant in the transmission of Jer. 31(38).15. However, in connection with the narrative of the massacre the addition is apt. The brief description in Mt. 2.16 contains three exaggerations: Herod becomes *very* angry, and *all* boys in Bethlehem and *all* its surrounding area are killed. No wonder then that, according to the quotation, such great enmity results in great sorrow. The addition of πολύς serves to attune narrative and quotation to each other.[53] So it seems that Matthew removed a redundant word, and made up for it by adding πολύς, a word that fitted well into the context into which he inserted the quotation.

It has been observed that several details of the wording of the quotation found an explanation in the influence of the analogous verse Gen. 37.35. It is impossible to tell at what level of the transmission of Jer. 31(38).15 this influence has to be situated. The use of analogous texts was a widespread phenomenon; I do not see good reasons to ascribe this particular instance to Matthew.

There are two details in the quotation which are very probably pre-Matthean. In the previous section, we have concluded that ἐν 'Ραμά in the first line may come from the LXX (the words are found in LXX B) but also from independent translation of the Hebrew. It can be shown that Matthew found the geographical name in his biblical text. In the first section of this study, I observed that geographical interest is obviously present in Matthew 2, and that the Evangelist has tried to eliminate the tension between Ramah and Bethlehem by adding the words καὶ ἐν πᾶσι τοῖς ὁρίοις αὐτῆς in v. 16. That means that Matthew *found* a text with a geographical name;[54] otherwise it is incompre-

51. For the addition see, for example, Mt. 14.24 // Mk 6.47; Mt. 26.47 // Mk 14.43; for omission see, for example, Mt. 13.34 // Mk 4.33; Mt. 17.14 // Mk 9.14.
52. See, for example, Exod. 2.11; Ps. 21(22).17; Isa. 2.6; Ezek. 38.12.
53. So also Gnilka, *Matthäusevangelium*, I, p. 53.
54. Cf. Strecker, *Weg der Gerechtigkeit*, pp. 58-59; Luz, *Matthäus*, I, p. 127.

hensible why he used the verse from Jeremiah at all, and even adapted the preceding narrative to it. And if he found a text with a geographical name, it was probably a Greek one, not a Hebrew one in which an ambiguous ברמה could be read in two ways.

That in the third line of the quotation τέκνα is used to translate בנים, is another feature that should be evaluated as very probably pre-Matthean. We have seen that the translation is easily understood when the Jeremian context of Jer. 31(38).15 is taken into account. In the Matthean context, however, the word τέκνα causes some tension, for the preceding narrative concerns the killing not of children in general but of boys only. That is at least the obvious meaning of Mt. 2.16 when read in connection with the story of the visit of the Magi to Herod (2.1-8): the expected 'king of the Jews' (v. 2) was supposed to be male, not either male or female. It is also the obvious meaning of v. 16 when we read it against the background of the story of the birth of Moses (Exod. 1.15–2.10), in which Pharaoh orders male children only to be killed. If then πάντας τοὺς παῖδας in v. 16 should be understood as 'all the male children', the translation of בנים by υἱοί in Jer. 31(38).15 would have served Matthew better. So he found the translation by τέκνα.[55] That Matthew was responsible for the translation, as some interpreters think,[56] is unlikely, not only on account of the tension just pointed out, but also because Matthew uses τέκνον almost exclusively when he finds it in his source.[57] The people's declaration of responsibility in 27.25 ('his blood on us and on our children', ἐπὶ τὰ τέκνα ἡμῶν) may constitute an exception, and it shows together with other passages that for Matthew, τέκνα can mean 'posterity'. It is also possible that Matthew saw a link between the quotation in 2.18 and the declaration of responsibility in 27.25: the posterity will suffer from the consequences of what their ancestors have done. That link, however, would

55. So also Strecker, *Weg der Gerechtigkeit*, pp. 58-59 (with 59 n. 2); Brown, *Birth of the Messiah*, p. 222; Luz, *Matthäus*, I, p. 127 n. 7; Harrington, *Matthew*, pp. 44-45; New, *Old Testament Quotations*, p. 113.

56. Rothfuchs, *Erfüllungszitate*, pp. 64-65; Soares Prabhu, *Formula Quotations*, pp. 254-56; B.M. Nolan, *The Royal Son of God: The Christology of Matthew 1–2 in the Setting of the Gospel* (OBO, 23; Fribourg: Editions Universitaires; Göttingen: Vandenhoeck & Ruprecht, 1979), p. 138; Gundry, *Matthew*, p. 36; Gnilka, *Matthäusevangelium*, I, p. 53; Davies and Allison, *Saint Matthew*, I, p. 270; Knowles, *Jeremiah in Matthew's Gospel*, p. 37; Becking, '"Voice"', pp. 231-32.

57. See Mt. 3.9; 7.11; 9.2; 10.21; 15.26; 19.29; 22.24; 23.37. The *Sondergut*-passages 18.25; 21.28 very probably also belong to this series.

have functioned equally well with υἱοί in the quotation (see Mt. 1.20; 27.9).

I conclude that with the exception of the omission from and addition to the second line, there is no positive evidence of Matthean redaction in the quotation. On the other hand, two elements of it (ἐν 'Ραμά and τέκνα) are almost certainly pre-Matthean.

4. *Conclusion*

Matthew took the quotation from Jer. 31(38).15, which he offers in 2.18, from a continuous biblical text, and integrated it in its present, Matthean context. His biblical text was a revised LXX. In the case of the verse in question, the revision involved a better translation of the Hebrew, as well as an adaptation to the context of the verse in Jeremiah and to the analogous verse Gen. 37.35. There are no positive indications that Matthew was responsible for the revision. It seems that his editorial work on the quotation was limited to removing a redundant duplicate expression and adding the adjective πολύς.

It appears then that the hypothesis of Matthew using a revised LXX for his fulfilment quotations holds true in the case of the quotation in 2.18 as well. As far as I can see now, it is the best explanation for the textual form of the quotations in 2.18; 4.15-16; 12.18-21; 13.35; 21.5. For the very short quotations in 2.15 and 8.17 in themselves it is not possible to demonstrate that they come from such a revised LXX, but in these two instances the brief Old Testament passage quoted (Hos. 11.1; Isa. 53.4) was translated in the LXX in such a way that a revision can hardly be distinguished from a fresh translation. In any case, even these two quotations can be shown to come from a pre-Matthean Greek biblical text. It remains to be examined whether the textual form of the other formula quotations can be plausibly explained on the same basis, and where this revised LXX has to be situated. Another question which must not be neglected, is how Matthew's use of a revised LXX in the formula quotations relates to his use of the Old Testament in other contexts.[58]

58. I am grateful to Mrs K.M. Court for checking my English.

JESUS INSPECTS HIS PRIESTLY WAR PARTY (LUKE 14.25-35)

Crispin H.T. Fletcher-Louis

In Lk. 14.25-35 there is a collection of logia, three of which clearly deal with the demands of discipleship (vv. 26, 27, 33). Besides these three the opening verse is a familiar Lukan narrative setting and vv. 34-35 are also variously related to discipleship. The two parables in vv. 28-32 are also traditionally read as prescriptive for the would-be disciple. However, this collection—which is sandwiched between two discrete units (14.1-24; 15.1-32)—has been the cause of some interpretative difficulties.

Chief among such difficulties is the impression that Lk. 14.25-35 'is not a carefully designed argument but, rather, a loose conjunction of diverse source-material'.[1] In particular there has been uncertainty as to the place of the two parables (vv. 28-32) in their present Lukan context.[2] It is claimed that if these verses are removed—as their absence from Matthew (10.37-38) suggests they should—there is created a smoother flow of thought for the remaining verses.[3] 'The teaching of the paragraph is about the necessity for renouncing everything and putting Christ first, whereas the parables [as normally read] are concerned with self-testing rather than self-sacrifice...'[4] Luke's opening

---

1. R.A. Piper, *Wisdom in the Q-Tradition* (SNTSMS, 61; Cambridge: Cambridge University Press, 1989), p. 202. Cf. R. Bultmann, *The History of the Synoptic Tradition* (Oxford: Basil Blackwell, 1968 [1921]), pp. 170-71.

2. For example P.G. Jarvis, 'Expounding the Parables: V. The Tower-builder and the King Going to War (Luke 14.25-33)', *ExpTim* 77 (1965–66), pp. 196-98, (196); Piper, *Wisdom*, p. 202; B. Heininger, *Metaphorik, Erzählstruktur und szenisch-dramatische Gestaltung in den Sondergutgleichnissen bei Lukas* (NTAbh, 24; Münster: Aschendorff, 1991), p. 132.

3. For example J.D.M. Derrett, 'Nisi Dominus aedificaverit domum: Towers and Wars (Lk xiv 28-32)', *NovT* 19 (1977), pp. 241-61 (242).

4. Jarvis, 'Expounding the Parables', p. 196.

narrative comment (v. 25) has been judged inconsequential to the content of what follows, and the saying about salt losing its saltiness is easily detached from what precedes. It is frequently noted that various elements in vv. 25-35 pick up themes from the previous parables and teaching;[5] however, the internal logic of this section has remained obscure.

On the normal reading of the two central parables the man who wants to build a tower and the king who wants to go to war are treated as exemplary for the life of every would-be believer, in carefully considering beforehand whether they have the means to complete the task: these are typically Lukan non-allegorical example stories. There are some, however, who have raised objections to this individualistic interpretation. For example, Peter G. Jarvis has pointed out that 'it is uncharacteristic of Jesus to advise people to work things out beforehand. His usual attitude being that God is to be trusted for the future...'[6] Picking up Jarvis' own solution to the problem, and developing suggestions made earlier in this century by William Manson and Claus-Hunno Hunzinger, Duncan Derrett has argued for a fundamentally Christocentric and, therefore, theocentric interpretation.[7] On this reading Jesus is the man who wants to build a tower and Jesus is the king preparing to go to war. In doing so Jesus assesses the fitness of his resources—his disciples. There are a number of obvious strengths to this interpretation.

Hunzinger noted that the parables are examples of the common Lukan parabolic form which opens with the phrase τίς ἐξ ὑμῶν ('Who among you...').[8] In Luke these are always fundamentally theocentric.

---

5.   Chief among these: (1) the theme of socio-economic attachments preventing entry into the Jesus community (14.18-19, 33), (2) a qualification of any mistaken reading of 14.15-24 to the effect that, for example, Jesus requires faith without an appropriate lifestyle of obedience (cf. Mt. 22.11-13); (3) the reference to hating one's wife responds to the marital excuse not to come to the banquet in 14.20.

6.   Jarvis, 'Expounding the Parables', p. 197. Cf. Derrett, 'Nisi Dominus', pp. 248-49. Luke 9.56-62 does not furnish examples to the contrary: there the call is to accept the rootless life of faith, not to calculate the extent of one's *own* resources.

7.   Derrett, 'Nisi Dominus'. W. Manson, *The Gospel of Luke* (London: Hodder & Stoughton, 1930), p. 175; C.-H. Hunzinger, 'Unbekannte Gleichnisse Jesu aus dem Thomas-Evangelium', in W. Eltester (ed.), *Judentum-Urchristentum-Kirche* (BZNW, 26; Berlin, Alfred Töpelmann: 1960), pp. 209-20 (213-217). Hunzinger compares *Gos. Thom.* p. 97. Cf. also J. Louw, 'The Parables of the Tower-Builder and the King Going to War', *ExpTim* 48 (1936–37), p. 478.

8.   'Unbekannte Gleichnisse', pp. 214-15.

In each instance of the parabolic use of this phrase the narrative proceeds to describe the nature of God represented by one of its lead roles. In Lk. 11.5-6, 11-12 and 17.7 God's nature lies behind that of the shameless friend, the father and the master of an estate. Alternatively, in the behaviour of the hypothetical protagonist there is revealed the nature of Jesus' own action, which in turn reveals God's nature (15.4, cf. 14.5). As in rabbinic parables so in the Jesus tradition—a king usually stands in for God (Mt. 18.23-35; 22.1-14, cf. Lk. 19.11-27).

Derrett pushes the allegorical nature of this interpretation further by pointing to the common use of the word tower (πύργος) as a euphemism for the Jerusalem Temple or specifically the sanctuary within the temple. This is a feature of Second-Temple Jewish literature rooted in the biblical parable of the vineyard in Isaiah 5. The tower of the second verse of that text was normally taken to refer to the sanctuary (the wine vat representing the altar, and so on).[9] Jarvis and Derrett also discern a possible allusion in the threat of popular derision at an abortive attempt to build the tower (14.29b) to the tower in Genesis 11 mockingly called 'Babel'.[10] Of course, read in this way, Jesus is not preparing to build any material temple or sanctuary, rather he is building a community of believers.[11] This is an allegorical interpretation thoroughly consistent with the use of οἰκοδομεῖν and temple language throughout the New Testament.[12]

The perceived inconsistency between the parables and their contexts

---

9.   For the history of this interpretation rooted in earliest targumic tradition see Craig A. Evans, 'On the Vineyard Parables of Isaiah 5 and Mark 12', *BZ* 28 (1984), pp. 82-86 (83-84). Derrett and Evans compare *1 En.* 89.50, 56, 66b-67, 73; *Barn.* 16.1-5; *t. Me'il* 1.16 and *Suk.* 3.15. See also Josephus *War* 7.427 and *Sib. Or.* 5.424-5 (discussed below); *T. Mos.* 2.4 (following the conjectural emendation of the Latin *ferram* to *turrem* [R.H. Charles, (*The Assumption of Moses* London: A. & C. Black, 1897)], p. 62) or *turrim* (J. Tromp, *The Assumption of Moses: A Critical Edition with Commentary* [SVTP, 10; Leiden: E.J. Brill, 1993], pp. 8-9, 157); *Jos. Asen.* 2.1; 14.5 (discussed by G. Bohak, *Joseph and Aseneth and the Jewish Temple in Heliopolis* [Early Judaism and its Literature; Atlanta: Scholars Press, 1996], pp. 68-70, 73-74); *Jub.* 29.16, 19 where Abraham has a tower which receives offerings in a quarter-yearly cycle (cf. 31.6); Sir. 49.12 (MS A); *Exod. R.* 20.5.

10.   Jarvis, 'Expounding the Parables', p. 198; Derrett, 'Nisi Dominus', p. 252.

11.   For πύργος as a symbol of the church see especially the Shepherd of Hermas (e.g. *Vis.* 3.2.4–3.7.6; *Sim.* 8.2; 9.3-31) where the identification is made 149 times in all.

12.   See 1 Cor. 3.9-12; Eph. 2.19-22; Rom. 15.20, cf. Acts 4.11; 9.31; 20.32.

is now removed: having told a parable which celebrates the dawn of the eschatological banquet (14.15-24), Jesus launches into the most uncompromising demands on his followers. They are to hate their own kith and kin, even their own life, being willing to take up their cross in coming after him. In a society which valued highly family and racial ties his hearers and Luke's readers could be forgiven for questioning the ruthlessness of Jesus' demands. Verses 28-32 explain the rationale behind Jesus' testing of his disciples' and the crowds' faith (trust and faithfulness). He is building a new Temple and preparing an army for battle. He needs trustworthy resources for the project. They are to bid farewell to everything in their possession as they join his journey to Jerusalem (v. 33).

On this reading the opening narrative setting provided by Luke (v. 25) suits perfectly the contents of the pericope as a whole (vv. 26-35). Jesus is speaking to the crowds of followers many of whom, no doubt, were of uncertain commitment to his cause. Whilst the size of his following would give Jesus and his closest followers confidence that they have the social muscle to achieve great things as they march towards Jerusalem, Jesus perceives the need for stringent and essentially cross-centred criteria of discipleship.

The second parable, vv. 31-32, corresponds to the purpose of v. 26 in dealing with the question of human resources. The effect of Jesus' words in v. 26 is to sift the workforce he has at his disposable. By such sifting he risks greatly reducing the number of his followers. Like the king going to war with an empirically smaller force than his enemy he needs to know whether his force is actually better trained and committed (cf. v. 27) and thus able to meet the greater numerical force of the enemy. The first parable (vv. 28-30), on the other hand, corresponds to the focus of v. 33—the issue of financial resources. The tower-builder needs to ascertain the extent of his financial resources. So too, by pressing upon his followers the need to surrender their possessions in v. 33, Jesus establishes a community with the necessary financial muscle to carry through his vision for his new temple community (cf. Acts 2.42–6.15).

Jesus is on his way to Jerusalem; the centre of both military power and the activity of the priestly/Levitical institution. For Jesus to tell a parable about a man building a temple (tower) and establishing a military force 'whilst still far away from his enemy' in the context of Jesus' own journey to Jerusalem surrounded by crowds of followers can only possibly mean that he is telling these parables about himself: the traditional interpretation thus fails to pay sufficient attention to the very specific context in the Lukan narrative.

While the minority interpretation of these two parables must be essentially correct, various objections to Derrett's interpretation have been raised by Craig Blomberg. Blomberg argues that in 12.25 ('*Who among you* by worrying is able to add a single hour to the span of your life?') Luke provides an exception to the rule, claimed by Hunzinger, that τίς ἐξ ὑμῶν parables are always either Christocentric or theocentric.

But in defense of the minority reading, Lk. 12.25 is not at all parabolic as are all the other instances of the phrase τίς ἐξ ὑμῶν in Luke (and this includes Lk. 14.25-35). So Lk. 12.25 provides no justification for not treating it on analogy with its parabolic purpose elsewhere in Luke. Blomberg's other objection—that the image of God as the inferior of two kings who considers the possibility of surrendering to the enemy is inappropriate—is also beside the point. Luke is particularly fond of parables which draw on the imperfection of the human world of affairs to accentuate the workings of God's Kingdom and character. These parables operate within the thoroughly Jewish logic of a *qal waḥomer* (an *a fortiori* argument, cf. Lk. 11.13, πόσῳ μᾶλλον). In Lk. 11.5-8, 11.11-13, 16.1-8 and 18.1-8 the friend at midnight, the father, the steward and the judge, being human and evil (11.13, πονηροὶ ὑπάρχοντες), could not in their totality stand for God; yet, to the extent that these characters are good, wise and just, they clearly do. So too, the image of God as tower-builder unsure of his resources or of a king with inferior means should not be pressed.

In any case the image of Jesus as a king marching to Jerusalem to do battle with one whose power is apparently greater suits perfectly the claims and counter-claims of the prince of darkness. In Lk. 4.6 the devil claims that he possesses all the authority and glory of the kingdoms of the inhabited world, and that he has the power to give them over to Jesus. In Lk. 10.22 this claim is refuted since the Son is the one to whom God has bestowed all authority and power.[13] Satan has little power during Jesus' ministry (4.13); however, in the Passion he has his hour of apparent triumph (22.53). If Jesus appears to have the weaker

13. Luke's language at 4.6 is different from that at Mt. 4.8-9 in a way which ties the temptation to the Great Thanksgiving. Note especially the Lukan use of παραδίδωμι, and the similar phrases καὶ ᾧ ἐὰν θέλω δίδωμι αὐτήν and καὶ ᾧ ἐὰν βούληται ὁ υἱὸς ἀποκαλύψαι in 4.6 and 10.22.

force, as 14.31 implies, that is in any case consistent with the Lukan theology of glory through suffering and weakness, which, is central to his Christology (for example, 24.26).

In the rest of this study I wish to demonstrate that there is much more to this approach. In particular it will be supported, and the passage further illuminated, by a close examination of the verses—individual parts in their history of religions context and by paying attention to the intertextuality of Luke's language. In particular we find that the temple imagery of the first parable is the tip of a bigger cultic iceberg lying just beneath the surface of the whole of Lk. 14.25-35.

1. *The Tower and the Temple*

On closer inspection Derrett's allegorical interpretation of the tower as a symbol for the community as temple is more thoroughly integrated into the material in the rest of this section. The following considerations substantially confirm the tradition of allegorical interpretation of vv. 28-32 which he represents.

a. *The Temple-Builder and Political Satire*
We have already mentioned the possibility that the foolish tower-builder is meant to recall the tower of Babel of Genesis 11, a story which was understood in the first century as a political satire on the founding of Babylon.[14] Of all the Gospels, Luke's is the most interested in political commentary. At times it is harsh and bleak (for example, Lk. 13.1-9; 19.41-44). At others he is happy to reference political events with a touch of satire. For example, in Lk. 19.12-15 the prince travelling to a foreign land in order to receive his kingdom is clearly an allusion to the journeys of the Herodian rulers to receive power over Israel from pagan Rome.[15]

Derrett noted that the Jerusalem temple (both Herodian and pre-Herodian) was built in two stages—foundation first (Ezra 3; Josephus, *Ant.* 8.63; 15.391). Luke 14.28-29 envisaged the construction in the same way.[16] The building of the Herodian temple was evidently a

---

14. Especially Josephus *Ant.* 1.109-21.

15. See Josephus on Herod the Great (*War* 1.282-5; *Ant.* 14.374-89), and Archelaus (*War* 2.14-100; *Ant.* 17.224-340).

16. See also the importance for Luke of the laying of a proper foundation in another Temple parable (6.48, diff. Mt. 7.24).

massive project, consuming considerable time, energy and resources, and taking over 80 years to complete. Unfortunately, too little is known of the political and economic vicissitudes surrounding its construction. However, in the speech which Josephus has Herod make to the populous announcing his plans for the rebuilding of the Temple there is awareness of precisely the problems envisaged in Lk. 14.28-30.

> These were Herod's words, and most of the people were astonished by his speech, for it fell upon their ears as something quite unexpected. And while the unlikelihood of his realizing his hope did not disturb them, they were dismayed by the thought that he might tear down the whole edifice and not have sufficient means to bring his project (of rebuilding it) to completion. And this danger appeared to them to be very great, and the vast size of the undertaking seemed to make it difficult to carry out. Since they felt this way, the king spoke encouragingly to them, saying that he would not pull down the temple before having ready all the materials needed for its completion. And these assurances he did not belie. For he prepared a thousand wagons to carry the stones, selected ten thousand of the most skilled workmen, purchased priestly robes for a thousand priests, and trained some as masons, others as carpenters, and began the construction only after all these preparations had diligently been made by him (*Ant.* 15.388-90, cf. 15.381).

Whether or not at this point Josephus is slavishly following his source, Nicolaus of Damascus, is unclear. The issue at stake is very similar to that described in the Lukan parable: a man undertakes a building project and, conscious of the popular ridicule that would ensue if he did not bring it to completion, he reassures all concerned that he has the necessary wherewithal. But is the negative reaction of the Jewish populace no more than Nicolaus's record of the initial reaction to the building project's plans? Would Luke's readers, or for that matter any hearers of the parable's original telling by Jesus of Nazareth, have any memory of this issue 50 or more years later?

In the first instance it is quite understandable that the Jewish populace should be anxious at the prospect of a rebuilding project which might leave the sanctuary permanently exposed. However, since in fact the rebuilding was not completed until the early 60s of the first century CE it is highly likely that the words Josephus puts on Herod's lips actually reflect an issue that was of considerable political consequence throughout the final years of the Second Temple. From what follows it is evident that Josephus' desire to have Herod reassure his hearers that he was prepared to carry through the project is borne of Josephus's own desire to reassure his readers that, despite events to the contrary, the building project was well conceived from its inception. Josephus writes in *Ant.* 15.391:

> After removing the old foundations, he [namely, Herod] laid down others, and upon these he erected the temple, which was a hundred cubits in length and twenty more in height, *but in the course of time this dropped as the foundations subsided and this part we decided to raise again in the time of Nero.*

A passing notice of what must be the same incident is provided in Josephus' *Jewish War*, where we are told how John of Gischala uses for his defensive purposes some of the timber which Agrippa II had brought into the Temple to shore up its subsiding foundations (5.36). There is here, then, an embarrassing admission that in fact Herod's plans and projections were not sufficient and that precisely the problem which Jesus warns against in Lk. 14.28-29 dogged Herod's rebuilt temple throughout its short-lived existence. No doubt those close to Herod and his political power-structure did everything to minimize this public relations disaster. His opponents—perhaps the majority of the Jewish populace—would surely at times have mocked Herod and his dynasty for his efforts in the way Lk. 14.29b-30 describes. There was perhaps within such quarters a well-established tradition of religio-political satire against Herod, his family and their temple-building projects of which Jesus' short parable is itself a good example.[17]

It is probable too that the same Jewish populace suffered the mockings of the wider Gentile population, inasmuch as the latter would have regarded Herod's temple as essentially a Jewish temple. The Jews claimed their Temple held unique cosmological significance providing stability in the universe and surety for Israel against famine, pestilence and sword.[18] But the shaky foundations of the Jerusalem Temple hardly persuade the sceptical: on the contrary they would have provided plenty of ammunition for the anti-Semitic. So, among the implied hearers of Jesus' parable, not only would emotions have run high they would also

---

17. For another aborted building project by one of the Herodian family see *War* 5.152.

18. On this see generally C.H.T. Fletcher-Louis, 'The Destruction of the Temple and the Relativization of the Old Covenant: Mark 13.31 and Matthew 5.18', in K.E. Brower and M.W. Elliott (eds.) *'The Reader Must Understand': Eschatology in Bible and Theology* (Leicester: Apollos, 1997), pp. 145-69, and the secondary literature cited there.

have been conflicting. Many of Jesus' hearers, and Luke's Jewish read-ers, would have been caught in a complex web of loyalty to their Temple; pride, mingled with deep dissatisfaction at its Herodian spon-sorship, and the knowledge that their leadership's failure to plan ahead at its inception was costing them sorely in their bid to be the hierocratic leaders on the world stage.

This Lukan parable, then, relates to a very specific and well-known religious and political debate. That context prescribes a communal inter-pretation in which the protagonist is Israel's true leader and temple-builder. It is highly unlikely that Luke's readers would have thought of the individualistic and ahistorical reading which has dominated modern interpretation.[19]

b. *Tower, Temple and Community: The Oniad Temple at Leontopolis*
The Lukan parable is not simply, however, a satire against Herod or his rebuilt Temple. Thus far, we have suggested the parable is also a claim by Jesus that in asking so much of his followers he is laying the foun-dations of a temple community which he can be sure to complete. For Luke's Jesus the temple is one composed not of bricks and mortar but of human persons. The church as temple is a well-established theme in early Christian literature, though it is normally judged to be absent from Lukan theology.[20] On closer inspection there is much in these closing verses of Luke 14 to suggest here, at least, Luke articulates a priestly ecclesiology.

19. My reading is not dissimilar to that recently proposed by N.T. Wright who sees in the images of a tower-builder and king going to war dire warnings against Israel's desire to take up a holy war against Rome (*Jesus and the Victory of God* [London: SPCK, 1996], p. 405). However, in the Lukan context the precise nature of Wright's understanding of the parables' political comment is unlikely: too much in Lk. 14.25-35 sounds like an agenda for a revolutionary movement, not a critique of one particular type of revolution. It is much more likely that 'the Tower' (and 'King Going to War') are a satirical mockery of competing and dominant claimants to power with which the 'crowds' would feel sympathetic, rather than an attack on prevalent nationalistic expectations. In his otherwise laudable endeavour to read the Gospels in the context of Jewish nationalism and Jesus' critique of the holy war tradition Wright's interpretation looses sight, in at least the present passage, of the reappropriation of the imagery of that tradition in a specifically christological direction.

20. P.W.L. Walker, *Jesus and the Holy City: New Testament Perspectives on Jerusalem* (Grand Rapids: Eerdmans, 1996), p. 68 n. 47.

The best known Jewish parallel to such an ideology in Christian literature is, of course, the self-perception of the Qumran community behind the Dead Sea Scrolls. Their attitude towards the Jerusalem Temple and any eschatological physical temple is complicated, but there is no doubt that while estranged from the former and in anticipation of the latter they considered themselves a spiritual temple. They were, in the memorable and polyvalent, phrase of 4Q174 a *miqdāš ādām*—'a sanctuary of men', or 'of Adam'.

Though in the extant Qumran texts the community is nowhere described as a tower, there are hints that the Essenes would have at once identified with Jesus' parable.[21] In a number of important passages the Qumran community thinks of itself as laying the *foundation* of a new Temple community.[22] Joseph Baumgarten and George Brooke have recently discussed a fragmentary Qumran text (4Q500 frag. 1) where the allegorization of Isaiah 5, widely known from extra-biblical sources and taken up in the Gospels' Parable of the 'Wicked Tenants', is assumed. It is this biblical passage which provided the scriptural anchor for the temple-as-tower symbolism, and though in what is left of the Qumran fragment that connection is not made, the use of similar imagery of the community to that in 4Q500 elsewhere in the scrolls may indicate that the temple/tower/community constellation was well known at Qumran.[23]

The probability that this was the case is heightened by the importance the Isaiah 5 passage evidently played for the Oniad-led movement which broke away from the Jerusalem hierocracy in the first half of the second century and built a temple at Leontopolis in lower Egypt. Josephus in *War* 7.427 specifically says that the Leontopolis temple resembled a tower (πύργος). The Oniad justification for their actions on the basis of the prophecy in Isa. 19.19 ('On that day there will be an altar to

---

21. For the *individuation* of the temple/tower imagery in application to the community member see 1QH 15.8 [7.8] and 1QSb 5.23-4. At the centre of the northern face of the site at Khirbet Qumran there are the remains of a large tower (see R. de Vaux, *Archaeology and the Dead Sea Scrolls* [London: Oxford University Press, 1973], pp. 5-6, 25). However, the structure does not have obvious sanctuary features in its relation to the rest of the complex.

22. for example, 1QS 5.5; 8.8; 9.3.

23. See G.J. Brooke, '4Q500 1 and the Use of Scripture in the Parable of the Vineyard', *DSD* 2 (1995), pp. 268-94 and J.M. Baumgarten, 'The Qumran Sabbath Shirot and Rabbinic Merkabah Traditions', *RevQ* 13 (1988), pp. 199-213. For Lukan interest in Isaiah 5 (besides Lk. 20.9-19), cf. Isa. 5.11-13 with Lk. 21.34.

the Lord in the centre of the land Egypt, and a pillar to the Lord at its border') is well-known and is clearly stated by Josephus (*War* 7.432; *Ant.* 13.64, 68). In a perceptive discussion C.T.R. Hayward has demonstrated the extensive Oniad reliance on Isaianic prophecy, including the probability that the Temple's tower-like shape was inspired by Isa. 5.2.[24] This means that Isaiah 5 and its description of Israel as a vineyard with a tower at its centre had already been used by one breakaway temple movement some two hundred years before Jesus' ministry is remembered to have taken up the image. Like the Oniad family whose aim was 'to rival the Jews at Jerusalem' (*War* 7.431), Jesus sees himself building a new true Temple, while the one in Jerusalem remains standing. Unlike the Oniad temple, which was built of 'huge stones' (*War* 7.427), Jesus is building his from flesh and blood.[25]

In assessing the significance of the tower imagery we have already noted a possible slighting allusion to the tower of Babel. This symbolism, incidentally, was recognized in patristic interpretation.[26] Any allusion to the tower of Babel may also have a positive function for the identity of the Christian community. In Acts 2 the Pentecostal community is formed as an undoing of the judgment consequent upon the sin of the generation at Babel (Gen. 11). The idea that the eschatological community would recapitulate the fate of that generation is also evident in the description of the eschatological temple in *Sib. Or.* 5.414-433. There the eschatological temple contains

> a great and immense tower (πύργον) over many stadia touching even the clouds and visible to all (5.424-425).

24. C.T.R. Hayward, 'The Jewish Temple at Leontopolis: A Reconsideration', *JJS* 33 (1982), pp. 429-33, (432-33). Beside the application of Isa. 5.2 and 19.19 Hayward demonstrates that behind Josephus' reference to the temple standing for 343 days there lies an interpretation of Isa. 30.26 parallel to that found in the Targum (pp. 436-37).

25. The degree to which the sanctuary-as-tower symbolism fed the Oniad Temple community at Leontopolis may now be seen in the use of tower imagery in *Joseph and Aseneth*. Gideon Bohak has persuasively argued that the text as a whole provides an aetiological allegory for the founding of the Leontopolis Temple. Aseneth's tower (2.1; 14.5) represents the sanctuary to the pagan goddess Bubastis which was taken over by the Oniad Jews and dedicated to Israel's god (see Bohak, *Joseph and Aseneth*, pp. 68-70, 73-74).

26. For the constellation of Babel, tower and church in St Ephrem see R. Murray, *Symbols of Church and Kingdom: A Study of Early Syriac Tradition* (London: Cambridge University Press, 1975), pp. 219-24.

There is a clear allusion to Babel as Andrew Chester has noted.[27]

It may be asked: why, if a temple is meant, Luke's Jesus did not use the word ἱερός or ναός? The obvious answer is that to have done so, when his hearers were the crowds in general, not just his committed inner group, would have been to risk the misunderstanding of a potentially dangerous political claim (cf. Mk 14.58, Acts 6.14; 7.48). The true eschatological Temple would be built at the very least by a human Davidic messiah, if not by God himself.[28] As throughout his parables, Jesus veils a bold and politically confrontational claim in parabolic metaphor.

The word 'tower' on its own, of course, need not have any symbolic reference.[29] Jerusalem had many towers (Ps. 47.13; 2 Chron. 26.9; Neh. 3.1, 11, 19, 25; Tob. 13.17; 1 Macc. 1.33; *Aristeas* 101-105), besides the one tower of symbolic strength at its centre. Yet, (1) the widespread use of the tower image for the temple in debt to Isaiah 5,[30] (2) the specific religio-political context of the scenario described by Luke in 14.28-30, and (3) the fact that such a reading here lends literary structure to an otherwise disjointed passage go together to justify the view that such symbolism was intended at least by Luke, if not the tradition before him also.

---

27. A. Chester, 'The Sibyl and the Temple', in W. Horbury (ed.), *Templum Amicitiae: Essays on the Second Temple Presented to Ernst Bammel* (JSOTSup, 48; Sheffield: JSOT Press, 1991), pp. 37-69 (56).

28. Cf. Chester, 'The Sibyl and the Temple', pp. 50-56. In *Sib. Or.* 5.414-433 it is built by 'a blessed man...from the expanses of heaven' (5.414).

29. Although Luke did not choose to include reference to the Isaianic tower in his version of the 'Wicked Tenants' parable (20.9-19, diff. Mt. and Mk), this in no way detracts from our claim that he knows very well its temple symbolism. The sacral symbolism of the vineyard was itself ubiquitous and did not need the support of details unessential to the thrust of the parable of the tenants.

The tower of Lk. 13.4 is evidently part of the larger temple complex—Siloam being of considerable cultic significance—though clearly, in the non-parabolic teaching material of Lk. 13.1-5 it does not stand so simply as a symbol for the temple or its sanctuary.

30. Besides Isa. 5, the parabolic description of the 'tower of the flock' in Micah's description of Zion as locus of God's coming dominion (4.8), will also have played a prominent role in the development of tower as sanctuary symbolism. Micah 4.8 has perhaps already influenced *1 En.* 89.50, 67 where the tower is set up for Israel depicted as flock of sheep. Is it a coincidence that in the Lukan context there follows a parable in which the repentant are similarly described as sheep?

2. *Levitical Discipleship*

The interpretation of the Parable of the Tower-Builder as one describing Jesus' own building of a temple community does not stand on its own. The rest of the material in Lk. 14.25-35 is replete with language and imagery which means Jesus' followers are being gathered into a specifically Levitical or priestly community. This is clearest in three of the passage's individual parts: (1) the call to social estrangement in v. 26, (2) the call for a renunciation of possessions in v. 33, and (3) the saying about salt.

a. *Levitical Discipleship through Social Estrangement (Luke 14.26)*
Jesus's teaching in this section begins with one of his harder sayings:

> Whoever comes to me and does not hate his father (τὸν πατέρα ἑαυτοῦ), and his mother (τὴν μητέρα) and his wife and his children (τὰ τέκνα) and brothers (τοὺς ἀδελφούς) and sisters, even his own life, is not able to be my disciple (Lk. 14.26).

Commentators regularly note, though do not fully explore, the fact that Jesus' words allude to Moses' blessing of Levi in Deut. 33.9 (LXX):

> The one saying to his father (τῷ πατρί) and his mother (τῇ μητρί) 'I have not seen you' and his brothers (τοὺς ἀδελφούς) he did not acknowledge and his children (τοὺς υἱούς) he disowned.

This is the only place in the Old Testament where there is such a combination of father, mother, siblings and children. It is also one of the few biblical texts where such a clear-cut rejection of family ties is praised.[31]

The thrust of both Luke and Deuteronomy is essentially the same, suggesting that Luke has Jesus call his disciples to a specifically priestly community. In Mt. 10.37 there is also a possible allusion to Deut. 33.9; however, the similarity is weakened by Matthew's less rigid separation of the believer from his family and the preference for Mic. 7.6 as the scriptural base in the previous verse (Mt. 10.36). Both Matthew and Luke envisage a conflict that does not respect familial loyalties. However, Luke sees that conflict paradigmatically rooted in the formation of the Levitical community over against the rest of Israel. There is no reason, of course, to think that Luke's Jesus calls only those of *racial* Levitical descent, however the biblical principle of a group

---

31. See also 1 Kgs 19.19-21 which has influenced Lk. 9.62.

spiritually set apart from the rest of racial Israel is followed.

There are several important points at which Luke differs from Deuteronomy 33. First, to the list of relations he adds a reference to hating one's wife (diff. Mt. 10.37). Elsewhere I have demonstrated this is an example of a larger Lukan concern to record traditions which legitimate the existence of a celibate, angelomorphic Christian community.[32] That identity is rooted in pre-Christian priestly traditions of purity and cultic worship. Hating one's wife is a logical extension of the social and ontological separation of the priestly calling, exemplified by Deut. 33.9.

Second, the hyperbolic 'hate' is a semitic idiom (for example Prov. 13.24; 2 Sam. 19.6). Its presence here (diff. Mt. 10.37) alerts us to the fact that we are dealing with a fundamentally Jewish cultural milieu. Since Deut. 33.9 would naturally be interpreted with reference to Exod. 32.27-29—the Levitical vengeance on those in Israel who had worshipped the golden calf—it is possible that that act of priestly zeal (that is, of *hatred* for the sinful brother) has influenced the choice of language here.[33] Indeed, it is specifically in the Dead Sea Scrolls (1QS 2.4-17; 9.21) and Josephus' description of the Essenes (*War* 2.139: 'he will forever hate [μισήσειν] the unjust') that we find a similar call to hate those outside the true (priestly) community.

A third difference is the context of following *Jesus*. The Levites give themselves solely to *God*, their portion. The Christological implications of allegiance to Jesus in this saying are not to be missed.[34] (They are appropriately accentuated in Matthew's version.)

Fourth, to the denial of family Lk. 14.26 adds a denial of oneself. There is some, admittedly limited, evidence that this was a common interpretation of Deut. 33.9. In one of his references to Deut. 33.9, Philo says that Levi exemplifies the man who 'forsakes father and mother, *his mind and material body*, for the sake of having as his portion the one God' (*Leg. All.* 2.52).[35] This may be simply a piece of Philonic allegorization. Alternatively it may belie a common exegetical tradition: some

---

32. C.H.T. Fletcher-Louis, *Luke–Acts: Angels, Christology and Soteriology* (WUNT, 2.94; Tübingen: J.C.B. Mohr [Paul Siebeck], 1997), pp. 78-96, 193-95.

33. For Deut. 33.9 interpreted with reference to Exod. 32.27-29 see later rabbinic texts (for example *Num. R.* 1.12; 15.12; *Eccl. R.* 4.8 § 1; *b. Yom.* 66b; *Sifre* 349-50; *Frag. Targ.* and *Targ. Onq.*).

34. Cf. Jarvis, 'Expounding the Parables', p. 196.

35. Cf. *Mut. Nom.* 127; *Fug.* 88-89; *Ebr.* 72.

Jews understood the call to the denial of kith and kin on joining the priesthood to mean that one's own well-being, physical and mental is surrendered. This would be natural since social deprivation may inevitably entail a more individual and personal deprivation.[36]

The importance of Deut. 33.9 for the whole of this pericope may also be present by an intertextual awareness of the rest of Deuteronomy 33. In the surrounding words of the blessing of Levi there is a reference to his being *tested* at Massah and Meribah (33.8; cf. Exod. 17.1-7; Num. 20.2-13) and Deut. 33.9 itself can be taken as a reference to the Levites slaying idolatrous fellow Israelites at Sinai (Exod. 32.25-29). In rabbinic tradition this event could itself be regarded as a moment when God *tested* Levi and found him faithful.[37] Just as God tested Israel and found Levi faithful, so now Jesus tests the crowds (note the repeated 'whoever does not...', οὐ δύναται εἶναί μου μαθητής, vv. 26, 27, 33) in the hope of finding some who will take up their cross in the formation of a new priesthood.

b. *Through Renunciation of Possessions (Luke 14.33)*
After the initial testing of his followers (vv. 26-27) and the explanation of the rationale behind that testing (vv. 28-32), Jesus reiterates the challenge. The resumptive οὕτως οὖν of v. 33 introduces yet another demanding criterion of discipleship; dispossession of wealth. The theme is Lukan (12.33; 18.22). Once again a strongly Levitical subtext is evident when it is remembered that within Israelite society it is the Priests and Levites who were to be landless, ministering to the Lord in dependence on the tithes of the rest of the nation (Num. 18.20, 23; Deut. 10.9; 18.1-2; cf. Neh. 13.10).

It is well-known that this law was kept only loosely in the late Second Temple period. Josephus's aristocratic priestly family, for example, had considerable land holdings in the Jerusalem area.[38] But for our purposes it is sufficient to note that elsewhere Luke is evidently keen to see the fulfilment of the original ideals of the Torah in the formation of a landless priesthood. In Acts 4.35-36, within a general account of the early Christians' communitarian lifestyle, Luke makes specific mention

36. This may also be reflected in the combination of an ascetic (and angelomorphic) and priestly identity in various Jewish traditions (see Fletcher-Louis, *Luke–Acts*, pp. 193-95, 199).
37. *Num. R.* 1.12 and *Num. R.* 15.12 where the event is associated with Ps. 11.5.
38. See his *Life* 422, 425.

of Barnabas who, being a Levite, sold a field in his possession bringing the proceeds to the feet of the disciples.[39] This is both a fulfilment of the Old Testament's landless Levitical ideal and sound proof that Luke understood such surrender of property as a priestly calling.

c. *Levitical Discipleship through the Life of the Living Sacrifice (Luke 14.34-35)*

Finally, the pericope ends with the Lukan form of the saying on salt common to all three Synoptic Gospels (Lk. 14.34-35; Mk 9.49-50; Mt. 5.13). The saying, particularly in its Markan form, has been a *crux interpretum*. Various suggestions as to the conceptual background have been offered, among which a sacrificial setting has been a strong candidate.[40] In Lev. 2.13 and Ezek. 43.24 salt is added to sacrifices (cf. Ezra 6.9; Num. 18.19; 2 Chron. 13.5). There was evidently some dispute as to the extent of the required use of salt in the sacrifices as *Jubilees* and 11QTemple both stipulate, in a somewhat polemical vein, its use in all offerings (*Jub.* 21.11; 11QT 20.13a-14b; cf. *T. Levi* 9.14). Though space prevents a thorough examination of each occurrence of the saying, it can be argued that this was always its fundamental sense.[41]

In all three versions the presence of salt is affirmed (Mk. 9.49; Mt. 5.13a), in Mark and Luke this presence is specified as being 'good' (Mk. 9.50a; Lk. 14.24a). In all three versions there follows the puzzle: what happens if the salt ceases to fulfil its intended function? In Matthew and Luke (and perhaps implicitly in Mark) this is answered with the threat that useless salt is to be destroyed by one means or another. Now if the 'salt' be taken as a metonym for the whole sacrificial institution, then the salt saying fits perfectly into the flow of thought within the Gospel as well as the early Christian attitude towards the Jerusalem temple as the place of its sacrificial cult within the

---

39. The language is Lukan in both Acts 4.36 and Lk. 14.33; see especially ὑπάρχοντος (Acts 14.36) and ὑπάρχουσιν (Lk. 14.33).

40. For options see W.D. Davies and D.C. Allison, *A Critical and Exegetical Commentary on the Gospel According to Saint Matthew* (ICC; Vol. 1; Edinburgh: T. & T. Clark, 1988), I, pp. 472-73.

41. For the sacrificial interpretation see O. Cullmann, 'Das Gleichnis vom Salz: Zur frühesten Kommentierung eines Herrenworts durch die Evangelisten', in K. Froehlich (ed.), *Vorträge und Aufsätze* (Tübingen: J.C.B. Mohr [Paul Siebeck], 1966), pp. 192-201; R. Schnackenburg, *Schriften zum Neuen Testament: Exegese in Fortschritt und Wandel* (Munich: Kösel, 1971), pp. 195-96.

dispensations of salvation history: if the sacrificial cult has ceased to fulfil its intended soteriological function then it is destined to destruction (cf. Mk. 11.12-25, and parallels).

This is an interpretation which particularly suits the Lukan context. Not only is Jesus setting up a new temple and priesthood around himself, which would implicitly relativize the one in Jerusalem, his second parable concerning a king going to war strikes a note of warning to any enemy which stands in his way. As the Gospel story unfolds it becomes clear that 'the enemy' has now found a base in Jerusalem and the power structures of the temple state (see 22.53). If their salt has μωρανθῇ ('become insipid'), then the participants in the Temple Cult are destined to be cast outside. Let those who have ears to hear, hear!

In the context of the Markan form of the saying the sacrificial sense is perhaps less self-evident. However, there are several features which do suggest such an interpretation. The disciples are said to have salt in themselves. They are like the hearers of Jesus' sermon in Matthew 5–7 who are 'the salt of the earth'. This is an important point to make if, like Luke, Mark sees the temple cult in Jerusalem as now relativized. The functions of that cult are now transferred to the salted lifestyle of the Christian community itself (cf. Col. 4.6). One such function was the maintenance of peace among the people of God by the removal of sin which would otherwise create enmity between its members. Thus it follows naturally that because they have salt in themselves, the disciples have peace with one another (Mk 9.50d).

The Matthean form of the saying also suits a sacrificial interpretation as Ithamar Gruenwald has seen in a persuasive reading of the Sermon on the Mount as an implicit relativization of the Jerusalem cult.[42] This time the function of the temple cult is transferred to the people of God, Israel, as a whole. They are to be God's means of dealing with sin in the world as their history had always intended.[43] When Matthew's Jesus refers to the people of God as a light set on a hill he is specifically thinking of popular perceptions of the Jerusalem temple as a gleaming

---

42. I. Gruenwald, 'From Priesthood to Messianism: The Anti-Priestly Polemic and the Messianic Factor', in I. Gruenwald (ed.), *Messiah and Christos: Studies in the Jewish Origins of Christinity; presented to David Flusser on the Occasion of His Seventy-Fifth Birthday* (Tübingen: J.C.B. Mohr [Paul Siebeck], 1992), pp. 75-93.

43. Cf. especially N.T. Wright, *The New Testament and the People of God* (London: SPCK, 1992), pp. 262-72.

white wonder of the world, reflecting the sun's rays with its white marble and gold plating, visible from afar to every approaching visitor.[44] Matthew 5.13-16 is part of a larger temple-mythology theme which gives a literary and conceptual structure to the whole of Matthew's Sermon on the Mount, as I have argued elsewhere.[45]

Conclusion

Thus Luke concludes 14.25-35 with a pericope which was throughout the tradition understood to refer to matters of cult and temple in the history of God's purposes. The whole of this section is dominated by priestly concerns. In as much as it has a specific scriptural base Deut. 33.9 is a hook upon which the author has hung material devoted to Jesus and his movement. When read in this way these verses are a literary whole devoted to Jesus' inspection of his priestly community as it advances to war against the enemy.

44. See especially K.M. Campbell, 'The New Jerusalem in Matt. 5.14', *SJT* 31 (1978), pp. 335-63.
45. Fletcher-Louis, 'Destruction of the Temple', esp. pp. 167-69.

NARRATIVE ANALYSIS AND SCRIPTURE IN JOHN

Judith Lieu

More than in any of the other Gospels, Scripture provides the indispensable reference point and scaffolding for the argument and the thought of John. From apparently inconsequential allusions through to John's distinctive Christology, it is Scripture that makes the Gospel 'work'. This has become obvious enough in recent years, which have seen a flood of monographs and articles devoted to the subject.[1] Yet if this is as yet unquenched, it is because there is much that remains unplumbed. John's 'formula' quotations are erratic, clustering mainly in the final part of the Gospel, and not obviously chosen because of any consistent key role either in the narrative nor in the theological argument. Elsewhere both direct and indirect echoes abound, but the apparent lack of any self-consciousness about this means that there are few constraints on the inventiveness of the scholar detecting hitherto 'unrecognised allusions'.[2] Whether some, any, or all of these were recognized by the author, let alone by his (sic) immediate audience, remains not just unanswerable, but probably crucial for any reconstruction of the setting of either, and of their relationship, past or present, with Judaism and its exegetical activity. Was the author unreflectedly drawing on a rich treasury of literary and symbolic resources, some of which would fortuitously resonate no less with those from a Gentile background than with those bred in and with the Scriptures? Or was he

---

1. E.g. M. Menken, *Old Testament Quotations in the Fourth Gospel: Studies in Textual Form* (Kampen: Kok, 1996); A. Obermann, *Die christologische Erfüllung der Schrift im Johannesevangelium* (WUNT, 2.83; Tübingen: Mohr, 1996); B. Schuchard, *Scripture within Scripture: The Interrelationship of Form and Function in the Explicit Old Testament Citations in the Gospel of John* (SBLDS, 133; Atlanta: Scholars Press, 1992).

2. J.D. Derrett, τί ἐργάζῃ; (Jn 6,30): An Unrecognized Allusion to Is 45,9', *ZNW* 84 (1993), pp. 142-44, could be joined by countless other monographs and articles which add to the stock of Johannine allusions.

aggressively claiming that the scriptural images and aspirations of Israel found their complete and unrepeatable expression in Jesus? And how is this to be related to the still debated—perhaps antithetical— questions of John's 'Jewishness' and of 'the Jews' in his Gospel?

Some contribution to an answer to these dilemmas may be made by exploring how different players within the Gospel make use of Scripture. This has not hitherto been adequately explored.[3] John's use of Scripture has been seen either as a 'seamless robe', or, alternatively, as a sometimes discordant patchwork of sources and redaction, best unstitched to properly appreciate the different fabrics. As with other Johannine conundra, recent text- and reader-sensitive approaches may bypass this dichotomy, and allow us to focus on the way Scripture plays its part in the dynamic effect of the text's construction.[4] It should be emphasized that this approach operates within an entirely independent framework from the proper analysis of the degree to which the evangelist is drawing on earlier or wider exegetical traditions, whether Jewish or 'Christian', and of his dependence on or redaction of specific versions or forms of the text.[5] To that extent it is a 'virgin reader' who is envisaged, as a matter of convenience more than of principle.

In what follows, the use of Scripture will be explored as found in the mouths of the various participants in the Johannine drama. To attempt this with every whisper of scriptural allusion and symbolism would take more than the present exercise has space for, and risk running aground in the swamps of verification already referred to. I shall, therefore, limit myself to explicit, acknowledged, references to Scripture—unmistakable quotations together with appeals to what is written, to the Law or to the prophet(s)—while recognizing that to do so can only be a preliminary stage.

3. A start is made by J. Beutler, 'The Use of "Scripture" in the Gospel of John', in A. Culpepper and C. Black (eds.), *Exploring John: In Honor of D. Moody Smith* (Philadelphia: Westminster/John Knox Press, 1996), pp. 147-62. See also more generally on the narrator, B. Olsson, *Structure and Meaning in the Fourth Gospel: A Text-linguistic Analysis of John 2:1-11 and 4:1-42* (CONBNT, 6; Lund: C.W.K. Gleerup, 1974), pp. 262-66.

4. Narrative studies of the Fourth Gospel tend to ignore issues such as the use of Scripture, and see Jesus' journey and that of the believer as available to the reader without mediation; see for example R.A. Culpepper and F. Segovia (eds.), *The Fourth Gospel from a Literary Perspective* (Semeia, 53; Atlanta: Scholars Press, 1991)

5. As analysed and documented by Menken, *Old Testament Quotations*.

The primary division must be between the implied narrator who frequently adds his own comments or explanations, and the various actors within the drama; among the latter Jesus stands over against various 'others', particularly, but not exclusively, his opponents. In practice it will be seen that at times identities are blurred, particularly as the narrator encroaches on the verbal space occupied by other players (1.23; 2.17; 7.38-39; 9.7). Moreover, as commonly noted, the different actors often speak in the same accents—the Johannine voice may appear markedly undifferentiated; once again, it is the narrator who sets the tone.

The Narrator

The narrator's voice is heard not only in the straight narrative but also in the interpretative comments which in this Gospel play such an essential part. In this he goes far beyond Mark, despite the latter's decisive opening appeal to Isaianic prophecy (Mk 1.2), an assertiveness which is not sustained elsewhere in that Gospel. Luke goes little further (Lk. 3.4), although it is too infrequently noted that the programmatic passage from Isa. 61.1-2 is not put on Jesus' lips but is retained by narrator's privilege (Lk. 6.17-20); Luke prefers to allow his 'actors' to utter scriptural or quasi-scriptural interpretation (1.67-79; 4.10). Matthew is more decisive, liberally sprinkling his narrative, especially in the opening stages, with declarations of Scripture fulfilled (Mt. 1.22; 2.17; 3.3; 4.14; 8.17; 12.17-21 etc.); yet he has no qualms about allowing his characters to use the same fulfilment construction as does his narrator (2.5-6).

In this, as we shall see, John is perhaps closest to Matthew. Yet, in contrast to Matthew, in the initial stages of Jesus' ministry the relationship with Scripture remains oblique. If the opening prologue is the narrator's most definitive act of interpretative self-exposure, we can hardly ignore the absence of any explicit appeal to Scripture as such, as that which has been written and which now can be respoken. This is not to deny the many echoes of Scripture which have been found there, particularly of the wisdom traditions; yet for our purposes a distinction needs to be made between such echoes and the author's explicit signalling of them. The former undoubtedly belong to the Gospel's *use* of Scripture, but their place in the narrator's *understanding* of Scripture is less secure. This is underlined when the prologue climaxes with the far from lucid affirmation, 'The Law was given through Moses, grace and truth came through Jesus Christ' (1.17). The absence of any conjunctive particle, characteristic of the prologue, leaves unstated how the two clauses relate to each other;[6] neither 'Law' nor 'Moses' have been met before, nor will be used again by the narrator, although other participants will return to the theme; here, however, the aorist passive 'was given', together with the preposition 'through' rather than 'by', allows for the divine origin of the Law. The preceding promise of 'grace in place of grace' could be taken to give Law the value of 'grace',[7] but this is qualified by the explicit sourcing of 'grace and truth' in Jesus Christ, whom the reader will identify with the 'only begotten, full of grace and truth' in v. 14. This alone suggests a degree of contrast between the two, but not a contrast that can be expressed in terms of any model of fulfilment, supersession or conflict. Since the language of 'grace' is also dropped by the narrator in the rest of the Gospel, a source-critical reading might well now conclude that the verse is redactional or reflects concerns self-evident only in its original setting. My reading can only recognize the proleptic reference to Moses and the Law which will be taken up by Jesus (5.45-46; 7.19; 8.17; 10.34) and by his opponents (9.28; 19.7).[8]

That the 'grace and truth' echoes the divine self-revelation in Exod. 34.6 seems likely, and the following verse, the affirmation that 'no-one has ever seen God', surely in this context contrasts Moses' experience then with Jesus now. Yet this does not amount to a 'theory' of Scripture and offers no clear guidelines for how we are to proceed. We may compare what happens in ch. 6. Here, as I will show, it is Jesus' interlocutors who introduce the scriptural reference, albeit with a formula characteristic of the narrator (6.31: Exod. 16.4, 15; Ps. 78.24).[9] Not surprisingly, Jesus not only picks up the reference, significantly both making

6.   Contrast the addition of δε in 𝔓66, implicitly followed by some English translations.

7.   On this translation and its implications see R.B. Edwards, 'XAPIN ANTI ΧΑΡΙΤΟΣ (John 1.16) Grace and Law in the Johannine Prologue', *JSNT* 32 (1988), pp. 3-15.

8.   See below, pp. 156-59.

9.   See below pp. 157-58. On the debate regarding the source for the quotation see M.M. Menken, 'The Provenance and Meaning of the Quotation in John 6:31', *NovT* 30 (1988), pp. 39-57 (reprinted in *Old Testament Quotations*); P.N. Anderson, *The Christology of the Fourth Gospel* (Valley Forge, PA: Trinity Press International, 1997), p. 202.

Moses explicit and at the same time denying his role, but himself alludes to the wider context (6.49: Num 14.23).[10] Yet the narrator too draws on the same context when he makes the Jews 'murmur' (6.41-43; cf. Exod. 16.2), so that we are no longer dealing with a discussion between Jesus and his opponents about scriptural event, but the whole drama in which all the actors are involved is played on the template of that Scripture.[11] Again, this falls outside any simple model of fulfilment, typology or salvation history.

It is this which dogs any investigation of the Fourth Gospel's understanding of Scripture: for the sufficiently—or over—sensitive reader scriptural echoes are to be found everywhere, yet by failing to make them explicit or to interpret them, the narrator gives no clue as to what they might mean. Some, such as the locating of Jesus' meeting with the Samaritan woman by reference to Jacob's gift of Sichem to Joseph (4.5; Gen. 48.22; Josh. 24.32), may indicate local knowledge and tradition rather than any appeal to Scripture as such; although the reference also prepares for the woman to pick up the claim (4.12), it is not self-evident how crucial this is to the interpretation of the narrative as a whole. More ambiguous details such as the 38 years of the paralysed man's sickness (5.3), arguably an allusion to the wilderness wanderings of Deut. 2.14, may invite an allegorical interpretation of the miracle, yet reference to the commentaries quickly demonstrates that the precise mechanism of any allegory remains unclear and perhaps illusory.

In the examples so far, only the crowd's question in 6.31 has provided an explicit link between the written text of Scripture ('as it is written') and the narratives or experience ('history') recorded there— the identification of the one with the other may be more obvious for the modern reader for whom written text is the primary point of access to narrative and experience, than for the first-century reader who might think more of recited, confessed and heard tradition.[12] Yet elsewhere

10. See Anderson, *Christology*, pp. 206-208; J.M. Lieu, 'Temple and Synagogue in John', *NTS* 45 (1999), pp. 51-69, 65.

11. Lieu, 'Temple and Synagogue', pp. 64-66. Olsson, *Structure and Meaning*, pp. 102-109; 281-89 talks of a 'Scripture screen'; Anderson, *Christology*, pp. 200-208 speaks of 'rhetorical use of the manna tradition' and parallels it to the midrashic development found in Ps. 78.

12. Although, as already noted, the immediate source of the quotation in Jn 6.31 is disputed, while the chapter as a whole draws on the complex of traditions found in Num. 14 and Ps. 78 as well as Exod. 16; see nn. 10-11.

the narrator does appeal to 'what is written', and here his use appears very different. It has often been observed that explicit fulfilment formulae (ἵνα πληρωθῇ) cluster in the second part of John's narrative, focusing essentially on the passion of Jesus (12.38-39; 19.24; 19.28; 19.36-37; cf. 13.18; 15.25; 17.12 spoken by Jesus, discussed below).[13] As we shall see, the narrator can also use the same formula of Jesus' 'word', again in the passion context (18.9, 32).

The first of these fulfilment formulae, 'Although he had done so many signs before them, they did not believe in him, so that the word of Isaiah the prophet might be fulfilled, which he spoke... (Isa. 53.1) ...again Isaiah said... (Isa. 6.10)', introduces the concluding reflection on Jesus' ministry (12.37-50), thus confirming that this section serves equally as a transition to what follows. The dramatic quality of this pair of quotations, reflecting on the failure of Jesus' signs to evoke belief, is not sustained by those that follow. It stands alone also in identifying the quotation as 'the word' and its source as 'Isaiah the prophet', the former perhaps because of the reference to 'hearing' and 'report' in the quotation itself, the latter because of the subsequent appeal to Isaiah's Temple vision. This is the only point at which the narrator suggests a rationale for fulfilment—Isaiah saw his (= Christ's) glory and spoke about him (v. 41). It is a rationale which can not be transferred to the other fulfilment quotations.

This emphasis on Isaiah recapitulates, and possibly explains, the one reference by the narrator to Scripture that falls outside the pattern which will be explored in this section. In 1.23 John the Baptist identifies himself through the words of Isa. 40.3—in contrast to the Synoptic use of this passage where the citation is put into the mouth of the narrator. Yet the identifying gloss 'as the prophet Isaiah said' probably should be ascribed not to John the Baptist (so RSV) but to the narrator (so REB; NRSV). Thus the narrator has begun and ended the public ministry with what 'Isaiah said' (1.23; 12.39).[14]

Yet this attention to source and significance does not seem to be replicated by the remaining fulfilment quotations: these refer only to 'the scripture' (ἡ γραφή), which, while it may denote a specific text, more probably treats Scripture *qua* Scripture. One of them (19.24; Ps. 22.18) can be clearly identified and follows its source closely; of the others, those in 19.28; 19.36 cannot be certainly identified, while that in

13. John shares this fulfilment formula with Matthew; cf. also Mk 14.49.
14. See Beutler, 'Use of "Scripture"', p. 147.

19.37 follows a deviant text. The narrator is more concerned with emphasizing the fulfilment of 'scripture' as such than with particular proof-texting. A classic example of this and of the narrator's technique is seen when Jesus says 'I thirst', 'in order', adds the narrator parenthetically, 'that scripture might be completed'(19.28).[15] The distinctive 'completed' (τελειωθῇ), only here in John, has been deliberately chosen to reinforce Jesus' knowledge 'that all had been completed' and to anticipate his final cry 'it is completed'—narrator and Jesus speak and think the same language. Jesus' immediate cry 'I thirst' is not obviously a quotation from Scripture, although various sources have been suggested (Ps. 63.1). It is more likely that it is not his words which fulfil Scripture but the response of offering him the vinegar on a 'hyssop'; thus Jesus is presented as provoking this fulfilment by his words—although whether this is presented as Jesus' conscious intention or as the narrator's incontrovertible knowledge remains ambiguous. Even so, the allusion is contested: Ps. 69.21 is an obvious source, and is certainly reflected in the synoptic parallel, with which John shares some distinctive wording;[16] but the Psalm does not explain the 'hyssop', and this may be a Passover reference (cf. Exod. 12.22). There seems to be no specific reason why it is this Scripture that must be fulfilled, and no doubt it came to the evangelist from the tradition; his point is that 'scripture' must needs be fulfilled and that Jesus ensures this.

The final fulfilment quotation, again identified only as 'the scripture' (19.36), similarly merges a Psalm and a Passover reference (Ps. 34.21; Exod. 12.10, 46). Despite its specific reference to the failure to break Jesus' legs, its climactic position and introductory 'these things happened', together with the 'for' (γάρ) which links the verse to the preceding call to faith, extend that reference to include the whole of Jesus' passion, a reference reinforced by the appended citation of Zech. 12.10 which is brought under the same rubric. Perhaps this finale thus

15. On the characteristic Johannine use of parenthesis see G. van Belle, *Les parenthèses dans l'évangile de Jean* (Leuven: Peeters/Leuven University Press, 1985).

16. Mk 15.35-36; Mt. 27.46-49 share with John σπόγγον (not in Ps. 69.21) ...ὄξους and περιτίθημι; they are closer to Ps. 69.21 than John in the verb ἐπότιζεν. The εἰς τὴν δίψαν μου of the Psalm has probably inspired John's διψῶ. In the Synoptics they are responding to Jesus' cry of dereliction, and they offer the sponge on a reed. In John the identity and motive of those who respond is passed over in silence—they have no independent significance.

forms an inclusio with the otherwise more banal first formula quotation from Ps. 22.18 which supports the failure of Jesus' tunic to be split (19.24). More probably it matches the first fulfilment passage in 12.38-39, for both consist of two quotations, the second joined to the first by the words 'again Isaiah/another scripture said/says'. With pointed irony, whereas the first declared 'he has blinded their eyes...lest they see', the second rejoins 'they shall look on the one they have pierced'. The effect of such 'looking' is left for the reader to determine.[17]

For the narrator, then, each moment of Jesus' crucifixion happened in order to fulfil Scripture; yet Scripture, like Jesus' passion, functions as a unity and not as a patchwork of details to be matched. There is, moreover, a touch of irony: the apparently inconsequential words, 'I thirst', and the ambiguous response to them are determined by Jesus' knowledge, shared by the narrator, that 'all things had been completed'; Scripture finds its own consummation in the eschatological consummation of all things, unmarked.[18] The reader who observes all this through the lens of fulfilment provided by the narrator is left wondering what, and with what effect, those who watched 'saw'.

For the narrator, however, the first point at which Jesus fulfils Scripture comes earlier, although here the introductory intentional ('in order that...') formula is not used. In 12.14 Jesus' finding of and sitting on the ass are parenthetically glossed 'as it is written', followed by Zech. 9.9—again not an exact quotation and perhaps modified by Isa. 35.4. On one level this reinforces the focus of scriptural fulfilment on Jesus' passion, towards which the Gospel now moves; on another it introduces another facet of the author's understanding. Although the narrator here has implicitly intruded himself, he modifies this by the subsequent comment that Jesus' disciples did not recognize this at the time, but only when Jesus was glorified 'remembered that these things were written concerning him and they did these things for him' (12.16). This explanation forms an inclusio with Jesus' first visit to Jerusalem and his action in the Temple when once again the disciples are presented as *remembering* that 'it was written, "Zeal for your house shall consume

---

17. See R. Schnackenburg, *The Gospel According to St John* (3 vols,; ET; New York: Crossroad, 1982), III, pp. 293-94, who concludes '...mankind... [They] will and must look to him whom they have pierced, for their salvation or destruction'.

18. This is underlined by the failure to provide a subject for the climactic τετέλεσται.

me"' (2.17).[19] Although ambiguous in context, this remembering is probably also understood as happening only later, as is made explicit in 2.22: here, although there has been no scriptural reference, the 'omniscient' narrator not only explains that Jesus had referred 'to the shrine of his body' but adds that 'when he was risen from the dead his disciples remembered that he said this and believed the scripture...'

It has often been argued that these verses provide the rationale for the Gospel and its distinctive presentation of Jesus—a remembering through the mediation of the Scriptures and through the spirit (14.26; cf. 15.26-27; 16.14).[20] That this is a fruitful way of understanding the method of this Gospel is undoubtedly true, but it is not the case that the author is thereby simply justifying his own activity. In describing the disciples' ignorance and subsequent remembering the narrator is indeed aligning himself with them, for he shares what they come to know; by calling this a 'remembering' and not a new 'understanding' or 'proclaiming', he affirms the rightness of their, and therefore of his, reading. The reader who is brought to share that knowledge is thereby brought into the circle of discipleship. Yet by describing what the disciples do not at the time know, and, in 12.14-15, by citing the Scripture before acknowledging their ignorance of it, he claims the primacy of an omniscient narrator over his characters. He also acknowledges the difference between what was done and experienced then and its (subsequent) interpretation; in this he could be said to be more conservative than Mark who weaves the Zecharian allusion into his narrative.[21] Moreover, neither Jesus nor the narrator relates the activity of the spirit to the interpretation of Scripture—this is not a spirit-inspired activity.[22]

A variation on the remembering theme comes in the narrator's comment which closes the visit of the two disciples to the empty tomb, 'for they did not yet know the scripture that he must rise from the dead'

19. In contrast to Mk 11.17 and parallels Jesus himself does not appeal to what has been written.

20. E.g. R.A. Culpepper, *Anatomy of the Fourth Gospel* (Philadelphia: Fortress Press, 1987), pp. 28-30; A.T. Hanson, *The Prophetic Gospel: A Study of John and the Old Testament* (Edinburgh: T. & T. Clark, 1991), pp. 246-53.

21. Similarly the Synoptics weave the allusion to Ps. 22.18 into their narrative while John separates it into a fulfilment quotation, neither do they make the reference to Ps. 69.21 explicit.

22. This needs careful nuancing since many interpreters do elide the remembering, the understanding of and in the light of Scripture, and the activity of the Paraclete; see above n. 20, and Olsson, *Structure and Meaning*, p. 263.

(20.9). There are a number of problems here which have led some to see the verse as redactional;[23] first, in contrast to other New Testament traditions, John does not otherwise speak of the resurrection as a fulfilment of Scripture—and in those other traditions it is 'the third day', passed over in silence by John, which seems an indispensable part of the scriptural reference. Secondly, the verse follows on strangely from the statement that the 'other disciple' saw and believed, for it seems to qualify that belief in terms alien to the general Johannine debate about faith and sight: once again the narrator is claiming an omniscience that challenges any simple identification of him with the Beloved Disciple.[24] It seems likely that a cross reference to 2.22 is intended, for they share a contextual reference to Jesus' death and resurrection, an appeal to 'the scripture', and the anticipation of an understanding only attained when Jesus rose from the dead.[25] Despite the evocation of 2.17 with its explicit citation of Ps. 69.10, it is more likely that in both cases 'the scripture' is to be understood absolutely. In 2.22 'the scripture' is coupled with 'the word which Jesus spoke', and it has even been suggested that 'the scripture' in 20.9 refers to or includes Jesus' own symbolic prophecy of his death. However, while in John Jesus' word is coming to have the same authority as Scripture, it is unlikely that the two are identified through common terminology as ἡ γραφή.[26] A more persuasive possibility would be that this is a conscious correction of the tradition that even during his ministry Jesus himself had spoken of its necessity (δεῖ) (Lk. 22.37; 24.44): in John, again more conservatively, such scriptural recognition belongs to the future—yet in speaking of what the disciples did not yet know, the narrator shares with the readers his own knowledge.

Thus in 2.17, 22; 12.16; and 20.9 the narrator envelopes the ministry and particularly the Passion of Jesus with the affirmation that what has happened was already written in Scripture. Yet with the privilege of omniscience and retrospection the narrator acknowledges that recognition of the fulfilment of Scripture will be something granted to the disciples alone; moreover, it belongs not to the time of Jesus' ministry

23. See the discussion in R.E. Brown, *The Gospel According to John* (2 vols.; New York: Doubleday, 1970), II, pp. 987-88.

24. As argued by D. Tovey, *Narrative Art and Act in the Fourth Gospel* (JSNTSup, 151; Sheffield: Sheffield Academic Press, 1997), pp. 144-46.

25. Although in 2.22 ἐγείρειν is used, whereas in 20.9 the verb is ἀναστῆναι.

26. See below, p. 155.

but will only be 'remembered' later. In this the evangelist adopts a very different stance from that of Matthew or indeed of the other Gospels, and establishes a hermeneutic that clearly distinguishes the time and events of Jesus' ministry from the faithful, spirit-led recollection of the believing community: this is quite the opposite of the merging of the horizons of which this evangelist is often accused.

One further passage belongs to this framework, the contested quotation in 7.37-38. Here, instead of the 'remembering' theme, the future reference is created as the narrator interprets Jesus' words as being 'about the spirit': 'this he spoke concerning the spirit, which those who believe[d] in him would receive. For spirit as yet was not, because Jesus was not yet glorified' (7.39). The implication again is that this would only be realized later, once Jesus was glorified, and that since it would pertain only to 'those who believed in him', it would be they who would perceive this. The issues for debate concerning the citation in vv. 37-38 are well known: (a) are the words 'the one who believes in me' part of what precedes, providing the subject for 'let them drink', or, assuming a stop at the end of v. 37, part of what follows, and thus the antecedent of '*his* belly'?; (b) does the citation formula, 'as the scripture said' refer to what precedes or to what follows?; (c) in either case, assuming a reference to one or more specific passages of Scripture, how are these to be identified?; (d) does the '*his* belly' refer to Jesus or the believer? For our purposes these conundra need not be fully resolved. Yet more important is the identity of the speaker in 38b: is it Jesus who appeals to Scripture, or the narrator, who is clearly speaking in the following verse (v. 39)? Even if v. 38 is taken as the sense unit, with the citation formula interposed in the middle of Jesus' declaration, that interposition might be the narrator's comment, signalling a truth not perceptible at the time: 'The one who believes in me', *(as scripture said)*, 'rivers...'[27] If the citation formula begins a new sentence, both the appeal to Scripture and the proleptic reference to the spirit could naturally be assigned to the narrator: '...and let the one who believes in **me** drink'. *As scripture said, 'Rivers of living water will flow out of* **his** *belly'*. This ambiguity of voices is characteristic of the evangelist (see below), and, while in the light of the other passages discussed it would

27. Compare the narrator's identification of John the Baptist's quotation from Isaiah at 1.23. Olsson, *Structure and Meaning*, pp. 262-63 nn.16, 28 acknowledges that v. 38 could be read as the narrator's comment.

be attractive to assign this reference to the narrator, a final decision remains impossible.

In each instance of the narrator's voice being heard during the ministry of Jesus, the focus of such Scripture and remembering is Jesus' death and resurrection. Otherwise, Jesus' ministry is not scripturally determined. This means that when the reader comes to the fulfilment quotations within the narrative of Jesus' passion which have been discussed above, s/he knows that these too are written from the prerogative of later knowledge; only here do the two horizons of event and meaning merge, and even here the evangelist signals their separation: the Scripture is to be fulfilled, and so the soldiers act (19.24)—where these two meet, in the divine purpose, in the believing response, in the narration of the event, or in its actuality, remains unstated.

Moreover, the narrator has introduced alongside Scripture the word of Jesus, neither identifying them nor determining their relationship. At two key points, again in the passion narrative, what happens is described as 'in order to fulfil the word...he said' (18.9, 32). In the first it is by the protection and sovereign ('I am') will of Jesus that the disciples are free to go—in, perhaps deliberate, contrast to the Markan Jesus' citation of Zech. 13.7, 'I shall strike the shepherd and the sheep shall be scattered' (Mk 14.27).[28] In the second there is an unmistakable irony that the Jews' rejection of Pilate's invitation for them to 'judge him according to [their] law' ensures the fulfilment of Jesus' word signifying the manner of his death.[29] In this way, in the events of Jesus' passion the narrator reinforces what he said in 2.22 about the disciples' post-resurrection remembering of and faith in 'scripture and the word Jesus said'.

The Actors in the Drama

Jesus
In a variety of ways the narrator's voice is difficult to distinguish from that of Jesus. This has often been remarked with reference to 3.14-21, 31-36 where the disappearance of first and second person forms leaves commentators and translators at a loss as to where to mark the end of

28. See further below, p. 155.
29. On the reference to their law see below p. 156; for his signalling of his death see 12.32-34; 3.14; 8.28. This only underlines the failure to appeal to Isa. 52.13 which many interpreters see as lying behind John's 'lift up'.

Jesus' discourse. This may suggest that 7.37-39 discussed above fall under the same rubric, and that the blurring of the distinction between speakers here is intentional. Similarly, as we have seen, in 19.28 *Jesus* says 'I thirst', in order to fulfil or to provoke the fulfilment of Scripture, an intention *the narrator* identifies. This comment comes as the last of the narrator's claims to discern the inner knowledge of Jesus (13.1, 3; 18.4; 19.28); the intention of these claims is not just to present Jesus' prophetic foreknowledge (as at 2.24), but to bind all the events of the Passion together 'sub specie aeternitatis'. It is, therefore, not surprising that in these chapters Jesus himself also speaks of the purposeful fulfilment of Scripture, using the same formula as does the narrator, 'in order that scripture might be fulfilled' (13.18; [15.25]; 17.12). Again, the specific points and texts may seem arbitrary, and there are other allusions to Scripture which are not marked as such (15.1; 16.21-22), but on closer analysis they do echo some of the issues already discussed.

In 13.18 the quotation from Ps. 41.9 is one that in Mark is embedded within the narrative (Mk 14.18); as in 19.24, 28-29, by making the quotation explicit, Scripture and event retain their separate identity. In the overall context the reference anticipates Judas's betrayal of which Jesus is about to speak (13.21)—again (cf. 19.24) the necessary fulfilment of Scripture precedes the event—although the immediate context allows a more open-ended interpretation.[30] More importantly, the disciples will only know its meaning later (v. 19) and be brought to faith. The citation in 15.24, 'they hated me without cause', also appears in a context where the later experience of the believing community, including persecution, continues that of Jesus; it is followed by the promise of the testifying work of the Spirit who is yet to come (cf. 7.39). This citation comes from the Passion Psalm tradition (Ps. 69.5; 35.19), again suggesting that the evangelist took over an earlier citation tradition while reinterpreting its significance. In this case the sonorous introductory 'that there might be fulfilled the word which was written in their law' recalls Jesus' own earlier use of this formula in the preceding narrative of his ministry (cf. 8.17; 10.34 and below). This, however, is as near as Jesus gets to predicting his death as the fulfilment of Scripture (contra Mk 14.49; Lk. 18.31); even in these two cases the fulfilment formula is loosely attached, 'but that the scripture/the word...might be fulfilled', so that

30. A 'community history' reading might see the anticipation of later betrayal and apostasy.

once again the precise link between event and fulfilment remains unstated.

The final example, that in 17.12, is contentious: 'When I was with them I kept them in your name which you have given me, and guarded them, and none of them has been lost except the son of destruction, that scripture might be fulfilled'. No scriptural passage explicitly anticipates the destruction of a proleptically named 'son of destruction', and hence many interpreters have seen here a further reference to the theme of betrayal in Ps. 41.9, already cited at 13.18.[31] This seems unlikely, for in the immediate context there is nothing to recall that Psalm.[32] Instead, the context does suggest that the reference is not to the exceptive clause but to the affirmation of Jesus' protection of those for whom he now prays; yet for this too there is no obvious Scripture in mind. A closer parallel is provided by Jesus' own earlier assurance as given in 6.37, 39, that he would not cast out or lose any given to him by God, prompting some to see this as the 'scripture'.[33] Yet when Jesus at his arrest urges his captors to let his disciples go, the narrator adds the explanation, 'in order that the word might be fulfilled which he said, that "of those whom you have given me I have lost not one"' (18.8-9). Here the reference might equally be to those words in ch. 6 or to the present text in 17.12 or to a combination of both.[34] However, here, as at 2.22, and also later in 18.32, it is the narrator who speaks, and he is careful to distinguish 'the word which Jesus spoke' from Scripture even if ascribing it some of the same value as that which is to be fulfilled; it is then unlikely that even a narrator who merged Jesus' voice with his own would allow Jesus himself to refer to his own word as 'scripture'. Whether or not a specific passage was in mind, Jesus is surely in 17.12 presented as consciously fulfilling Scripture through the coming events.

As these cases show, although the narrator has signalled the recognition of the fulfilment of Scripture as belonging to the time beyond

31. For the epithet see Isa. 57.4 LXX; Prov. 24.22 LXX; for a reference to Ps. 41 see Hanson, *Prophetic Gospel*, pp. 174-75, 197-98.

32. So rightly W. Sproston, ' "The Scripture" in John 17:12', in B.P. Thompson (ed.), *Scripture: Meaning and Method. Essays Presented to Anthony Tyrrell Hanson* (Hull: Hull University Press, 1987), pp. 24-36.

33. So Sproston, 'The Scripture'.

34. The textual variant at 17.12, 'those whom you have given me' (A D Θ 𝔐 etc.), rather than 'in the name which you have given me', would make the cross-reference more precise and thereby indicates that it is secondary.

Jesus' death and resurrection, Jesus himself can anticipate this because he shares the omniscience of the narrator (or perhaps vice versa) and also because Jesus' words within chs. 13–17 themselves anticipate the events which in the narrative sequence are yet to take place.[35] Thus in the passage just discussed (17.12), Jesus uses a past tense ('guarded' imperfect, 'protected' aorist) of an event yet to take place within the narrative sequence, and at that later moment (18.9) an earlier past tense ('lost') can be seen as prophetic of the present. As the reader moves on into the narrative of Jesus' arrest and death s/he already knows that these events are encompassed by the goal of Scripture, yet s/he equally knows both that all this was known to the Jesus who knew all (13.1), and that for the believing community this insight belongs to the future when all could now be spoken in the past tense. At the same time, there are but three explicit quotations, and they are outnumbered by the emphasis on Jesus' own words spoken before the event in order to be recognized beyond it (13.19; 14.25, 29; 15.11; 16.1, 4, 33; cf. 18.9, 32); as we have seen, the work of the spirit will be to continue the remembering of *Jesus'* words (14.26), and the Jesus of the Farewell Discourses does not interpret Scripture.

Jesus and his Opponents
Within the public ministry Jesus' use of Scripture is very different. Again, we must exclude unmarked allusions, however precise and obvious they may seem to us (e.g. 1.51). Here fulfilment formulae are absent, and Scripture is the subject of argument and counter-argument. For the most part the term 'scripture' (ἡ γραφή) is absent, except at 10.35; 5.39[pl] by Jesus without specific reference, and at 7.42 by the crowds, probably again of Scripture as a whole. Instead the appeal is to what 'is written', an appeal made both by Jesus—'in the prophets' (6.45 = Isa. 54.13), or 'in your Law' (8.17 = Deut. 17.6 etc.; 10.34 = Ps. 82.6)—and by the crowds (6.31 = Ps. 78.24). In each case, although the context is one of debate, this is not a polemic over the interpretation of Scripture or of the law (as in Mk 10.2-9), nor the use of Scripture to condemn (as in Mk 7.6-7; 8.18; Mt. 13.14-15), nor the appeal to the fulfilment of Scripture in the dramatic events surrounding Jesus' ministry or coming death (Mk 9.13; Mt. 11.10; 21.42). It seems unlikely

---

35. On this see Gail O'Day, '"I have overcome the world" (John 16:33) Narrative Time in John 13–17', in Culpepper and Segovia (eds.), *The Fourth Gospel*, pp. 153-66.

that '*your* law' when spoken by Jesus signals disassociation as in the Matthaean '*their* synagogues';[36] the discussion of circumcision and sabbath in 7.19-24 gives no hint that such prescriptions of the law are under fire, and the introductory 'Did not Moses give you the law' does not contain any negative overtones.

So too, Jesus' opponents do indeed claim to be the seed of Abraham (8.33) and 'disciples of Moses' (9.28-29); they protest that it is the sabbath (5.10), object that 'no prophet arises from Galilee' (7.52), and despise the crowd 'who do not know the law' (7.49). Yet the application and interpretation of the law or of the Scriptures does not provide the stuff of debate. Obviously this claim demands careful qualification: objections that Jesus blasphemes, that he makes himself God (10.33), are founded on the Torah and can be readily illustrated there. The point is that appeal to and citation of Scripture are not made explicit (contra Mt. 19.7; 21.42; 22.29; 22.41-45). Despite 9.28-29, there is no suggestion that Jesus presents himself as an alternative and opposing authority to Moses.[37] Instead Jesus is presented as one who can engage like them in the clever exegesis of Scripture to prove his point, and who agrees that 'scripture cannot be annulled' (10.35).

There is, however, little consistency or discernible pattern. Chapter 6 illustrates this well, as it does the wider problems in interpreting John's use of Scripture. This is the one occasion where Scripture is cited against Jesus—by the crowds who introduce the quotation from Ps. 78.24 with the formula, 'as it is written', otherwise used only by the narrator at 12.14.[38] The formula is matched by Jesus' concluding 'it is written in the prophets, "And they shall all be taught by God"' (6.45; Isa. 54.13). A number of scholars have compared the development between the two quotations, and the interim exegesis, with the midrashic techniques familiar from Jewish sources, and have treated vv. 31-59 as

36. So also A. Obermann, *Die christologische Erfüllung*, pp. 57-60.

37. This should qualify suggestions that the Johannine Christians saw themselves as disciples of Jesus and their Jewish opponents as disciples of Moses. The references to Moses in 3.34 and 6.31-32, although often interpreted as polemical, can only be read as such by presupposing underlying traditions or views regarding his significance; on the surface of the text the relationship between Jesus and Moses is much more ambivalent.

38. It would be attractive to see this as a remark by the narrator, and Olsson, *Structure and Meaning*, p. 263 n. 28 seems to allow for this, but the logic demands that the actual quotation must be ascribed to the crowds.

a homiletic unity.[39] This is to ignore that it is the crowds who speak in v. 31 and that their use of Scripture is as a challenge to Jesus, implicitly rejecting any recognition of what he has already done.[40] Jesus effectively corrects their exegesis and so redefines the significance of the manna tradition. As we have already seen, the narrator exercises his own scriptural irony by making the crowd/Jews who appeal to their 'fathers'' wilderness experience repeat their fathers' murmuring (v. 41), and risk receiving the same sentence of death given to those who ate the manna (v. 49), but further analysis of this falls outside the task of the present paper.[41]

What is remarkable in the quotations ascribed to Jesus is that the interpretation given them is not notably christological.[42] This is in stark contrast to what Jesus says about Scripture: 'You search the scripture's—and it is they which bear witness concerning me' (5.39); 'If you believe Moses you would believe me, for he wrote about me. If you do not believe what he wrote, how will you believe my words' (5.46-47). Yet the only point which might illustrate this claim is the comparison in 3.14 between Moses' lifting of the serpent (Num. 21) and the lifting up of 'the Son of Man'.

After all this, and particularly after the under-stated role of Scripture in explicit controversy, it is then the more ironical that at Jesus' trial his opponents claim, 'We have a law and according to that law he ought to die' (19.7). In the context of the Gospel the reference is not just to a specific ruling, for example that concerning the death penalty for blasphemy (Lev. 24.16), but to the law as such. In the immediate context there is an unmistakable tension with 18.31 where Pilate challenges them to 'judge him according to your law'—the same phrase as in 19.7—provoking their response 'We are not permitted to kill anyone'. The tension can be, and frequently is, resolved by the argument that, although they considered Jesus merited death by their law, they did not, under Roman rule, have the right to carry out that sentence. Irrespective of the historical arguments involved, this may miss the Johannine irony which has them undermine their own appeal to the law even before they

39. P. Borgen, *Bread from Heaven: An Exegetical Study of the Concept of Manna in the Gospel of John and the Writings of Philo* (NovTSup, 10; Leiden: E.J. Brill, 1966)

40. This is persuasively argued by Anderson, *Christology*, pp. 200-204, 213-16.

41. See above pp. 145-46 and nn. 9-11

42. Unless at 10.34 there is a reference to Jesus as the pre-existent logos.

make it.[43] The previous references to the law reinforce this: until this point, after the enigmatic statement of the narrator in 1.17, the law has been claimed by Jesus in his own support even while conceding that it is 'their law' (8.17; 10.34).[44] For the discerning reader there is a further irony: when Jesus appealed to the demand for two witnesses as written 'in their law' (8.17), the passages to which he referred spoke not of witnesses to the claims made by someone but of the witnesses needed for the passing of a death penalty (Deut. 17.6; 19.15); in 10.34 his appeal to their law (in fact to Ps. 82) authenticated his claim, as the one who embodied the word of God, to be not just Son of God but perhaps 'God', the charge they now bring against him; in 15.25 Jesus again referred to 'their law' the Psalmist's affirmation, 'they hated me without cause'. In 7.51 Nicodemus had objected that their law did not condemn anyone without first having heard from them; the subsequent chapters have fulfilled that condition. After this, the reader is unlikely to concede their appeal to the law for his death.

It is difficult to know how to interpret the conflicting impressions given by the combination of the surfeit of arguably scriptural echoes, of the apparently inconsequential and random appeal to explicit Scripture by Jesus, and of the undemonstrated claims that Scripture and Moses are essentially about Jesus. It is not surprising that such contrasting conclusions have been drawn concerning John's attitude to Scripture. For the reader, however, a pattern does emerge: since the fulfilment of Scripture belongs to the insight gained by the disciples after Jesus' death, and focuses particularly on his death and resurrection, it has little place within Jesus' encounter with others during his ministry. That the Scriptures testify to Jesus and that Moses wrote about him is not something that could be ascertained independently, by comparing the details of his life with unmistakable prophecies (e.g. Mt. 2.5-6); indeed, when the crowd attempts such an appeal to the very Scripture used by Matthew, they fall into division and uncertainty (7.41-43). Like so much else, it has to be taken on trust, a trust that will only be vindicated for those who become disciples, and even for them only after Jesus' death and resurrection. The solution to the dilemma of 5.47 is not that they should become more faithful students of Moses and the Scriptures,

---

43. Note ἔξεστιν ἀποκτεῖναι at Mk 3.4 of what is (not) permitted in the Torah, even on the sabbath.

44. Also 1.45, 'The one of whom Moses wrote in the law, and the prophets'.

so that they then will believe also in Jesus and perhaps become disciples, but rather the reverse.

Narrative Sequence and Scripture

A quick overview of explicit references to Scripture confirms this conclusion. In the first chapter the law, given through Moses, and Jesus, source of grace and truth, are brought together in an as yet unexplained relationship; John the Baptist's preparatory role is located in the words of the prophet Isaiah. The narrator has prepared the ground, and the reader will not be surprised when Philip identifies Jesus as the one written of by Moses in the law, and by the prophets. Yet ch. 2 points the reader beyond any superficial expectation of proof-texting: a real understanding of Scripture, as written about Jesus in his death and resurrection, was not patent during Jesus' ministry; it was reserved for disciples, and even for them became the lens through which they remembered Jesus only after his death; moreover, already Jesus' word is set alongside Scripture as the focus of such remembering. Only once this foundation is laid by the narrator, do the participants take up the theme; here the initiative lies with Jesus, yet on the overt level the debate is patchy. There is little conflict over the interpretation and observation of the law, and Jesus does not claim a radically different reading of God's law from theirs; rather he shows himself able to argue from it as well as they. That, in contrast, so much scriptural imagery lies below the surface of the narrative perhaps reinforces the reader's awareness that this belongs not to the level of the events of Jesus' ministry but to that of a believing remembering. Only as Jesus' public ministry draws to a close does the narrator re-enter with a further reminder of the role of such remembering, and then with a return to Isaiah, who had introduced the narrative. Now a new theme is introduced, that of the necessary fulfilment of Scripture. It is this, with its focus on Jesus' death, which will provide a thread through the following chapters. Jesus' total control is reinforced as he and the narrator share this impulse driven by Scripture; other actors unwittingly play their role to the same end. Yet the intensification of scriptural reference comes to an abrupt end with the death of Jesus. The final explicit quotation displays before the readers' eyes the scriptural image of the pierced Jesus; for the first time the narrator addresses the readers directly, inviting them ('you') to share in the faith and understanding that scriptural fulfilment had first inspired in the disciples (19.35).

Even so, much remains unsolved; we are left uncertain whether Scripture has any continuing role after Jesus' climactic cry that completes it. How does, and will, Scripture function alongside the word of Jesus, whose words come from God (17.8)?[45] And now, after the death of Jesus, we must add the testimony of sight which is the immediate foundation for the belief to which readers are summoned in 19.35, and even more 'that which is written' now 'in *this* book' (20.31; cf. 21.24-25)—and might there be room for yet more to come?

---

45. Cf. 6.63, 68; 3.34; 12.47-48; the issue is complicated by John's use of ῥήματα here, although note λόγος in 17.6.

JESUS' PRAYER IN JOHN 11[*]

Wendy Sproston North

Anthony Hanson and Max Wilcox, co-founders of the Seminar on the use of the Old Testament in the New, identified the opening words of Jesus' prayer in Jn 11.41 as an allusion to Ps. 118.21 (LXX 117.21), and did so working independently of one another. Hanson was first to get into print in an article in 1973. Wilcox published four years later, by which time the coincidence had been discovered.[1] The aim of this study is to offer support for this joint identification by approaching Jn 11.41-42 from the broader perspective of the composition of the Lazarus story as a whole.

I have argued elsewhere that the Fourth Gospel and 1 John are linked indirectly by virtue of their mutual reliance at points on the same traditional material.[2] On that basis, I have proposed that the epistle can take its place alongside the Synoptic gospels and the Pauline literature as a control to isolate tradition in the Gospel text. I have also claimed that, with the added advantage of 1 John's contribution to the identification of tradition in the Gospel, we are now in a position to render a plausible account of the processes of creative interpretation of tradition which

[*]   The substance of this argument was given as part of a paper at a meeting of the Old Testament in the New Testament Seminar in 1994. For Lionel, ever Browning's 'not-incurious, picker-up of learning's crumbs', in appreciation of the joy of scholarship shared.

1.   See A.T. Hanson, 'The Old Testament Background to the Raising of Lazarus', in E.A. Livingstone (ed.), *Studia Evangelica* (6 vols.; Texte und Unter-suchungen zur Geschichte der altchristlichen Literatur, 112; Berlin: Akademie-Verlag, 1973), VI, pp. 252-55 (254); M. Wilcox, 'The "Prayer" of Jesus in John XI.41b-42', *NTS* 24 (1977), pp. 128-32 (130 n. 5); see further A.T. Hanson, *The New Testament Interpretation of Scripture* (London: SPCK, 1980), p. 210 n. 21.

2.   W.E. Sproston, 'Witnesses to What Was ἀπ' ἀρχῆς: 1 John's Contribution to our Knowledge of Tradition in the Fourth Gospel', *JSNT* 48 (1992), pp. 43-65, reprinted in S.E. Porter and C.A. Evans (eds.), *The Johannine Writings* (The Biblical Seminar, 32; Sheffield: Sheffield Academic Press, 1995), pp. 138-60.

gave John's text its final form. It is this approach that I intend to adopt in analysing John's story of the raising of Lazarus and, in particular, the prayer John has Jesus offer immediately before the miracle. Before we embark on that, however, a brief description of my position on the Lazarus story in general will help speed the argument.

First, I am in agreement with the view that the Lazarus story was not originally part of the Gospel but was added to it by John at a later stage, probably in the process of a second edition.[3] This is an important point because it affects our understanding of how John has worked: it means that the story was almost certainly interpolated into already existing material and that therefore, in composing it, John also designed it to fit its new surroundings. While this policy of assimilation can be detected in relation to most other parts of the Gospel, nowhere is it more in evidence than with the material in ch. 12. Quite clearly, John has intended the two chapters to be taken as a unit. This is immediately obvious in 11.2, John's typically heavy-handed reference directing us forward to the anointing in 12.3,[4] and there are numerous other points of continuity—one study lists more than 50[5]—all of which suggest that the con-

3. See, for example, B. Lindars, *Behind the Fourth Gospel* (Studies in Creative Criticism, 3; London: SPCK, 1971), p. 60; *idem, The Gospel of John* (NCB; London: Marshall, Morgan & Scott, 1972), pp. 50, 381-82; J. Ashton, *Understanding the Fourth Gospel* (Oxford: Clarendon Press, 1991), pp. 201-203.

4. John's prompt in 11.2 reads oddly because, as the Gospel now stands, the actual event does not take place until the following chapter. Nevertheless, this is best regarded as a casualty of John's interpolation of the Lazarus story into an existing text rather than put down to the bungling intrusion of a later editor. Among commentators who accept 11.2 as authentic are C.K. Barrett (*The Gospel According to St John* [2nd edn; London: SPCK, 1978], p. 390); G.R. Beasley-Murray (*John* [WBC, 36; Waco, TX: Word Books, 1987], p. 187) and K. Grayston (*The Gospel of John* [Epworth Commentaries; London: Epworth Press, 1990], p. 90). See also D.A. Lee, *The Symbolic Narratives of the Fourth Gospel: The Interplay of Form and Meaning* (JSNTSup, 95; Sheffield: JSOT Press, 1994) who dubs the idea of a later editor 'unnecessary' (p. 193 n. 3). The verse is retained as genuine by G. van Belle in his detailed study, *Les parenthèses dans l'évangile de Jean: Aperçu historique et classification, texte grec de Jean* (Studiorum Novi Testamenti Auxilia, 11; Leuven: Leuven University Press, 1985), p. 84.

5. P. Mourlon Beernaert, 'Parallelisme entre Jean 11 et 12: Etude de structure littéraire et théologique', in A.-L. Descamps *et al.* (eds.), *Genèse et structure d'un texte du Nouveau Testament: Etude interdisciplinaire du chapître 11 de l'évangile de Jean* (Lectio Divina, 104; Paris: Cerf; Louvain-La-Neuve: Cabay, 1981), pp. 123-49.

tent of ch. 12 had no small part to play in the making of the Lazarus story. My second point concerns the *Sitz im Leben* of John's narrative. The message to the reader here is overwhelmingly one of assurance, particularly in relation to the promise of resurrection to eternal life. This, together with the call to follow Jesus in times of personal danger (cf. 11.7-10, 16), convinces me that ch. 11 belongs to the same period as 16.2, the text in which John's fears that the lives of his flock may be forfeit on account of their faith are most clearly voiced, and which is also generally held to belong to a later stage in the Gospel's composition. The final and, for my purposes, the most important point is the general character of the composition itself. For the most part, John's story has every appearance of a superb piece of redaction based on detectable source-material which is largely outside the chapter itself. To put this another way, while I have no doubt that John's account is grounded in a miracle story about Jesus raising someone from the dead, the sheer weight of theologizing John has obliged this miracle to bear has ensured that what lies before us is almost entirely extrapolated from other tradition-based material. It is precisely this extensive process of 'signification' which renders the final product vulnerable to the kind of analysis I intend to pursue with the help of 1 John.

John 11.41-42: A Crux Interpretation

As Hanson and Wilcox were well aware when they wrote, Jn 11.41-42 is notoriously difficult to interpret. My first task, then, must be to examine the text of the prayer and attempt to establish its implications for John's presentation of Jesus at that particular point in his narrative.

Although John's reference in 11.41 to Jesus lifting his eyes is a clear signal that what follows is intended to be understood in the context of prayer,[6] the declaration, πάτερ, εὐχαριστῶ σοι ὅτι ἤκουσάς μου. ἐγὼ δὲ ᾔδειν ὅτι πάντοτέ μου ἀκούεις (RSV: 'Father, I thank thee that thou hast heard me. I knew that thou hearest me always'), is not a petition at all; rather, it is a confident acknowledgment that on this occasion, as always, Jesus has the ear of God. Needless to say, this representation of

---

6. So, for example, Barrett, *Gospel*, p. 402; R.E. Brown, *The Gospel According to John* (2 vols.; Anchor Bible, 29, 29a; Garden City, NY: Doubleday, 1966; London: Geoffrey Chapman, 1971), pp. 427, 436; J.H. Bernard, *A Critical and Exegetical Commentary on the Gospel According to St John* (2 vols.; ICC; Edinburgh: T. & T. Clark, 1928), p. 397.

Jesus at prayer has evoked a series of responses from commentators. Broadly speaking, the range of opinion falls into three categories.

First, there is the suggestion that the prayer is a complete artifice, a hollow gesture whose sole purpose is to impress the bystanders (cf. 11.42b). Loisy's phrase 'prière pour la galerie' ('prayer to the gallery') is to the point here, as is also Holtzmann's report of the prayer dubbed by some as a *Scheingebet* ('sham prayer') or *Schaugebet* ('show prayer').[7] Among modern commentators, Lindars inclines most to this view. Strictly speaking, he argues, the prayer is unnecessary but is included specifically for the crowd.[8] By and large, however, the suggestion of a pretence prayer is dismissed today on the grounds that this is no bid for self-aggrandizement on Jesus' part, but a demonstration of the Son's dependence on the Father which ensures that the miracle is for the glory of God (cf. 11.4, 40).[9]

A second response is to assume that Jesus' thanks for having been heard presupposes not only that a petition has been made but also that the moment of request can be pin-pointed by sifting through the story so far. Accordingly, while suggestions vary, Jesus' inner turmoil and distress at v. 33 proves the most popular option.[10] The problem here is, of course, that John has not specified an actual moment of petition,

---

7. See A. Loisy, *Le quatrième évangile* (Paris: Alphonse Picard et Fils, 1903), p. 651; H.J. Holtzmann, *Evangelium, Briefe und Offenbarung des Johannes* (HKNT, 4; Freiburg: J.C.B. Mohr [Paul Siebeck], 1908), p. 139. R. Bultmann quotes Wrede and Heitmüller to this effect (*The Gospel of John: A Commentary* [ET G.R. Beasley-Murray; Oxford: Basil Blackwell, 1971], p. 409 n. 1). See also the references in M.-J. Lagrange, *Evangile selon Saint Jean* (5th edn; Etudes bibliques; Paris: J. Gabalda, 1936), pp. 307-308) and E.C. Hoskyns, *The Fourth Gospel* (ed. F.N. Davey; 2 vols.; London: Faber & Faber, 1940), pp. 474-75.

8. Lindars, *Gospel*, pp. 401-402.

9. See, for example, Barrett, *Gospel*, pp. 402-403; Brown, *Gospel*, pp. 436-37; D.A. Carson, *The Gospel According to John* (Leicester: InterVarsity Press; Grand Rapids: Eerdmans, 1991), p. 418; R. Schnackenburg, *The Gospel According to St John* (3 vols.; New York: Herder & Herder; London: Burns & Oates, 1968–82), II, p. 339.

10. Bernard, for example, assumes that the aorist ἤκουσας in v. 41 indicates some definite act of prayer, perhaps before v. 4 (*Gospel*, p. 397). For the suggestion that the prayer was offered during the agony at v. 33, see Lagrange, *Evangile*, p. 308; Barrett, *Gospel*, p. 402; J.N. Sanders, *A Commentary on the Gospel According to St John* (edited and completed by B.A. Mastin; London: A. & C. Black, 1968), p. 275; also J.E. Davey, *The Jesus of St John: Historical and Christological Studies in the Fourth Gospel* (London: Lutterworth Press, 1958), p. 126.

which means that any proposal of this kind is forced to rely on conjecture. As for the suggestion that the petition was offered at v. 33, this is highly improbable given that the story itself makes clear that Jesus knew he would raise Lazarus as early as v. 11.[11]

The third approach, which is widely held, interprets the prayer as a demonstration of the Son's perfect unity with the Father, which is such that Jesus' petitions are always granted without their needing utterance. This was Bultmann's position[12] and, in fact, such is Bultmann's towering influence even yet that this theme of the Son's constant prayerful attitude continues to echo in the work of most commentators on this passage up to the present time.[13] There is much to be said for this third argument. On the one hand, it fits in well with evidence elsewhere in the Gospel for Jesus' utter dependence on and unity with the Father and, on the other, it makes it possible to maintain the view that Jesus really prays while also accounting for the fact that no petition is recorded earlier in the narrative. Yet even this interpretation is not without its problems. For example, it is difficult to see why John would have chosen to present his readers with an insight into the Son's unique union with the Father when it must, by definition, exclude themselves. To put this another way, how far can we be certain that purely christological concerns were as much a priority to the fourth evangelist as they evidently are to those who interpret him for today? A second problem is that this interpretation is inconsistent with John's presentation of Jesus at prayer elsewhere in the Gospel. Thus, if the meaning here is that uttered prayer on Jesus' part is always unnecessary, it is noticeable that no such consideration has weighed in the case of the actual prayers John records at 12.27-28 and in ch. 17. Indeed, in the latter instance, John has no hesitation in presenting Jesus uttering petition to the Father, and doing so at considerable length.

---

11. As Carson correctly remarks, v. 11 'assumes that the raising of Lazarus had been determined for some time' (*Gospel*, p. 418).

12. Bultmann, *Gospel*, p. 408.

13. See Barrett, *Gospel*, p. 402; Brown, *Gospel*, p. 436; Schnackenburg, *Gospel*, II, p. 339; Beasley-Murray, *John*, p. 194; Lindars, *Gospel*, p. 401; C.H. Dodd, *The Interpretation of the Fourth Gospel* (Cambridge: Cambridge University Press, 1953), p. 256; H. Van der Loos, *The Miracles of Jesus* (NovTSup, 8; Leiden: E.J. Brill, 1965), p. 585; and especially R.H. Fuller, *Interpreting the Miracles* (London: SCM Press, 1963), pp. 107-108. Fuller is quoted approvingly by Beasley-Murray. See also R.A. Culpepper, *The Gospel and Letters of John* (Interpreting Biblical Texts; Nashville: Abingdon Press, 1998), p. 17.

As this brief survey shows, it is no easy matter to arrive at an interpretation of John's meaning in these verses that is satisfactory on all counts. However, if one conclusion is to be drawn from the discussion so far, it is surely that a strictly christological approach, whether devoted to defending the genuineness of the prayer or to extolling the unique qualities of the Son's union with the Father, is unlikely to provide the key. In fact, with Christology so high on the agreed agenda in this case, it is perhaps not surprising that what has been missed by most is the simple observation that this prayer develops logically out of Martha's confidence, earlier in v. 22, that Jesus can have from God whatever he asks. I suggest, therefore, that if we seek to unlock John's meaning in vv. 41-42, we need to begin with the faith of Martha from a previous scene in his narrative. With that in mind, my next task will be to investigate the context and content of v. 22.

Martha's 'Confession'

By the time Jesus finally arrives at the outskirts of Bethany in v. 17, Lazarus has been dead and in the tomb four days. Martha goes out to meet Jesus and, as Mary will do later, she draws attention to the fact of Jesus' absence during her brother's fatal illness (v. 21, cf. v. 32). Unlike her sister, however, Martha has more to say. In v. 22, she adds, καὶ νῦν οἶδα ὅτι ὅσα ἂν αἰτήσῃ τὸν θεὸν δώσει σοι ὁ θεός ('And even now I know that whatever you ask from God, God will give you'). In order to capture the full flavour of what is being implied here, we need to be aware of exactly what kind of statement this is. In the first place, we must surely resist any suggestion that this is some wistful, half-baked hint on Martha's part.[14] There is nothing tentative about Martha's οἶδα ('I know') here; it carries all the certainty of an agreed truth. Indeed, its presence tells us that Martha is as certain about this as she is, two verses later, about the fact that her brother will rise again at the last day, a conviction which draws on common assumption.[15] As Bultmann

---

14. *Pace* Sanders, *Gospel*, p. 268; Lindars, *Gospel*, p. 394; Barrett, *Gospel*, p. 395; Bultmann, *Gospel*, p. 401; Brown, *Gospel*, p. 433; E. Haenchen, *A Commentary on the Gospel of John* (2 vols.; ET R.W. Funk: Hermeneia; Philadelphia: Fortress Press, 1984), II, p. 61.

15. Although a well-known constituent of Pharisaism, belief in resurrection was

rightly observes, v. 22 'is formulated not as a request but as a confession'.[16] Even so, however, it is difficult to see how the actual substance of the statement can be classed as 'confessional' in the usual Johannine sense. Thus, while Martha's confidence in the power of Jesus' prayer is no doubt proper to faith, it is scarcely of the same order as, for example, the lofty Christology of the triple title she bestows on Jesus at v. 27. In other words, if, according to John, Martha 'knows' that God always grants Jesus' requests, what is the basis for that certainty in this case? In order to discover something of the background to the statement, we will need to consult 1 John on the issue of prayer.

While Martha's faith in Jesus as a man mighty in prayer is not reproduced in the Christology of the epistle writer, nevertheless, on the subject of prayer itself, we find 1 John lyrical indeed. Twice he refers to it in glowing terms and, on the second occasion, he signals clearly that this is a matter involving the shared knowledge of tradition. I will make this second reference my starting-point.

As the epistle draws to its close, 1 John's theme of assurance concentrates on the language of having and knowing.[17] By 5.12, he has already stated that the faithful, those who have God's witness (v. 10), are those who have life. This last thought is uppermost in his mind as he embarks on the final section.

In 5.13, 1 John announces to his readers that his aim in writing is so that those who believe in the name of God's Son may know that they have eternal life. This verse is often compared with the very similar valedictory formula at Jn 20.31. Nevertheless, the evangelist has nothing to match 1 John's ἵνα εἰδῆτε ('that you may know') here and the confidence that it implies.[18] In fact, confidence or boldness (παρρησία) is 1 John's next topic (5.14). This they all have before God (note the return of the 'we' of joint witness with ἔχομεν) and it is such that if they petition God according to his will he hears them. In v. 15, this privilege is affirmed in the strongest possible terms (οἴδαμεν, twice):

widely held in Judaism at the time; see Barrett, *Gospel*, p. 395; Beasley-Murray, *John*, p. 190; Brown, *Gospel*, p. 434; Lindars, *Gospel*, p. 394; also Grayston, *Gospel*, p. 91.

16. Bultmann, *Gospel*, p. 401.

17. There are eight instances of ἔχειν in 5.10-15 alone, and six of οἶδα in vv. 13-20.

18. See especially R.E. Brown's comments in *The Epistles of John* (AB, 30; New York: Doubleday, 1982; London: Geoffrey Chapman, 1983), p. 634.

certainty of a favourable hearing[19] carries the equal certainty that they have their requests granted. Having set out the principle, 1 John now turns to apply it in the case of intercessory prayer for an erring brother (vv. 16-17). Precisely what he means here by sin which is and is not πρὸς θάνατον ('unto death') is a difficulty not easy to resolve.[20] Nevertheless, this does not obscure the point of the application, which is that prayer by one of the faithful in such an instance is guaranteed success. Thus, one who sees his brother sinning shall ask, and God will give him life (αἰτήσει καὶ δώσει αὐτῷ ζωήν).[21] With this final assurance on prayer, 1 John's language of asking and being given by God takes us back to Martha's address to Jesus in the very different setting of Jn 11.22: ὅσα ἂν αἰτήσῃ τὸν θεὸν δώσει σοι ὁ θεός ('whatever you ask from God, God will give you').

So far, then, when it comes to what 1 John and his readers 'know' about prayer, and where his diction coincides with that of Martha in the Gospel, the focus is not on Jesus but on the privileged status of those who believe in him. In fact, this position is unaltered from the epistle writer's previous reference to prayer where much the same terminology is used. I will now complete the evidence from the epistle with a brief examination of the earlier passage.

Following an argument on conscience of some considerable obscurity (3.19-20),[22] 1 John turns to the subject of boldness (παρρησία) before God (v. 21, cf. 5.14). As in the later passage, this leads immediately to an assurance of successful prayer (v. 22). The wording is slightly different here but the point is the same. Thus, whereas in 5.14 true prayer was according to God's will, here it holds for those who keep God's

---

19. ἐάν with οἴδαμεν here does not imply a condition but draws a consequence (= 'since'), so R. Schnackenburg, *The Johannine Epistles* (ET R. and I. Fuller; New York: Crossroad, 1992), p. 248; Brown, *Epistles*, p. 610. On the use of ἀκούειν with the meaning 'to hear favourably', see I.H. Marshall, *The Epistles of John* (NICNT; Grand Rapids: Eerdmans, 1978), p. 244; S.S. Smalley, *1, 2, 3, John* (WBC, 51; Waco, TX: Word Books, 1984), p. 295.

20. See the lengthy discussion in Brown, *Epistles*, pp. 612-19.

21. Despite the awkward shift, the implied subject of δώσει here is almost certainly God and not the petitioner; see Schnackenburg, *Epistles*, p. 249; Marshall, *Epistles*, p. 246 n. 17; Smalley, *1, 2, 3 John*, p. 300; K. Grayston, *The Johannine Epistles* (NCB; Grand Rapids: Eerdmans; London: Marshall, Morgan & Scott, 1984), p. 142; see further, the discussion in Brown, *Epistles*, pp. 611-12.

22. See especially Brown's remarks in *Epistles*, p. 453.

commandments and do what pleases him.[23] Similarly, the assurance itself is slightly altered: whereas in 5.14-16 reference was made to asking and being heard or to asking and being given, here the form used is asking and receiving. In 3.23, however, the verbal parallelism resumes with the reference to belief in the name of God's son (cf. 5.13).

Thus, our initial impression is confirmed: when 1 John speaks of prayer whose answer is certain, he consistently refers it to the confidence of the faithful before God and not, as in Martha's statement, to that of Jesus himself. Strictly speaking, then, as far as he is concerned, the tradition on prayer is about Christianity rather than Christology.

If we take this perspective seriously, it suggests that if John and 1 John are linked through tradition in this case, the direct equivalent in the Gospel is not 11.22 but some other text related to it which is orientated towards discipleship. In fact, it takes the combined witness of both passages in the epistle to identify conclusively this key text as a Jesus logion on prayer in the Gospel's final discourse material. The logion appears in its entirety on Jesus' lips in 16.23b-24:

> ἀμὴν ἀμὴν λέγω ὑμῖν, ἄν τι αἰτήσητε τὸν πατέρα ἐν τῷ ὀνόματί μου δώσει ὑμῖν. ἕως ἄρτι οὐκ ἠτήσατε οὐδὲν ἐν τῷ ὀνόματί μου· αἰτεῖτε καὶ λήμψεσθε, ἵνα ἡ χαρὰ ὑμῶν ᾖ πεπληρωμένη.

> 'Truly, truly, I say to you, if you ask anything of the Father, he will give it to you in my name. Hitherto you have asked nothing in my name; ask, and you will receive, that your joy may be full.'

Note the double ἀμήν opening, which can serve as a tradition signal,[24] and the combination of αἰτεῖν not only with διδόναι as in 1 Jn 5.16/Jn 11.22 but also with λαμβάνειν as in 1 Jn 3.22. Note also the

23. On the equivalence of these expressions in Johannine thought, see especially W. Loader, *The Johannine Epistles* (Epworth Commentaries; London: Epworth Press, 1992), pp. 46, 74, and Marshall, *Epistles*, p. 200.

24. Barnabas Lindars's suggestion that John's characteristic double ἀμήν can signal a traditional Jesus-saying (see *Behind the Fourth Gospel*, p. 44; *idem*, *Gospel*, p. 48) is dismissed as 'unnecessary' by Margaret Davies, who prefers to define the formula as 'a stylistic device which draws attention to crucial assertions'; see M. Davies, *Rhetoric and Reference in the Fourth Gospel* (JSNTSup, 69; Sheffield: JSOT Press, 1992), p. 269. However, Lindars himself did not resist the view that John was capable of using this feature purely for effect (cf. *Behind the Fourth Gospel*, p. 46). Moreover, since what John deems to be 'crucial' could well involve traditional material in any case, there is no reason to suppose that either position excludes the other.

reference to Jesus' name which is an accompanying feature in both 1 John passages.[25] All told, including Jn 11.22, this logion is variously reproduced no fewer than seven times in the Gospel and epistle (Jn 11.22; 14.13-14; 15.7, 16; 16.23-26; 1 Jn 3.21-23; 5.14-16).

It is not difficult to identify New Testament equivalents to this tradition linking John and 1 John. This is clearly a version of the well-known 'ask, and it will be given' logion. Perhaps its most famous occurrence is in the Sermon on the Mount as 'Ask, and it will be given you...for everyone who asks receives', where it is part of a triple saying (Mt. 7.7-8//Lk. 11.9-10). However, in one context or another, this logion actually surfaces in all three Synoptics as well as in the epistle of James, and does so in much the same variety of form as in the Johannine texts (Mt. 7.7-8; 18.19-20; 21.22; Mk 11.24; Lk. 11.9-10; Jas 1.5-6; 4.2-3).[26] A glance at its use in the New Testament as a whole quickly reveals that there are two features that are typical of its presentation. First, the giver in the saying is always assumed to be God[27] so that the logion is consis-

---

25. In fact, 1 John never uses the expression 'in the name of Jesus/God's Son' *except* in connection with this logion (3.23; 5.13). This reinforces the impression that the two are organically linked in the Johannine tradition (cf. also Jn 14.13-14; 15.16; 16.26).

26. See further the studies of similarities in pattern and substance between the Johannine and Synoptic references by C.H. Dodd in *Historical Tradition in the Fourth Gospel* (Cambridge: Cambridge University Press, 1963), pp. 349-52, and Brown (*Gospel*, pp. 634-35). The striking resemblances between Jn 16.23-24 and Mt. 7.7-8//Lk. 11.9-10 prompt W.D. Davies and D.C. Allison to suggest that the Johannine version may be an adaptation of the tradition from Q (*A Critical and Exegetical Commentary on the Gospel According to Saint Matthew* [3 vols.; ICC; Edinburgh: T. & T. Clark, 1988–97], I, p. 685). See also Schnackenburg's remark that these parallels are 'another indication of the fact that the Johannine school preserved and gave further consideration to many early traditional statements of Jesus' (*Gospel*, III, p. 160). On the link between the Epistle of James and the Q traditions, see P.J. Hartin, *James and the Q Sayings of Jesus* (JSNTSup, 47; Sheffield: JSOT Press, 1991), especially pp. 173-79 on asking and prayer.

27. The similitude which accompanies the Q references (Mt. 7.9-11; Lk. 11.11-13) confirms that the giver is meant to be God, which means that the verb δοθήσεται in the logion is a 'divine' or 'theological' passive (see Davies and Allison, *Matthew*, p. 679; Schnackenburg, *Gospel*, III, p. 72; Loader, *Epistles*, p. 45; Grayston, *Epistles*, p. 116). The reference to Jesus himself as the respondent in Jn 14.13-14 is not really an exception to this rule: as the context makes clear, prayer in this case is to the glorified Jesus in union with the Father (see, for example, Lindars,

tently placed in a prayer context. Indeed, explicit reference to prayer is included in two of the Synoptic examples (Mt. 21.22; Mk 11.24); compare also the reference to having παρρησίαν πρὸς τὸν θεόν ('confidence before God') in the 1 John passages (3.21; cf. 5.14). Second, the logion usually appears hedged about with conditions and qualifiers.[28] This is hardly surprising: after all, it would not do for everyone to think that it was suddenly open season on requests! Accordingly, the instructions in the Synoptics and James are that the request itself be a matter of Christian agreement and that the asking be done in faith (Mt. 18.19; 21.22; Mk 11.24; Jas 1.6). Similarly, the Johannine texts refer to keeping God's commandments, pleasing him, asking according to his will, and abiding in Jesus (1 Jn 3.22-23; 5.14; cf. Jn 14.15; 15.10, 12, 17; Jn 15.7; cf. 1 Jn 3.24).[29] There is no qualifier, however, in the case of Jn 11.22. Nor is the reason hard to find, for in this verse John has made the characteristically original move of applying the logion, not to those who believe in Jesus, but to Jesus himself—who, of course, invariably does God's will, keeps his commandments, and pleases him always (Jn 4.34; 15.10; 8.29). Thus, in an interesting case of role reversal, what is proper to Christianity has, in the hands of the fourth evangelist, become Christology.[30]

On this showing, then, the basis for Martha's certainty in 11.22 consists in the fact that her words to Jesus are a version of the 'ask, and it will be given' logion from tradition, although this identification is almost never made in the commentaries and elsewhere.[31] In context,

---

Gospel, p. 476; Barrett, *Gospel*, p. 461; Sanders, *Gospel*, p. 325). This evidence in general lends support to the argument that the intended subject of δώσει in 1 Jn 5.16 is God (see above, n. 21).

28. This is recognized by most commentators but see especially the discussion by Grayston (*Epistles*, p. 116).

29. For further references outside the New Testament corpus, see D. Goldsmith, '"Ask, and it will be given...": Toward Writing the History of a Logion', *NTS* 35 (1989), pp. 254-65 (254 nn. 2-4); Brown, *Epistles*, p. 461; Davies and Allison, *Matthew*, p. 680.

30. *Pace* C.H. Dodd, *The Johannine Epistles* (MNTC; London: Hodder & Stoughton, 1946), p. 93; Brown, *Epistles*, p. 480; Smalley, *1, 2, 3 John*, pp. 206, 296; and D. Rensberger, *1 John, 2 John, 3 John* (Abingdon New Testament Commentaries; Abingdon Press: Nashville, 1997), p. 105, the attribution was not to Jesus first in this case.

31. Among commentators, Lindars comes closest in remarking that Martha's

this application serves to focus attention on Jesus' God-given powers and so provides a point of entry into the teaching on Jesus as life-giver and agent of resurrection (vv. 25-26). This in turn prompts yet another expression of Martha's faith, which draws the interview to a close. I will conclude my comment on this scene with a brief examination of her confession in v. 27.

Asked if she believes what Jesus has told her, Martha gives her assent in full measure. In fact, so extensive is her response in v. 27 that it is the only occasion in the entire Gospel where John puts the three titles she uses all together. The first two are fairly standard Johannine fare and are linked again by John in his own statement of purpose in 20.31.[32] The third, however, which is really more of a messianic description than a title,[33] has probably been added with an eye to neighbouring material. The expression, ὁ ἐρχόμενος ('he who comes'), used here and in 6.14 with reference to Jesus' mission in the world, is derived from Ps. 118.26. According to the Gospel tradition, this Scripture was applied to Jesus by others, most notably by the crowd on his triumphal entry into Jerusalem (Mk 11.9 and parallels).[34] John is well aware of that tradition. Indeed, at this stage he has already reproduced it in his own account of Jesus' entry into the city, which is now in the following chapter (12.12-19). Given his general intention to present the material in chs. 11 and 12 as a unit, it is more than likely that the psalm reference to Jesus as ὁ ἐρχόμενος in 12.13 has prompted his addition of the third element in Martha's confession in 11.27.

I have now completed my investigation of Martha's statement in 11.22 and taken account of its immediate context. However, as I have

words are 'reminiscent' of Mt. 7.7 and in also citing the later references to the logion in John (*Gospel*, p. 394). Although listed by Goldsmith ('"Ask, and it will be given..."', p. 254 n. 1), this reference is missing from the special studies of the logion by Dodd and Brown (see above, n. 26). More seriously, perhaps, it is also missing from J.D. Crossan's *Sayings Parallels: A Workbook for the Jesus Tradition* (Foundations and Facets; Philadelphia: Fortress Press, 1986), cf. p. 42, despite the author's claim to cite all instances in the corpus specified (p. xiii).

32. For Jesus as ὁ χριστός , cf. 1.41, also 1.20; 3.28 (by default); for ὁ υἱὸς τοῦ θεοῦ cf. 1.34; 1.49; cf. 10.36.

33. On this point, see Beasley-Murray, *John*, p. 192; Ashton, *Understanding*, p. 254 n. 29.

34. See especially the discussion on references to Jesus as ὁ ἐρχόμενος in the Synoptics, John, and elsewhere in the New Testament in J.K. Elliott, 'Is ὁ ἐξελθών a Title for Jesus in Mark i.45?', *JTS* NS 27 (1976), pp. 402-405.

already hinted, Martha's confidence in Jesus here has a bearing on later events in John's story. The logion expresses the certainty that requests made to God in prayer will be granted. I suggest that John's christological application of it in v. 22 has virtually dictated the terms in which he eventually describes Jesus at prayer before raising Lazarus. With that in mind, I will now return to the prayer and its context and attempt to follow John's tactics at that point.

The Prayer in Context

By 11.38, a certain amount of water has passed under the Bethany bridge since Jesus and Martha last met. In the meantime, there has been Jesus' intensely emotional encounter with Mary to a chorus of comment from a crowd of sympathizing Jews. Now, however, the stage is set for Jesus to return Lazarus to life. John fully intends that this miracle will be a σημεῖον ('sign') of Jesus' teaching to Martha, a sample fulfilment of the promise that those who believe in him now will be raised to life at the last day. To that end, he makes a point of including reminders of the earlier pericope in the present text: here is the tomb (v. 38, cf. 17); here is Martha—note also that she is admonished to remember what she was told (vv. 39-40, cf. 25-26); and here is the reference to Lazarus dead four days (v. 39, cf. v. 17). And here also, by the same token, is Jesus at prayer, predictably exhibiting the confidence that confirms the truth of Martha's certainty in v. 22 that whatever Jesus asks, God grants. If the opening words of the prayer take the form of a second allusion to Psalm 118, that is surely less than surprising in this context of general reference to the earlier scene. Moreover, if the allusion itself, taken from v. 41 of the psalm, consists in an expression of thanks placed on Jesus' lips, that is surely no more than the logical choice of wording in the circumstances. It may be, however, that the expression εὐχαριστῶ σοι ὅτι ἤκουσάς μου ('I thank thee that thou hast heard me') has also held an attraction for John because it introduces a perspective on Jesus as one whom God hears.

So far, I have argued from evidence within the Lazarus story itself that the prayer in 11.41-42 is the logical outcome of John's application to Jesus of the 'ask, and it will be given' logion in v. 22 and that the two are plainly linked. Nevertheless, a glance at the presentation of the logion in 1 John 5 leads one to suspect that the link between it and the prayer in the Gospel text may rest on rather more than logic. Note the ease with which the author of the epistle accommodates the assurances that God *hears* the faithful into his references to the logion in 5.14-15. In fact, 1 John's ἀκούει ἡμῶν ('he hears us') actually penetrates the logion there to become the mid-point between the asking stage and the receiving/being given stage. It is worth reminding ourselves at this point that the epistle writer is not in the business of forging radical new policies; on the contrary, he is bent on assuring his readers of their loyalty to tried and tested teaching.[35] This attitude, together with the comfortable manner in which the hearing references are introduced into the logion, suggest that the association of the two is a familiar and longstanding one in Johannine circles. The likelihood of this is increased when we consider that the description of God as a 'hearer' of prayer, which is a distinctive feature of the Johannine writings,[36] is also a significant element in the Old Testament presentation of God and in Judaism generally.[37] Thus, the link we find in the epistle writer's text probably goes back to the community's Jewish roots. In other words, it is not impossible that what comes to light in 1 Jn 5.14-15 reflects something of the network of unspoken communication between the evangelist and his own readers in John ch. 11. If this is so, then we may safely assume, for reasons behind the text as well as in it, that those who first heard the Lazarus story will have had no difficulty in connecting the reference to God hearing Jesus in the prayer with the statement of the logion earlier placed on the lips of Martha.

In so doing, John's readership, perhaps already in danger on account of their faith, will surely have been comforted. Here John has shown them Jesus at prayer, supremely fulfilling all the promise of the 'ask, and it will be given' logion. He is not only aware of having been heard specifically in relation to raising Lazarus from the dead (11.41), but also, with the words ἐγὼ δὲ ᾔδειν ὅτι πάντοτέ μου ἀκούεις ('I knew

35. Note, for example, 1 John's appropriation to himself of the language of original eye-witness (1.1-4) and his appeal to the tradition ἀπ' ἀρχῆς (1.1; 2.7; 2.24).

36. Apart from the Johannine references, the New Testament as a whole has only six instances where God is associated with verbs of hearing. Two of these are in quotations from the Old Testament (Acts 7.34; 2 Cor. 6.2) and the remaining four all use the 'divine' passive (Mt. 6.7; Lk. 1.13; Acts 10.31; Heb. 5.7).

37. See especially G.F. Moore, *Judaism in the First Centuries of the Christian Era: The Age of the Tannaim* (3 vols.; Cambridge, MA: Harvard University Press, 1927–30), II, pp. 215, 231.

that thou hearest me always') (v. 42), he is secure in the knowledge of the Father's immediate affirming response to any petition he might make.[38] In that security lies the evangelist's message to his beleaguered flock, for it confirms them in their faith as Christians. On this basis, they can be certain that prayers offered by those who believe in Jesus will always be heard by God. Indeed, as the Johannine Jesus himself repeatedly insists in references to the logion elsewhere in the Gospel, those who continue his work in the world should ask the Father ἐν τῷ ὀνόματί μου ('in my name') and their requests will be granted (14.13-14; 15.16; 16.23-24).[39]

Thus, on this analysis, it seems that John's purpose in 11.41-42 was neither to promote debate on whether or not Jesus really prays nor to afford a glimpse into the Son's unique communion with the Father. On the contrary, when Jesus' words are interpreted within the context of the story they were designed to fit, it emerges that what John has provided in this instance, and created through the medium of Scripture, is a demonstration of the power of Christian prayer in the person of Jesus himself.[40]

Summary and Conclusion

If the argument in this study offers a valid description of John's methods, then I may claim to have established the following points with reference to Jesus' prayer in 11.41-42. First, the prayer is a thanksgiving and not a petition because it is the corollary of John's application to Jesus of the 'ask, and it will be given' logion on Martha's lips in v. 22. Secondly, the allusion to Psalm 118 which opens the prayer comes as no surprise given that the influence of the same psalm is already apparent in Martha's confession in v. 27 and given also John's general inten-

38. *Pace* Bultmann *et al.*, the ideal of a constant prayerful attitude is not implied by this text (see above, p. 166).

39. Schnackenburg is surely correct in insisting that the phrase 'in my name' is not a condition but represents a Johannine development of the logion which belongs to a context of mission (*Gospel*, III, pp. 72-73). See also Dodd, *Historical Tradition*, p. 351 and Brown, *Gospel*, p. 635, both of whom compare the partial parallel in Mt. 18.20. Thus, those who pray in Jesus' name are those whom Jesus has sent, who represent him on earth and who ask in his place (see Schnackenburg, *Gospel*, III, pp. 73, 160; Lindars, *Gospel*, pp. 476, 492, 511; Sanders, *Gospel*, pp. 324, 342).

40. Among commentators I have consulted, only Hoskyns favours this 'democratic' approach to Jesus' prayer in John 11 (*Gospel*, p. 475).

tion to remind his readers of that earlier scene before the raising miracle finally takes place. Thirdly, the choice of wording from v. 21 of the psalm is not only entirely appropriate to the intended function of the prayer in relation to v. 22, but its content also serves John's purposes well by enabling him to focus on Jesus as one whom God hears, a familiar concept in Johannine circles and one which, to judge from the evidence in 1 John, is intimately bound up with the 'ask, and it will be given' logion itself.

My overall aim was to support the identification by Anthony Hanson and Max Wilcox of an allusion to Ps. 118.21 in Jn 11.41, and it is hoped that this compositorial approach to John's narrative has plausibly achieved that aim. In the process of the investigation, however, certain factors have emerged which also have a bearing on the issue of John's use of Scripture in general and its place in his scheme of things. I will comment briefly on these broader implications by way of conclusion.

If these proposals on the nature and function of the prayer are correct, then we must allow that, even though the prayer has been partly framed using words from Scripture, Scripture itself has not dictated the subject-matter of the prayer. That had already been settled by v. 22, at the point where John applied the 'ask, and it will be given' logion to Jesus. In other words, there is reason here to resist the view that John's narrative is primarily Scripture-driven. This is really where Hanson's proposal that John saw Psalm 118 as a kind of prophetic timetable of events in these chapters leaves us.[41] In this instance, at least, it appears that Scripture is written into John's narrative because it was already embedded in the Christian tradition from which he drew inspiration. Accordingly, as I have suggested, Martha's ὁ...ἐρχόμενος in 11.27 was taken from Ps. 118.26 in deference to the tradition in 12.13, and so a further reference to the same psalm in 11.41, as the earlier pericope is recalled, is hardly surprising. Perhaps, however, we should also look for something else in the immediate context of the prayer which has brought the psalm to John's mind at that precise point, and so triggered the allusion.

This is the real strength, in my opinion, of Wilcox's observation that there must be more than coincidence in the fact that John refers in v. 41 to removing the *stone* immediately before alluding to a Scripture right next door to the well-known 'stone' text of Ps. 118.22.[42] On this basis,

---

41. See Hanson, 'Old Testament Background', p. 255; *idem, New Testament Interpretation*, p. 167.

42. See Wilcox, '"Prayer"', pp. 131-32.

Wilcox proposes, first, that the reference to Ps. 118.21 in the prayer is to be taken as part of a wider context including at least the 'stone' verse next to it and, secondly, that the mention of 'stone' in the story itself has somehow acted as a keyword which has linked narrative and psalm together at some unspecified pre-Johannine stage. My only reservation about this is that I see no reason to suppose that all this interesting editorial activity must have happened at the pre-Johannine level. Indeed, I have found nothing in my own investigation to indicate that John has relied on source-material of any kind for this prayer, far less on something that needed to be explained or 'explained away'.[43] The alternative is that the word 'stone' has acted as a keyword for John himself. If so, then the following scenario presents itself: as he turns to compose the prayer, probably with Psalm 118 in his head from Martha's earlier words, John's reference to the removal of the stone (v. 41a) puts him in mind of the rejection of the stone in the psalm, from which point it is but a short step to finding the words of the neighbouring verse conveniently to hand for Jesus' opening words. Even if we cannot be certain of the nuts and bolts, however, there can be little doubt that the link we find in v. 41 between the stone reference and the prayer is John's own handiwork. Notice the nice little pun where 'lifting the stone' moves on to 'lifting the eyes' in a prayerful gesture (cf. 17.1) and so, finally, on to the prayer itself.

43. Wilcox, '"Prayer"', p. 132.

SOMETHING GREATER THAN SOLOMON:
AN APPROACH TO STEPHEN'S SPEECH*

Peter Doble

Σολομῶν δὲ οἰκοδόμησεν αὐτῷ οἶκον ('But Solomon built a house for him') (Acts 7.47). In this verse lie the roots of two exegetical traditions about Stephen's speech. Those who read Luke's δὲ in an adversative sense[1] tend also to read its οἶκον as a contrast to the σκηνῶμα (7.46) which David wanted to establish. Neudorfer,[2] for example, understands this sense to signal the beginnings of a Jerusalem cult, a cause of contention among the Diaspora. Hansen takes one further step, finding here evidence of a christian catechetical tradition about the Temple.[3] Other, fewer voices question this anti-cultic reading of Stephen's speech.[4]

This paper suggests a new approach to an old problem by asking two questions. First, is there a discernible Lukan treatment of Solomon which might explain his final appearance at this point?[5] Second, if there is, what might an exegete then make of the scriptural passages around Luke's reference to Solomon? Reading the speech as an anti-Temple polemic produces a sense of disjunction at 7.51; this paper's approach takes Luke's strands seamlessly into his ongoing narrative.

Stephen's speech stands at an important point in Luke's story, its

---

*   Presented to the *Annual Seminar on the Use of the Old Testament in the New* meeting in Hawarden, Wales, 2–4 April 1998; a revision of a paper read to the New Testament Research Seminar, University of Leeds, 1996.

1.   So, e.g., C.K. Barrett, *Acts* (2 vols.; ICC; Edinburgh, T. & T. Clark, 1994), I, p. 374.

2.   In I.H. Marshall and D. Peterson (eds.), *Witness to the Gospel* (Grand Rapids, MI: Eerdmans, 1998), p. 290.

3.   *Witness to the Gospel*, p. 314.

4.   E.g. D. Ravens, *Luke and the Restoration of Israel* (JSNTSup, 119; Sheffield: Sheffield Academic Press, 1995), p. 66.

5.   This point is significant because Solomon built the first Temple and the Temple is at the heart of accusations against Stephen.

vision makes plain the way things 'really' are, and it is the junction of
some major narrative strands. Acts 1.8 implies a Lukan schema: the
apostles are to bear witness first in Jerusalem, then in Judaea and
Samaria, finally, to the ends of the world. Because the Stephen unit
brings the Jerusalem period to a close, it is summative: it ends with an
account of Stephen's proto-martyrdom (7.57-60); it offers a long and
vivid picture of Stephen and of his apologia (6.8–7.56); it introduces
the person of Saul (8.1a), thereby connecting this unit with the remainder of Acts, particularly its third phase; it comments on a general persecution and a widening of the community's influence (8.1b). Everyone
agrees that Stephen's martyrdom leads to the first major transition in
Acts: at 8.1b begin both the Christian diaspora and their mission beyond
Jerusalem; at 7.58 and 8.1a readers are darkly prepared for the unfold-
ing of another drama. These events flow from Stephen's martyrdom,
itself the result of his peroration; but this is peroration only if it
properly concludes his speech—talk of disjunction at 7.51 rots all
notion of peroration. If, however, 7.51-53 can be shown to relate organically to 7.46-50, then speech, peroration, vision and martyrdom constitute a unity.

So, before Acts 7.46-47, what evidence is there of Lukan interest in
Solomon? Matthew and Luke agree on Jesus' Davidic descent. Luke
makes much of this: Joseph is twice said to be of the house/lineage of
David (Lk. 1.27; 2.4); twice Jesus is said to have been born in David's
city, Bethlehem (Lk. 2.4, 11); crucially, the Annunciation (Lk. 1.32)
promises Jesus 'the throne of his father, David,' amplified by 'He will
reign over the house of Jacob forever, and of his kingdom there will be
no end' (Lk. 1.33). Matthew and Luke have each three references to the
person Solomon;[6] Mark and John have none.[7] Matthew and Luke share
two references (Lk. 11.31/Mt. 12.42; Lk. 12.27/Mt. 6.29): Luke has one
in Acts; Matthew has one in his genealogy (1.6)–where Luke has none,
choosing to trace Jesus' descent[8] through Nathan (Lk. 3.31).

---

6.   Lk. 11.31; 12.27; Acts 7.47; cf Mt. 1.6; 6.29; 12.42.

7.   Jn 10.23 refers to Solomon's portico; such references are excluded from
examination at Acts 3.11 and 5.12.

8.   For discussion of Luke's form of Jesus' genealogy see: J.A. Fitzmyer, *The
Gospel According to Luke I–IX* (AB, 28; New York: Doubleday, 1981), pp. 490-
505; cf. R.E. Brown, *The Birth of the Messiah* (New York: Image Books, 1979),
pp. 505-12 for discussion of Jesus as a Davidid. Luke did not invent Nathan as Jesus'
ancestor: see 1 Chron. 14.4, 2 Sam. 5.14, where Nathan stands before Solomon as

A. *An Exegesis of Luke's Silence about Solomon*

Why did Luke 'remove' Solomon from Jesus' genealogy only to 'place' him elsewhere? This question pushes readers first into the Infancy Narratives where, *pace* Conzelmann, Lukan scriptural roots abound. Because earlier study has confirmed that in a 'sign' Luke echoed Isaiah's opening words about a manger (Lk. 2.7, 12, 16, (20); cf. Isa. 1.2-3), this study begins by examining Luke's use of σημεῖον ('a sign') at Lk. 2.12, and asks what Luke's readers might make of its companion ἐσπαργανωμένον ('wrapped in cloth').

Taking seriously Luke's use of σημεῖον, this study considers whether 'sign' includes ἐσπαργανωμένον in the same way that it probably includes ἐν φάτνῃ ('in a manger'), concluding that in his prologue the evangelist opened two narrative themes—scripture and Solomon—by echoing what Wisdom had to say of the young Solomon. This process examines Lk. 2.12 before reflecting on Lk. 1.32.

1. *Echoes of Wisdom in Luke's Infancy Narrative?*[9]

καὶ τοῦτο ὑμῖν τὸ σημεῖον, εὑρήσετε βρέφος
ἐσπαργανωμένον καὶ κείμενον ἐν φάτνῃ (Lk. 2.12).

And this shall be the sign for you; you shall find a baby wrapped in cloth bands and laid in a manger.

a. καὶ τοῦτο ὑμῖν τὸ σημεῖον. This is an 'angelic' sign, echoing scripture's assurance that what is disclosed through the visible points to a deeper, God-given reality. This sign is both different in kind from those which receive a bad press in the body of Luke's first volume (e.g. Lk. 11.29-32), and has especial force because it is offered by 'an angel of the Lord'; it thus belongs to a series of such signs, hallowed in biblical

---

one of David's sons born in in Jerusalem. But see *var lect* D which retains a Solomonic line for Jesus.

9.   For this section I am indebted to Mary Hayward who indicated similarities between Luke's 'infancy narrative' and Wisdom's account of Solomon's youthful 'autobiography', especially its reference to 'swaddling bands'. After presenting a draft of this paper to the NT Research Seminar at Leeds I encountered J. Winandy, 'Le signe de la mangeoire et des langes', *NTS* 43.1 (1997), pp 140-46; we follow significantly different lines of development. See also, R.E. Brown, 'The Meaning of the Manger: The Significance of the Shepherds', *Worship* 50 (1976), pp. 528-38.

tradition,[10] which confirm for humans what God has done or intends to do for them. Consequently, at this point in his narrative careful readers take seriously Luke's use of 'sign', by which he points them to a 'disclosure event'. In this event, the shepherds returned, glorifying and praising God for all they had heard and seen, just as it had been told them (Lk. 2.20; cf. 2.7, 16)—both manger and 'swaddling bands'.

b. εὑρήσετε βρέφος ἐσπαργανωμένον ('you shall find the baby wrapped in cloths'). Some commentators, following the lead offered by ἐν φάτνῃ have found significance in Isaiah's opening oracle (Isa. 1.2-3);[11] but, if one, then the sign's other element, σπαργανόω, must be included, and, for the moment, this study assumes the φάτνη reference to be an allusion to scripture. Fortunately, both φάτνη and σπαργανόω ('I wrap in bands of cloth') are 'Lukan'. φάτνη appears in the New Testament only at Lk. 2.7, 12, 16 and 13.15. Hengel[12] notes a 'surprising emphasis' on this word in the infancy narrative; if that is so, Hengel's note must be equally true of σπαργανόω which in the New Testament does not appear outside Luke's first two chapters and is wholly linked with this evangelist's use of φάτνη. Further, Luke's σπαργαν- element is as rare in the LXX as it is in the New Testament: the LXX has only two occurrences of the verb (Job 38.9; Ezek. 16.4) and two of the noun (Wis. 7.4; Ezek. 16.4).

Ezekiel 16.4 stands at the opening of a long, passionate, prophetic denunciation of Israel; vv. 4-6 offer a vivid picture of an unwanted baby girl, abandoned and exposed, denied care. What Ezekiel reported she was denied presumably constituted the basic care routinely offered to neo-nates who *were* wanted and properly nurtured: ἐν ᾗ ἡμέρᾳ ἐτέχθης, οὐκ ἔδησαν τοὺς μαστούς σου, καὶ ἐν ὕδατι οὐκ ἐλούσθης οὐδὲ ἁλὶ ἡλίσθης καὶ **σπαργάνοις οὐκ ἐσπαργανώθης**... ('On the day you were born they did not bind your breasts, nor were you washed with water to cleanse you, nor rubbed with salt, nor wrapped in cloth bands') (Ezek. 16.4). By ἐσπαργάνωσεν, then, Lk. 2.7 evokes a sense of a cared-for baby; while this scene may convey nothing more than that, its 'surprising emphasis' on φάτνη and σπαργανόω, especially

10. E.g., Exod. 3.12; Judg. 6, 13; 1 Sam. 2.34; 9.1–10.8; 14.10; 2 Kgs 19.29 cf. Isa. 37.30; 2 Kgs 20.9 cf. Isa. 38.7.

11. See C.F. Evans, *St Luke* (London: SCM, 1990) who refuses this linkage, commenting: 'This is surely far-fetched' (p. 200).

12. Hengel, 'Φάτνη', *TDNT*, IX, p. 53.

their joint presence in Luke as angelic sign, invites attentive readers to examine Luke's scene more closely.

There remain two passages to examine. First, Job 38.9 also offers birth imagery, this time concerning the founding of the world:

> ἐθέμην δὲ αὐτῇ νέφος ἀμφίασιν,
> ὁμίχλῃ δὲ αὐτὴν ἐσπαργάνωσα...
>
> ... when I made cloud its garment,
> and swaddled it in mist.

This adds nothing to the imagery of caring. Second, in Wis. 7.4 there is a swaddled human babe in a personal, historical sense: ἐν σπαργάνοις ἀνετράφην καὶ φροντίσιν... ('I was carefully nursed in cloth bands') and it is this 'personal' dimension which demands further reflection on the context of this verse in Wisdom.[13]

At 7.4, Wisdom opens something like an 'infancy' narrative, significantly, that of Solomon, and this parallel is set out in an appendix. However, it is well to be clear about what is and is not claimed for parallels now proposed between Luke and Wisdom:

> this argument depends on allowing its proper force to Luke's σημεῖον;
>
> one strand of this σημεῖον, is Luke's repeated ἐσπαργανωμένον;
>
> of four LXX occurrences of σπαργανόω *only* Wis. 7.4 leads to a comparable 'infancy/youth' narrative, and this seems to be unique in scripture.

Given this basis, the Appendix (see below) shows that the Luke and Wisdom narratives initially share a reference to σπαργανόω (section 1) and an emphasis on both youths' growth in σοφία ('wisdom') (section 2). The tables move this study into the Lukan scene in the Temple (2.41-52) where there is affirmation of the Holy Spirit as the source of both boys' σοφία (section 6); a strong accent on the youth (section 3) of both figures; the presence during serious discussion of 'elders' as admirers of both youths' σοφία (section 3); clear reference to both receiving the throne (section 5) of 'father David.' These shared features then prompt recognition of references to Adam (section 7—uniquely taken up in Luke's genealogy) and to mortality (Theophilus would have

---

13. Evans (*St Luke*, p. 200) noted that 'some' (unnamed) give the details here a more recognizable content by reference to Old Testament passages such as Wis. 7.4; this paper puts a large question-mark against Evans's judgment in this matter.

known how Jesus' story ended, and in his second volume Luke was to say much about God's raising of Jesus beyond corruption). Further, perhaps these similarities should not be detached from the Gospel's setting its 'boyhood of Jesus' scene in the Jerusalem Temple where the name 'Solomon' could scarcely be ignored.[14]

How might this Lukan construct contribute to his work's narrative development? Solomon's fame was ambiguous: when young, Solomon was admirable, but as king he failed and, consequently, was not really χριστός; the flaw in his character stands at the heart of Israel's divided history:

> ... you brought in women to lie at your side, and through your body you were brought into subjection. You stained your honour, *and defiled your family line*, so that you brought wrath upon your children, and they were grieved at your folly, because the sovereignty was divided and a rebel kingdom arose out of Ephraim (Sir. 47.19-21, italics added).

This is the roughly contemporary climate within which Luke's christological position is developed, fundamentally different from the Chronicler's bland assessment (2 Chron. 9.29-31),[15] but generally in line with the fiercer judgments of 1 Kgs 11.1-13. 'You stained your honour, *and defiled your family line*', suggests adequate reason for Luke's removal of Solomon from Jesus' ancestry; the restoration of Israel was to follow a different,[16] still Davidic, route.

2. *Luke made Jesus' Davidic Messiahship Central to his Programme*
Sirach, like Luke, knows that while Solomon was certainly not the Χριστός, God's promise to David still stands:

> But the Lord will never give up his mercy, or cause any of his works to perish; he will never blot out the descendants of his chosen one, *or destroy the family line of him who loved him*. So he gave a remnant to Jacob, *and to David a root from his own family* (Sir. 47.22, italics added; cf. Lk. 1.32-33).

---

14. At some time one needs to ask what significance, if any, on the basis of this study's reading, attaches to Luke's noting that the young church tended to meet in Solomon's portico; see Barrett (*Acts*, pp. 272-73).

15. One marvels at the editorial diplomacy of 2 Chron. 8.11 alongside 1 Kgs 11.1-8; evidently Sir. 47.19-20 trusts the harsher account.

16. By ascent rather than descent! See Lk. 20.41-43 which is used by the writer at Acts 2.34-35 to make precisely this point.

It is such conviction that underlay the hope of those who looked for the fulfilling of God's promises variously preserved in scripture. Luke appropriated this hope in his opening sequences: καὶ δώσει αὐτῷ κύριος ὁ θεὸς τὸν θρόνον Δαυὶδ τοῦ πατρὸς αὐτοῦ ('...and the LORD God will give to him the throne of his father David') (Lk. 1.32b). Here is the beginning of Luke's David-strand, of which his Solomon material is a necessary subset. The force of this study's argument depends entirely on the place in Luke's work of David—including psalms attributed to him—from the Annunciation through to the apostolic christological arguments in Acts.

In the interests of this theme, Luke needed to clarify the relation between David and Jesus, particularly because, while Sirach carried a tradition that Solomon had defiled David's family line, there persisted a parallel tradition of Solomonic greatness, for example, Mt. 6.29; 12.42 and parallels, and pseudonymous works like Wisdom.[17] One way for Luke to incorporate both traditions in his Christology was to show that the boy Jesus, like the man, was no whit inferior to Solomon; another was through Jesus' genealogy: ... τοῦ Ναθὰμ τοῦ Δαυὶδ τοῦ Ἰεσσαὶ τοῦ Ἰωβὴδ τοῦ Βόος ('... son of Nathan, son of David, son of Jesse, son of Obed, son of Boaz...') (Lk. 3.31-32). At a stroke, Luke's Christology replaced the Solomonic, flawed line from David (e.g. Sir. 47.20), choosing another of David's sons, Nathan, born in Jerusalem and named in 1 Chron. 14.4 immediately before Solomon. But Luke apparently refused to part with one key element in this Solomonic thread: from his childhood, like Solomon, Jesus too was *Wisdom*'s boy, although *his* descent may now 'resonate' with happier echoes of David's forthright and better-known prophet Nathan (but readers know that Luke's genealogy speaks of another man with the same name!).

Luke's Temple scene is a construct to open the curtain on the remainder of his work, prefiguring:

> the resurrection;[18]
> the conflict days before Jesus' arrest and trial, as he was with

---

17. At Hawarden, Dr Alan Lowe wondered whether in view of the late attribution of Wisdom to Solomon, Luke and his readers would have 'heard' this 'infancy' material as relating to Solomon. Internal evidence strongly suggests that Solomon is the alleged speaker; until it is certainly otherwise, this study warily assumes that Paul and Luke knew of no other attribution than to Solomon.

18. Cf. J.K. Elliott, 'Does Luke 2, 41-52 Anticipate the Resurrection?', *ExpTim* 83 (1971–72), pp 87-89.

the teachers in the Temple area, once more answering and
asking questions;

the christological certainties of Acts.

This approach strongly suggests that Lk. 2.41-52 is not an afterthought
but, rather, an integral part of Luke's narrative overview. And if that be
the case, it strongly supports, and is supported by, evidence for Luke's
knowledge and use of Wisdom in the accounts of Jesus' conflicts and
passion in Jerusalem.[19] This leaves open one much-discussed issue: Τί
ὅτι ἐζητεῖτέ με; οὐκ ἤδειτε ὅτι ἐν τοῖς τοῦ πατρός μου δεῖ εἶναί
με; ('Why were you searching for me? Did you not know that I had to
be about my father's business?') (Lk. 2.49).

Does 'father' here refer to God or to David? In the light of Lk. 1.32
and the evangelist's depiction of Solomonic wisdom, the latter should
now be thought at least a possibility.

3. *Review*

This opening section claims only that in his first two chapters, by clari-
fying Jesus' relation with David, Luke orchestrated the prelude to his
two-act 'opera', drawing on motifs and themes from Israel's past and
hinting at the drama yet to unfold.

When Theophilus first heard (or read) Luke's work, he came to it
having already been 'catechised' (Lk. 1.4).[20] Consequently, he probably
knew more than the mere outline of the apostolic κήρυγμα ('preaching,
proclamation'). He had probably heard apostolic arguments from scripture about Jesus' being heir to David's throne—was not this why Jesus
was called 'Christ?' He probably knew of objections raised both to
these scriptural arguments and to the κήρυγμα, particularly to presenta-
tions of Jesus' passion and talk of his resurrection—which is the reason
for Luke's offering Theophilus ἀσφάλειαν ('security, assurance')
(Lk. 1.4).

Theophilus, and all like him, hearing the 'scriptural' harmonics of the
prologue's closing scene, and of the genealogy which followed, would
have recognized that Luke had pictured the boy Jesus as David's
'proper' descendant, no less admirable than the young Solomon, yet the

---

19. See, e.g., P. Doble, *The Paradox of Salvation* (SNTSMS, 87; Cambridge:
Cambridge University Press, 1996), Chapter 7.

20. This reference to 'Theophilus' indicates no more than the present writer's
echoing Luke's own dedication to 'a reader'.

one destined to embody the promises made by God to David concerning a χριστόν who should rule Israel. By indicating the theological substructure of his Nativity and Temple scenes Luke prepared his readers for things to come, including the conclusion of his version of the Solomon strand, very different from Matthew's. Perhaps there is, after all, a genuine narrative-theological reason for Solomon's being the last-named character in Stephen's speech.

Before confirming that fact, because in Stephen's speech Solomon is tightly-linked with argument from scripture, Luke's uses of scripture need to be characterized.

B. *Luke and the Pursuit of Scripture*

Readers may object that the earlier exploration of 'swaddling bands' expects far too much of Theophilus's scriptural facility; four features of Lukan narrative combine to meet their objection.

First, in his prologue (Lk. 1.1-4) Luke refers to 'things fulfilled among us,' a notion which relates most naturally to scripture.

Second, in his first volume, Luke makes much of Jesus' transmission to the apostles of *his own* hermeneutic of the Scriptures concerning himself (e.g. Lk. 24.27, 32, 45-46); that is, Luke affirms that the apostles were instructed in Christ's Christology. Set first in the Emmaus narrative, and subsequently in Jesus' appearance in Jerusalem to the eleven, this twice-reported formal transmission to the apostolic band of the risen Lord's scriptural self-understanding sharply focuses Luke's understanding of the central role of scripture in his community's life and thought. This strand runs backwards as well as forwards, so readers are invited to reconsider the first volume's portrayal of Jesus.

Third, in Acts, Luke then shows the apostles liberally using scripture, and throughout their speeches he makes much use of scriptural allusion and citation. As Haenchen remarks in an admiring note on Luke's authorial skill, Acts without speeches would be like a gospel without Jesus' words.[21] But those same speeches without their quotations and allusions would be nothing, for, with the exception of Paul's Areopagus speech, they are wrought entirely around scripture. It is inconceivable that Luke, who had emphasized Jesus' transmission to his disciples of his own 'christological hermeneutic', would understand his presentation

21. E. Haenchen, *The Acts of the Apostles* (Oxford: Basil Blackwell, 1971), p. 212.

of the apostolic hermeneutic to be different from that legitimized by their Lord.

Fourth, within Acts, Luke strongly implies that the apostles explored scripture specifically to prove that Jesus was the χριστός:

Paul (17.2-3, παρατίθημι ['explain'], cf. 11) and Apollos (18.24-28, ἐπιδείκνυμι ['exhibit, prove']) are portrayed 'proving' from scripture that Jesus was the messiah;

Paul (9.22, συμβιβάζω ['prove']; cf. 13.27-37) 'proving' that Jesus was the messiah;

Paul (26.22-23, 27) and Peter (3.18; 4.25-28) 'proving'[22] that the messiah should suffer. Given both this clear christological focus and the centrality of scripture in the speeches, why should twentieth-century readers imagine some other aim and process for Stephen's speech within Luke's overall plan? One response may be that the speech is self-evidently about the Temple; this paper challenges this 'obvious', but difficult, answer.

Together, these four features suggest that one of Luke's characteristics is his exploring of scripture as the major interpreter of the Jesus-event. Luke's writing presupposes that his readership was attuned to the same kind of sensitivity, and that at least that community for which he was writing was already convinced that in *Torah*, psalms and prophets (Lk. 24.44) they would find clues to God's plan of salvation, given by Jesus himself, to help them grasp what was really 'going on' in Jesus' life, death and exaltation. So Luke's earlier, cryptic signals to Theophilus concerning the 12-year-old Jesus' visit to the Temple, should lead later readers to expect similar stylistic tautness in other notes of scripture.

This understanding of Luke's practice is kin to that noted by many scholars. Time would fail to tell of Dodd, Lindars, Stanton, Hays, Marcus, Wright and others[23] who have in their own ways urged that what

22. None of the above verbs is involved; Luke's apostles simply affirm God's having fulfilled what the prophets announced in advance (cf. 24.14f; 28.23).

23. C.H. Dodd, *According to the Scriptures* (London: James Nisbet, 1952); B. Lindars, *New Testament Apologetic* (London: SCM, 1961); G.N. Stanton, *Jesus of Nazareth in New Testament Preaching* (SNTSMS, 27; Cambridge: Cambridge University Press, 1974); R.B. Hays, *Echoes of Scripture in the Letters of Paul* (New Haven: Yale University Press, 1989); J. Marcus, *The Way of the Lord* (Edinburgh: T. & T. Clark, 1993). Marcus's insight is that Mark's theological substructure is in dialogue with his text and that his 'meaning' is discerned *dialogically*. That is the

in the text of the New Testament appear to be citations or allusions, are, in fact, markers, or signals, or headlines which call into play a larger, whole context.[24] Section A earlier showed how an appeal to a theological substructure 'works' in the case of brief signals in the Infancy Narrative as Luke developed his Solomonic reference;[25] his signal evokes the larger text, inviting readers to make substantial inter-textual links. Is there similar intertextuality in Luke's final reference to Solomon (Acts 7.46-47), with its accompanying scriptural allusions and references?

C. *Luke's Use of Scripture: Acts 7.46-56—Exploratory Exegesis*

The 'obvious' reading of these verses is not without its own difficulties: commentators have identified an adversative δὲ at v. 47; others have complained of disjointedness between vv. 50 and 51. For example, Haenchen writes: 'The *swift passage* to the string of charges in verses 51-53 which goad the audience into fury can only be explained if the preceding verses form a radical denunciation of the Temple worship',[26] while Bruce comments, 'This *sudden* invective may have been occasioned by an angry outburst against what he had just said. It was clear that he was attacking some of their most cherished beliefs about the Temple.'[27] There is indeed an awkwardness about these verses—but only if one limits one's reading to the printed verses and also thinks them to be essentially about the Temple; the alleged awkwardness disappears under a different reading.

This paper earlier established three 'notes' which underlie this exploration. First, references to scripture should be understood to involve the

argument of this study of Luke's Solomonic narrative strand. See also N.T. Wright, *Jesus and the Victory of God* (London: SPCK, 1996), p. 348 on Mk 13.12.

24. In fact, as Dodd put it, the *substructure* of New Testament theology. Marcus's extension of this is helpful: 'Mark has certainly learned much of what he knows about Jesus Christ from the scriptures. He would never have learned it, however, if he had not already known that Jesus Christ is the key to the scriptures' (Marcus, *The Way of the Lord*, p. 203). See also Franklin: 'Equally important is the unity of outlook...the quotations are not peripheral...but flow into and control the theology of Luke' (E. Franklin, *Christ the Lord* [London: SPCK, 1975], p. 75.)

25. At Mk 12.26 is ἐπὶ τοῦ βάτου a similar marker to that in Lk. 2.12, a mnemonic device predating chapters and verses?

26. Haenchen, *The Acts of the Apostles*, p. 286. Emphasis mine.

27. F.F. Bruce, *The Acts of the Apostles* (London: Tyndale Press, 1952), pp. 176-77. Emphasis mine.

whole context of an allusion or citation; second, the Lukan Solomon-thread is to be taken seriously as an important subset of his interest in David; third, Luke's use of scripture in the apostolic speeches is normally christological. Together, these three 'notes' suggest that within Stephen's speech readers should set out the larger context of each reference to scripture, and build it into the framework of Luke's argument. In the following pages that is done for Acts 7.46-56.

Such expanded rearrangement clearly demonstrates one good economic reason for Luke's mode of 'referencing': had he printed in full each scriptural passage on which his argument relied, then he would have needed at least one more scroll. However, readers' ability to recall where in scripture a particular passage was to be found, or their knowing it by heart, suggests that the essence of Luke's argument is found not simply in quotations but in the unexpressed portions of those scriptures to which he drew attention. Section B (above) indicates that Luke's community had so struggled with those scriptures which appeared to them to make sense of Jesus' story that readers could quickly access them.

Luke's final reference to Solomon is sandwiched between two references to scripture. The second reference is clear: Luke has cited Isa. 66.1-2a; the earlier reference is a probable allusion to Ps. 132.5. If a reader takes seriously the possibility that scripture references in Acts are to be read not as proof-texts but as 'headers' or 'footers' signalling longer passages, then, to explore what part such passages might play in the amplified Lukan argument, he or she needs first to set out in fuller form Luke's allusion to Psalm 132.

1. *Luke's Primary Reference: Psalm 132.5*
NA[27] and many commentators note that at v. 46 Luke alludes to Ps. 132.5 (LXX Ps. 131.5). If this allusion is intended to evoke a larger part of the psalm, then the latter's four principal themes need to be explored.

First, the psalm's Temple theme is obvious: the ark (of the covenant) is a central notion; the Temple itself is referred to in many ways—'dwelling place', 'footstool', 'resting place' and 'habitation' are used alongside the simple 'place' (τόπος). The building initiative is entirely David's (vv. 1-5) although the psalm affirms that a habitation in Zion is also God's choice (vv. 13-15). The tone of this theme is entirely positive.

A second theme, important in Acts, is that of God's sure promise to David that his kingdom will continue:

> The LORD swore to David *a sure oath*
> from which he will not turn back:
> 'One of the sons of your body
> I will set on your throne ... [28]
> their sons also, forevermore,
> shall sit on your throne' (Ps. 132.11-12).

The one who will continue this Davidic line is the 'anointed one', a χριστός, who may appeal to God's goodwill toward David in support of himself: 'For your servant David's sake, do not turn away the face of your χριστόν' (Ps. 132.10).

There is, however, a third thread, the christological conditional, which firmly relates God's promise to David to his sons' commitment to *Torah*. God's promise is not open-ended, but conditional: David is God's χριστός who is obedient. Psalm 132.12 spells this out clearly:

> *If your sons keep my covenant*
> *and my decrees that I shall teach them,*
> their sons also, forevermore,
> shall sit on your throne.

A fourth theme is that of vindication—first, vindication of God in respect of his 'sure promise', and, second, of David in respect of his line. This theme emerges at the psalm's conclusion. Referring to the Temple in Zion it affirms:

> There I will cause a horn to sprout up for David;
> I have prepared a lamp for my χριστόν.
> His enemies I will clothe with disgrace,
> but on him, his crown will gleam (Ps. 132.17-18).

Here, at Acts 7.46, immediately before Luke's final reference to Solomon, he places an allusion to a psalm linking Temple, David, χριστός and vindication. Now for two good reasons this should make readers pause:

Luke had earlier airbrushed Solomon out of Jesus' family portrait, so why does he figure at this point?

An important element in Luke's programme was that Jesus would sit on the throne of his father David: 'He will be great, and will be called

---

28. E.g. Acts 2.30 which is a clear allusion to Ps. 132.11, used with Ps. 16.8-11 and Ps. 110.1 to construct Peter's argument that David, a prophet, spoke of the resurrection of the χριστόν (Acts 2.31) and of his exaltation to God's right hand (Acts 2.34).

the Son of the Most High, *and the Lord God will give to him the throne of his father David'* (Lk. 1.32).[29]

But pondering this allusion presents a major problem to those who suspect that they have met this passage elsewhere: where was it?

> Now rise up, O LORD God,
> > and go to your resting place,
> you and the ark of your might.
> Let your priests, O LORD God,
> > be clothed with salvation,
> and let your faithful rejoice
> > in your goodness.
> O LORD God, do not avert your face from your χριστόν.
> Remember your mercy for your servant David.

Of course–this is also the LXX ending of Solomon's prayer at the dedication of the Temple (2 Chron. 6.41-42) and a reader carefully notes that while Psalm 132 began, 'O LORD, *remember* in *David*'s favour…', Solomon's prayer ends, 'O LORD God… *remember* your steadfast love for your servant *David*'. In relation to Psalm 132, the last couplet of Solomon's prayer is inverted and its LXX form is much more reminiscent of the psalm than is the MT. This presents readers with a problem: because the scriptural allusion at Acts 7.46-47 is most likely to Ps. 132.5, should the whole psalm now lead also to Solomon's prayer? It did lead this reader, who suspects that, on the principle of analogy, it would have done so for Theophilus and all like him.[30] Unquestionably, at Acts 7.47 Luke focused his readers' attention on Solomon's building God's οἶκος ('house'); this seems to suggest that, taken together, both the psalm and Luke's text point to what scripture said about Solomon's dedication of the temple. Consequently, readers *should* explore Solomon's prayer. The only way to be sure, is to examine that prayer to discover whether it adds to one's understanding of Stephen's speech.

2. 'But Solomon built him a house': A Case of Lukan Intertextuality? (2 Chronicles 6)

Like Psalm 132, this Solomonic prayer comprises a number of strands: the Temple, the sure promises to David, and the christological condi-

---

29. Further, Ps. 132.17-18 relates to Luke's account of Stephen's martyrdom.

30. Discussion at Hawarden highlighted the place of the educated Godfearer in Luke's understanding of the expansion of the apostolic mission; Luke's readership *knew* the scriptures.

tional. Confirmation of the prayer's being a middle term in Luke's argument emerges in discovering how it eases readers from Psalm 132 to Isaiah 66, removing all sense of disjointedness from Stephen's argument.

The Temple. The Temple thread in 2 Chronicles 6 affirms that David was minded to build a house[31] (οἶκος) for the Lord, the God of Israel, but that God willed that it be David's son who should do so (6.8), and that Solomon was now on the throne (6.7-10).[32] Yet what probably most characterizes Solomon's prayer is its oft-repeated insistence that heaven[33] is really God's dwelling place[34] and that the house built by Solomon could never aspire to be that. The Temple may be the place (τόπος)[35] where God sets his name; where the ark (of the covenant) rests; towards which Israel, God's people, pray; where foreigners may also come to pray—'in order that all the peoples of the earth may know your name and fear you as do your people Israel' (6.32-33)—but heaven is emphatically God's 'home' though even that cannot hold God (6.18). This understanding of God's relation to the Temple is so emphatically repeated that it must surely be one key element in the prayer; so must be the non-pejorative use of οἶκος throughout, and its conjunction with τόπος, either alone or coupled with 'dwelling' or 'resting.' Consequently, if Solomon's prayer is the middle term between Psalm 132 and Isaiah 66, then those exegetical attempts must fail which find in Stephen's speech a polemic against what Solomon actually built,[36] something alleged to be very different from what David (and God) intended; there *is* no implied contrast between σκηνῶμα ('tent, tabernacle') and οἶκος ('house') at Acts 7.46-47. Luke's concern lies elsewhere, with Solomon and his successors rather than with the

---

31. So at 2 Chron. 6.2, 5, 7, 8, 9, 10, 18, 20, 22, 24, 29, 32, 33, 34, 38, fifteen occurrences; used of the Temple in relation to David's purpose, see 6.7, 8, 10. This usage must put a question mark against attempts to force a distinction between σκηνῶμα and οἶκος in Stephen's speech (Acts 7.46, 47), *contra* Neudorfer, *Witness to the Gospel*, pp. 289-90.

32. Note Lk. 1.32 lurking in the background.

33. So at 2 Chron. 6.13, 14, 18, 21, 23, 25, 26, 27, 30, 33, 35, 39, twelve occurrences.

34. So at 2 Chron. 6.21, 30, 33, 39, four instances.

35. 2 Chron. 6.2; *this place*, 6.20, 21, 26, 40.

36. See, e.g., J. Kilgallen, *The Stephen Speech* (AnBib, 67; Rome: Pontifical Biblical Institute Press, 1976), pp. 90-95.

Temple itself: Solomon proved an unworthy heir of David, unfit to succeed to God's promise.

The Sure Promises to David. The Chronicler, however, understood God's promises to David to be twofold. The first related to his building of the οἶκος (see 2 Chron. 6.4-10, 14).[37] This building's significance is plainly spelt out:

> I have succeeded my father David, and sit on the throne of Israel, as the LORD promised, and have built the house for the name of the LORD, the God of Israel. There I have set the ark, in which is the covenant of the LORD that he made with the people of Israel (2 Chron. 6.10-11).

One element in God's promise had been fulfilled, and there was no question but that this house, now being dedicated, was what David had willed and God had approved. The second part had to do with David's succession, already noted in the passage quoted above: 'I have succeeded my father David, and sit on the throne of Israel, *as the LORD promised* ... ' but extended formally in:

> Therefore, O LORD, God of Israel, keep for your servant, my father David, that which *you promised him*, saying, 'There shall never fail you a successor before me to sit on the throne of Israel, if only your children keep to their way, to walk in my law as you have walked before me.' Therefore, O LORD, God of Israel, let your word be confirmed, which you promised to your servant David (2 Chron. 6.16-17 my emphasis, but cf. 2 Sam. 7.12-16).

This strong sense that God's promise to David concerning the succession will not fail is sustained within Solomon's prayer and on into the Acts. But, as elsewhere (save in 2 Samuel), God's promise of the Davidic succession is conditional.

The Christological Conditional. At the opening, as at the end, of the Chronicler's Solomonic prayer stands this christological conditional which is closely, necessarily related to God's promise to David. It may be that Solomon now occupies David's throne (6.10, 16) but that is conditional (6.16): he must 'walk in my *Torah*'. Perhaps a classic expression of this conditional appears in Ps. 132.10 in an inverted form from: ' ...O LORD God, do not reject your χριστόν. Remember your steadfast love for your servant David' (2 Chron. 6.42).

---

37. Note 6.8–9 which 'foreshadows' Acts 7.46-47.

Behind this innocent prayer stand two important confirmatory passages: first, Solomon's dream-vision (2 Chron. 7.12-22, cf. 1 Kgs 9.1-9) spelled out the close relation between Solomon's entering upon his kingdom (vv. 17-20) and Israel's fate (vv. 21-22). Second, David's testamentary benediction (1 Chron. 29.10-19) before Solomon was anointed carefully prepared readers for what was to follow:

> Grant to my son Solomon that with single mind he may keep your commandments, your decrees, and your statutes, performing all of them, and that he may build the temple for which I have made provision (1 Chron. 29.19).

To recall Solomon's prayer at the Temple's dedication is also to recall Solomon's vision with its weightily worded conditional—the result of Solomon's not walking by *Torah* was to be the shattering of the house for God that Solomon built (2 Chron. 7.19-22). So when Theophilus read Luke's 'But it was Solomon who built a house for him' (Acts 7.47), the words came freighted with significance for Jesus' story which itself began with an annunciation to Mary that God was to give David's throne to her son (Lk. 1.32).

The themes of Luke's secondary, internal allusion (2 Chronicles) were those of Psalm 132, although now, naturally, with much greater emphasis on 'heaven' and 'house'. Again, on the principle of analogy, Stephen, Theophilus and all like them, would look to these words and themes to lead them to comparable passages which would extend their understanding. Luke and his church knew that, in the context of another age's reflection on the Temple, the prophet 'Isaiah' had digested Solomon's story, consequently, 'heaven' and 'house' stand out in Luke's quotation of Isa. 66.1 at Acts 7.49, 50—a natural, smooth transition from Psalm 132, through the Chronicler's version of Solomon's prayer and on into the heart of the matter—'obedience' and 'disobedience'.

Introducing Luke's reference to Solomón, Acts 7.46 invited Theophilus to reflect on Psalm 132; Acts 7.47 then conspired with Ps. 132.8-10 to lead him to 2 Chronicles 6 and to 7.12-22; Solomon's prayer led naturally into Isaiah's reflection (66.1-6)[38] on the rebuilding of the now-shattered Temple. A problem remains: how might Luke's *quoting*

---

38. The extent of this 'suppressed quotation' is determined solely by its relation to the material in Acts which follows the 'marker' citation. In this paper it extends to Isa. 66.6 because vv. 3-6 form an important element in Stephen's peroration and vision.

Isaiah move Theophilus forward to Stephen's verbal onslaught on his accusers without its alleged sense of disjointedness? Again, the answer lies in an unexpressed, powerful portion of what 'Isaiah' had said.

3. *A Lukan Quotation: Isaiah 66.1-2a.*

> Thus says the LORD: Heaven is my throne and the earth is my footstool; what is the house that you would build for me, and what is my resting place? All these things my hand has made ... (Isa. 66.1-2a). [39]

Two facts are immediately obvious: first, relating to the Temple, there are strong, unusual verbal links between this quoted passage and Psalm 132: ὑποπόδιον ('footstool'),[40] and τόπος τῆς καταπαυσεώς ('place of rest') catch the eye; second, given that 2 Chronicles 6 is probably the co-text of an extended reading of Psalm 132, Luke's move to Isaiah's opening words would not surprise a reader, nor would they be read as a rebuke to Solomon (or David) for building the Temple. Obviously, 'heaven' is God's dwelling place and equally obviously no Temple can accommodate God. Solomon's prayer had made that repetitively plain, so why might Luke cite these verses? The exegetical principles underlying this present exercise suggest that by this brief extract Luke invited Theophilus to read further and deeper.

In Acts, this unexpressed, yet powerfully present, prophetic text is essentially concerned with the outworking of the christological conditional. 'Isaiah' knew, as Luke and Theophilus knew, that David's succession broke up under Solomon;[41] both Luke and Isaiah wrote knowing that God's as-yet-unfulfilled promise to David still hung potently in the air.[42] Readers enter this stage of Luke's 'outworking' through a substructure comprising a Song of Ascents (Ps. 132), the Chronicler's

---

39. For an earlier attempt to explore this suppressed quotation see P. Doble, 'The Son of Man Saying in Stephen's Witnessing: Acts 6.8–8.2', *NTS* 31 (1985), pp. 68-84 (80-82).

40. This is an interesting example; there are seven occurrences of the word in the Old Testament and New Testament. Ps. 132.7, which in LXX implies rather than uses 'footstool', links not only with Isa. 66.1 but with 1 Chron. 28.2 and with Ps. 99.5 in this usage; Acts 7.49 thus echoes a common view found clearly expressed in Mt. 5.35. Another use of 'footstool' derives from Ps. 110.1 and is echoed in Lk. 20.43; Acts 2.35; Heb. 1.13; 10.13.

41. See n. 15 above.

42. See, e.g., Isa. 55.3, cf. 38.5; and Luke's Jesus introduced, defined and shaped his ministry by reference to Isa. 61.1.

report of Solomon's prayer and then the extended Isaiah reflection on that prayer. Isaiah's fierce polarization of the obedient and disobedient carries the shared themes of these three texts into Luke's dramatic scene of Stephen's vision and martyrdom.[43]

'But this is the one to whom I will look, to the humble and contrite in spirit, who trembles at my word'. Like Acts 7.51, Isa. 66.2b initially appears disjointed from its antecedent. However, all sense of abruptness disappears when Isaiah's text is read within the framework of what Luke's catena of scriptural allusions had said about the continuity of David's line and the Temple. In passages directly concerned with the Temple, in their shared verses, both Psalm 132 and 2 Chronicles 6 prayed that for David's sake God would not turn his face away from his χριστόν. In an overtly 'Temple' context, Isaiah now commented that God had made his response to this prayer: the one on whom God would look attentively,[44] the one for whom God would have regard (cf. Lk. 1.48), would be τὸν ταπεινὸν[45] καὶ ἡσύχιον καὶ τρέμοντα τοὺς λόγους μου...('the humble and quiet, who quakes at my words')—that is, one who took seriously both *Torah* and *mitzvot*. Isaiah's implied comment on the christological conditional in Solomon's prayer is plain: Solomon may have built a magnificent Temple, but he failed God's christological conditional.[46] Israel's future lay with a different kind of person; this dialogue between Isaiah and Solomon's prayer must be read as one

---

43. The *unexpressed* portion of this Isaianic text provides readers with both the *co-text* for Stephen's allegedly abruptly-introduced, disjointed, peroration at Acts 7.51-53 and a strong *context* for Stephen's vision at 7.55-58 (both examined below).

44. καὶ ἐπὶ τίνα ἐπιβλέψω ἀλλ᾽ ἢ ἐπὶ τόν ταπεινὸν... ('and upon whom should I look but upon the humble?') (Isa. 66.2b). The verb has to do with looking attentively, studiedly at an object or person. It is probably not accidental that the notion appears in Luke's Annunciation: ὅτι ἐπέβλεψεν ἐπὶ τὴν ταπείνωσιν τῆς δούλης αὐτοῦ. ἰδοὺ γὰρ ἀπὸ τοῦ νῦν μακαριοῦσίν με πᾶσαι αἱ γενεαί: ('for he has looked with favour on the lowliness of his servant. Surely, from now on all generations will call me blessed') (Lk. 1.48). Here, the underlying thought is of 'choice', and it would be appropriate to 'hear' this sense in Stephen's speech.

45. See Doble, *The Paradox of Salvation*, pp. 112-26, especially n. 31, for a fuller discussion of the relation of ταπεινός to the Jesus story in Luke's work.

46. The significance of Sir. 47.12-22 for this position is not clear. The least that can be said is that it indicates a general view very like that of Luke, who took great pains to rewrite Jesus' genealogy (see 47.22b) and who wrote a core strand of his christology in line with Sir. 47.22c.

more step in the process of Stephen's proving Jesus as τὸν χριστὸν of God's promises to David, for questions about the Temple will always be questions about the king and the kingdom.

The Quaker, the Quakers and their Enemies. Further, built into Isaiah's passage (66.2b) is a little vignette of this primitive 'quaker' (ταπεινός, ἡσύχιος, τρέμοντα τοὺς λόγους μου, 'the humble and quiet, who quakes at my word') who also proves to be plural (66.5b); these quakers are promised that God will put their enemies to shame. These two brief passages belong to a well-established humiliation/vindication pattern found in the Psalms (the righteous sufferer), in Wisdom (ὁ δίκαιος), in Deutero-Isaiah (the Servant) and in Daniel (the son of man). In each of these, a symbolic singular represents the plural faithful whose humiliation is engineered by those opposed to God as much as to them. It comes, therefore, as no surprise to discover that this Isaianic passage also includes a vignette of his quaker's enemies: the prophet affirms (66.3b-4) that these are they who did what was evil in God's sight, who went their own ways, who did not listen when God called.[47] Their contrast with the quaker is heightened by 66.3a with its distinct echo of Solomon's Temple-dedication and its vast sacrificial offerings.[48] This humiliation/vindication pattern normally leads to a strong affirmation that God will ultimately vindicate his faithful and punish their enemies (and God's). Consequently, the quaker's (and quakers') haters and rejecters should expect to be mocked by God and disgraced (66.4a; cf. Ps. 132.18), but, before then, their conflict is sharp, and Stephen's fate symbolized for Theophilus's church wider conflicts and further martyrs. It is this close relation between Isaiah's words and Stephen's peroration that removes the alleged 'abruptness' or 'disjunction' at Acts 7.51, to which verse attention now turns.

D. *Stephen's Peroration (Acts 7.51-53) and its Scriptural Substructure*

Nearly half a century ago, when Dodd published his work he offered a

---

47. Isa. 66.4 There is a close parallel to this phrasing in 65.12, and, at a little more distance, in 50.2.

48. 'Then the king and all the people offered sacrifice before the LORD. King Solomon offered as a sacrifice twenty-two thousand oxen and one hundred twenty thousand sheep. So the king and all the people dedicated the house of God' (2 Chron. 7.4-5).

possibility and uttered a warning.[49] The possibility was that beneath allusions by New Testament writers to scripture, or half-quotations from it, there lay a body of unquoted material whose presence, if acknowledged, might enrich a later reader's understanding of the New Testament text. With that possibility came also Dodd's warning of 'the dangerous ground of speculation and fancy, where associations of ideas arising in the critic's own mind have been treated as evidence for original connections'.[50] So far, this study's hypothesis of Luke's scriptural substructure, sharply focused on Solomon, has been inferred from evidence within Luke's text; it now moves to confirm that the thrust of Stephen's speech derives from this scriptural substructure that also underlies Stephen's peroration and vision.

A Scriptural Framework for Stephen's Peroration
If this 'Solomonic' substructure was in Theophilus's mind as he read the speech, then he would find no disjunction between vv. 50 and 51. Stephen's speech simply carries over Isaiah's denunciation into his present; its words hang in the space between these allegedly disjunct verses, and readers should 'feel' the punch of Isa. 66.3-4, now directed against Stephen's accusers. These verses are a natural springboard for Stephen's attack: Σκληροτράχηλοι καὶ ἀπερίτμητοι καρδίαις καὶ τοῖς ὠσίν, ὑμεῖς ἀεὶ τῷ πνεύματι τῷ ἁγίῳ ἀντιπίπτετε, ὡς οἱ πατέρες ὑμῶν καὶ ὑμεῖς ('Stiff-necked people, uncircumcised in heart and ears, you are always opposing the Holy Spirit, just as your fathers used to do ... ') (Acts 7.51). Lying behind Stephen's words is the implication that his hearers were God's enemies. It was *they* who did not listen, *they* who did what was evil in God's sight, *they* who were the true descendants from Solomon, the last-named of the fathers—as your fathers,[51] so are you. Solomon's offence was that he did not keep *Torah*; they also did not keep *Torah*: οἵτινες ἐλάβετε τὸν νόμον εἰς διαταγὰς ἀγγέλων, καὶ οὐκ ἐφυλάξατε (' ... who received the law as

---

49. Dodd, *According to the Scriptures.*
50. Dodd, *According to the Scriptures*, p. 28.
51. This reading of Luke's scriptural substructure clarifies the difference between Stephen's 'our fathers' at 7.44-46 and 'your fathers' at 7.51-53. Stephen shares Israel's history to Solomon, but not beyond, for he knows who David's true descendant is. By their actions, his accusers have taken on the role of those who have chosen their own way, and consequently, as Isaiah had seen, have rejected Stephen as well as Jesus.

ordained by angels, yet you have not kept it') (Acts 7.53).[52]

Further, as throughout Ps. 132.18 and Isa. 66.5-6, the speech's substructure strongly implies retribution for God's enemies, so in Stephen's peroration retribution hangs heavily in the air, as it does in the δίκαιος model at Wis. 5.1-23. Of course Stephen is martyred, but his vision is his own proleptic vindication: like his Lord, he forgives his tormentors and entrusts himself to safer hands in heaven.[53]

A Scriptural Substructure for Stephen's Vision

Within Luke's substructure, Isaiah's oracle has also provided a context for better understanding Stephen's vision. For Stephen, heaven was opened and he saw the glory of God.

> ὑπάρχων δὲ πλήρης πνεύματος ἁγίου ἀτενίσας εἰς τὸν οὐρανὸν εἶδεν δόξαν θεοῦ καὶ Ἰησοῦν ἑστῶτα ἐκ δεξιῶν τοῦ θεοῦ, καὶ εἶπεν, Ἰδοὺ θεωρῶ τοὺς οὐρανοὺς διηνοιγμένους καὶ τὸν υἱὸν τοῦ ἀνθρώπου ἐκ δεξιῶν ἑστῶτα τοῦ θεοῦ (Acts 7.55-56).

This affirmation, twice repeated—and therefore to be heard—would surely have alerted Theophilus to what was really going on here. Theophilus would have heard in these words clear echoes from two passages in their Isaian substructure. First, 'Your own people who hate you and reject you for my name's sake have said, "Let the LORD be glorified, so that we may see your joy ..."' and second, 'Thus says the LORD: heaven is my throne and the earth is my footstool ...' (Isa. 66.1). Obvious verbal links between Luke and Isaiah are 'heaven' and 'δόξα' ('glory'); other thematic threads are basically those of the humiliation/vindication pattern, particularly the thread of God's retribution for those who have done what is evil, who have ignored *Torah*. The important question is, are these links structural or not?

Heaven. In quoting from Isaiah's reflection on 'Temple', Luke highlighted the word 'heaven', a key word, echoing Solomon's prayer of dedication of the earlier Temple and preparing his readers for Stephen's opened heaven:[54]

---

52. φυλάσσω is also the verb used at 2 Chron. 7.17 where Solomon's dream is the vehicle for a fleshing out of the significance of the christological conditional.

53. For a defence of Jesus' forgiveness of his tormentors see Doble, *The Paradox of Salvation*, pp. 179-83.

54. ...thereby reversing the effects of Acts 1.9! He was received out of their sight; Stephen now sees him.

But filled with Holy Spirit, he gazed into heaven and saw the glory of
God and Jesus standing at the right hand of God. 'Look,' he said, 'I see
the heavens opening and the Son of man standing at the right hand of
God!' (Acts 7.55-56).[55]

In fact, heaven is itself a theme for which a reader has been well-pre-
pared within Luke's own writing: it was to heaven, reports Luke, that
Jesus ascended (Acts 1.2, 10, 11), there to remain until the right time
(Acts 3.20-21);[56] there he is to be seen by Stephen, his *shaliach* and
martyr, seen as the Lord Jesus, at God's right hand. But Isaiah had
affirmed that heaven was God's throne and earth God's footstool; the
language is that of kingship. Consequently, given Luke's explicit reference at this point to the Son of man (7.56), all the imagery of Daniel's
'heaven' with its thrones will also come to a reader's mind, for heaven
is as much Daniel's as Luke's focus of the Son of man theme (see Dan.
7.9-10, 13-14).

Given Luke's programmatic commitment to Jesus' reception of
David's throne (Lk. 1.32), his references to the cloud in Acts 1.9, to
Jesus' passage to heaven (1.10), to Stephen's seeing God's δόξα
('glory') (7.55) and to his clear identification of Jesus with the Son
of man (7.56), it is not difficult to deduce that Theophilus would
most naturally 'hear' Luke's report of Stephen's vision as that of the
enthronement of the Son of man,[57] not, of course, on God's throne, but
on David's.[58]

How might such a 'hearing' come about? In Stephen's peroration and
vision Luke has melded three distinct christological terms,

First, perhaps the most obvious is 'Son of man' (7.56), on Jesus' lips
his distinctive way of speaking of his humiliation and suffering, but

55. In spite of the witness of P74, the logic of the argument suggested above
tends to confirm the υἱὸς ἀνθρώπου in the text of N–A[27]; but see Kilpatrick, 'Acts
vii. 56: Son of Man?', *TZ* 21 (1965), p. 14 (209) and 'Again Acts vii. 56: Son of
Man?', *TZ* 34 (1978), p. 232.

56. These verses preserve a Christology which underlies Luke's attitude to
David and to Solomon.

57. See Wright, *Jesus and the Victory of God*—'Sharing the throne of God'
(pp. 624-29) Cf. Lk. 21.28 with its echo of the vindication element in the humilia-
tion/vindication models. This verse concludes a long 'eschatological' passage
which begins with Luke's reference to the Temple's impending destruction (Lk.
21.5-6) and moves immediately to the question of who is χριστόν (Lk. 21.8); cf.
Acts 3.19-21 for an extension of this Christology leading to the Stephen-unit.

58. For the literally-minded: *thrones were set* (Dan. 7.9; cf. Lk. 22.23-30).

here brought to its glorious conclusion envisioned in Daniel; the humiliated Son of man has come into his kingdom.

Second, if this study's reading of Acts 7.46-56 is valid, then Stephen's argument is that although Solomon failed the christological conditional, God's promise to David of an everlasting kingdom has been fulfilled in the exaltation of Jesus (7.55), the one whose resurrection ensured that he would not see corruption, the one who at the Lord's right hand, was truly Lord and Christ.

Third, in his suffering and dying, the Lord was recognized as ὄντως ('genuinely, really') δίκαιος ('righteous one' [as in Wisdom 1–5]) (Lk. 23.47); Stephen accused his accusers of betraying and murdering the δίκαιος (Acts 7.52); at Wis. 5.1 the vindicated δίκαιος, like Jesus, stands in God's assize.[59] Although the word does not figure in Stephen's speech, the notion of Χριστός runs through Luke's scriptural substructure, emphasizing Solomon's failure and God's unfailing promise to David. According to Isaiah's oracles, the way to be Χριστός was to be truly δίκαιος, which, in Daniel, was to walk the suffering path of the Son of man. This is why the crucified Jesus can be properly spoken of as Χριστός (Acts 3.20).

'Heaven is my throne ... ' thus evoked a substructure which ended in both an opened heaven and Stephen's seeing the glory of God, and the 'Lord Jesus,' Son of man, enthroned as Χριστός.

Glory. A second verbal link is Luke's δόξα (Acts 7.55; cf. Isa. 66.5b): 'Your own people who hate you and reject you for my name's sake have said, "Let the LORD be glorified, so that we may see your joy ... " ' At this point the LXX of Isaiah is not easy to grasp,[60] but it probably suggests the quaker's opponents taunting him in ways very like the practical atheism of Wisdom's 'ungodly' (Wis. 1.16–2.22). Their taunt seems to demand evidence that the quaker's trust in God can be verified, perhaps by a sight of the *shekinah*; there just may be an echo here from 2 Chron. 7.1–3, with its implied validation of Solomon, but it is not to be strained after.

Like 'heaven', δόξα is a Lukan theme: he shared with Mark and Matthew two *logia* concerning the Son of man's ultimate δόξα (Lk.

59. See Doble, *The Paradox of Salvation*, pp. 142-45.

60. The confusion probably initially emerges from a misunderstanding of the MT's particle which can be either 'for the sake of' or 'in order that'; but that does not adequately explain the degree of opaqueness in LXX.

9.26; 21.27). Extending this understanding of suffering issuing in 'glory,' Luke shaped his transfiguration narrative by having Moses and Elijah present, οἳ ὀφθέντες ἐν δόξῃ ἔλεγον τὴν ἔξοδον αὐτοῦ ἣν ἤμελλεν πληροῦν ἐν Ἰερουσαλήμ ('...who appeared in glory and were speaking of his exodus, which he was about to fulfill in Jerusalem') (9.31), where ἔξοδον should be allowed both its senses, exodus and death; note also that Peter and those with him ...εἶδον τὴν δόξαν αὐτοῦ καὶ τοὺς δύο ἄνδρας τοὺς συνεστῶτας αὐτῷ ('...they saw his glory and the two men who stood with him') (9.32), anticipating Stephen's vision of the exalted Lord. On the Emmaus road, Luke's risen Christ took up the same theme: οὐχὶ ταῦτα ἔδει παθεῖν τὸν Χριστὸν καὶ εἰσελθεῖν εἰς τὴν δόξαν αὐτοῦ ('Was it not necessary that the messiah should suffer these things and enter into his glory') (Lk. 24.26), which is echoed in Paul's summary of his witness to Jesus (Acts 26.22). Consequently, Luke had already associated 'Son of man', 'Christ' and 'Jesus' with an ultimate δόξα. Moreover, δόξα links directly with Stephen's opening of Israel's story, Ὁ θεὸς τῆς δόξης ὤφθη τῷ πατρὶ ἡμῶν Ἀβραάμ ('The God of glory appeared to our father Abraham...') (Acts 7.2), and leads to its climax in 7.55.

Stephen's vision of the opened heaven and of God's δόξα is a direct answer both to the opponents' taunt in Isa. 66.5b, and, by implication, to Stephen's (and Jesus') opponents.

E. *Conclusion*

One good reason for Solomon's appearance at 7.47 is his focusing an intertextual substructure moving from Psalm 132 through Solomon's dedication prayer and vision, to Isaiah's reflection on 'Temple' and 'faithfulness'. Read 7.46-56 as a series of signals of this substructure and the nature of Stephen's response to his accusers becomes clearer: 'What kind of house will you build for me?' (Isa. 66.1, LXX). There is studied ambiguity in this Septuagintal question, for had not 'house' been used of both Temple and Davidic kingship?[61] God's question, 'Did not my hand do all these things?' will then refer more widely to the story of God's dealing with Israel and lead more naturally into Stephen's peroration.

---

61. So, e.g., Lk. 1.27, 33, 69; 2.4; cf. Acts 2.36, 7.46.

Stephen's speech began with a reference to God's appearing to Abraham (Acts 7.2; note τῆς δόξης) and ended with an appearing to Stephen—this time with Jesus at God's right hand. Between these theophanies lay one to Moses (Acts 7.30-31) and one, by allusion, to Solomon (2 Chron. 7.11-22)—who knew what kind of house he should build, but did not.

Stephen's accusers thus heard their charges answered: Jesus was not the Nazarene, but God's Χριστός; what really mattered was that with the Temple went Israel's responsibility to keep *Torah*; what Jesus had said of the Temple was a continuation of God's warning to Solomon. So the first major section of Acts concludes with a theophany and clearly-implied enthronement of Jesus, the Χριστός in David's line. As Acts 7.46 had itself strongly implied by its psalm's closing verses:

> [In Zion] I will cause a horn to sprout up for David;
> I have prepared a lamp for my Χριστός.
> *His enemies I will clothe with disgrace,*
> *but on him, his crown will gleam* (Ps. 132.17-18).

APPENDIX

Wisdom's Infancy Narrative	*Luke's Infancy Narrative*
1	
I was nursed with care in swaddling cloths. (Wis. 7.4)	καὶ τοῦτο ὑμῖν τὸ σημεῖον, εὑρήσετε βρέφος ἐσπαργανωμένον καὶ κείμενον ἐν φάτνῃ. (Lk. 2.12; cf. 2.7, 16)
2	
Therefore I prayed, and understanding was given me; I called on God, and the spirit of wisdom came to me. (Wis. 7.7)	τὸ δὲ παιδίον ηὔξανεν καὶ ἐκραται-οῦτο πληρούμενον σοφίᾳ, καὶ χάρις θεοῦ ἦν ἐπ᾿ αὐτό. (Lk. 2.40)
For wisdom, the fashioner of all things, taught me. There is in her a spirit that is intelligent, holy, unique, manifold, subtle, mobile, clear, unpolluted, distinct, invulnerable, loving the good, keen, irresistible (Wis. 7.22)	καὶ Ἰησοῦς προέκοπτεν ἐν τῇ σοφίᾳ καὶ ἡλικίᾳ καὶ χάριτι παρὰ θεῷ καὶ ἀνθρώποις. (Lk. 2.52)

Wisdom's Infancy Narrative	Luke's Infancy Narrative

3

Because of her I shall have glory among the multitudes and honor in the presence of the elders, though I am young.

I shall be found keen in judgment, and in the sight of rulers I shall be admired. (Wis. 8.10-11)

καὶ ἐγένετο μετὰ ἡμέρας τρεῖς εὗρον αὐτὸν ἐν τῷ ἱερῷ καθεζόμενον ἐν μέσῳ τῶν διδασκάλων καὶ ἀκούοντα αὐτῶν καὶ ἐπερωτῶντα αὐτούς· (Lk. 2.46)

ἐξίσταντο δὲ πάντες οἱ ἀκούοντες αὐτοῦ ἐπὶ τῇ συνέσει καὶ ταῖς ἀποκρίσεσιν αὐτοῦ. (Lk. 2.47)

4

As a child I was naturally gifted, and a good soul fell to my lot; (Wis. 8.19)

Cf. Lk. 2.40, 52

5

Then my works will be acceptable, and I shall judge your people justly, and shall be worthy of the throne of my father. (Wis. 9.12)

οὗτος ἔσται μέγας καὶ υἱὸς ὑψίστου κληθήσεται, καὶ δώσει αὐτῷ κύριος ὁ θεὸς τὸν θρόνον Δαυὶδ τοῦ πατρὸς αὐτοῦ, καὶ βασιλεύσει ἐπὶ τὸν οἶκον Ἰακὼβ εἰς τοὺς αἰῶνας, καὶ τῆς βασιλείας αὐτοῦ οὐκ ἔσται τέλος. (Lk. 1.32-33)

6

Who has learned your counsel, unless you have given wisdom and sent your holy spirit from on high? (Wis. 9.17)

καὶ ἀποκριθεὶς ὁ ἄγγελος εἶπεν αὐτῇ, πνεῦμα ἅγιον ἐπελεύσεται ἐπὶ σέ, καὶ δύναμις ὑψίστου ἐπισκιάσει σοι· διὸ καὶ τὸ γεννώμενον ἅγιον κληθήσεται, υἱὸς θεοῦ. (Lk. 1.35, Cf. 3.21-22; 4.18)

7

I also am mortal, like everyone else, a descendant of the first-formed child of earth; and in the womb of a mother I was molded into flesh ... (Wis. 7.1)

... τοῦ Ἐνὼς τοῦ Σὴθ τοῦ Αδὰμ τοῦ θεοῦ. (Lk. 3.38)

EPISTLES AND REVELATION

'FOR THIS HAGAR IS MOUNT SINAI IN ARABIA' (GALATIANS 4.25)

J.C. O'Neill

In warm tribute to Lionel North, a philologist who has patiently kept alive concentrated study of the use of the Old Testament in the New, I offer a study on a passage in Galatians which another philologist, Friedrich Nietzsche, called 'jenes unerhörte philologische Possenspiel um das alte Testament' ('that unprecedented philological buffoonery concerning the Old Testament'), whereby the church supposedly withdrew the Old Testament from the Jews by asserting that it contained nothing but Christian doctrine.[1]

Before we come to Hagar, let us begin with the allegory of the two sons, Gal. 4.21-24a. The allegorist addresses 'those who wish to be under the law'. The allegorist asks his readers to hear the law itself. Can the allegorist be Paul? Can Paul be writing to the Gentile Christians in Galatia, who are being persuaded by missionaries hostile to him to accept circumcision in order to become proper Christians? Hardly.

If this were Paul writing to Gentile Christians in Galatia, he would be using *law* in two different senses: you, who wish to be under the ceremonial law that demands circumcision, should listen to the Law of Moses which recounts the story of Ishmael and Isaac. If the Galatians accepted this argument, they would resolve not to be circumcised because of the authority of a story in the Law of Moses. They might well ask, Why should we continue to accept the authority of the Law of Moses, which, you argue, should persuade us to desire no longer to be under the Law of Moses?

---

1. *Morgenröte*, I.84, *Werke* I (ed. Karl Schlechta; Munich: C. Hanser, 1954), pp. 1067-68; *Kritische Gesamtausgabe* V/1 (ed. Giorgio Colli; Mazzino Montinari; Berlin: W. de Gruyter, 1971), p. 75; cited in full by H.J. Schoeps, *Paul: The Theology of the Apostle in the Light of Jewish Religious History* (English trans; London: Lutterworth, 1961), p. 235; referred to by Hans Dieter Betz, *Galatians: A Commentary on Paul's Letter to the Churches in Galatia* (Hermeneia; Philadelphia: Fortress Press, 1979), p. 244.

The most natural way to take the rhetorical question at the start of Gal. 4.21 is as directed to those who both always did want to live properly under the law and wished to continue to live under the law. The allegorist is assuming that his hearers claim to be genuine adherents of the law. His allegory is designed to deepen their understanding of the true meaning of the law. The word *law* means the same in both instances.

The allegory cannot have been chosen in order to meet the issue of whether or not Gentile Christians should be circumcised, since both Ishmael and Isaac were circumcised, Ishmael on the same day as Abraham himself (Gen. 17.23-37; 21.4). The allegorist's audience can hardly be other than fellow Jews.[2]

What is the point of the allegory? There is a great contrast between Ishmael and Isaac, Ishmael being begotten κατὰ σάρκα, 'from the slave-woman', and Isaac being begotten δι' ἐπαγγελίας, 'from the free woman'. Timothy Lim has drawn attention to Philo's argument that Sarah, like Leah, Rebecca and Zipporah, conceived directly from God.[3] In *Cher.* 43-47 Philo refers to Gen. 21.1, 'And the Lord visited Sarah as he had said and the Lord did unto Sarah as he had spoken.' The verb in the LXX is ἐπεσκέψατο, (meaning 'visited', but the verb could mean 'behind') and Philo interprets this by noting that Moses introduces Sarah as conceiving ὅτε ὁ θεὸς αὐτὴν μονωθεῖσαν ἐπισκοπεῖ, 'when God beheld her by herself'. The note that sounds again and again in Gen. 21.1-2 is 'as the Lord said', 'as he had spoken', 'at the set time of which God had spoken to him', referring back to Gen. 17.15, 16, 19, 21 and Gen. 18.10-15. Isaac, and he alone, was conceived through the express promise of God. This promise was given when God commanded Abraham to circumcise all male children, and the promise was that Sarah would become nations, and that kings of peoples would be of her (Gen. 17.1-22).

---

2.   Gijs Bouman, 'Die Hagar- und Sara-Perikope (Gal 4, 21-31): Exemplarische Interpretation zum Schriftbeweis bei Paulus', *ANRW* II.25.4, pp. 3135-55, argued that Paul was facing incomers from Jerusalem who wanted the Galatians circumcised precisely because they were descended from Hagar. I find it difficult to imagine how the Galatians could have been connected with Arabs. Bouman relied heavily on the supposition that the unusual vocabulary and tortuous line of argument can be accounted for on the hypothesis that Paul was constrained to use the terminology of these supposed opponents. This is a desperate remedy.

3.   Timothy H. Lim, *Holy Scripture in the Qumran Commentaries and Pauline Letters* (Oxford: Clarendon Press, 1997), pp. 54-55.

Presumably, the audience addressed by the allegorist was in danger of forgetting the promise that in Abraham's seed all the nations of the earth would be blessed (Gen. 22.18; cf. Gen. 12.3; 18.18; 26.4). The audience, desiring to be under the law in the sense of being faithful to the law, was forgetting the promise that accompanied the birth of their father Isaac; they were behaving like descendants of Ishmael.

The allegorist pushes home the point by drawing attention to the two mothers. They represent two covenants. The convenant concerning Hagar and Ishmael is presumably God's promise that the son of the bondwoman would be made a great nation (Gen. 21.13, 18). Hagar bears a son destined for servitude. In so bearing Ishmael, Hagar is said to be ἀπὸ ὄρους Σινᾶ (literally 'from Mt Sinai') (Gal. 4.24). All the commentators I have consulted assume that somehow Hagar's giving birth is equivalent to the giving of the Law at Mt Sinai.

But how has Mt Sinai got into the allegory? If anyone should still think that we are reading the words of Paul to Gentile Christians, Mt Sinai can scarcely be the issue, for the covenant at Mt Sinai concerned the moral law and the ceremonial law of the sabbath, not circumcision.[4] Did Paul want the Gentile Christians to stop keeping the moral law? Is the Sabbath the great issue? (Gal. 4.10, *days*, is hardly proof that Paul was facing trouble over the sabbath.) If he did want to attack the law, why did he come to Sinai by way of Hagar?

Let us look closely at Gal. 4.24. The αὗται are, of course, the two women. Lightfoot, Lipsius, and Hans Dieter Betz then take the μία to refer to one of the covenants, not to one of the women. They assume that a verb is to be supplied; Lightfoot suggests 'given': 'one of them, which was given from Mount Sinai, bearing children unto bondage'.[5]

In so doing, these commentators are following a line that had already been followed subconsciously by the scribes, who omitted the article before δύο διαθῆκαι. The article is read by ℵ* Ψ 491 623 Origen[2:1] Chrysostom Cyprian. With the article, the two covenants become the subject of the sentence, αὗται becomes the complement, and the re-

---

4. At Sinai, circumcision seems only to be referred to allegorically, meaning circumcision of the heart, Deut. 10.16; 30.6.

5. J.B. Lightfoot, *Saint Paul's Epistle to the Galatians: A Revised Text with Introduction, Notes and Dissertations* (London: Macmillan, 7th edn, 1881), p. 180 on Gal. 4.24; R.A. Lipsius, *Briefe an die Galater, Römer, Philipper* (HKNT; Freiburg: J.C.B. Mohr [Paul Siebeck], 2nd edn, 1892), pp. 53-54; Betz, *Galatians*, p. 244.

sumptive μία relates to the women, not to the covenants.

That this is right is confirmed by the participle dependent on μία, γεννῶσα: the woman gives birth, not the covenant. This is all allegory, and every step in the allegory must start with the women and their sons.

But what are we to make of the strange clause ἀπὸ ὄρους Σινᾶ... γεννῶσα (literally, 'born from Mt Sinai')? What does ἀπό mean? The preposition cannot go with the participle γεννῶσα in the sense that Hagar brought forth a son in some way dependent on Mt Sinai. The preposition ἀπό must bear a sense akin to its sense when motion is in view, the sense of 'away from' or even 'far from'. In Gen. 23.4, 8 Abraham's burying of Sarah ἀπ᾽ ἐμοῦ renders the Hebrew מלפני, 'out of my sight'. The prophet Hosea condemned the idolatrous people by saying that 'they have gone a whoring from under their God', ויזנו מתחת אלהיהם, which the LXX translates ἐξεπόρνευσαν ἀπὸ τοῦ θεοῦ αὐτῶν (Hos. 4.12). They have removed themselves from obedience to their God; they committed fornication far from their God. Genesis 21.21 tells us that Ishmael was born in Paran, and Paran, according to Num. 10.12 (cf. 12.16) was one stage or more from Sinai. The allegorist takes the physical distance of Paran from Sinai—out of sight of Sinai—as a spiritual fact. Ishmael was born far from the marvellous mountain where God gave his people the law. So Ishmael was destined to be a slave whereas Isaac (the one who was promised by God as the origin of a seed as numerous as the stars in the sky, by whom all nations would be blessed) would be free.

Hagar bears unto slavery because she bears out of sight of Sinai. Paradoxically, obedience to the law given at Sinai spells freedom. *m. Ab.* 6.2:

> And it is written, And the tables were the work of God, and the writing was the writing of God graven [חָרוּת, a hapax legomenon of uncertain meaning] upon the tables (Ex 32.16). Read not חָרוּת but חֵרוּת [freedom], for thou findest no freeman excepting him that occupies himself in the study of the Law.[6]

The same point is made in a rabbinic tradition, playing on the account of Ishmael's sporting with Isaac (Gen. 21.9). This tradition takes it that Ishmael *mocked* Isaac. Of what did the mocking consist? Ishmael mocked Isaac by boasting that he had been circumcised when he was

---

6. Herbert Danby, *The Mishnah* (Oxford: Clarendon Press, 1933), p. 459. Cf. *'Erub.* 54a.

thirteen years old and so could choose (Gen. 17.25), whereas Isaac was only circumcised on the eighth day (Gen. 21.4). Isaac replied that he was ready to do something far greater than accept circumcision at the age of thirteen. 'Were the Holy One, blessed be He, to say unto me: "Sacrifice yourself before me" I would obey.' The tradition concludes: 'Straightway, "God did tempt Abraham (Gen. 22.1)" ' (*b. Sanh.* 89b).[7] The account of Ishmael's mocking Isaac, which led to the expulsion of Hagar and Ishmael, comes immediately before Isaac's willing submission to being sacrificed on Mt Moriah, Genesis 22. Obedience, willingness to give up one's life, means freedom.

If this reading of Gal. 4.24 holds good, the straight identification of Hagar with Mt Sinai in Arabia in the next verse, Gal. 4.25, cannot be right. In fact neither P[46] nor the important witnesses א C F G Supplement to 1241 (from St Catherine's monastery at Mt Sinai) 1739 and Epiphanius read *Hagar*. The usual explanation, that Hagar dropped out accidentally because of the γάρ, does not convince. As Ian Moir pointed out, P[46] reads δέ for γάρ, and P[46] also lacks Hagar.[8] Since Hagar can no longer be identified with Mt Sinai in Arabia, we should accept the readings of Gal. 4.25a which do not have Ἁγάρ.

However, a massive problem still remains: Why should the allegorist, who assumes a close and detailed knowledge of Scripture, make the banal observation that Sinai is a mountain in Arabia?

In order to make a start on the interpretation of Gal. 4.25-27 we need to see that there is no connection of argument between Gal. 4.25-27 and Gal. 4.21-24 (see Table). Of course there is a congruence of belief, but no author is responsible for the transition from Gal. 4.21-24 to Gal. 4.25-27. The on-the-surface banal statement that Sinai is a mountain in Arabia is the start of a new argument.

The mention of Sinai in the scriptural argument preserved for us in Gal. 4.21-24 reminded the collector of the traditions of another scriptural argument concerning Sinai and Hagar. An author would have developed the first argument with some praise of Sarah, and Marcion's Galatians, according to Tertullian, contains such a praise of Sarah (Tertullian, *adv. Marcionem* 5.4.8). Yet even Marcion's Galatians is not

---

7. Cited by Richard N. Longenecker, *Galatians* (WBC, 41; Dallas, TX: Word Books, 1990), p. 202. Cf. *Targ. Ps.-Jon.* Gen 22.1, cited by Longenecker on p. 203.

8. Ian Moir, Review of *A Textual Commentary on the Greek New Testament* by Bruce M. Metzger (1971), *Bible Translator* 24 (1973), pp. 329-33 at p. 332: 'Gal 4:25. More needs to be said here. P[46] & c. had no γάρ and still got rid of Hagar!'.

the development of Gal. 4.21-24 by an author; the praise of Sarah in Marcion's Galatians is also an independent tradition. The very banality of the assertion that Sinai is a mountain in Arabia alerts us to the likelihood that we are reading the start of a new allegorical reading of the law. Arabia, I think, stands for the desert, and the desert is contrasted with the city. Isaiah 54.1 is to be cited in Gal. 4.27, and this verse in Isaiah contrasts the woman who has a husband with the woman who is, literally, a desert:

> ὅτι πολλὰ τὰ τέκνα τῆς ἐρήμου
> μᾶλλον ἢ τῆς ἐχούσης τὸν ἄνδρα (Gal. 4.27).

> for more numerous are the children of the desert
> than of the woman who has a husband (Gal. 4.27).

The city in the context of Gal. 4.25 is the present city of Jerusalem. What the present city of Jerusalem should be was revealed to Moses on Mt Sinai (Exod. 25.9, 40; 26.30; Num. 8.4; 1 Chron. 28.19; Acts 7.44; Heb. 8.5). In *2 Bar.* 4.2-6 the heavenly Jerusalem is contrasted with 'this building that is in your midst now', and the heavenly Jerusalem is said to have been revealed to Adam before he sinned, to Abraham on the night the torch passed between the portions of the victims, as well as to Moses.

Mount Sinai is explicitly linked with the heavenly Jerusalem in the tradition preserved in Hebrews 12. Moses at Mt Sinai and the people waiting at the foot of Sinai to be sure are contrasted with the readers of Hebrews 12:

> For ye are not come unto the mount that might [not] be touched, and that burned with fire, nor unto blackness, and darkness, and tempest, and the sound of a trumpet, and the voice of words; which voice they that heard intreated that the word should not be spoken to them any more...and so terrible was the sight, that Moses said, I exceedingly fear and quake (Heb. 12.18-21).[9]

The contrast, however, is not between an earthly Sinai and a heavenly Jerusalem to be taken as some Platonic form. Rather, it is a contrast between the proper fear and awe that accompanied the giving of the law in Exod. 19.1–24.8 and the extraordinarily privileged closer access to God and the vision granted to Moses and Aaron, Nabad and Abihu and 70 of the elders of Israel. They saw the God of Israel on Mt Sinai, 'and there was under his feet as it were a paved work of a sapphire stone...

---

9. Conjecturing μὴ ψηλαφωμένῳ with O. Holtzmann.

They saw God and did eat and drink' (Exod. 24.9-11). The recipients of the tradition preserved to us in Gal. 4.25-27 lived in Arabia, and Arabia means The Desert. Mount Sinai is in Arabia and by their obedience to the law they are given the highest vision, the vision of the heavenly Jerusalem.

> But ye are come...unto the city of the living God, the heavenly Jerusalem, and to an innumerable company of angels, to the general assembly and church of the firstborn, which are written in heaven, and to God the Judge of all, and to the spirits of just men made perfect, and to Jesus the mediator of the new covenant, and to the blood of sprinkling, that speaketh better things than that of Abel (Heb. 12.22-24).[10]

The present Jerusalem ought to have been patterned after the heavenly Jerusalem, but here in Gal. 4.25 it plainly is not. We are reminded of the description in documents found at Qumran of Jerusalem as 'a fortress of wickedness'; they 'shed blood like water upon the ramparts of the daughter of Zion' (4QTestim [= 4Q175] 1.29-30). 'For Zion, the mother of us all, is in deep grief and great affliction' (*4 Ezra* 10.7).

The usual printed texts of Gal. 4.25 identify Hagar, first with Mt Sinai and then with the present Jerusalem. I have given reasons for rejecting the identification of Hagar with Mt Sinai, for in the tradition they are opposites. I have suggested that we accept the text that does not read Ἁγάρ in Gal. 4.25a. However, we do need the word Ἁγάρ to make the connection in Gal. 4.25b between Hagar and the present Jerusalem. I suggest that the word γάρ after δουλεύει may be a corruption of Ἁγάρ; I conjecture that Ἁγάρ should be restored at that place. The verb συστοιχεῖ in Gal. 4.25b is left without a subject by my acceptance of the shorter text in Gal. 4.25a; its subject can hardly be Σινᾶ. I suggest there is much to be said for regarding the MS D* as providing the true text of the second line of my text of Gal. 4.25: συστοιχοῦσα τῇ νῦν Ἰερουσαλήμ: 'having joined ranks with the present Jerusalem, Hagar continues a slave with her children'. Hagar and her children have allied themselves with the present Jerusalem, and so the present Jerusalem becomes a slave like them—perhaps a reference to Herod the Great of Idumaea, who could have been a native of Ascalon in Philistia.[11]

10. Omitting by conjecture Σιὼν ὄρει καὶ as a Marcionite gloss designed to introduce a contrast between Sinai and the heavenly city.

11. See Emil Schürer, *The History of the Jewish People in the Age of Jesus Christ (175 B.C.–A.D. 135)*, I (rev. and ed. Geza Vermes and Fergus Millar; Edinburgh: T. & T. Clark, 1973), p. 234 n. 3.

The heavenly Jerusalem is, of course, free, and she is the mother of these true children of Isaac. Because the present Jerusalem is allied with the descendants of Ishmael, she shares their essential slave nature. Those who preserve the vision of the Jerusalem above that was revealed on Mt Sinai are forced to move back into the desert, into Arabia where Mt Sinai is.

They do not lose hope, for the words of prophecy in Isa. 54.1 apply to them: the children of the desert will be more numerous than the children of the city. The celibate communities of the desert will rejoice to see their numbers grow, and they will share in the eventual victory when the heavenly Jerusalem will come down and recover the earthly Jerusalem.

I suggest that Gal. 4.28-30 and Gal. 4.31–5.1 are two separate oracles working on the same theme. Each begins with the vocative ἀδελφοί, but 4.28-30 is in the second person and 4.31–5.1 is in the first person. What possible reason would an author have had for changing from second person to first person? A collector is at work, not an author. Galatians 4.28-30 reminds the brothers that, although they are children of promise, they must face persecution. They are to prepare to expel the oppressive children of Ishmael. There is no way that this little oracle can be made to fit the circumstances of Paul's letter to the Galatians. Paul has prided himself on keeping the terms of the agreement reached between him and the pillars in Jerusalem, and he can hardly now turn round and identify them or the trouble-makers in Galatia with Ishmael.

The final oracle in Gal. 4.31–5.1 provides a number of teasing textual problems. I have tentatively constructed a text in which every word that is found in different positions in the manuscripts, or in none, is omitted. The 'yoke of slavery again' seems to refer to Egypt: the children of the free woman Sarah, although enslaved for 450 years in Egypt, should not spiritually return to slavery now, as though they were children of Hagar. Christ has indeed freed them.

The four oracles show no signs of having been written by Paul in order to deal with the crisis in Galatia. That crisis arose because some were pressing the Gentile Galatians, who had come to believe that Jesus was the Messiah and saviour of the world, to become Jews by circumcision. I can see no way that four allegorical treatments of Ishmael and Isaac could have been employed by Paul in this case, since both Ishmael and Isaac were circumcised.

Galatians 4.21-24 is a call to Israel to return to full obedience to the law, not to behave like descendants of Ishmael whose mother Hagar gave birth far away from Sinai. Hagar's children are born to slavery. In obedience to the law lies freedom. Isaac is the type of freedom, as shown by his willingness to offer himself a sacrifice to God.

Galatians 4.25-27 was written from within a monastic community that withdrew to the desert because the earthly Jerusalem had been corrupted by spiritual Ishmaelites who were the slaves of evil. The prophet Isaiah foretold the eventual victory of the free community over the sons of Belial.

Galatians 4.28-30 takes Ishmael's mockery of Isaac as a type of the persecution endured by the true Israelites, spiritual descendants (as well as physical descendants) of Isaac. God in Scripture addresses Sarah's words to Abraham (Gen. 21.10) to the community. They must prepare themselves for battle against the sons of darkness.

Galatians 4.31-5.1 reminds the community that the rock that accompanied the desert generation was Christ. Christ had freed them and they must not return to the fleshpots of Egypt.

The native soil in which these traditions were nourished was probably the order of Essenes whose communities (both lay and monastic) flourished from the early second century BCE to the fall of Jerusalem.[12]

The traditions were loaded into Paul's epistle to the Galatians because they emphasized themes dear to him, the theme of God's promise to Abraham which Abraham believed, and 'it was counted to him for righteousness', and the theme of freedom.

Unfortunately the anti-Jewish temper of many of the scribes who copied Galatians in the first three centuries made it all too easy to connect Hagar and Sinai. The connection made Gal. 4.21–5.1 one of the classic places for the entirely unhistorical conclusion that 'The Law and the Gospel cannot co-exist; the Law must disappear before the Gospel… The Apostle thus confidently sounds the death-knell of Judaism…'[13] Paul's argument was that Jews who believed Jesus was Messiah should continue as Jews, while Gentiles who also believed this should remain

---

12. Abraham was important for the Qumran community (Genesis Apocryphon; CD 3.2-4; 12.11; 16.6; 4Q378 22 1.4; 4Q379 17 1.4; 5Q22 1 1.5) Perhaps 1QH 9.34-36 (17.34-36) is a reference to the binding of Isaac. The frequent conjunction of *faith* and *righteousness* in 1QSb 5.25-26; 1QM 13.3; 1QH 16.7 (8.15); 17.13-15 (4.13-15) and 1QpHab 8.1-3 may well reflect the tradition that *Abraham believed God and it was counted to him as righteousness* (Gen. 15.6; Hab. 2.4; cf. Rom. 4.3; Gal. 3.6; Jas 2.23).

13. Lightfoot, *Galatians*, p. 184 on Gal. 4.30.

Gentiles.[14] The Bible the Gentiles should use would continue to be the Law and the Prophets and the Writings: this they could inherit as Gentiles. Their salvation, alongside that of Israel, was promised in its pages.

Galatians 4.21–5.1

4.21 Λέγετέ μοι, οἱ ὑπὸ νόμον θέλοντες εἶναι,
τὸν νόμον οὐκ ἀκούετε;
22 γέγραπται γὰρ ὅτι Ἀβραὰμ δύο υἱοὺς ἔσχεν,
ἕνα ἐκ τῆς παιδίσκης
καὶ ἕνα ἐκ τῆς ἐλευθέρας.
23 ἀλλ᾽ ὁ μὲν ἐκ τῆς παιδίσκης κατὰ σάρκα γεγέννηται,
ὁ δὲ ἐκ τῆς ἐλευθέρας δι᾽ ἐπαγγελίας.
24 ἅτινά ἐστιν ἀλληγορούμενα.
αὗται γάρ εἰσιν αἱ δύο διαθῆκαι,   [add αι: ℵ* Ψ 491 623 Or²·¹
μία μὲν ἀπὸ ὄρους Σινᾶ   Chrys Cypr]
εἰς δουλείαν γεννῶσα,
ἥτις ἐστὶν Ἀγάρ.

25 τὸ δὲ Σινᾶ ὄρος ἐστὶν ἐν τῇ Ἀραβίᾳ.   [𝔓⁴⁶ cf. το γαρ Σινα ℵ C
συστοιχοῦσα τῇ νῦν Ἰερουσαλήμ   F G 1241ˢ 1739 Epiph]
δουλεύει Ἀγὰρ μετὰ τῶν τέκνων αὐτῆς.   [cf. Αγαρ for γαρ]
26 ἡ δὲ ἄνω Ἰερουσαλὴμ ἐλευθέρα ἐστίν,
ἥτις ἐστὶν μήτηρ ἡμῶν.
27 γέγραπται γάρ, Εὐφράνθητι, στεῖρα ἡ οὐ τίκτουσα,
ῥῆξον καὶ βόησον, ἡ οὐκ ὠδίνουσα·
ὅτι πολλὰ τὰ τέκνα τῆς ἐρήμου
μᾶλλον ἢ τῆς ἐχούσης τὸν ἄνδρα.

28 ὑμεῖς δέ, ἀδελφοί, κατὰ Ἰσαὰκ ἐπαγγελίας τέκνα ἐστέ.
29 ἀλλ᾽ ὥσπερ τότε ὁ κατὰ σάρκα γεννηθεὶς ἐδίωκεν τὸν κατὰ πνεῦμα,
οὕτως καὶ νῦν.
30 ἀλλὰ τί λέγει ἡ γραφή;
Ἔκβαλε τὴν παιδίσκην καὶ τὸν υἱὸν αὐτῆς·
οὐ γὰρ μὴ κληρονομήσει ὁ υἱὸς τῆς παιδίσκης
μετὰ τοῦ υἱοῦ τῆς ἐλευθέρας.

4.31 διό, ἀδελφοί, οὐκ ἐσμὲν παιδίσκης τέκνα
ἀλλὰ τῆς ἐλευθέρας.
5.1 τῇ ἐλευθερίᾳ Χριστὸς ἠλευθέρωσε.
στήκετε, καὶ μὴ πάλιν ζυγῷ δουλείας ἐνέχεσθε.

14. J.C. O'Neill, 'Paul's Missionary Strategy', *Irish Biblical Studies* 19 (1997), pp. 174-90.

ADAM *REDIVIVUS*: PHILIPPIANS 2 ONCE MORE

Morna D. Hooker

This paper is an attempt to respond to the article by Markus Bockmuehl published in the *Journal of Theological Studies* a few years ago on the meaning of the phrase ἐν μορφῇ θεοῦ.[1] That article had two main conclusions, the first of which was that there was 'insufficient evidence to establish an *explicit* link, or even a deliberate allusion, to Adam'.[2] The Adamic interpretation was accordingly described as being an 'interpretative cul-de-sac'.[3] The other, more positive, conclusion, was that the meaning of the word μορφή was 'visible form', and that the background of Paul's usage here was to be found in Jewish mystical tradition. With the second of these conclusions I have no quarrel. The evidence, though somewhat scanty, does indeed suggest that μορφή had this visual meaning, though whether or not this came to Paul via the mystical tradition I am not so sure. What I want to challenge is Bockmuehl's first conclusion, that the belief that the passage should be read in the light of the story of Adam is an 'interpretative cul-de-sac'.

Those of us who have argued for Adamic influence have found links with Adam not only in the phrase 'in the form of God' in v. 6, which *may* be reminiscent of Gen. 1.26, but in the implicit contrast between Adam, who grasped at equality with God, and Christ, who did not grasp at/cling to/exploit that equality.[4] Whereas Adam was stripped of his privileges, Christ deliberately emptied himself, becoming what Adam had become—a slave, subject to death. In favour of this interpretation

---

1. M. Bockmuehl, ' "The Form of God" (Phil. 2:6): Variations on a Theme of Jewish Mysticism', *JTS* NS 48 (1997), pp. 1-23.
2. M. Bockmuehl, ' "The Form of God" ', p. 11.
3. M. Bockmuehl, ' "The Form of God" ', p. 6.
4. My own interpretation ('Philippians 2:6-11') was published in E.E. Ellis and E. Grasser (eds.), *Jesus und Paulus: Festschrift für W.G. Kümmel* (Göttingen: Vandenhoeck & Ruprecht, 1975), pp. 151-64, and reprinted in M.D. Hooker, *From Adam to Christ* (Cambridge: Cambridge University Press, 1990), pp. 88-100.

we may point to Paul's use of Adam elsewhere (most clearly in Rom. 5.12-21 and 1 Cor. 15.21-22, 42-50), and to the language Paul uses at the end of Philippians 3 (where the implications of the 'hymn' for Christians are set out), language which echoes that which he uses elsewhere to describe the restoration of men and women to the glory which Adam lost (Rom. 8.18-30, 39; 1 Cor. 15.35-57; cf. 2 Cor. 3.12-4.6).

Bockmuehl begins by dismissing the traditional assumption that the phrase ἐν μορφῇ θεοῦ is the equivalent of κατ᾽ εἰκόνα θεοῦ, the LXX translation of בצלם אלהים in Gen. 1.26-27. He refers to an article by D. Steenburg, who argued that εἰκών and μορφή were not synonyms.[5] Although it is at least worthy of note that some of the Fathers believed εἰκών and μορφή to be synonyms,[6] I have to agree that Steenburg's case is a persuasive one: we cannot simply pretend that ἐν μορφῇ θεοῦ and κατ᾽ εἰκόνα θεοῦ are the same thing. However, I find myself uneasy with the analogy that Bockmuehl then employs to illustrate this conclusion. With εἰκών, μορφή and δόξα he compares 'corn flakes, toast, and orange juice', which may all, he says, 'be discrete aspects of the same breakfast'.[7] So they may, but I do not think they are related in quite the same way as are εἰκών, μορφή and δόξα. Corn flakes, toast and orange juice are separate items on the menu, very different in origin, character and taste; their only connection is that they may follow one another at the same meal. The fact that εἰκών, μορφή and δόξα are not synonyms does not mean that they do not belong together; it is possible that they overlap in a way that corn flakes, toast and orange juice do not. Bockmuehl's own discussion shows that this is in fact so.

The Problem

The question of whether the figure of Adam is in view in Philippians 2 is linked with the debate as to whether or not in describing Christ as 'in the form of God' Paul is thinking of him as pre-existent, though the two issues should not be confused. Some of those who have supported the Adamic interpretation have tried to exclude the idea of pre-existence from Philippians 2, and have argued that it is the actions of the *human*

5. D. Steenburg, 'The Case Against the Synonymity of *Morphê* and *Eikôn*', *JSNT* 34 (1988), pp. 77-86.

6. E.g. Ambrosiaster, in his Commentary on Phil. 2.6; see *PL* 17, col. 407 254C.

7. ' "The Form of God" ', p. 8.

Jesus that are contrasted with those of Adam. Since the man Adam was created in the image of God, the phrase 'in the form of God' must, they suggest, refer to the earthly Jesus. One of the strongest advocates of this interpretation has been James Dunn,[8] though he seems to have modified his views in his recent book on Paul's theology.[9] It is, however, difficult to make sense of what Paul says in v. 7 without acknowledging that it was the *pre-existent* Christ who became man: so difficult, I suggest, as to be impossible.

The attraction of the theory that Paul is thinking of the human Jesus is, of course, that it allows for a real comparison and contrast between Adam and Christ. If, however, we maintain that it was the pre-existent Christ who was 'in the form of God', then Adam and Christ are no longer in alignment. The problem that now confronts us is this: How can we have a figure who is described in Adamic terms who then *becomes* man, and takes on Adam's likeness? Bockmuehl dismisses the notion of what he terms 'an eternally pre-existent *human* Jesus'.[10] But is this in fact the necessary alternative to the view that eliminates pre-existence in favour of an earthly Jesus? Is it possible, in other words, to combine the ideas of pre-existence and the comparison with Adam *without* thinking of the *human* Jesus as 'eternally pre-existent'?

Incarnation

Now the idea that Christ became man is found elsewhere in Paul, and it is perhaps wise to begin looking for an answer to this conundrum there. Particularly interesting is Rom. 8.3, since what we have there is in many ways similar to Phil. 2.6-7: ὁ θεὸς τὸν ἑαυτοῦ υἱὸν πέμψας ἐν ὁμοιώματι σαρκὸς ἁμαρτίας... Instead of Philippians' ἐν ὁμοιώματι ἀνθρώπων we have ἐν ὁμοιώματι σαρκὸς ἁμαρτίας. The verse comes towards the climax of Paul's extended argument about the redemption of mankind in Christ, who has by his obedience reversed what Adam did when he brought sin and death into the world. In the rest of the chapter we read of the renewal of creation and the restoration of the glory lost by Adam. God, we are told, sent his Son in the likeness of

8. J.D.G. Dunn, *Christology in the Making* (London: SCM Press, 1980), pp. 113-21.

9. J.D.G. Dunn, *The Theology of Paul the Apostle* (Grand Rapids: Eerdmans; Edinburgh: T. & T. Clark, 1998), pp. 281-88, 292-93.

10. Bockmuehl, ' "The Form of God" ', p. 10.

sinful flesh; the result is that men and women are delivered from slavery, and themselves become children (lit. 'sons') of God (Rom. 8.14-17), having been destined to be conformed (συμμόρφους) to the image (εἰκών) of his Son (8.29). Paul's expectation reflects the hope of future restoration found in later Judaism, which looks forward to a time when men and women will again be like God. Thus *Gen. R.* 21.7 interprets Gen. 3.22 of the world to come, when God will say 'Behold the man *has become* as one of us'.

The same idea is expressed in Galatians 4: ἐξαπέστειλεν ὁ θεὸς τὸν υἱὸν αὐτοῦ, γενόμενον ἐκ γυναικός, γενόμενον ὑπὸ νόμον. This time we find verbal echoes in the word γενόμενον (although it is used in a slightly different sense) in a context which implies that, in being born of a woman under the Law, Christ became a slave in order that those who were slaves might become sons. In both Romans 8 and Galatians 4, unlike Philippians 2, the initative is taken by God, who sends the one described as his Son. A parallel to Christ's *self*-emptying in Phil. 2.7 is found in 2 Cor. 8.9, where he is said to have become poor for the Corinthians' sake, with the result that they have been made rich. All three of these passages describe what we may term 'incarnation'.

Now Gal. 4.4-5. and 2 Cor. 8.9 are two of the so-called 'interchange' formulae, where the result of Christ becoming man is that men and women are made what he eternally is.[11] Romans 8.3 and Phil. 2.6-11, on the other hand, though also about what we would call 'incarnation', appear to tell us only about Christ becoming man—until, that is, we read a little further; when we do, we discover that here, too, believers are transformed and take on Christ's likeness. In Romans 8, as we have just seen, this is spelt out later in the chapter; in Philippians, it occurs at the end of ch. 3. I find it intriguing that the idea of Christ's incarnation is always linked with the destiny of believers. Whether 2 Cor. 5.21 and Gal. 3.13 should also be classified as incarnational formulae is open to debate, though my own belief is that it is a mistake to regard them as concerned solely with the death of Jesus; the notion of Christ becoming 'sin' in 2 Corinthians 5 is remarkably similar to Rom. 8.3, while that of Christ being made a curse in Galatians 3 is linked with the statement that he came under the Law in Gal. 4.4. What Christ was in his death is the logical outcome of what he became by his birth, as Phil. 2.6-11

---

11. See, in particular, 'Interchange in Christ', *JTS* NS 22 (1971), pp. 349-61, reprinted with other essays on the same theme in Hooker, *From Adam to Christ*.

reminds us. Certainly there is a link in both 2 Corinthians 5 and Galatians 3 with what believers become in Christ: the righteousness of 2 Cor. 5.21 and the blessing of Gal. 3.13 belong to those who are also 'in Christ', and therefore the children of God, sharing the glory and riches of Christ (cf. Rom. 8.14-21; Gal. 3.26–4.7; Phil. 3.8-9, 20-21).

Image

In Romans 8, this idea of becoming like Christ is expressed in terms of being conformed to the image of God: συμμόρφους τῆς ἐικόνος τοῦ υἱοῦ αὐτοῦ (v. 29). It is worth noting the close proximity of ἐικών with σύμμορφος and with δοξάζω in v. 30; even though εἰκών, μορφή and δόξα are not synonyms, they have *something* to do with each other, and their relationship is apparently closer than that of orange juice, cereal and toast. We find the same idea, expressed in the same language, in two other passages. In 2 Cor. 3.18, Christians see the glory of the Lord reflected in the face of Christ, and are transformed into the same image; this time we have εἰκών, **μετα**μορφόομαι and δόξα linked together. In 2 Cor. 4.4 we learn that Christ is himself 'the image of God'. Similar ideas are developed in Colossians, where Christ is described as 'the image of the invisible God' (Col. 1.15), while Christians are said to have taken off 'the old man' and to have put on the new, which is being renewed after the image of his creator (Col. 3.10; the 'sexist' language here is necessary if we are to grasp the point). The figure of Adam is surely lurking in the background in all these passages; first of all the language is 'Adamic', since Adam was created after the image of God, and was understood to have reflected the glory of God before the Fall; secondly, the context in each case points to Adam. Romans 8, as we have already noted, is the climax of an argument about Adam's fall and humanity's restoration in Christ, and the chapter ends with creation itself being set to rights. 2 Corinthians 4.6 is a quotation from Gen. 1.3, but already in ch. 3 the midrash on the story of Moses on Mt Sinai in Exodus 33 has reminded us of the glory lost by Adam which, according to rabbinic legend, was almost restored to Israel through Moses. Colossians 1.15-20 is about Christ's primacy in the universe, and 3.10 sets the idea of our renewal according to the image of the creator side by side with the metaphor of taking off the old man and putting on the new. Similar ideas are certainly present in 1 Corinthians 15, and may well lie behind the passage at the end of Philippians 3, for though the word εἰκών is not used there, we are told that the Lord Jesus Christ will transform our bodies of humiliation and conform them (σύμμορφος) to his own body of glory.

There is one other εἰκών passage which we ought to include, though it is something of a conundrum, and that is 1 Cor. 11.7. Here we are told that man (but not woman!) is the image and glory of God. The statement is backed up by references to Gen. 2.18 and 22, and is clearly based on Gen. 1.27, even though the phrase used there is **κατ' εἰκόνα θεοῦ**. The real problem with this passage is, of course, that Paul is attempting to use the biblical material to support a sexist hierarchy that conflicts with the view he expresses in Gal. 3.28 that male and female are equal in Christ. It seems that his social conditioning when dealing with a practical situation is in conflict with his theological insight in Galatians. I suggest that he has tied himself up in a muddle here because he has tried to combine what is said in Genesis 1 (where both male and female are created in the image of God) with a justification for social convention based on Genesis 2 (where the woman is subordinate to the man). By interpreting Genesis 1 in the light of Genesis 2, he is able to argue for an important *difference* between male and female, for although he does not in fact deny that woman is 'the image of God', his argument clearly depends on the denial that she is the *glory* of God.

What is intriguing about this statement in 1 Cor. 11.7, however, is the fact that Paul uses a phrase that we might expect him to use of Christ (εἰκὼν καὶ δόξα θεοῦ) of 'a man'. The assumptions that led him to do this are set out earlier in the chapter: if man is the glory of God, and woman is the glory of man, this is because the head of a woman is her husband, the head of a man is Christ, and the head of Christ is God. Yet we see at once that a stage in the 'hierarchy' is missing in v. 7: instead of God—Christ—man—woman (v. 3), we now have God—man—woman. What Paul *ought* to be saying in v. 7 is that it is the *head* of man (= Christ) who is the image and glory of God. Moreover, having said that *man* is the image and glory of God, he immediately has a problem in trying to draw a parallel with the relationship between man and woman, since now he is unable to say that woman is the image of man. Paul has approached the question with presuppositions of male superiority derived from Genesis 2, but these presuppositions do not fit with the idea expressed in Genesis 1, that both male and female were created in the image of God.

1 Corinthians 11 appears to be an aberration in Paul's usage, since elsewhere the phrase εἰκών θεοῦ refers to Christ. Moreover, like the passages which refer to Christ's incarnation, these other εἰκών passages are all linked with the destiny of believers (both men and women), who become *like* Christ.[12]

Adam

Let us turn now to two passages where the comparison between Adam and Christ, implicit in so many of these εἰκών passages, is made explicit. In Rom. 5.12-21, this comparison is the climax of the argument in the preceding chapters, and we are told that what happened in Christ was in many ways *not* the equivalent of what happened in Adam (vv. 15-17), both because the grace of God was at work in Christ, and because Christ's actions were the very reverse of Adam's—a point which is then underlined in the comparisons of vv. 18-19, which are in effect contrasts. The nature of God's overwhelming grace was spelt out in the opening verses of the chapter, where we were told that Christ died 'for us' (v. 8), that is 'for the ungodly' (v. 6), and that we have been reconciled to God through the death of his Son (v. 10), being 'justified' or 'rightwised' (δικαιωθέντες) by his blood (v. 9).

In 1 Cor. 15.21-22, Christ stands over against Adam as the one who brings life instead of death, and who is then identified as the Son who reigns until he hands everything over to his Father (vv. 24-28). Later in the chapter, Adam is described as the first man, who became a living soul (v. 45, quoting Gen. 2.7), whereas Christ is the last Adam, who is a life-giving Spirit. Verse 46 underlines the fact that the σῶμα ψυχικόν, ('the physical body') comes before the σῶμα πνευματικόν ('the spiritual body'). We are then told that the first man is from the dust, the second man from heaven, and just as men and women have borne the image of the first, so they will bear the image of the second (vv. 47-49). If 1 Cor. 15.47 describes Christ as 'the second man', that is surely because, *as man*, Adam preceded Christ; in terms of our own experience, also, we share in the physical body of Adam *before* we are transformed into the spiritual body of Christ. The fact that Paul found it necessary to emphasize this point is unlikely to be because he knew the

---

12. Even in 1 Cor. 11, Paul is appealing to what men and women were created to be—and perhaps also to what they *should* be in the Christian community; the angels referred to in v. 10 may be present to see that creation's purpose is fulfilled.

teaching of Philo and wished to contradict it; it is more likely that he stressed it because he knew that it would have been natural for the Corinthians to think of the heavenly man as *preceding* the earthly since, of course, his heavenly origin meant that he was pre-existent. Paul is concerned here with the way in which humanity bears the image first of the earthly, then of the heavenly (v. 49) and not the question as to whether Adam or Christ existed first.

Once again, then, we find the idea that we bear Christ's image, which is here directly contrasted with the image of Adam. The point of Paul's argument is the nature of the future resurrection, when Christians will share the glorious body of Christ. In both 1 Corinthians 15 and Romans 5, Paul is again concerned with the destiny of men and women, and as elsewhere, this is to be like Christ. Christ is understood to have reversed the effects of Adam's fall, and the reason that he is able to do so is that he is both Man and Son of God. The relationship between Adam and Christ is not that of two competitors in a task, the first of whom fails while the second succeeds. Rather, Christ has to *undo* the failure of Adam, *reverse* his disobedience, and bring life where Adam brought death. He is thus *greater* than Adam. Christ and Adam are never regarded by Paul as equals. Rather he sees Christ as the pattern of what Adam was meant to be, and the eschatological goal of what men and women are to become.

Son of God

We are not surprised, therefore, to find that both these passages about Adam are associated with language about the Son of God. In Romans 5, Paul uses this title immediately before the 'Adam' passage. The summary in vv. 8-9 of what God has done in 'rightwising' sinners through Christ's death, and what he may therefore be relied upon to do—namely save us from wrath—is repeated in vv. 10-11, this time in terms of our reconciliation to God through the death of his Son and the fact that we may therefore rely upon him to save us by his love. If the 'he's in that summary are ambiguous, that is because the agent of the passive verb σωθησόμεθα is ambiguous; this is hardly surprising, since the parallel reminds us that God and Christ are at one. I suspect that the title 'Son of God' is used here because it expresses both Christ's unity of purpose with his Father and his obedience to God's will. These, as we have already seen, are important themes in vv. 12-18.[13]

These, too, are ideas which belong to 1 Cor. 15.28, the verse which concludes the paragraph that begins, in vv. 21-22, with the comparison of Adam and Christ. The resurrection that comes through Christ will take place at his coming (v. 23), and this is followed by his reign, in fulfilment of Ps. 8.6, a passage which, significantly, refers to all things being put under *Man's* feet. What happens in Christ is the realization of God's purpose for humanity. But at the end Christ will hand over the kingdom to the Father, and the Son will himself be subject to God, as Ps. 8.5 suggests (vv. 24, 28).

'Son of God' language is also prominent in Romans 8, another passage we have already looked at; in fact, all the themes I have so far considered—incarnation, image and Adam—are to be found there. It is God's Son who is sent in the likeness of sinful flesh in v. 3—a way of reminding us that what Christ achieved was the work of God. It is to the image of God's Son that believers are conformed (v. 29)—a way of reminding us that in being conformed to Christ, we too become children of God and so like him (vv. 14, 19). Verse 32 repeats the theme of 5.8-11: if God did not spare his own Son, but gave him up for us, we may expect him to give us all things.

Romans 8 may well be a later development of ideas already spelt out in Gal. 4.1-7, where Paul again tells us that God sent his Son; the Greek verb is different,[14] but the brief clause combines once again the ideas of God's purpose and Christ's obedience. God also sent the Spirit of his Son, with the result that we, too, become 'sons'. Sayings about the Son of God, like those about Christ's incarnation, about εἰκών, and about Adam, seem to tell us as much about human destiny as about Christ himself.

Most of the remaining references to Jesus as 'Son of God' occur in brief references to the gospel, but there is one of these in particular which we should examine, and that is Rom. 1.3-4. This passage is often said to be a pre-Pauline summary of the Gospel, a view which I do not share, but if it is indeed such a summary, Paul has certainly made it his own; as usual with these introductory summaries, it is entirely appropriate to the theme of the letter. The Gospel is said to be about God's

---

13. Cf. M.D. Hooker, *Pauline Pieces/A Preface to Paul* (London: Epworth; New York: Oxford University Press, 1979), pp. 53-68.

14. Rom. 8.3 uses πέμπω, Gal. 4.4 ἐξαποστέλλω.

Son, who was born of the seed of David; the word γενομένου puts us in mind immediately of the γενόμενος in Gal. 4.3 and Phil. 2.7. We, of course, tend to think of the phrase 'of the seed of David' as a messianic claim, and therefore interpret it as though it were some kind of exalted title; but Paul puts it in the context of σάρξ, using his familiar phrase κατὰ σάρκα. We see, then, that for him the statement that the Son of God was 'born of the seed of David according to the flesh' is the equivalent of 'being born in human likeness', or 'being born of a woman, under the law'. The Son of God shares in our humanity, and even his Davidic lineage is a part of being human. The second part of the summary speaks of his being 'declared to be Son of God in power by the resurrection of the dead, Jesus Christ our Lord'. Here we have the equivalent of the second half of the Philippian 'hymn', where Christ is highly exalted and given the name that is above every name, so that all creation acknowledges him as Lord. In Philippians it is God who exalts Christ; Romans uses the divine passive and the phrase ἐν δυνάμει, 'in power', but also the phrase κατὰ πνεῦμα ἁγιωσύνης, balancing the κατὰ σάρκα in the first clause.

There are two interesting points for my purposes in this summary. The first is the fact that it speaks of the Son of God becoming man and then, at the resurrection, being declared Son of God. Is that first reference to 'Son of God' an indication of pre-existence? If so, what is the difference in status between what he was then and what he becomes at the resurrection? Is the resurrection simply an open acknowledgment of what he always was? Or should we understand the verb ὁρίζω to mean 'appoint' rather than declare. These are familiar problems, which have been met before in Philippians 2, suggesting that what we have here is a parallel summary. This passage even ends in a similar way to Phil. 2.6-11, with the reference to Jesus Christ being proclaimed as Lord. The second point of interest is Paul's use of those phrases κατὰ σάρκα and κατὰ πνεῦμα, which are taken up in Romans 8, where we are told that Christ came ἐν ὁμοιώματι σαρκὸς ἁμαρτίας, ('in the likeness of sinful flesh'), so that those who have lived κατὰ σάρκα might live κατὰ πνεῦμα (vv. 3-4). What it means to live κατὰ σάρκα, and the way in which men and women come to a new life κατὰ πνεῦμα is in fact the theme of the first eight chapters of Romans, and is summed up in the key passage in 5.12-21, where the same idea is expressed in terms of the contrast between life in Adam and life in Christ. It is only by concentrating on Rom. 1.3-4 in isolation and ignoring the argument of Romans 1–8 as a whole that one can deny the relevance of Adam to this passage.

Philippians

I suggest, therefore, that the links between these various passages indicate that they are united by an underlying coherent theme. The relationship between them is not that of separate items on a breakfast menu, but rather that of differently coloured threads which have been woven together into a tapestry. The fact that Adam seems to be present in so many of the passages I have mentioned, and not simply those where he is named, encourages me to suppose that Adamic imagery underlies Philippians 2–3, where we have similar ideas of Christ becoming man with the result that men and women become what he is. 'Adamic' language is used, moreover, in Phil. 3.21, where we have several interesting echoes of 1 Corinthians 15. In Phil. 3.21 we expect a Saviour from heaven (cf. the man from heaven in 1 Cor. 15.47), we have an echo of Ps. 2.6 (cf. 1 Cor. 15.27-28), and we wait for our bodies to be changed and to be conformed to Christ's (cf. 1 Cor. 15.35-49). How, then, are we to deal with the objection that Phil. 2.6 cannot be intended as a contrast between Adam and Christ, since the *result* of Christ's action is that he became man, and took on human likeness? *I suggest that it is precisely in this anomaly that we find the solution to the problem.* As we have already seen, Paul does not regard Adam and Christ as exactly parallel, since for him Christ is always greater than Adam. In Romans 5, Adam and Christ are, as it were, placed in the two pans of a pair of scales, but the finger of God rests on one of the pans, with the result that what happens in Christ is *far greater* than what happens in Adam. In 1 Corinthians, the first man was created out of the dust, a living being, but the second man is from heaven, and is a life-*giving* spirit. As man, Adam precedes Christ; but as the pattern according to which Adam was created, Christ precedes Adam. Christ is the *true* 'image of God', after whom Christians are now being recreated, while Adam is the distorted copy, whose disobedience meant that humanity became enslaved to sin and death. If for a moment we assume that the background of Philippians 2 is to be found in this Adamic imagery, and attempt to set out the two actions of Adam and Christ diagramatically, the pattern would be:

not

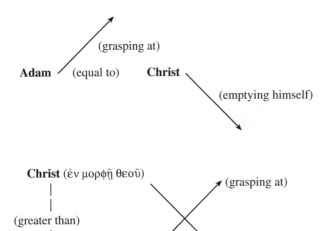

but

The chief problem with the idea that Adam is in mind in Phil. 2.6 is due to the assumption that Adam and Christ are being viewed as equals; they are not. To make sense of any parallel with Adam in Philippians, we have to understand Christ to be the 'blueprint' of what Man was *meant* to be, the perfect image of God and the reflection of his glory. If Paul has chosen to use the phrase ἐν μορφῇ θεοῦ rather than the one used of Adam in Genesis, that is with good reason, for it would make no sense at all to say that one who was 'in the image of God' (i.e. man) *became* man! The pre-existent one was *not* κατ᾽ εἰκόνα θεοῦ, but ἐν μορφῇ θεοῦ.

Why is it, then, that Paul here uses this particular term μορφή, whereas similar statements in Romans 1 and 8 and Galatians 4 refer to God's Son? It has, indeed, often been assumed that what we have in Philippians 2 is an example of Son-of-God Christology, and this idea has been explored by C.A. Wanamaker,[15] who examined Phil. 2.6-11 alongside Gal. 4.4, Rom. 1.3-4, 8.3-4 and 1 Cor. 15.24-28. If the basic meaning of the word μορφή is 'visible form', as Bockmuehl argues, then the suggestion that the phrase ἐν μορφῇ θεοῦ is in fact comparable

---

15. C.A. Wanamaker, 'Philippians 2.6-11: Son of God or Adamic Christology?', *NTS* 33 (1987), pp. 179-93. Cf. H. Conzelmann, who includes it, without apology, in his summary about Christ as 'Son of God', in *An Outline of the Theology of the New Testament* (ET London: SCM Press, 1969), pp. 79-80.

to the title 'Son of God' is a viable one, since children are often like their parents. This visible form is perhaps to be identified with God's glory, which features in Old Testament theophanies (cf. Exod. 32). Or perhaps, since Bockmuehl objects to the assumption that these terms are synonyms, we should understand it rather as the expression of the inner reality that is at one and the same time concealed by and revealed by the glory. The idea that God has a 'form' which normally cannot be seen by humans is found in various Jewish writings.[16] Particularly interesting is the well-known passage in the Talmud quoted by Bockmuehl which interprets Gen. 1.27 as meaning that God created Man 'in the image (צלם) of the likeness (דמות) of his form (תבנית)' (*b. Ket.* 8a). We do not know how early this particular interpretation is, but the fact that it distinguishes image (צלם is frequently translated in the LXX by εἰκών), likeness (דמות, commonly translated by ὁμοίωμα) and form (תבנית is mostly translated by ὁμοίωμα or παράδειγμα, but once, in Isa. 44.13, by μορφή), may be significant. A parallel idea is found in Philo who, however, uses the term εἰκών to describe what is *closest* to God. So God is the pattern of the image (who is also God's Word) and this image is in turn the pattern for humanity, since 'God made the Man after the image of God' (κατ᾽ εἰκόνα θεοῦ, *Leg. All.* 3.96). Does a similar idea lie behind Paul's hierarchy in 1 Cor. 11.3 (though there expressed in terms of κεφαλή), where we have God–Christ–Man? Is this why Christ is presented as *the* εἰκὼν τοῦ θεοῦ, to whom men and women must be conformed? And if μορφή is the 'visible form' of God, do we have a similar idea, expressed this time in terms of δόξα, in 2 Corinthians 3, where Christ is the image of God and the embodiment of his glory, and therefore superior to the *reflected* glory of the Law? What Israel glimpsed at Sinai is embodied in Christ.

This parallel between Phil. 2.6-11 and 2 Cor. 3–4.6 is an interesting one, since the setting of the so-called 'hymn' in Philippians 2 is reminiscent of the Sinai traditions of Exodus and Deuteronomy. Just as God's revelation of himself to Moses on Sinai was followed by the demand for obedience from the people, so now the idea that the nature of God—the visible form of his glory—is revealed in the actions of Christ is followed by the demand that the Philippians are obedient to the gospel. In contrast to the Israelites, who grumbled and argued (Exod. 16.1-12; 17.1-7), and proved to be 'a crooked and perverse gen-

---

16. See Bockmuehl, ' "The Form of God" ', pp. 11-23.

eration' (Deut. 32.5), they are to be 'blameless and innocent children of God'. Following the implicit contrast of Christ's obedience with Adam's disobedience, the obedience expected from those who belong to Christ is now contrasted with the disobedience of Israel, who repeated the sin of Adam when they turned their back on God's revelation in the Exodus and on Sinai and worshipped other gods.[17] Philippians 2 sets the theme of 'Adam' in the context of the Law. So, too, in 2 Corinthians 3, where the 'midrash' on God's revelation on Sinai reaches its climax in the description of the way in which Christians are being transformed into the image of Christ, and reflect his glory.[18] For Paul, Christ is the wisdom of God (1 Cor. 1.24, 30), through which God created the world (Col. 1.15-17), a wisdom that was partially revealed in the Law at Sinai (2 Cor. 3.7-18). But this same wisdom can be described also as the image of God and the reflection of his glory (2 Cor. 4.4; Col. 1.15).[19]

Ideas about the creation of Adam such as those expressed in the Talmud and in Philo may well lie behind Paul's use of Adamic language. For him, Christ is the *true* 'image of God' (2 Cor. 4.4; Col. 1.15), the one who is 'in his form' and therefore Son of God, whereas Adam, who was created 'after' God's image, became subject to sin and death because of his disobedience (Rom. 5.12-21), and is now only a distorted copy of what he was meant to be, a slave to the στοιχεῖα τοῦ κόσμου. Those who have borne the image of the first Adam may, in turn, bear the image of the last Adam (1 Cor. 15.42-49)—last, not in the sense that he came into existence last, but because he represents the eschatological goal of humanity, God's original purpose for creation. He is the one through whom all things exist (1 Cor. 8.6; Col. 1.15-16), the embodiment of God's glory, according to whose image men and women are being restored (Rom. 8.28-30; Col. 3.9). I have no difficulty with Wanamaker's suggestion that Phil. 2.6 should be read alongside those passages which speak of *the Son of God* becoming man, but we do well to ask why Paul chose to use the phrase ἐν μορφῇ θεοῦ here

17. For the way in which Paul links the sin of Adam and of Israel in Romans, see Dunn, *The Theology of Paul the Apostle*, pp. 93, 97, 99-100. Jewish tradition also linked the two.

18. This 'Adamic' language is continued in ch. 4, with the reference to Christ as the image of God (v. 4), and the reference to the creation narrative (v. 6).

19. These ideas are, of course, already associated in the Wisdom tradition and in Philo.

rather than 'the Son of God'. I suspect that part of the answer at least to this question is to be found in the contrast between ἐν μορφῇ θεοῦ and μορφὴν δούλου, for the logic of the passage demands a contrast—between 'the form of a slave', which expresses the condition into which Adam fell, and 'the form of God', which expresses the condition of the one who is *greater* than Adam. *If Paul wished to emphasize the contrast between Adam and Christ*, then 'the Son of God' was not the most appropriate term to use. As we have already seen, **κατ᾽** εἰκόνα θεοῦ was also inappropriate. He might, of course, have written ὅς εἰκὼν θεοῦ ὑπάρχων, the 'Adamic' phrase he uses elsewhere. Why does he not use it here? Is it possible that part of the explanation is to be found in 1 Corinthians 11, where Paul surprises us by using εἰκών of man—and even more astonishingly, of the male of the species? Was εἰκὼν τοῦ θεοῦ perhaps insufficiently clear to be used in the context of Phil. 2.6, where Paul wished to make a *contrast* between Christ and Adam? Might the phrase εἰκὼν τοῦ θεοῦ have suggested, in this context, that Adam and Christ were equal figures on a level playing-field? Or was it, after all, simply the parallel with μορφὴν δούλου λαβών that made him prefer ἐν μορφῇ θεοῦ ὑπάρχων?[20]

I am not sure of the answers to these questions, but the fact that Paul does not use the word 'image' here is certainly no reason to reject the reference to Adam. Contrary to the views of both Wanamaker and Bockmuehl, therefore, I want to suggest that Paul may well have used the phrase ἐν μορφῇ θεοῦ precisely because the theme of the contrast with Adam is fundamental to the argument of the passage, and because it was in fact the best and clearest way to express both that contrast and the superiority of the one who was and who remained, even during his humiliation, 'in the form of God'. If we take due note of all the evidence, we shall I think discover that the so-called Adamic cul-de-sac leads us to the key ideas underlying the Philippian hymn, and to fresh insights into Pauline Christology.

20. Those who regard Phil. 2.6-11 as a pre-Pauline 'hymn' have no need to wrestle with these problems!

ONCE MORE, ISAIAH 66: THE CASE OF 2 THESSALONIANS

Ivor H. Jones

I

Recent biblical studies have drawn attention yet again to the traditions developed from Isaiah 66 and used by the early church. Two contributions in particular relate closely to the Thessalonian correspondence. Professor Horbury in his *Jewish Messianism and the Cult of Christ* presents the thesis that messianism was prevalent in the Second Temple period. He develops this in part by means of the rich vein of messianic interpretation to be found in the LXX Prophets and Psalms, and in the connections made in Qumran material and the Targumim between passages such as Isa. 66.7 and Isa. 9.5(6). He notes the glorification of the messiah in Ps. Sol. 17, a glorification probably adapted from Isaiah 66, and notes also the bringing together of the messianic judgment of the great adversary, 'the Wicked One', and the reception of the nations' gifts by the messiah in 2 Esdras 13, again based on Isa. 66.5-24. He suggests that in the link between these passages and the traditional exegesis of Isa. 11.4 we can recognize the influence of the Isaianic passages on 2 Thessalonians, in the expectation of the Lord's coming with angels for vengeance (2 Thess. 1.7-8), the messianic woes and the judgment of the 'Wicked One' (2 Thess. 2).[1] This current article will hope to corroborate that judgment. It is also worth adding, irrespective of any decisions on the authorship of 2 Thessalonians, that the main Pauline letters and 2 Thessalonians have this in common, that the LXX of Isaiah, especially the section of Isaiah usually nowadays called Trito-Isaiah, provides an important backdrop for these writings:[2] the interlocking themes of disobedience, the woes, the absence of a saviour,

---

1. W. Horbury, *Jewish Messianism and the Cult of Christ* (London: SCM Press, 1998), pp. 55, 62, 99, 103, 115.
2. Horbury, *Jewish Messianism*, p. 81.

anger, destruction, fire, messianic deliverance and judgment proved a valuable resource for many generations of writers.[3]

A second relevant contribution is Rainer Riesner's *Paul's Early Period*, where he relates a text-critically reconstructed form of Isa. 66.18-21 to Paul's geographical fulfilment of his mission to Jews and Gentiles. Riesner considers the geographical and chronological detail of 1 Thessalonians against that background.[4] Although some details regarding the individual geographical regions in the text of Isa. 66.19 can be regarded as speculative, there remains as a result of Riesner's work a strong likelihood that, early in his career, Paul reflected on Isa. 66.18-21 from the standpoint of his vocation's role within the divine purpose. I shall hope to provide confirmation of that view.

Previous attempts to build specific links beween Isaiah 66 and the Thessalonian correspondence have found some approval, albeit with some quite justifiable limitations.[5] The key links with 2 Thessalonians are impressive: the phrase ἐν πυρὶ φλογὸς (if that is the original reading)[6] is unique to 2 Thessalonians within the New Testament material, rare in the LXX,[7] and appears in 2 Thess. 1.8 with διδόντος ἐκδίκησιν, a close approximation to Isa. 66.15 ἀποδοῦναι ἐν θυμῷ ἐκδίκησιν and ἀποσκορακισμὸν ἐν φλογὶ πυρός. 2 Thessalonians 1.8 has also a similarity with Isa. 66.4 ἐκάλεσα αὐτοὺς καὶ οὐχ ὑπήκουσάν μου (see also 2 Thess. 3.14). The context of Isa. 66.4 has in 66.3 a reference to and a

---

3.   See Rom. 9–11; also Mk 9.48; Acts 7.45-50; Jn 16.22; 2 Pet. 3.33; Rev. 12.2, 5; 21.1; on Isa. 66, B. Lindars, *New Testament Apologetic* (London: SCM Press, 1961), pp. 245-46. On the issues of method involved in this article see S. Porter, 'The Use of the Old Testament in the New Testament', in C.A. Evans and J.A. Sanders (eds.), *Early Christian Interpretation of the Scriptures of Israel* (JSNTSup, 148; Sheffield: Sheffield Academic Press, 1997), pp.79-96.

4.   R. Riesner, *Paul's Early Period* (Grand Rapids, MI: Eerdmans, 1998), pp. 245-306.

5.   On the work of R.D. Aus to be referred to later, see 'The Liturgical Background of the Necessity and Propriety of Giving Thanks according to 2 Thessalonians 1:3', *JBL* 92 (1973), pp. 432-38; 'God's Plan and God's Power: Isaiah 66 and the Restraining Factors of 2 Thess 2:6-7', *JBL* 96 (1977), pp. 537-53, and 'The Relevance of Isaiah 66:7 to Revelation and 2 Thessalonians 1', *ZNW* 67 (1976), pp. 252-68; see also C. Wanamaker, *The Epistles to the Thessalonians* (Grand Rapids, MI: Eerdmans, 1990), pp. 224, 251; R. Jewett, 'A Matrix of Grace', in J. Bassler (ed.), *Pauline Theology*, I (Minneapolis: Fortress Press, 1991), p. 67; and M. Menken, *2 Thessalonians* (London: Routledge, 1994).

6.   On this point see Wanamaker, *The Epistles to the Thessalonians*, pp. 224-26.

7.   Exod 3.2; Sir. 8.10; 45.19; Isa. 66.15.

definition of ὁ ἄνομος, 'the lawless one' (see 2 Thess 2.3). 66.7 has ἔτεκεν ἄρσεν, traditionally understood as a messianic reference; and in the previous verse there is language appropriate to the messianic woes (66.6).[8] An impressive, cumulatively significant list.

It is also true that the language of 2 Thessalonians has resemblances to a wider range of LXX material than simply Isaiah 66. There are unusual compound verbs shared with the LXX such as ἐγκαυχᾶσθαι (2 Thess. 1.4),[9] ἐνδοξασθῇ (2 Thess. 1.12),[10] καταξιωθῆναι (2 Thess. 1.5);[11] there are phrases in 2 Thessalonians unique to the New Testament, such as τῆς δόξης τῆς ἰσχύος (2 Thess. 1.9),[12] unusual features of syntax only here in the Pauline Corpus such as ἀνθ' ὧν (2 Thess. 2.10) but which are common in the LXX, and important idioms such as ἐκ μέσου γένηται (2 Thess. 2.7) for which LXX parallels are adduced. All these features indicate an important LXX background for 2 Thessalonians.

The question is whether these findings contribute anything substantial to our understanding of 2 Thessalonians. A brief review of some of the main arguments concerning the authorship of 2 Thessalonians suggest that they may. The findings so far referred to could be regarded as trivial. They are described as such by Hartman in his work on eschatology in 2 Thessalonians: they make a small contribution to the prehistory of constellations of motifs and traditions, but, according to Hartman, hardly address the relation of such constellations to the letter as a communication.[13] That the text of 2 Thessalonians appears to use Isaiah 66 and some of the traditions which flowed from it may locate one possible source of inspiration for the letter, but that gives little hint of how, why and for what purpose the source was used.

Hartman, like many contemporary scholars, leans toward non-Pauline authorship for 2 Thessalonians. The author of 2 Thessalonians, he argues, working within the Pauline tradition, is not so much concerned

8.   φωνὴ κραυγῆς ἐκ πόλεως, φωνὴ ἐκ ναοῦ, φωνὴ κυρίου ἀνταποδιδόντος ἀνταπόδοσιν τοῖς ἀντικειμένοις.

9.   See Pss. 51(52).3; 73(74).4; 96(97).7; 105(106).47.

10.   See especially Isa. 45.25; 49.3; Ps. 88(89).8.

11.   See 2 Macc. 13.12; 3 Macc. 3.21; 4.11; and in the Passive, 4 Macc. 18.3.

12.   See Isa. 2.16, 19, 21; 1 Chron. 16.28.

13.   L. Hartman, 'The Eschatology of 2 Thessalonians as Included in a Communication', in R.F. Collins (ed.), *The Thessalonian Correspondence* (BETL, 87; Louvain: Leuven, 1990), pp. 470-84 (470, 484).

with the time of the parousia as with a strained situation of persecution in which the hearers find themselves and which could tempt them to fall away. It is within that framework that the usage of the sources has to be located. So, for example, Hartman notes the similarities between 2 Thessalonians and Matthean material, particularly material which is usually described as a 'later strand' of the synoptic tradition: the false prophets work 'mighty signs and wonders, so as to lead astray, if possible, even the elect' (Mt. 24.24). This motif is used in 2 Thessalonians to expand the picture of the 'lawless one', so that the readers may be aware of the satanic wickedness that will be let loose and which is in fact already active in their situation.[14]

Hartman may well be right that the aspect of communication in 2 Thessalonians requires a fresh evaluation of the letter's eschatology, and I shall take that aspect into account in section 3. He is probably also right to consider the importance for the letter of the book of Daniel and of the impact of Deuteronomy 13 on the development of the tradition on false prophets. But it is not clear why, in addition to the use of Danielic and Deuteronomic traditions, the author should have judged also to be relevant the particular elements paralleled in Isaiah 66. Hartman appears to think they may be relevant, but does not seem to commit himself as to why.[15] The issue whether Pauline authorship of 2 Thessalonians might provide a satisfactory answer to that question is one which will be taken up in due course.[16]

If Hartman considers an emphasis on 2 Thessalonians as communication relevant to the theory that it is a post-Pauline letter, Schmidt offers him statistical support for post-Pauline authorship. Schmidt's evidence deserves careful attention, but once again we shall find that Isaiah 66 and the LXX evidence are of crucial importance in our

14. Hartman, 'The Eschatology of 2 Thessalonians', pp. 480-82. With regard to the argument against Pauline authorship of 2 Thess. drawn from agreements with Matthean material, it should be noticed that the same argument would have to be used in relation to 1 Thess. 2.15 and its parallel in Mt. 23.32, where the 'filling up of the fathers' measure' appears in an addition to Q material.

15. Hartman, 'The Eschatology of 2 Thessalonians', p. 484 n. 70.

16. For other uses of Isa. 66 see H.A. Brehm, 'Vindicating the Rejected One', and G. Beale. 'Solecisms in the Apocalypse as Signals', in C.A. Evans and J.A. Sanders (eds.), *Early Christian Interpretation of the Scriptures of Israel* (JSNTSup, 148; Sheffield: Sheffield Academic Press 1997), pp. 266-99, 421-46; also T. Holtz, *Die Christologie der Apokalypse des Johannes* (Berlin: Akademie Verlag, 1962), pp. 102-103.

assessment of his work. With the aid of a GramCord statistical research programme Schmidt finds that a study of the opening thanksgiving in 2 Thessalonians places it with Ephesians, a letter normally considered pseudepigraphic. He also compares the phrase strings in 2 Thessalonians with those of other letters in the Pauline Corpus, with the same result, that 2 Thessalonians appears to belong with Ephesians and Colossians rather than with the main-line Pauline correspondence.[17] In Schmidt's view the stylistic distinctiveness of 2 Thessalonians about which many scholars have been so far been unable to satisfy themselves, emerges with a greater clarity in GramCord surveys.

The flaws in Schmidt's statistics are, however, fatal to his argument. First, Schmidt argues that 2 Thessalonians exhibits a high degree of sentence complexity. By this he means that it employs a considerable number of, and variations of, constituent clauses in a sentence. Adopting the terminology of generative linguistics Schmidt writes of constituent clauses being embedded into the matrix sentence. So 2 Thess. 1.3-12 is described as having 23 sentence units; that is we have there a matrix and 22 embedded clauses. On this basis the numbers for the longest sentence in the opening thanksgiving section of each of the letters in the Pauline Corpus show 2 Thessalonians on a level with Ephesians and Colossians. For example, the number of embedded clauses in 2 Thess. 1.3-12 is given as 22, and in Ephesians as 18. By contrast 2 Corinthians is listed as having five. Schmidt's method is however faulty. The thanksgiving section of 2 Corinthians is understood as 2 Cor. 1.3-7, whereas the actual thanksgiving vocabulary, crucial for the definition of an opening thanksgiving,[18] does not appear in 2 Corinthians until 1.11; so the opening thanksgiving can only properly be spoken of as being 1.3-11. If that definition is followed, then the figures for number of embedded units is quite different: the longest sentence in terms of embedded units in 2 Corinthians is 15. Schmidt's statistical case for sentence complexity in 2 Thessalonians is unreliable. Secondly, the danger of the GramCord statistics is apparent in the low figures that such small literary units as the letters of the Pauline Corpus

17. D. Schmidt, 'The Syntactical Style of 2 Thessalonians: How Pauline is it?', in R.F. Collins (ed.), *The Thessalonian Correspondence* (BETL, 57; Louvain: Leuven, 1990), pp. 383-93.

18. J. Lambrecht, 'Thanksgivings in 1 Thessalonians 1–3', in R.F. Collins (ed.), *The Thessalonian Correspondence* (BETL, 57; Louvain: Leuven, 1990), pp. 183-205.

produce. In the statistical details of the phrase strings the actual figures are so low that it would take only a single additional example to change the overall proportional summary for each letter dramatically. Given that we have seen above that there are several distinctive LXX phrases in 2 Thessalonians, and since 2 Thessalonians includes such features in all the three phrase constructs which Schmidt identifies, an interesting issue of interpretation arises: are the figures for 2 Thessalonians (marginal in terms of numbers: Ephesians 77, Colossians 47, 2 Thessalonians 22), evidence for a distinctive non-Pauline style, or indications of a particular use of Old Testament material, a use which would in itself satisfactorily explain the marginal numerical differences? Thirdly, the assumption behind Schmidt's method is that once a survey is produced of a particular stylistic or syntactical feature using GramCord material the statistical results can stand unchecked. But everything depends on the accuracy with which the search is set up, and it is almost always necessary to check 'by hand' how accurate that is.[19] Schmidt offers no check on the stylistic surveys.

Frank Witt Hughes's arguments on behalf of a Deuteropauline character for 2 Thessalonians centre on a series of nine antitheses. These antitheses he regards as basic to rhetoric, and basic to a genus of deliberative rhetoric which is designed to test the addressees' honourable attitude to true Pauline faith.[20] The presence of rhetoric is not, of course, in itself an argument against Pauline authorship. A clutch of special studies recently has demonstrated the use of rhetorical argument within the main-line Pauline letters.[21] But Hughes is arguing that the

19. A useful illustration is to be found in the use of the GramCord material to study the Genitive Absolute in the LXX and New Testament. A 'hand search', adding a sharper grammatical definition to the units embedded in the matrix, brought to light several false entries. See the Appendix in I.H. Jones, *The Matthean Parables* (Leiden: E.J. Brill, 1995), pp. 482-520.

20. F.W. Hughes, *Early Christian Rhetoric and 2 Thessalonians* (JSNTSup, 30; Sheffield: Sheffield Academic Press,1989).

21. D. Hellholm, 'Enthymemic Argumentation in Paul: The Case of Romans 6', in T. Engberg-Pedersen (ed.), *Paul in his Hellenistic Context* (Minneapolis: Fortress Press, 1995), pp. 119-79; on Paul and his rhetoric see Part IV of S. Porter and T. Olbricht (eds.), *The Rhetorical Analysis of Scripture* (JSNTSup, 146; Sheffield: Sheffield Academic Press, 1997). P. Esler defines the nature of Paul's rhetoric in Galatians as closely matched to the factual context, and analyses it by means of a process communication theory: P. Esler, *Galatians* (London: Routledge, 1998), chapters 1–3.

rhetorical antitheses are a clear indication of the letter's post-Pauline purpose. His designation of nine antitheses as crucial to the argument and purpose of 2 Thessalonians does, however, involve several significant misreadings of the text. Again LXX parallels are involved. One illustration must suffice: the antithesis 'the readers who are being afflicted' who are part of the elect, versus 'those who are afflicting', whom God will pay back with affliction (1.5-9).[22] In the case of this antithesis Hughes is not reflecting the precise way in which the contrast is employed in 2 Thessalonians. The actual text of 2 Thessalonians, in the two places where the contrast is found, 1.6-7a and implicitly 2.10, gives a much stronger emphasis to one side of the contrast rather than to the other. The two parts of the antithesis are not in balance. It is the present state and the future fate of the oppressors, 1.7b-9 and 2.10-12, which carries the emphasis. As we have already seen in relation to Isaiah 66 the fate of the oppressors is a part of the wider framework of thought in Trito-Isaiah, and in section 3 we shall see that it is precisely because of the future fate of the oppressors that the elect, according to 2 Thessalonians 2, have no need to be afraid of the experience of oppression. To concentrate on the simple antithesis is to miss the point the antithesis (and therefore the letter) is making.

A fourth substantial case for non-Pauline authorship of 2 Thessalonians centres on the eschatology of the letter. Erlemann, in his major treatment of New Testament near-expectation, follows many scholars in setting 2 Thessalonians apart from other main Pauline letters. He makes the case that 2 Thessalonians 2 belongs in the 'context of an argument about the dating of the Parousia'.[23] It is the concentration on the sequence of events leading up to the Parousia of Christ which, he argues, distinguishes 2 Thessalonians from the Pauline tradition, and represents, within the life of the early church, an 'inadmissible form of near-expectation'.

Section 3 will suggest that to concentrate on the sequence of events leading up to the Parousia is to impose our contemporary interests on the text.[24] We shall see in section 3 that a more careful attention to the

22. F.W. Hughes, *Early Christian Rhetoric and 2 Thessalonians* (JSNTSup, 30; Sheffield: Sheffield Academic Press,1989), p. 76.

23. K. Erlemann, *Naherwartung und Parusieverzögerung im Neuen Testament* (Tübingen: Francke Verlag, 1995), p. 209. For a similar position see M. Menken, *2 Thessalonians* (London: Routledge, 1994), p. 29.

24. Hartman, 'The Eschatology of 2 Thessalonians', p. 484.

text of 2 Thessalonians provides an eschatological picture containing a number of typically Pauline features. In this attention to the text the LXX background of 2 Thessalonians, and particularly Isaiah 66, will play a significant role, as indeed it has already in section 1. In section 2 I shall address some of the issues of method that need attention preparatory to embarking on a careful reading of the text.

II

The first issue of method concerns the appropriateness to Thessalonians of Philip Esler's communication theory. Esler's conclusion on using that theory in relation to Galatians is that in Galatians Paul is intent on

> explaining and justifying a particular type of largely domestic religion tied to kinship patterns and local politics, and having a strong emphasis on normative behaviour which finds its source in the Spirit, who is poured out on those who believe. He does this above all by generating a sense of the glorious identity enjoyed by the members of his congregations.[25]

To reach that conclusion Esler uses Oberg's description of 'culture shock'; it monitors the distress encountered as a result of being cut loose from familiar signs of social interaction. Esler also employs Tajfel's social identity theory. He identifies the exigencies of the letter (the imperfection of relationship requiring communication), the audience (especially the ethnic factors), and the constraints (especially those involving social differentiation).

To provide a brief comparison with Galatians Esler sketches out some implications of this method for the Thessalonian correspondence. The Thessalonian letters do not yield themselves quite so neatly to that kind of analysis as the Galatian letter, but the headings of 'imperfection of relationship', 'audience' and 'constraints' nevertheless serve as helpful guidelines. The difficulties are, in the first place, that the ethnicity to be taken account of in the Thessalonian correspondence is harder to define than in the case of the Galatians. Are the Thessalonian followers of Christ primarily Gentiles,[26] or is Jason an indication that early work

---

25. Esler, *Galatians*, p. 239.

26. For recent studies on this see J. Barclay, 'Thessalonica and Corinth: Social Contrasts in Pauline Christianity', *JSNT* 47 (1992), pp. 47-74 and 'Conflict in Thessalonica', *CBQ* 55 (1993), pp. 512-30.

in the Thessalonican synagogue produced Jewish converts?[27] The jury is still out on that particular problem; there is much to be said for both alternatives. In the second place the issue of social differentiation is more difficult to define in the case of Thessalonica. Meggitt's plea for a reading of élite letters such as those in the New Testament letters 'upside down' (e.g. to see how vocabulary is used to fight wars of identity and exclusion) leads to interesting insights on social differentiation.[28] It could well be that the social background to the Thessalonian correspondence is one where mutuality is the strategy of survival (2 Thess. 3.6-12) rather than one in which patronage encourages dependence. Thirdly, the nature of the 'culture shock' experienced by the early followers of Jesus in Thessalonica depends to a large extent on the answers to the two previous questions. Is the culture shock essentially that of an apocalyptic evangelist losing contact with previous kinship and family ties, or does a re-reading of the Thessalonian correspondence with a reduced emphasis on eschatological timetables, as hinted by Hartman, suggest that the reason for the distress and difficulty among Thessalonican Christians was caused by unexpectedly violent reactions from neighbours and friends—hence the reference in Acts 17.6-7 to 'acting against the decrees of Caesar'?

Not only is it difficult in the case of the Thessalonian correspondence to specify with certainty the exigencies, audience and constraints behind the act of communication, there is also the difficulty that 2 Thessalonians, even if it is Pauline, is so brief and so textually close to 1 Thessalonians that the particularities of the communication involved in 2 Thessalonians cannot easily be determined.

A further problem in applying Esler's method to 2 Thessalonians emerges when we recall the opening comments in Section I concerning the use there of Isaiah 66 and the LXX. Supposing that the primary basis

27. On Jason see F. Morgan-Gillman, 'Jason of Thessalonica', in R.F. Collins (ed.), *The Thessalonian Correspondence* (BETL, 57; Louvain: Leuven, 1990), pp. 39-49, who argues in support of Marshall's view: that συμφυλέται in 1 Thess. 2.14 should be taken in a local rather than a racial sense and thus should not exclude the Jewish population of Thessalonica, and that to refer 1 Thess. 2.14 to Gentile antagonism leaves vv. 15-16 quite unmotivated and tangential.

28. J. Meggitt, *Paul, Poverty and Survival* (Edinburgh: T. & T. Clark, 1998). See also A. Malherbe, *Paul and the Thessalonians* (Philadelphia: Fortress Press, 1987), and J. Murphy-O'Connor, *Paul: A Critical Life* (Oxford: Oxford University Press, 1996).

of the Thessalonian Christian community was Gentile, what intercul-
tural issues would be involved if Paul were addressing a primarily
Gentile community with reference to a Greek Jewish text? Perhaps at
this point the issue turns on the nature of language and whether the
somewhat stark distinction made by Esler between the process model of
communication and the semiotic model, can do full justice to intercul-
tural translation. We might turn for guidance in the case of 2 Thessalonians to Dalferth's more nuanced philosophical base for the use of language. The translatability of created communication needs to take
preference over social identity as the basis of harmonizing perspectives.[29]

Despite these reservations about the use of Esler's method in the
study of the Thessalonian correspondence, his reminder of the distance
between our contemporary culture and that of the ancient Mediter-
ranean world, particularly in terms of kinship and identity, is invalu-
able. We need to pay particular attention to the Thessalonian texts as a
form of communication, and to formulate as clearly as our texts and
information allow the exigencies, audience and constraints behind that
communication.

III

So finally I turn to the text of 2 Thessalonians. I shall use the rhetorical
indications of the text to guide me as I follow the trend of the communication.

The first major section of 2 Thessalonians is 1.3-12. The rhetorical
description of 1.3-12 as an exordium reminds us that it occupies a role
within the process of persuasion.[30] It has two balancing sentences, 1.3a
and 1.11a, and a confirmation of the divine grace at work in the process
described. These balancing sentences provide the context of thanksgiving and intercession which the author and readers share, a context such
that the latter (the intercession) is consequentially related to the former
(the thanksgiving); note the εἰς ὅ in 1.11a.[31] The thanksgiving appears

29. I. Dalferth, *Theology and Philosophy* (Oxford: Basil Blackwell, 1988),
pp. 141-48.

30. A similar case has been made for 1 Thess. 2–10.

31. Compare and contrast W. Wuellner, 'The Argumentative Structure of
1 Thessalonians as Paradoxical Encomium', in R.F. Collins (ed.), *The Thessalonian
Correspondence* (BETL, 57; Louvain: Leuven, 1990), pp. 117-36.

to be an expansion of the content of the thanksgiving in 1 Thess. 1.2 (πίστις, ἀγάπη), as the intercession expands the 1 Thessalonians reference to intercession; and both thanksgiving and intercession in 2 Thessalonians 1 envisage a consequence: the thanksgiving envisages the cause for pride in the readers' patient perseverance, and the intercession envisages the mutual glorification of the readers and the Lord Jesus. This mutual glorification includes a future reference, as it does in 2 Thess. 1.10a. The thanksgiving for public pride in their patient perseverance has its focus in particular present circumstances, namely the experience of opposition (1.4), and in two particular interpretations of that experience: God's righteous judgment (1.5 τῆς δικαίας κρίσεως) is at work in it, and God's intention is that the readers should be deemed worthy of the Kingdom (1.5; the Kingdom is both a future hope and a present responsibility or reality).[32] Those two particular interpretations of the experience of opposition are cautiously (see the εἴπερ in 1.6) explained in terms of God's righteousness (δίκαιον παρὰ θεῷ) as reversing the respective fates of persecutors and persecuted. The writer thereafter paints himelf into the picture and gives a timing for the realization of the reversal of those fates (μεθ' ἡμῶν, ἐν τῇ ἀποκαλύψει 1.7). What follows is the powerful double evocation, using Isaiah 66 imagery, of the fate of those who do not know God and who are disobedient to the Gospel. They will come face to face with the glory of the Lord Jesus and his holy ones; those who have believed the writer's testimony will greet the moment with amazement. This will happen 'on that day'.

This opening section of 2 Thessalonians uses a language system built in and from worship (see the time references within it).[33] It spells out the disrupted relationships with which the letter has to struggle. But above all it places the experience of the readers within a profound discussion of the relation of disobedience to divine wrath drawn from Jewish sources. The problem is to define which Jewish sources and how they are used. The crucial phrase within the discussion is 1.5: ἔνδειγμα τῆς δικαίας κρίσεως. As we have already seen this phrase is paralleled in 1.6 with δίκαιον παρὰ θεῷ where it refers to the reversal of the fates of persecutors and persecuted. This suggests that τῆς δικαίας κρίσεως could at the very least imply the judgment that leads to that reversal; it

32. See Rom. 14.17; 1 Cor. 4.20, and 2 Thess. 1.5c ὑπὲρ ἧς καὶ πάσχετε, but see also 1 Thess. 2.12.

33. See Aus, 'The Liturgical Background', pp. 432-38.

cannot simply refer to the faith and perseverance of the faithful. But to what then does ἔνδειγμα ('evidence') refer? What is the evidence of this 'divine judgment'? Detailed discussion among scholars has suggested that the 'evidence' is the persecution and affliction of the Thessalonians, and that their persecution and affliction is evidence of divine righteousness in various senses, all of which can be recognized in Jewish sources: evidence in suffering which is retributive, a chastising of the pious, prophetic of reversal and a proof of election.[34] Excellent and illuminating though that background is for 1.5 there are two ways in which the interpretation of ἔνδειγμα τῆς δικαίας κρίσεως against that background is then limited by scholars unnecessarily. First 1.5 is, curiously, on the basis of that background, interpreted as having only a future reference rather than both a present and a future reference.[35] That the Jewish understanding of suffering implies a present evidence of divine judgment and righteousness can be illustrated in many respects, but perhaps most relevantly to 2 Thess.1.5 in Isa. 66.5: εἴπατε, ἀδελφοὶ ἡμῶν, τοῖς μισοῦσιν ἡμᾶς καὶ βδελυσσομένοις, ἵνα τὸ ὄνομα κυρίου δοξασθῇ καὶ ὀφθῇ ἐν τῇ εὐφροσύνῃ αὐτῶν... ('Declare, our brethren, to those who hate and detest us, that the Lord's name is glorified and seen in their gladness'). The present happy state of the oppressors is in itself visible evidence of divine power and purpose. The persecutors are unwitting evidence and, indeed, unwitting agents of a present divine purpose. Undoubtedly 1.5 has a future reference, as indeed 2 Thessalonians 1.12 has, ὅπως ἐνδοξασθῇ τὸ ὄνομα τοῦ κυρίου ἡμῶν Ἰησοῦ ἐν ὑμῖν ('So that the name of our Lord Jesus may be glorified in you'). (see 1.10a), although such a future glory cannot be dissociated from obedience now in the present (1.10b). But surely, against the background of Jewish discussions of suffering and health, the evidence of the present state of the persecutors cannot be automatically excluded from ἔνδειγμα τῆς δικαίας κρίσεως in 1.5. Secondly, the fourfold summary of how suffering was interpreted in Jewish sources is, as background material for 2 Thess. 1.5, unnecessarily limited in the sense that the eschatological context in the Thessalonian correspondence is

34. See Wanamaker's analysis in *The Epistles to the Thessalonians*, pp. 220-24 of the text of 1.5 and his discussion of J. Bassler's 'The Enigmatic Sign: 2 Thessalonians 1.5', *CBQ* 46 (1984), pp. 496-510 and W. Wichmann's *Die Leidenstheologie: Eine Form der Leidensdeutung im Spätjudentum* (BWANT, 4.2; Stuttgart: Kohlhammer, 1930).

35. Wanamaker, *The Epistles to the Thessalonians*, p. 223.

complicated by the presence of pagans among persecuted and Jews among the persecutors. The language of divine ὀργή ('wrath') is, of course, used in Jewish sources in relation to both pagans and Jews. In relation to both it can express the divine condemnation of injustice and disobedience and the divine intention that the wicked should repent. The Wisdom of Solomon provides useful evidence of this. Wisdom 18.10–19.17 notes three areas: that the Egyptians confess their acceptance of the final plague as evidence of their wickedness; that the righteous are touched by the trial of death in the final plague 'but the wrath did not long continue' (18.20), and, because of the intervention of the intercessor the destroyer conceded that 'the single trial of the wrath was enough' (18.25); and that the Egyptian forgetfulness of God's previous punishment led them to 'fill up the punishment lacking to their torments' (19.4).[36] Isaiah 66 provides complementary evidence. The fire of divine judgment will fall on all humanity, as it will on Jews who engage in forbidden practices (66.15-17); the Gentiles will be drawn to Jerusalem where all, Jew and Gentile, will see the evidence of the unquenchable fire of judgment (66.20-24). The further eschatological problem in the case of the Thessalonian correspondence is whether or not ὀργή in the early Christian context is understood as having fallen irreversibly on the Jews who have rejected Christ. The key passage which is thought to raise this problem is 1 Thess. 2.14-16. But the crucial phrase in that passage, ἔφθασεν δὲ ἐπ' αὐτοὺς ἡ ὀργὴ εἰς τέλος is hardly likely to imply an irreversible condemnation, particularly if εἰς τέλος means 'completely', that is either 'all inclusively'—inclusive of all Israel—or 'in every respect'[37]—as an extension of the temporal

36. See S. Cheon, *The Exodus Story in the Wisdom of Solomon* (JSPSup, 23 Sheffield: Sheffield Academic Press, 1997), chapter 5. The motif of 'filling up the punishments' is in Wis. 19.4 a metaphorical expression to contrast the results of Egyptian forgetfulness of past punishment with Israelite remembrance. I. Broer's discussion of this passage in 'Der ganze Zorn (1 Thess. 2.14-16)', in R. Collins (ed.), *The Thessalonian Correspondence* (BETL, 87; Louvain: Leuven, 1990), pp. 154-55, compares the theological treatments of the motif within German literature—a less satisfactory approach.

37. A possible sense in Hab. 1.4 LXX. T. Holtz finds a place for 1 Thess. 1.15-16 within the Pauline understanding of divine grace and uses Steck's outline of the prophetic tradition which sees persecution of the prophets as a means to call Israel to repentance (as Broer does, see n. 36 above, although Broer gives a greater stress to the intensification of the tradition in Paul); in contrast to Broer Holtz translates εἰς τέλος 'without exception': that is to say, as in Rom. 1–3 and 9–11, all without

πάντοτε in 1 Thess. 1.16b rather as its ultimate culmination. These are important eschatological factors, recognizable in other Pauline material, and present in the Thessalonian correspondence, and particularly in 1 Thess. 1.5.

How then can we summarize this section? The interpretation of 2 Thess. 1.5 should include a wide range of possibilities: the fourfold understanding of suffering, consideration of the divine control of all persecutors, including those who could (in Paul's mind, at any rate) be Jews (1.8b), and the rhetorical force of eschatological language about divine wrath which implies the need and availability of grace. Divine justice concerns on the one hand the persecutors who are unwitting agents and who are in danger of paying the price of disobedience, and the persecuted, who also are objects of divine judgment and who, according to 2 Thess. 1.11-12 must wait for their divine approval (according to 1 Thessalonians, approval of their holiness at the coming of Christ). So included within 2 Thess. 1.1-12 is an understanding of the Jews as among the instruments of the divine purpose, who are at the same time potential objects of divine judgment. This provides one of the keys to 2 Thessalonians.

The features of that summary of 2 Thess. 1.3-12 are worth expanding further. First, if Paul wrote 2 Thessalonians, whatever the composition of the community to which the letter is addressed (the 'you' of 1.4b-7a), there can be little doubt that phrases such as 'those who do not obey the gospel of our Lord Jesus', and 'they will suffer the punishment of eternal ruin cut off from the presence of the Lord' included, in Paul's mind at least, a reference to Jewish opponents. From the point where Paul associates himself with the readers (1.7b-12) that is the only conclusion to draw. Why then the language drawn from Isaiah 66? That Paul should have phrased 2 Thess. 1.8 in the language of Isaiah 66 may well mean that he was reflecting on the fate of his Jewish opponents in the light of the mysterious paradoxes of the divine purpose set out in that passage. As one who had given his testimony to the Thessalonians and prayed for them in their distress he had himself experienced opposition from his own race; he had perhaps considered their fate in the light of the terrible warnings of Isaiah 66, together with the affirmations there

exception who reject Christ stand under judgment, yet such certainty never excludes the possibility of a gracious release from judgment; see T. Holtz, 'Judgment on the Jews (1 Thess. 2.15-16)', in R. Collins (ed.), *The Thessalonian Correspondence* (BETL, 87; Louvain: Leuven, 1990), pp. 284-94 (293).

concerning the divine purpose behind the apparent disasters and intransigence. Are there hints here of his concern that a divinely ordained πώρωσις had afflicted some of his own people, a concern which he was later to express in terms of his concern to win them at all costs, even if it meant identification with them, even if it meant identification with all, both Jews and Greeks (τοῖς Ἰουδαίοις ὡς Ἰουδαῖος, τοῖς ἀνόμοις ὡς ἄνομος, 1 Cor. 9.20-21)?[38] Romans 9.3 provides the strongest expression of this concern; he would be gladly be an outcast from Christ on behalf of those of his own people, and Rom. 9.3 stands at the beginning of the long section which owes a great deal to the thought of the Isaiah LXX. Are we observing in 2 Thess. 1.1-12 evidence that the Isaiah LXX influenced his thinking about Jewish persecutors at an earlier stage in his apostolic work than 1 Corinthians and Romans?

Secondly, in the thanksgiving section 2 Thess. 1.3-12, 2 Thessalonians diverges from 1 Thessalonians in some important respects. They diverge despite the close literal parallels between the two thanksgiving sections. It is the introduction of Isaiah 66 and the traditions associated with it in 2 Thessalonians 1 which marks one such point of divergence.[39] The Isaianic pattern of thought seems to provide a picture of judgment and probably also a broader base for the understanding of the experience of persecution. In 1 Thessalonians Paul addresses the issue of persecution by Jews directly, concentrating on the extent to which divine wrath is falling on Israel. In 2 Thessalonians, although the threat of punishment is no less severe, another factor appears alongside it—a

38. The link between 1 Cor. 9.20-21 and the theme of 'imitation' (see 2 Thess. 3.7) is expounded by M.D Hooker, 'A Partner in the Gospel', *Epworth Review* 25 (1998), pp. 70-78: 'the imitation of Christ depends on union with him. But if Christ is truly formed in the Christian community, does this not mean that its members will share in his redeeming work?' (p. 77).

39. T. Holtz, *Der erste Brief an die Thessalonicher* (Zürich: Benziger, 1986) notes only three references to Trito-Isaiah in 1 Thessalonians: Isa. 48.12f, 54.13 and 59.17. The last of these is particularly interesting because 1 Thess. 5.8 appears, in quoting Isa. 59.17 (or perhaps Wis. 5.18), to avoid the word 'righteousness', a factor which Esler includes in his argument that 'righteousness' only emerges as a key term where Gentiles converts faced pressure to be circumcised. The role of Isa. 66, which suggests a differentiation between 1 Thess. and 2 Thess., appears to assist Paul in facing the question of opponents from among his compatriots. That role needs to be put in a biblical perspective: Isa. 66 is one of several attempts within the book of Isaiah (see also Isa. 32.3) to cope with Isa. 6.10 and Israel's 'hardening of heart'.

divine intention and purpose is recognized which affects disobedient and obedient alike.

In 2 Thess. 1.3-12 Paul may be revealing, not least by his use of Isaiah 66, early stages in his concern for his own race. When we turn to 2 Thessalonians 2 we find that the parallels with Isaiah 66 are fewer; but they are no less important. In 2 Thessalonians 2 Paul begs the readers that they should not quickly be disturbed or terrified in relation to the Parousia of Christ and their 'being gathered together to him'. The cause of the disturbance or terror is news that the day of the Lord had arrived (2.1-2). The meaning of that sentence 'the Day of the Lord has arrived' is much disputed.[40] Perhaps the solution closest to the text of 2 Thessalonians is that the Day of the Lord was associated by some readers with the messianic woes, understood as the beginning of that Day; an intensity of opposition suggested to some that the Day had dawned.[41]

Paul's response to their distress is that the news 'that the Day of the Lord has arrived' is a form of delusion (2.3). Apostasy has to precede the Day;[42] and associated with apostasy is the revelation of the 'lawless man'. The news that the Day has arrived is an example of delusion, and the delusion consists in thinking that the extremities of the woes have not yet been reached.

The status of this revelation of the 'lawless man' (see Isa. 66.3) is not clear. When in 2.8-10 the future revelation of the 'lawless man' is mentioned again, the verb ἀποκαλυφθήσεται could be used absolutely: 'he will be revealed'; or it could be accompanied by the dative τοῖς ἀπολλυμένοις: 'he will be revealed to those who are perishing'. In that case the revelation is to that specific group only. Alternatively, although less satisfactorily because of the following relative clause, τοῖς ἀπολλυμένοις could be taken with the immediately preceding phrase ἐν πάσῃ ἀπάτῃ ἀδικίας; in that case the revelation would be public but the effectiveness of the deceit would be limited to 'those who are perishing'. In either case the status of the revelation is limited, either limited to a group of persons, or limited in its deceitful effect on that

40. See Barclay, 'Conflict in Thessalonica', pp. 526-28.

41. Aus, 'The Relevance of Isaiah 66.7', p. 263: 'The concentration of these indications in the first chapter shows that the author considers this the most important issue with which he must deal'.

42. That is, if we regard the protasis in the text of 2.3b as having 2.2d as a form of its assumed apodosis.

group. The news that the Day has arrived is an example of delusion; such delusion belongs to the unfaithful, and such delusion is inappropriate to the readers. The readers are warned against this deceitful effect; it is the deceitfulness of wickedness (2.10). It is an outworking of Satan (2.9). It is also part of the divine purpose that those who take pleasure in injustice will put their trust in the lie and be judged for what they are, as those who refuse the truth and take pleasure in injustice.[43] Once again the divine purpose is seen as operating among the readers' opponents.

What then is the function of 2.1-12? The function of the unit 2.1-12, if indeed it is a unit, would seem to be a warning against being misled. The warning however is relevant to the readers only in so far as it is inappropriate for them to be misled, for example in the matter of the arrival of the Day of the Lord.

The section 2 Thess. 2.3-12 makes a contrast between what the readers have already been taught and ought to have remembered (2.5), and what they are aware of now (2.6). What they have already been taught is that there will be apostasy, characterized by the 'man of lawlessness', a boastful, blasphemous opponent of God.[44] This is well described as traditional teaching; it is based on the traditions developed from Isaiah and Daniel. What the readers are fully aware of now, at this present moment, is however something rather different; it is the outworking of the mystery of lawlessness now. They are aware of it because they can recognize it in the delusion to which God has already committed those who are perishing (Compare 2.7a with its present tense τὸ γὰρ μυστήριον ἤδη ἐνεργεῖται ['For the mystery is already at work'] [but see p. 250]) with 2.11 and its present tense πέμπει αὐτοῖς ὁ θεὸς ἐνεργείαν πλάνης ['God sends them a power that workes delusion']). The contrast within the section is therefore between an experienced present outworking of lawlessness and delusion, and the previously given traditional teaching of a future embodiment of lawlessness.

If the function of the section is a warning against being misled and

43. Taking διὰ τοῦτο in 2.11 as prospective, pointing toward εἰς τὸ πιστεῦσαι αὐτοὺς τῷ ψεύδει.

44. See n. 1 and Dan. 11.36 (MT). On this see L. Peerbolte, *The Antecedents of Antichrist* (Leiden: E.J. Brill, 1996). Peerbolte argues (pp. 90-92) that in *Dialogue with Trypho* 32.3-4 and 110.2 Justin does not use 2 Thess. but only a tradition related to that of 2 Thess.; Justin's use of Dan. 11.36c rather than 11.36b is, in his view, an indication of this.

the basis of the warning is a contrast between what is and what is to be, between what the readers have been taught and what will be revealed to the deluded, then the section as a whole is a warning to the faithful not to be misled because that would be inappropriate for instructed, faithful followers of Christ. It is appropriate only to those in whom the mystery of lawlessness is at work and to whom the 'lawless one' will be revealed.

The next step in the argument takes us into the two difficult verses 2 Thess. 2.6-7.[45] From what we have seen so far the likelihood is that εἰς τὸ ἀποκαλυφθῆναι αὐτὸν in 2.6b refers to the purpose or the timing of the same future revelation of the 'man of lawlessness' mentioned in 2.3. The γὰρ in 2.7a and the position of the ἤδη directly before the verb ἐνεργεῖται in v. 7a suggest that the present operation or outworking of lawlessness provides a reason for that purpose or timing. One purpose which the section has already identified is the deceiving of 'those who are perishing'. If the section is a coherent argument, then τὸ κατέχον is likely to serve that particular purpose: 'what you are at present aware of is τὸ κατέχον, so that he may be revealed in his own time; for already now the mystery of lawlessness is at work'.

This leads us to the key question of how to deal with τὸ κατέχον and ὁ κατέχων. Why is there a change from the neuter participle in 2.6 to the masculine participle in 2.7b, and how is the verb to be understood? An answer lying immediately to hand is that τὸ κατέχον in 2.6 is neuter because it refers to μυστήριον in 2.7a. A second answer is that, to make sense of 2.7a with its γὰρ, its present tense ἐνεργεῖται, and its τὸ μυστήριον placed first in the sentence and divided by the verb from τῆς ἀνομίας, some such sense for κατέχω is required as 'grasp', 'maintain', or even 'possess'[46]—now indeed you are aware of "that which possesses", so that the man of lawlessness may be revealed in his own time. For, at present, it is as a mystery of lawlessness that it operates.' That is what the followers of Christ recognize in the unbelievers who oppose them.

The mysterious working of lawlessness is identifiable and is recog-

45. For detailed discussions of these verses see the bibliography in J. Weima and S. Porter, *An Annotated Bibliography of 1 and 2 Thessalonians* (Leiden: E.J. Brill, 1998), pp. 246-72.

46. If the verb refers to evil, and in 2.7b to the 'evil one' then the available sense of 'possess' would be particularly appropriate. See C. Giblin, '2 Thess 2 reread', in R.F. Collins (ed.), *The Thessalonian Correspondence* (BETL, 87; Louvain: Leuven, 1990), pp. 459-69 (459).

nized as such by the followers of Christ. What follows in the text (2.7b) appears to be an incomplete sentence. However ἐνεργεῖται can be supplied from the previous sentence (2.7a) and read in 2.7b also. The opening word of the sentence μόνον carries considerable stress: 'it is only as "the possessor" that it operates'. The masculine participle ὁ κατέχων is a unique formulation; it could be parallel to ὁ πειράζων (1 Thess. 3.5), the participle designating Satan in a particular role. If that is the case here in 2.7b the participle designates the mysterious power of Satan which possesses the unbeliever. According to 2 Thess. 2.7b that remains the case until—ἕως ἐκ μέσου γένηται. The phrase ἐκ μέσου γένηται is usually taken to mean 'depart'. However a survey of the LXX, Aquila and Symmachus uses of ἐκ μέσου shows that the phrase depends for its force upon the verb which accompanies it. It indicates separation or departure with verbs of taking, departing, separating. However with verbs of place it can mean 'among'. In Num. 25.7 for example ἐξανέστη ἐκ μέσου τῆς συναγωγῆς means 'he stood up in the middle of the synagogue'. In the absence of a verb of separation and with the verb γένηται which could indicate place it is therefore unlikely that the phrase would indicate separation. Since γένηται can mean 'arrived', the whole phrase here may well be the equivalent of our idiom 'he arrives centre stage'. 2.7 then indicates that the mysterious work of lawlessness continues in the present; but it is only as 'the possessor' that Satan operates until he takes centre stage. Then Satan's true claim becomes apparent with the arrival of the 'lawless one'. The distinction is between 'the possessor' as possessor of individuals and as claimant to the world. Once he takes centre stage then the time of the 'lawless one', the embodiment of lawlessness, will begin.[47] There is no need for the believer to fear him, since the 'Lord will destroy him with the breath of his mouth' (2.8). But for the unbeliever his arrival, his parousia, means further delusion and the threat of ultimate destruction.

If this reading is correct, and it follows the rules of grammar, then the unit 2.1-12 is a warning against being misled; the basis of the warning is a contrast between what is and what is to be, between what is evident now and what will be revealed, between what believers are aware of as a mysterious power of possession and that which unbelievers will come to know as the claim of Satan to total possession. Through the appearance of the man of lawlessness, whom the Lord Christ will destroy,

---

47. See nn. 1 and 2 for references to 'the lawless man' in Isa. 66.

Satan misleads the unbelievers on their way to delusion and destruction.

There is a keen logic at work in the unit but not the strict rhetorical shape envisaged by Hughes. The relation of 2.1-2 and 2.3-12 is not that of partitio and probatio. Rather the answer given to the Thessalonians in their surprise and terror at the supposed news of the Day's arrival is that they are not to be misled; it is those who do not believe who will be victims of Satan's subterfuge. The answer to their surprise and terror is not in the form of a timetable of the last days; rather, it deals in a different way with the fear that persecution means the arrival of the Day. It quietens hearts and minds through the reminder that the tradition treats apostasy, the man of lawlessness and the work of Satan as the concern of unbelievers. The faithful are not to be misled.

If 2.3-12 are not part of a probatio, 2.13-17 cannot be either. The opening eight words of 2.13 are identical with those of the opening of the exordium (1.3). Rhetorically they give the impression of a resumée, shaped by the use of ἡμεῖς δὲ, to make clear the contrast between the fate of the faithless and the fulfilment of God's purpose through the gospel for those who believe. The elect are the firstfruits of the divine purpose,[48] and that is encouragement for them in the difficult times through which they are living. The conclusion is stated clearly in 2.15: they should stand by what they have been taught.

2.1-14 marks the limits of the influence of Isaiah 66 in 2 Thessalonians. But it is worth commenting briefly on the final chapter of 2 Thessalonians because of its relevance to the purpose of the letter. If the letter is Pauline, the reason for the addition of 3.1-16 is not immediately apparent. Paul asks for the prayers of the Thessalonians on the grounds that he too knows what evil men can do, and using Isa. 25.4-12 he draws on themes akin to Isaiah 66. Such a request for prayer of his behalf is only to be expected. However the repetition in 3.6-13 of what is contained in 1 Thessalonians 4 seems a strange waste of space. There is nevertheless a possible explanation. In 1 Thessalonians Paul used a phrase which, in the light of his argument in the whole letter, sounds foolishly ambiguous. Having advised the Thessalonians to keep awake, and having comforted them in the loss of those who had 'fallen asleep' Paul promises that all believers will live together with Christ (5.10)

---

48. G. Fee, 'On Text and Commentary on 1 and 2 Thessalonians', in E. Lovering (ed.), *SBL Seminar Papers* (Altanta: Scholars Press, 1992), pp. 165-83, makes the case for reading ἀπαρχην in 2.13, and comments: 'God has chosen a people for his own name—his firstfruits, if you will, of the great eschatological harvest.'

εἴτε γρηγορῶμεν εἴτε καθεύδωμεν. If some misread that to mean, as indeed they might well have done, that believers need not after all heed his warnings about morally 'keeping awake', then Paul would have had good reason to repeat in 2 Thessalonians what he had said about the style of living appropriate to those who belong to the community of Christ.[49]

Conclusion

The role of Isaiah 66 in 2 Thessalonians has sometimes been treated as of marginal importance. What we have seen in this article is that there is some truth in the judgment; the references in the letter to Isaiah 66 are few. They are however significant as far as the purpose of the letter is concerned, and, together with other LXX phrases, they raise some significant questions about both the purpose and the setting of 2 Thessalonians. Apart from assisting the rehabilitation of the Pauline authorship of the letter—and several of the main arguments against Pauline authorship have been shown in the light of LXX influence to be vulnerable—the shift from 1 Thessalonians to 2 Thessalonians which those references represent hints at an important perspective on a problem which over the years caused Paul great anxiety and pain: the presence of some of his own race among those who set obstacles to the progress of the gospel. The main body of the letter addresses the anxiety and pain which the Thessalonians felt at the opposition which they encountered, a pastoral concern which Paul met using traditions with Old Testament roots. But behind the pastoral concern for them and his advocacy of his apostolic style of life there emerges in 2 Thessalonians one of the fundamental issues with which Paul would wrestle for the rest of his life, and one on which the Isaianic material afforded him illuminating insights: how does the divine purpose relate to those of his compatriots who reacted against his preaching? 2 Thessalonians hints that there is no part of the experience of the Thessalonian Christians from which the influence and purpose of God can be excluded; even the experience of persecution is included, whether by Jews or Gentiles. In that is one of the most comforting, and at the same time cautionary, messages which Paul can offer to his suffering community; and in that is an emerging answer to the question of why his compatriots should oppose him.

49. On the ambiguity of 1 Thess. 5.10 see M. Lautenschlager, 'εἴτε γρηγορῶμεν εἴτε καθεύδωμεν', *ZNW* 81 (1990), pp. 39-59.

THE USE OF THE OLD TESTAMENT IN REVELATION 12

Ian Paul

There is little doubt that, while Revelation does not formally cite the Old Testament, it is saturated with allusive references to it. Its language is more dependent on the Old Testament than any other work of the New. H.B. Swete notes that the appendix to Westcott and Hort's commentary indicates references to the Old Testament in 278 of the 404 verses of Revelation—nearly 70 per cent.[1] R.H. Charles and Swete (following Lightfoot) both make extensive lists of allusions, some years prior to any concern to classify such lists and objectify the method behind their creation.[2]

Recent interest in the relation between the Old Testament and the New, and in particular the way the New 'uses' the Old, have naturally spilt over into studies on Revelation. Thus works have appeared on the use of particular Old Testament books—in particular Isaiah, Ezekiel and Daniel—as well as general works on the Old Testament in Revelation.[3] But a key question in looking at Revelation's use of the Old

1. H.B. Swete *The Apocalypse of St John: The Greek Text with Introduction, Notes and Indices* (London: Macmillan, 1917), p. cxl. G.K. Beale, *The Book of Revelation: A Commentary on the Greek Text* (NIGTC; Grand Rapids, MI: Eerdmans; Carlisle: Paternoster, 1999), p. 77 n. 16 lists a range of estimates of the number of allusions in Revelation, though he does not distinguish between the numbers of allusions and the numbers of verses which contain allusions.

2. R.H. Charles, *The Revelation of St John: A Critical and Exegetical Commentary* (Edinburgh: T. & T. Clark, 1920), pp. lxii-lxxxvi; Swete, *Apocalypse*, pp. cxxxv-cxlviii.

3. J. Fekkes, *Isaiah and Prophetic Traditions in the Book of Revelation* (JSNTSup, 93; Sheffield: JSOT Press, 1994); J.M. Vogelgesang, 'The Interpretation of Ezekiel in the Book of Revelation' (PhD dissertation, Harvard University, 1985); Jean-Pierre Ruiz, *Ezekiel in the Apocalypse: The Transformation of Prophetic Language in Rev. 16.17–19.10* (European University Studies, 23; Frankfurt, 1989); G.K. Beale, *The Use of Daniel in Jewish Apocalyptic Literature and in the Revelation of St John* (Lanham, MD: University Press of America, 1984). See also

Testament has been how, exactly, we can discern whether or not there is an allusion within the text. To see that this is a pressing question, one only has to look at the 'allusions' mentioned by different commentators. In the passages on the seven trumpets (Rev. 8.7–9.21 and 11.15-18) ten different commentators between them propose allusions to 288 Old Testament passages—and agree on only one![4]

In this article, I hope to look at some of the issues that are thrown up in studying Revelation's use of the Old Testament (many of which need further exploration), then examine verbal parallels to the Old Testament found in Revelation 12, and finally look at the significance of these allusions in the reading of this chapter. As with any individual work of analysis, an understanding of Revelation's use of the Old Testament is only one piece in a larger jigsaw, and its true significance can only be seen from the wider picture of how we might read the text.

The Interpretation of Allusion and Citation

The relation of the New Testament to the Old was less of a problem in pre-critical study. Where the apparent meaning of an Old Testament text was in conflict with the use of that text in the New, then the New Testament was seen as fulfilling the Old, providing the fuller meaning, the *sensus plenior*. Undergirding this was the belief in common, divine authorship of both texts, and in a consequent coherence in their theologies. Critical study, with its focus on the human authors and their variegated historical and literary contexts, could not rest easy with such an approach. Since it was difficult to make methodological sense of the variety of ways the New Testament writers 'interpreted' the Old, in modern hermeneutical terms at least, it was easy to conclude that such interpretation was arbitrary, and designed to serve the later writers' own apologetic ends. Barnabas Lindars is representative of this view:

numerous articles on the Old Testament in Revelation by Aune, Beale, Moyise and others.

4.   Jon Paulien, 'Elusive Allusions: The Problematic Use of the Old Testament in Revelation', *BR* 37 (1988), pp. 37-53 (37). The commentators were Charles, Dittmar, Hühn, Kraft, Ford, Mounce, Prigent, Westcott and Hort, and the tables given in NA 26 and UBS 3 Greek New Testaments. They all agree that Rev. 9.5 alludes to Job 3.21—not perhaps the most theologically significant element of this section of Revelation.

> The place of the Old Testament in the formation of New Testament theology is that of servant, ready to run to the aid of the gospel wherever it is required, bolstering up arguments, and filling out meaning through evocative allusions, but never acting as the master or leading the way, nor even guiding the process behind the scenes.[5]

In other words, both the new logic and the new context of the words cited override and obliterate the old. Schüssler Fiorenza appears to adopt this view when she comments that in Revelation John 'does not interpret the Old Testament but uses its words, images, phrases and patterns as a language arsenal in order to make his own theological statement'.[6]

But more recent work has shown this to be an inadequate account of how citation and allusions function. T.M. Greene, J. Hollander and others have shown (from a literary perspective) that the relationship between the text cited and the text citing is much more complex and dynamic; in the mind of the reader, the context and connotations of the original are not entirely left behind, but are brought to bear (positively or negatively) in the reading of the citation or allusion.[7] This notion of 'intertextuality' has been used with great effectiveness by Richard Hays, in his explication of the way that Paul uses Scripture; 'connotations bleed over' from the Old Testament into Paul's own writing.[8] Intertextuality has also been used to positive effect as a discipline in the study of Revelation, and has been shown to be of significance in arbitrating between conflicting readings where Old Testament allusion plays a part.[9] Richard Bauckham goes as far as to say that Revelation

---

5.   Barnabas Lindars, 'The Place of the OT in the Formulation of NT Theology', *NTS* 23 (1976), pp. 59-66 (66).

6.   Schüssler Fiorenza, *The Book of Revelation: Justice and Judgement* (Philadelphia: Fortress Press, 1985), p. 135.

7.   Thomas M. Greene, *The Light in Troy: Imitation and Discovery in Renaissance Poetry* (New Haven: Yale University Press, 1982); J. Hollander, *The Figure of Echo: A Mode of Allusion in Milton and After* (Berkeley: University of California Press, 1981).

8.   Richard B. Hays, *Echoes of Scripture in the Letters of Paul* (New Haven: Yale University Press, 1989), p. 142.

9.   See Steve Moyise's discussion of Rev. 1 'The Use of the Old Testament in the Book of Revelation' (Unpublished paper given at British NT conference) and Chapters 1, 3, and 6 of *The Old Testament in the Book of Revelation* (Sheffield: Sheffield Academic Press, 1995); Aune 'Intertextuality and the Genre of the Apocalypse', *SBL Seminar Papers* 30 (Atlanta, GA: Scholars Press, 1991), pp. 142-60.

'is a book designed to be read in constant intertextual relationship with the Old Testament'.[10]

It should be noted that intertextuality, as an approach, does not provide a method for interpretation, so much as highlighting the importance of considering the relation between the new context and the old in interpreting allusion and citation. In each case, only study of the texts in question can show the way in which the contexts interrelate.

The Detection of Allusion in Revelation

The issue that is distinctive to the study of Revelation in this area is how to discern the presence or otherwise of allusion. By far the majority of Paul's use of Scripture is explicit citation; none of John's is.

There have been several recent attempts to objectify the process of discerning allusions.[11] In his study of the way Daniel is used in Jewish apocalyptic literature and Revelation, Greg Beale classifies allusions fairly simply as 'clear allusions,' 'probable allusions (with more varied wording)' and 'possible allusion or echo'.[12] It is perhaps surprising that the setting out of these categories and a few related methodological points is limited to a single footnote at this stage. Beale does return to questions of methodology (and rather briefly authorial intention) in his conclusion, and expands his thoughts further in his recent commentary.[13]

Jon Paulien starts with a more developed explicit approach to method. He distinguishes between echoes and direct allusions. In discerning *direct allusions*, he uses three criteria internal to the text (verbal parallels, thematic parallels and structural parallels), together with any external evidence, in order to discern how probable an allusion is— certain, probable, possible, or not an allusion. Paulien's approach has the virtue of bringing some critical objectivity to the discussion, and

---

10. R. Bauckham, *The Climax of Prophecy: Studies in the Book of Revelation* (Edinburgh: T. & T. Clark), pp. x-xi.

11. In relation to Revelation, approaches of note include Beale, *The Use of Daniel*, Paulien, 'Elusive Allusions' and L.P. Trudinger, 'The Text of the Old Testament in the Book of Revelation' (Phd dissertation: Boston University, 1963), the latter being noteworthy because of its date.

12. Beale, *The Use of Daniel*, p. 43 n. 62.

13. See the concluding section of Beale, *The Use of Daniel*, and the discussion in *idem*, *Book of Revelation*, pp. 76-99. Interestingly, his comments on the detection of allusions still follow his threefold classification set out in 1984.

raising questions of method within the process of commentary. But it has two significant weaknesses.

First, his differentiation between *echo* and *allusion* depends entirely on whether he believes that occurrence of a verbal parallel was intentional on the part of the author.[14] As he provides no clear criteria for discerning whether something was in the author's mind or not, it could be argued that this does not get us very far. Moreover, since Freud it is clear that texts may communicate something about their authors of which the authors themselves are not yet aware.[15] Paulien also assumes that where an allusion is deliberate, we should necessarily then consider the original context of the allusion in interpreting it in the new context, even though an author could deliberately take something quite out of context.[16] And he assumes that where a text is taken to be referred to unconsciously (on the part of the author) this tells us less about the significance of the connexion. This is unfortunate, given that the allusions in Revelation may indeed be the product of 'a memory so charged with Old Testament words and thoughts that they arrange themselves... without conscious effort on [the author's] own part'.[17]

This suggests that Paulien does not pay enough attention to the problems inherent in discussing authorial intention. It is perfectly acceptable, on literary and methodological grounds, to talk meaningfully of authorial intention, and it is therefore also meaningful to discuss allusion. But it is important in both cases not to assume too much about the relation between intention and meaning, and to remember that any test of interpretation must be against coherence with the text, not against an imputed authorial intention.[18]

---

14. Paulien, 'Elusive Allusions', pp. 40 and 48: 'Where the author was consciously referring to previous literature, we call the parallel a "direct allusion"... Many of the allusions cited by major commentators are really echoes, and should not be listed as though the author had them in mind.'

15. Umberto Eco, *Interpretation and Overinterpretation* (Cambridge: Cambridge University Press, 1992), gives some personal examples of where readers have pointed out allusions in his own writings that he had not been aware of at the time of writing, which he nevertheless agrees in retrospect are allusions.

16. Paulien, 'Elusive Allusions', p. 41.

17. Swete, *Apocalypse*, p. cliv.

18. I have discussed the current hermeneutical debate about authorial intention in my thesis 'The Value of a Ricoeurian Hermeneutic of Metaphor in Interpreting the Symbolism of Revelation Chapters 12 and 13' (PhD dissertation, Nottingham Trent University, 1998), pp. 151-54.

The second shortcoming of Paulien's approach is that the classification of allusions is based on the interpreter's confidence, rather than the text's (or even author's) intention. It is surely more pertinent whether an allusion appears of major significance, minor significance, or is incidental to the passage as interpreted. We may be relatively uncertain about an allusion according to Paulien's criteria, and yet be clear that a text is of crucial importance in understanding a passage. For example, the allusion to Ps. 2.9 in Rev. 12.5 would not figure high up on the scale of probable allusions, according to Paulien's system. For whilst there are four words in common, so that it qualifies well as a 'verbal parallel', it features not at all as a thematic or structural parallel, which for Paulien are usually the more significant measures.[19] But within the context of the passage, the fact that the allusion comes 'out of the blue', as it were—there is a marked discontinuity with the surrounding verses—actually points up the importance of the allusion. It serves to identify unambiguously the male child as the Messiah figure of Jewish expectation.[20] This is of central importance in understanding the passage. The evaluation of allusion therefore needs two dimensions: an axis of confidence (the reader's perspective); and an axis of significance (the author's/text's perspective).

A more satisfactory classification (if classification is what is needed) follows from the way that allusion actually works for writers and within a text. Writers may allude to an earlier text by means of the occasional word or phrase, or may do this more systematically by developing an allusive theme. Conversely, they may allude to a single phrase or idea, and more or less discard the context, or may allude to a repeated theme in the work in question. I would therefore suggest a broad classification of allusion along these lines: verbal allusion to words; verbal allusion to themes; thematic allusion to words; thematic allusion to themes. We will come across examples of each of these types in Revelation 12. Criteria for identifying allusions are important, but in the process of reading such data cannot be separated from discussion of the theological significance of each case, as Greg Beale's recent commentary demonstrates.

19. Paulien, 'Elusive Allusions', p. 44: 'Of the three, verbal parallels are often the weakest criterion [*sic*].'

20. Even J.M. Ford, *Revelation* (AB, 38; New York: Doubleday, 1975), agrees with this identification, even though her theory of Baptist authorship makes her stop short of going on to identify this with the historical Jesus.

Paulien has noted that we should take account of the context of allusion in the allusive work (under 'structural' and 'thematic parallels'). But we need to take equal account of how the text alluded to has been understood in the intervening years, and particularly by communities that may have close links with Revelation and its readers. If a possible allusion appears to understand the earlier text in a way that other contemporary works have understood it, then this provides very strong corroboration for the identification of the allusion. This is an extension of Paulien's 'external evidence', and comes into play in an interesting new identification of an allusion in Rev. 12.8, as we shall see below.

In all this, it is important to remember that much interpretation consists in guess-work and intuition; objectivity comes to bear only in assessing the proposed interpretations.[21] In the same way, we need to rely on our own and others' insights and intuition in discovering allusions; objective methods are surely only valuable when we are assessing conflicting claims.

In order to help in this assessment, I have listed the text of Revelation 12 alongside the proposed texts alluded to.[22] In examining allusions in Revelation 12, I took as my starting point the lists of Charles, Swete and Ford as well as the work of Hendrik, van Henten and Beale. I have worked with Greek texts of the Old Testament for two reasons. In the first place, the whole notion of *verbal* allusion is thrown out when comparing across different languages. In order to match words, we would need to correlate terms used in translation. And the only meaningful data for that would be to return to Greek versions of the Old Testament. Secondly, despite Charles's thesis that much of Revelation's allusion is to the Hebrew text, translated by the author, there is no clear consensus that this is the case. Beale has shown that the situation is complex, and

---

21. This point is made at some length by Paul Ricoeur in *History and Truth* (Evanston: Northwestern University Press, 1965). Here he is in agreement with the comments of E.D. Hirsch in his discussion of *Validity in Interpretation* (New Haven: Yale University Press, 1967).

22. It is surprising how rarely this is done in studies that focus on intertextuality in specific passages. Beale, *The Use of Daniel*, lists only texts in English translation alongside Old Testament references—there is no clear presentation of the texts that are proposed as parallel. Despite Charles's separation of passages that owe more to the Hebrew of the Old Testament and those owing more to a Greek version in his listing of allusions, there are very few instances where a comparison with a Greek version misses anything.

there are even occasions where Revelation parallels the LXX in preference to θ'.[23] There do not appear to be any occasions where a parallel with the Old Testament is missed in Revelation 12 and 13 by considering the Greek only.

Allusions in Revelation 12

Isaiah 7.14 (Revelation 12.1)

Both texts include a pregnant woman as a sign; though the text in Isaiah has no christological overtones in its original context, it may well have acquired them for John and his readers due to the hermeneutical influence of the tradition represented by Mt. 1.23. The texts share the verbal parallel σημεῖον, but παρθένος is not a general synonym for γυνὴ, and the phrase ἐν γαστρὶ ἔχουσα/ἕξει, whilst appearing to be a strong verbal link, is a common Greek idiom, and thus adds little. (The same point undermines supposed connexions with Mt. 1.18 where the identical phrase to Rev. 12.2, ἐν γαστρὶ ἔχουσα, occurs.) There is no structural parallel, in that Isa. 7.14 appears to play no part elsewhere in Revelation, and the original context of the verse is not picked up. Further, the other allusions in the description of the woman are to corporate metaphors, and within the structure of Revelation the anti-type to this woman is the whore of ch. 17, who is also a corporate figure.[24]

The images of sun, moon and stars do have some minor precedents in the Old Testament, but these are not thematically developed, and there is no strong verbal parallel. These are better understood in terms of their general, 'archetypal' resonances, and the astral imagery of the cult with which the chapter has strong connexions.

---

23. G.K. Beale, 'A Reconsideration of the Text of Daniel in the Apocalypse', *Bib* 67.4 (1986), pp. 539-43.

24. It could be argued that the astral imagery echoes that associated with Artemis and Isis, and these are individuals. But it is not clear that this should affect our view of the allusion to the Old Testament. But note that single characters frequently have corporate significance in Revelation. For example, the antitype to the beast from the land in ch. 13 is the people of God (within the quasi-trinity of dragon, beast from the sea, and beast from the land—J.W. van Henten, 'Dragon Myth and Imperial Ideology in Revelation 12–13', *SBL Seminar Papers* 33 (1994), pp. 496-515 (496) and the beast itself may 'represent' the *Commune Asiae* (Swete, *Apocalypse*, p. lxxx).

Isaiah 26.17 and 66.7 (Revelation 12.2, 6)

The image of the people of God in the agonies of labour, and waiting to be delivered by God, seems to become more developed from 26.17 to 66.7. This image acquired especial significance during the Maccabaean period, when it came to have specifically Messianic connotations, the sufferings of God's people thus described being the birthpangs of the new (Messianic) age.[25] A parallel is found at Qumran, in 1QH 3.7-12, which contains some similarities, but also some important differences. There is no need to see a dependence between this and Revelation; rather, 'the most that can be argued is that they both used the same tradition'.[26]

Rissi saw the whole of Isa. 26.17–27.1 as seminal for Revelation 12.[27] The intervening verses (20-21) do have thematic parallels with Revelation—their images of judgment recur in Isaiah and elsewhere, and also occur thematically in Revelation—but that need not imply that these verses have such critical importance for Rev. 12.1-2. On the other hand, Hedrik is being too rigourous when he rules out the influence of Isa. 26.17 on the grounds that the 'woman' gives birth to wind (MT) or salvation (LXX), rather than a Messiah figure.[28] This fails to take into account the subsequent development of the woman-in-labour image.

Isaiah 66.7 has multiple verbal parallels to Rev. 12.2, 5 and 6; Zion is a woman in the pains of childbirth and longing to be delivered by God. Note that in some senses Zion/Jerusalem stands for the people who are suffering, but also Zion/Jerusalem 'gives birth' to the new people delivered by God. A corporate understanding of the woman in Revelation 12 leads to the same paradox, since she gives birth to the child and the 'rest of her offspring' (12.17). In the MT of Isa. 66.7, she is delivered of a son (וְהִמְלִיטָה, hiphil perfect of מלט). Now, מלט shares the ambiguity

---

25. See *m. Gen. R.* 85, *Lev. R.* 14.9 and *Targ. Jon. Isa.* 66.7, and R.D. Aus, 'The Relevance of Isaiah 66.7 to Revelation 12 and II Thessalonians 1', *ZNW* 67 (1976), p. 256 for comment, and pp. 260-61 for a discussion of the 'messianic woes' that constituted the pains of birth in Jewish understanding.

26. William K. Hedrik, 'The Sources and Use of the Imagery in Apocalypse 12' (ThD dissertation, Graduate Theological Union, 1971), p. 27, contrast P. Prigent, *Apocalypse 12: Histoire de l'exégèse (Beiträge zur Geschichte der biblischen Exegese)* (Tübingen: J.C.B. Mohr, 1959), p. 142.

27. M. Rissi, *Time and History: A Study on the Revelation* (Virginia: Richmond, 1966), pp. 36-37.

28. Hedrik, *Sources and Use*, p. 25. His case is not helped by his misquoting the LXX.

of the English verb 'to be delivered'—to give birth and to be saved, the meanings of מלט in the hiphil and niphal respectively. The LXX makes this explicit by translating it with two verbs, ἐξέφυγεν καὶ ἔτεκεν ἄρσεν, 'she fled and bore a son', and thus 'the ground is broken and the seed planted' for the idea of combining Exodus/desert imagery with the deliverance of God's suffering people through the birth of the Messiah.[29] That a Messianic dimension was seen in the verse is made clear in *Targum Jonathan Isaiah*, where this phrase becomes 'her king shall be revealed'.[30]

Micah 4.10 and 5.3(2) (Revelation 12.5, 17)

This is a further passage on the theme of Israel as a woman in childbirth, waiting on God to be delivered. Although the verbal parallels are not as close here as in the Isaiah passages, there is a structural parallel between 5.3-4 and Revelation 12. In Mic. 5.3 'they' will be given up until 'she who is in labour has brought forth'. Hedrik is right to point out that this says nothing specific about Israel as the woman—the thought as it stands is similar to that of Isa. 7.14, in saying that some woman who is pregnant now will just have given birth when God delivers his people, that is, the waiting time will be short.[31] But he does not notice the earlier reference in Mic. 4.10 to Israel's sufferings being likened to those of a woman in labour. This then allows the possibility of a Messianic interpretation of 5.3, the one in labour being Israel/Zion, and the one brought forth being the Messiah.[32] There is then a double structural parallel with Revelation 12: he will shepherd his flock (ποιμανεῖ) (Mic. 5.4) and be joined by the rest of his brethren (5.3).

Daniel 7.7, 8, 21 (Revelation 12.3, 8, 17)

Chapters 12 and 13 appear to allude to Daniel 7 extensively. The beast from the sea appears as a collation of the features of the four beasts in

---

29. The phrase is one coined by Hedrik (*Sources and Use*, p. 32) in relation to the idea of a personified Israel giving birth to a Messiah—though unfortunately he fails adequately to discuss Isa. 66.7, and underestimates the significance of Mic. 5, since he neglects to consider it in conjunction with Mic. 4.

30. See Aus, 'The Relevance'. Translation of the Targum cited is that by J.F. Stenning (Oxford: Clarendon Press, 1949).

31. Hedrik, *Sources and Use*, p. 30.

32. For a defence of this reading, see James L. Mays, *Micah* (Philadelphia: Westminster Press, 1976), p. 116.

Daniel 7, in having ten horns, and seven heads (the sum of the number of heads of the four beasts). The dragon in ch. 12 anticipates the beast in ch. 13 by sharing these features. The blasphemies of the arrogant horn on the fourth beast in Daniel, its power to make war on the holy ones, and its strength are all ascribed directly to the beast. The strength of the fourth Danielic beast is ascribed to the dragon.[33]

Psalm 2.9 (Revelation 12.5)
A clear verbal parallel exists in 12.5 identifying the male child as the expected Messiah figure. This psalm is frequently alluded to and quoted elsewhere in the New Testament, and 'from the perspective of early Christianity, it was a messianic psalm par excellence'.[34] It is only alluded to at one other place in Revelation (2.27), but imagery of divine kingship, similar to the psalm's, is present throughout (for instance in 1.5; 4.2; 6.17; 19.5).

Daniel 8.10 (Revelation 12.7)
The mixed identification of Daniel's horn and beast and Revelation's beast and dragon is also exemplified here, where the dragon throws down the stars in the same way as Daniel's little horn.

Daniel 10.13 and 20 (Revelation 12.7).
Revelation 12.7 mentions the figure of Michael as the opponent to the opponent of God and his people, in much the same way as Daniel. There is no need, however, to suppose a specific allusion to each text mentioning Michael. Note that 12.7 supplies the only occurrence of τοῦ with the infinitive in Revelation, which strengthens the case for seeing an allusion here.

Daniel 2.35 and Psalm 37(36).36 (Revelation 12.8)
The slightly unusual phrase οὐ(χ) (ὁ) τόπος εὑρέθη αὐτοῦ occurs only twice in the Old Testament, and τόπος with the passive of εὑρίσκω occurs nowhere else in the New Testament other than at Rev. 20.11.

In Daniel, the context is the divine judgment of the metal and clay figure of Nebuchadnezzar's dream, which stood for four kingdoms that would be destroyed by the coming kingdom of God. But in Psalm 37, the phrase is used of the wicked man; the psalm is an ethical injunction

---

33. For a fuller account of the use of Daniel in Rev. 12 and 13, see the relevant chapters in Beale, *The Use of Daniel.*
34. Peter C. Craigie, *Psalms 1–50* (WBC; Waco, TX: Word Books, 1983), p. 68.

not to fret because of the wicked, but to continue to trust in God. The interpretation of the psalm at Qumran shows how the general statement of reassurance in an ethical context becomes the prediction of God's judgment of an eschatological adversary. In 4Q171, the beginning of the psalm is interpreted as concerning all the wicked. But as the commentary continues, it focuses increasingly on the eschatological scenario involving the community. By v. 32 of the psalm, the commentary interprets it entirely in terms of the Wicked Priest and his opposition to the Teacher of Righteousness. Unfortunately, the manuscript does not include the interpretation of v. 37, but it is reasonable to suppose that the commentary continues along these lines.

Daniel's and Revelation's allusion to the psalm implicitly assume the same kind of hermeneutic. In Daniel, the judgment is not of a personified adversary, but is brought about by the advent of the Messianic kingdom. In Rev. 12.8, the judgment is of the cosmic enemy of God, Satan, and echoes the theme of the eschatological adversary that is found in a number of other places in the book.[35] In contrast, other New Testament allusions to the psalm (Mt. 5.5-11; 6.8-18; 1 Pet. 5.7; 1 Thess. 5.24-25) draw on the 'more natural, moral implications of the psalm'.[36]

The connexion of Revelation 12 with Psalm 37 and its interpretation at Qumran has not been noticed before, to my knowledge. As an allusion it has significance in three areas of discussion.

In the first place, its presence suggests that attempts to 'track' Satan from heaven to earth are misplaced; the significance of the episode is (proleptic) eschatological judgment, not cosmic geography.[37]

In the second place, its role within the passage follows the hermeneutical tradition within Daniel and at Qumran, where the understanding of the text is somewhat removed from anything that could be argued to be the author's intention in the original context of the psalm. In other words, the meaning of Old Testament texts cited within Revelation is not tied semantically to their original Old Testament context—they are

---

35. See A. Yarbro Collins, *The Combat Myth in the Book of Revelation* (Harvard Dissertations in Religion, 9; Missoula, MT: Scholars Press, 1976), Chapter 3.

36. Craigie, *Psalms 1–50*, p. 300.

37. See Yarbro Collins, *Combat Myth*, p. 131: 'If the dragon was cast down in act II [verses 7-9] then he must have been in heaven in act I [verses 1-6].' See also Minear's difficulties with cosmic geography in 'The Wounded Beast', *JBL* 72.2 (1953), pp. 93-101.

not like apples placed in a basket of other fruit that retain their semantic identity regardless of context.

Thirdly, the presence of two diverse interpretative traditions of this psalm within the New Testament may serve to shed light on the nature of the Christian communities, and their theological relation with other groups such as the community at Qumran. With regard to Revelation, there is more work to be done here.

Genesis 3.13, Job 1.6, Zechariah 3.1 (Revelation 12.9)

Revelation 12.9 draws together diverse elements of the Old Testament theme of a personified opponent to God. Again, there is no reason to think that the individual verses are being alluded to any more specifically than this.

Revelation 12.10 adds the appellation 'accuser', which picks up the theological idea of Job 1.9-11 without alluding to the specific text. The fall of Satan to the earth in 12.9 has theological similarities to Isa. 14.12 (as noted above), but there is little or no shared vocabulary between the two passages.

Isaiah 44.23 and 49.13 (Revelation 12.12)

Of the 52 occurrences of οὐρανός in Revelation, this is the only one in the plural. The context of both Isaiah texts is of celebration at God's act of redemption, in the forgiveness of sins and the comforting of his suffering people. Both chapters are alluded to a number of other times in Revelation. The allusion does not appear to have great structural significance within Revelation 12, but perhaps contributes to the hieratic, 'scriptural' feel that the widespread allusion to the LXX creates.[38]

Exodus 19.4 (Revelation 12.14)

The eagles' wings in Exodus 19 are identified as a metaphor for the Exodus deliverance. In Revelation 12, this Exodus imagery has been hinted at in the flight of the woman in v. 6, and is made explicit in v. 14 with the mention of the desert. This makes any connexion with Isa. 40.31 much less likely.

---

38. See E. Schüssler Fiorenza, *Revelation: Vision of a Just World* (Edinburgh: T. & T. Clark, 1985), p. 29; Yarbro Collins, *Combat Myth*, p. 109.

Daniel 7.25 and 12.7 (Revelation 12.14)
This clear verbal parallel comes in the context of the other thematic and structural parallels with Daniel, and is duplicated as 1260 days (12.6) and 42 months (13.5).[39]

Significance of Biblical Allusions in Revelation 12

All four types of allusion (verbal allusion to words, verbal allusion to themes, thematic allusion to words, thematic allusion to themes) occur in this chapter. Revelation 12.5, 8 and possibly 12 are verbal allusions to words and phrases. 12.9 and 14a appear to be verbal allusions to themes and ideas in the Old Testament. The use of the 'time, times and half a time' and its mutations into 1260 days and 42 months is a thematic development of a particular phrase in Daniel. And the image of the woman throughout ch. 12 develops a theme found in the Old Testament and in other apocalyptic literature.

Chapter 12 has five main characters in the narrative body of the chapter (vv. 1-6 and 13-18): the woman; the dragon; the male child; Michael; the rest of the woman's seed. Many of the allusions to the Old Testament function in such a way as to identify the characters, rather than describe the action of the plot. For example, the fact that the woman is in the agonies of childbirth serves to identify her with the expectant people of God. The dragon's throwing down of the stars connects him with the horn of Daniel, rather than describing anything within the main plotline. The description of the child as the one to rule with a rod of iron serves to identify him as the Messiah, and does not contribute anything to the action within the story. So the characters are biblical—but where does the shape of the narrative come from?

Building on the work of Hermann Günkel, Adela Yarbro Collins has demonstrated the importance of pagan mythology in shaping the text of Revelation 12. In her thesis of 1976, she set out the structural, historical and theological connexions between Revelation 12 and two particular versions of an ancient combat myth, one involving the conflict between Apollo and Python, and the other that of Horus with Seth-Typhon. The structural correspondences (which involve some reordering in the plot of Revelation 12, but are still clearly discernible) as is shown overleaf.

The dependence of Rev.12.1-6 and 13-18 on this mythology can help

---

39. On the equivalence of these periods, see Bauckham, *Climax of Prophecy*, p. 420.

to explain some of the structural oddities of the chapter, not least the theological lacuna left by the unusually brief summary of the Messiah's life, death and resurrection in 12.5—still a matter for comment in recent studies.

Leto—Python—Apollo	*Isis—Seth-Typhon—Horus*	*Woman—Dragon—male child (Rev. 12)*
1. Struggle for the sanctuary at Delphi	1. Struggle for kingship	
2. Leto pregnant by Zeus	2. Isis pregnant by Osiris	2. Woman about to give birth (2)
3. Python pursues Leto and tries to kill her	5. Birth of Horus	3. Dragon intends to devour the child (v. 4)
4. The north wind rescues Leto, who is then helped by Poseidon	3. Seth-Typhon pursues Isis and Horus	5. Birth of the child (v. 5a)
5. Birth of Apollo and Artemis	4. Ra and Thoth help Isis	7. Kingship of the child (5b)
6. Apollo overcomes Python	6. Horus overcomes Seth-Typhon	6. Michael defeats the dragon (7-9)
7.	7. Kingship of Horus	4. Woman is helped by God (v. 4), the great eagle (v. 14) and the earth (v. 16)
8. Apollo establishes the Pythian Games		3. Dragon pursues the rest of the woman's offspring.

I have shown elsewhere how Yarbro Collins's work provides the basis for seeing Revelation 12 as a series of four 'nested' units, where the second (vv. 7-9) and third (vv. 10-12) are each in turn epexegetical of the preceding unit, so that the theological lacuna is filled before the text returns to the mythologically-shaped plot in verse 13.[40]

In using the mythology as the basis for its narrative framework, the text has displaced the characters in this narrative with the biblical images. This displacement appears to have a polemical goal, since the myth was of especial significance as imperial propaganda.[41] Such polemical displacement is in fact characteristic of Revelation, as is shown by two other examples.

40. See my thesis 'The Value of a Ricoeurian Hermeneutic', pp. 178-81
41. As demonstrated by van Henten, 'Dragon Myth'.

First, David Aune has shown that the phrases 'I have the key to Death and Hades' (1.19), 'I am coming quickly' (five times) and 'I am the Alpha and the Omega' (four times) are all unique to Revelation in early Christian writings, have attested use in Graeco-Roman magic (particularly in the cult of Hekate), and are used in a way 'where the validity of the religious and magical assumptions behind are implicitly denied'.[42] In other words, they form part of an anti-magical polemic brought about by the displacement of pagan gods by the figure of Christ, a polemic that is re-enforced by the affirmation of magic as a vice (9.20) and that magicians will suffer the second death (21.8) and be shut out of the new Jerusalem (22.15).

Secondly, Allen Kerkeslager has argued convincingly that the figure of the rider on the white horse (in 6.2) stands not for Christ (as some have argued) but for Apollo, representing false religion that deceives the people.[43] It is the insertion of the Apollo figure into a story of deception and destruction that makes the polemical point, and this is re-inforced at other places: in 9.11 there is a pun on the word 'apollyon';[44] and the story of Apollo is (according to Yarbro Collins's theory) visited again in ch. 12.

The polemical displacement by biblical imagery of figures in a mythological framework serves to create a new perception of reality in the understanding of the reader. The process of opening up such a world by the juxtaposition of unlikes (in this case, the Old Testament and the Apollo myth) finds its theoretical (linguistic) foundation in Paul Ricoeur's hermeneutic of metaphor, set out most clearly by Ricoeur in *Interpretation Theory* and *The Rule of Metaphor* and applied to apocalyptic symbolism by André Lacocque.[45] According to Lacocque, both the images used and the reality to which they refer must be adapted and simplified in order that they should correspond to one another. The

42. D. Aune, 'The Apocalypse of John and Graeco-Roman Magic', *NTS* 33 (1987), p. 481.

43. A. Kerkeslager, 'Apollo, Greco-Roman Prophecy, and the Rider on the White Horse in Rev 6.2', *JBL* 112.1 (1993), pp. 116-21.

44. Kerkeslager ('Apollo', p. 119) mentions a rather pleasing contemporary parallel with this, in a poem about a singing doctor called Niketas. 'When Niketas sings, he is the Apollo of his songs. But when a physician, the Apollo [ie apollyon] of his patients.'

45. A. Lacocque 'Apocalyptic Symbolism: A Ricoeurian Hermeneutical Approach', *Bib Res* 26 (1981), pp. 6-15. I have explored the importance of Ricoeur's theory at some length in my thesis 'The Value of a Ricoeurian Hermeneutic'.

apocalyptic image is then the product of the fusion of an adapted image from the traditional 'store-house' of imagery with a simplified and stereotyped version of social and political realities. There is an *Epoche*, a distanciation for both the signifier (the image) and the signified (the reality in question). The image is given its new context, its *Sitz im Wort* (replacing its original *Sitz im Leben*), and the reality is caricatured by the association with the symbol. In Revelation 12 and 13, the social and political realities of the Empire in first-century Asia, the pagan mythological material, and the biblical imagery become fused in this *Epoche*, to produce a symbolized reality.

The twin concepts of caricature and polemical displacement within apocalyptic symbolization find a parallel with a more widely understood contemporary phenomenon—both are at the heart of a certain kind of political cartoon. Here, characters are drawn from one scenario (usually the one on which the cartoonist wishes to comment) and are placed in a plot or narrative framework from another scenario (the one being used as the vehicle of the cartoon). When Gordon Brown was shadow Chancellor, he 'drew' this cartoon of the Conservative government, picturing them as the disillusioned unemployed causing riots on the streets—at the time a topical picture:

> It is the familiar formula for trouble on the street—the build-up of tensions, noise, pushy and aggressive behaviour, territorial disputes, the long hot summer ahead in Downing Street and aggressive men with not enough to do, men whose future employment prospects are bleak, with no long-term stake in society. Even the constant police presence will not provide reassurance. Appeals from senior community leaders [such as Sir Edward Heath and Lord Archer]…will not be able to restore calm… By the Autumn, he will become a convert to Labour's new solutions for curbing persistently anti-social neighbours.[46]

As with Revelation 12, the characters belong to one setting, while the plot is drawn from another. The bringing together of these dissimilars has the effect of metaphorizing the situation, and opening up the possibility of perceiving the situation in a new way.

In the case of Revelation 12, the new understanding of the world opened up by the process of metaphorization actually inverts the dominant ideology of Empire. Instead of taking the role of the conquering hero Apollo, bringer of life, order and prosperity, the imperial figure

46. Text kindly supplied by Gordon Brown, taken from *Hansard*, 12 July 1995, p. 990.

becomes the chaos monster Python. Here he is portrayed as the biblical figure of Satan, the primeval opponent of God and his Messiah, who in his turn has become the one conquering through sacrifice portrayed elsewhere in Revelation as the lamb on the throne. This inversion of the dominant ideology puts those subscribing to Revelation's view of reality in the position of being a 'cognitive minority' living with a new mythology that is in direct opposition to that of the majority of the population.[47]

Conclusion

From a careful study of the Old Testament texts alluded to, understood within the structure of the text and its mythological influences, we have seen that Revelation 12 uses the Old Testament as a symbolic resource with which to metaphorize the world of its contemporary readers. It is less a case of Revelation 'interpreting' the Old Testament than Revelation using Old Testament categories to interpret its own world.

This use of biblical categories is perhaps the reason for Schüssler Fiorenza's comment on Revelation's 'language arsenal' noted at the beginning of this article. If the text of Revelation were 'moving backwards' from the present, in order to explain or expound the biblical texts, then we might expect a more careful treatment. But it is not doing this. It is moving forwards, using the biblical images and ideas to metaphorize the world in order to refigure it and thereby expose its reality.

> This is an indication of 'visionary language' rather than a deliberate attempt to write a commentary on these texts…this is not exegesis in any conventional sense.[48]

This is not an unusual phenomenon, in that it has a parallel in what are known as the 'charismatic' traditions, where the language of the Bible is taken up in prayer and conversation.[49] It is interesting to note that this is a group that, like John, sees its activity as closely related to the eschatological outpouring of the Spirit.[50] The invitation to the

47. On the Christian community as cognitive minority, see further D.A. deSilva, 'The Construction and Social Function of a Counter-Cosmos in the Revelation of John', *Forum* 9.1-2 (1993), pp. 47-61.

48. Rowland, *Revelation*, p. 6.

49. Rowland, *Revelation*, p. 6.

50. There is a developing corpus of systematic reflection on 'charismatic hermeneutics', most notably in the UK by Mark Stibbe. He notes the starting point of much of this (relatively unreflective) use of biblical vocabulary in contemporary

modern reader is perhaps to engage in a similar exercise of interpretation, in order to live in a biblical cognitive minority that keeps faith with a God who eschews the power structures of the world.

To see Revelation as using the Old Testament as a hermeneutical resource implies that the meaning of Old Testament texts in Revelation can never be tied rigidly to the meaning of those texts in their original context. But neither does it mean that the texts 'float free' from their Old Testament roots. John, it appears, is finding a 'correspondence of relationships' between the Old Testament and his own world, and in doing so is perhaps setting out a paradigm for the interpretation of Scripture—including the interpretation of the book of Revelation itself.[51] And whatever the apparent differences of meanings between the texts as alluded to in Revelation and in their Old Testament contexts, there remains for those in the faith community the theological task of holding such meanings together within the wider canonical context.

One further point is worth noting with regard to methodology. My discovery of an apparent allusion to Psalm 37 in Rev. 12.8, previously unnoticed, suggests that there is more work to be done in the analytical task of identifying possible allusions.[52] It is interesting to see that in his newly-published commentary Beale does not follow the pattern of Charles and Swete in tabling what he believes are allusions to the Old Testament—even though identifying the role of such allusion is central to his hermeneutical strategy.[53] It appears that explicit identification of what is assumed to be allusion to the text of the Old Testament remains an important potential set of data for future study, and for dialogue between commentators.

context is 'a sense of a rich harmony between biblical texts and present experience' ('This is That: Some Thoughts Concerning Charismatic Hermeneutics', *Anvil* 15.3 [1998], p. 183).

51. The term 'correspondence of relationships' is the one used by E. Schüssler Fiorenza of her own interpretative strategy in reading Revelation; see her *Revelation*, pp. 10-11.

52. I understand from a conversation with Jon Paulien that he is planning to publish a table listing all possible allusions in Revelation to the Old Testament, according to ten scholarly authorities. This may well be useful, though there is a danger that looking for a consensus amongst these authorities will given a minimal, rather than methodologically sound, position.

53. Beale, *Revelation*, p. xix.

Allusions to the Old Testament in Revelation 12

12.1 Καὶ σημεῖον μέγα ὤφθη ἐν τῷ οὐρανῷ, γυνὴ περιβεβλημένη τὸν ἥλιον, καὶ ἡ σελήνη ὑποκάτω τῶν ποδῶν αὐτῆς, καὶ ἐπὶ τῆς κεφαλῆς αὐτῆς στέφανος ἀστέρων δώδεκα, 12.2 καὶ ἐν γαστρὶ ἔχουσα, καὶ κράζει ὠδίνουσα καὶ βασανιζομένη τεκεῖν. 12.3 καὶ ὤφθη ἄλλο σημεῖον ἐν τῷ οὐρανῷ, καὶ ἰδοὺ δράκων μέγας πυρρός, ἔχων κεφαλὰς ἑπτὰ καὶ κέρατα δέκα καὶ ἐπὶ τὰς κεφαλὰς αὐτοῦ ἑπτὰ διαδήματα, 12.4 καὶ ἡ οὐρὰ αὐτοῦ σύρει τὸ τρίτον τῶν ἀστέρων τοῦ οὐρανοῦ καὶ ἔβαλεν αὐτοὺς εἰς τὴν γῆν. καὶ ὁ δράκων ἔστηκεν ἐνώπιον τῆς γυναικὸς τῆς μελλούσης τεκεῖν, ἵνα ὅταν τέκῃ τὸ τέκνον αὐτῆς καταφάγῃ. 12.5 καὶ ἔτεκεν υἱόν, ἄρσεν, ὃς μέλλει ποιμαίνειν πάντα τὰ ἔθνη ἐν ῥάβδῳ σιδηρᾷ. καὶ ἡρπάσθη τὸ τέκνον αὐτῆς πρὸς τὸν θεὸν καὶ πρὸς τὸν θρόνον αὐτοῦ. 12.6 καὶ ἡ γυνὴ ἔφυγεν εἰς τὴν ἔρημον, ὅπου ἔχει ἐκεῖ τόπον ἡτοιμασμένον ἀπὸ τοῦ θεοῦ, ἵνα ἐκεῖ τρέφωσιν αὐτὴν ἡμέρας χιλίας διακοσίας ἑξήκοντα.

12.7 Καὶ ἐγένετο πόλεμος ἐν τῷ οὐρανῷ, ὁ Μιχαὴλ καὶ οἱ ἄγγελοι αὐτοῦ τοῦ πολεμῆσαι μετὰ τοῦ δράκοντος. καὶ ὁ δράκων ἐπολέμησεν καὶ οἱ ἄγγελοι αὐτοῦ, 12.8 καὶ οὐκ ἴσχυσεν, οὐδὲ τόπος εὑρέθη αὐτῶν ἔτι ἐν τῷ οὐρανῷ. 12.9 καὶ ἐβλήθη ὁ δράκων ὁ μέγας, ὁ ὄφις ὁ ἀρχαῖος, ὁ καλούμενος Διάβολος καὶ ὁ Σατανᾶς, ὁ πλανῶν τὴν οἰκουμένην ὅλην— ἐβλήθη εἰς τὴν γῆν, καὶ οἱ ἄγγελοι αὐτοῦ μετ᾽ αὐτοῦ ἐβλήθησαν. 12.10 καὶ ἤκουσα φωνὴν μεγάλην ἐν τῷ οὐρανῷ λέγουσαν,

Isa. 7.14...σημεῖον ἰδοὺ ἡ παρθένος ἐν γαστρὶ ἕξει ...

Isa. 66.7 πρὶν ἢ τὴν ὠδίνουσαν τεκεῖν πρὶν ἐλθεῖν τὸν πόνον τῶν ὠδίνων ἐξέφυγεν καὶ ἔτεκεν ἄρσεν
Isa. 26.17 καὶ ὡς ἡ ὠδίνουσα ἐγγίζει τοῦ τεκεῖν καὶ ἐπὶ τῇ ὠδῖνι αὐτῆς ἐκέκραξεν

Dan. 7.7 θ᾽ ...καὶ κέρατα δέκα αὐτῷ

Dan. 8.10 θ᾽ ...ἔπεσεν ἐπὶ τὴν γῆν ἀπὸ τῆς δυνάμεως τοῦ οὐρανοῦ καὶ ἀπὸ τῶν ἄστρων...
[Mic. 4.10 ὤδινε...θύγατερ Σιων ὡς τίκτουσα...]
[Mic. 5.2 ...ἕως καιροῦ τικτούσης τέξεται...]
Ps. 2.9 ποιμανεῖς αὐτοὺς ἐν ῥάβδῳ σιδηρᾷ
Isa. 66.7 πρὶν ἐλθεῖν τὸν πόνον τῶν ὠδίνων ἐξέφυγεν καὶ ἔτεκεν ἄρσεν

Dan. 10.13 ...καὶ ἰδοὺ Μιχαηλ; 10.20 θ᾽...τοῦ πολεμῆσαι
Dan. 7.7 θ᾽ ...καὶ ἰδοὺ θηρίον... ἰσχυρὸν Dan. 2.35 θ᾽ ...καὶ τόπος οὐχ εὑρέθη αὐτοῖς...Ps. 36.36...καὶ οὐχ εὑρέθη ὁ τόπος αὐτοῦ
Gen. 3.13 ...ὁ ὄφις ἠπάτησέν με; Job 1.6 ...καὶ ὁ διάβολος ἦλθεν μετ᾽ αὐτῶν; Zech. 3.1 καὶ ὁ διάβολος εἱστήκει ἐκ δεξιῶν αὐτοῦ

Ἄρτι ἐγένετο ἡ σωτηρία καὶ ἡ
  δύναμις
καὶ ἡ βασιλεία τοῦ θεοῦ ἡμῶν
καὶ ἡ ἐξουσία τοῦ Χριστοῦ αὐτοῦ,
ὅτι ἐβλήθη ὁ κατήγωρ τῶν ἀδελφῶν
  ἡμῶν,
  ὁ κατηγορῶν αὐτοὺς ἐνώπιον
  τοῦ θεοῦ ἡμῶν ἡμέρας καὶ
  νυκτός.
12.11 καὶ αὐτοὶ ἐνίκησαν αὐτὸν διὰ
τὸ αἷμα τοῦ ἀρνίου
καὶ διὰ τὸν λόγον τῆς μαρτυρίας
αὐτῶν,
καὶ οὐκ ἠγάπησαν τὴν ψυχὴν
αὐτῶν ἄχρι θανάτου.

12.12 διὰ τοῦτο εὐφραίνεσθε, [οἱ   Isa. 44.23 εὐφράνθητε οὐρανοί;
  οὐρανοὶ   Isa. 49.13 εὐφραίνεσθε οὐρανοί
  καὶ οἱ ἐν αὐτοῖς σκηνοῦντες.
 οὐαὶ τὴν γῆν καὶ τὴν θάλασσαν,
  ὅτι κατέβη ὁ διάβολος πρὸς ὑμᾶς
ἔχων θυμὸν μέγαν,
  εἰδὼς ὅτι ὀλίγον καιρὸν ἔχει.
12.13 Καὶ ὅτε εἶδεν ὁ δράκων ὅτι
ἐβλήθη εἰς τὴν γῆν, ἐδίωξεν τὴν
γυναῖκα ἥτις ἔτεκεν τὸν ἄρσενα.

12.14 καὶ ἐδόθησαν τῇ γυναικὶ αἱ δύο
πτέρυγες τοῦ ἀετοῦ τοῦ μεγάλου, ἵνα   Exod. 19.4 ...ἐπὶ πτερύγων ἀετῶν...
πέτηται εἰς τὴν ἔρημον εἰς τὸν τόπον
αὐτῆς, ὅπου τρέφεται ἐκεῖ καιρὸν καὶ   Dan. 7.25 ...ἕως καιροῦ καὶ καιρῶν
καιροὺς καὶ ἥμισυ καιροῦ ἀπὸ   καὶ ἕως ἡμίσους καιροῦ; Dan. 12.7
προσώπου τοῦ ὄφεως. 12.15 καὶ   ...εἰς καιρὸν καὶ καιροὺς καὶ ἥμισυ
ἔβαλεν ὁ ὄφις ἐκ τοῦ στόματος αὐτοῦ   καιροῦ
ὀπίσω τῆς γυναικὸς ὕδωρ ὡς ποταμόν,
ἵνα αὐτὴν ποταμοφόρητον ποιήσῃ.
12.16 καὶ ἐβοήθησεν ἡ γῆ τῇ γυναικί,
καὶ ἤνοιξεν ἡ γῆ τὸ στόμα αὐτῆς καὶ
κατέπιεν τὸν ποταμὸν ὃν ἔβαλεν ὁ
δράκων ἐκ τοῦ στόματος αὐτοῦ. 12.17   Dan. 7.8 θ'...καὶ ἐποίει πόλεμον πρὸς
καὶ ὠργίσθη ὁ δράκων ἐπὶ τῇ γυναικί,   τοὺς ἁγίους...; Dan. 7.21 θ' ...ἐποίει
καὶ ἀπῆλθεν ποιῆσαι πόλεμον μετὰ   πόλεμον μετὰ τῶν ἁγίων...
τῶν λοιπῶν τοῦ σπέρματος αὐτῆς, τῶν   Mic. 5.2 ...καὶ οἱ ἐπίλοιποι τῶν
τηρούντων τὰς ἐντολὰς τοῦ θεοῦ καὶ   ἀδελφῶν αὐτῶν ἐπιστρέψουσιν...
ἐχόντων τὴν μαρτυρίαν Ἰησοῦ. 12.18
καὶ ἐστάθη ἐπὶ τὴν ἄμμον τῆς
θαλάσσης.

EPILOGUE

KAINA KAI ΠΑΛΑΙΑ: AN ACCOUNT OF THE BRITISH SEMINAR ON
THE USE OF THE OLD TESTAMENT IN THE NEW TESTAMENT

J. Lionel North

The distant origin of the British Seminar can be traced back to 1963, when the international organization *Studiorum Novi Testamenti Societas* (SNTS) began to make provision for what we nowadays call special interest groups, to be held alongside the main lectures and brief communications given at its annual meeting.[1] But more immediately it was not until 1975 that something like 'The Use of the Old Testament in the New Testament' became part of SNTS's seminar programme.[2] In that year and in 1976 Professor Matthew Black (St Andrews) led a group on 'The Christological Use of the Old Testament in the New Testament'.[3]

Even after only less than a quarter of a century some of the detail is not entirely clear, but the outline of the story is clear enough. In the summer of 1977 Black gave up the editorship of *NTS* and retired in 1978. It was probably because of these impending changes that in 1977 Professors Anthony Hanson (Hull) and Max Wilcox (Bangor, and formerly a postgraduate pupil of Black's) took over the leadership of Black's group. They had been regular attenders at the international meetings and both had already interested themselves in the issues raised

1. 'Seminar groups' were introduced into SNTS's programme in September 1963 and were first mentioned in *New Testament Studies* 10 (1963–64), p. 306. All journal references in these notes are to *NTS*.

2. This particular Seminar group's interest had of course been represented at earlier meetings of SNTS; a seminar on 'Jewish Exegesis in New Testament Times' was proposed in 1970 (17 [1970–71], p. 347) and was held in 1971 and 1973 (18 [1971–72] p. 377; 20 [1973–74], p. 463). Also cf. *New Testament Studies: Cumulative Index of Volumes 1–31 (1954–1985) and of the Bulletin I–III (1950–1952)* (1986), pp. 88-90.

3. Cf. 22 (1975–76), p. 353; 23 (1976–77), p. 353.

by the New Testament's use of the Old.[4] In taking over Black's group they widened its scope by dropping 'Christological' from its title. Henceforth it was to be devoted to examining the influence of the Old Testament on the New in all its facets, the redeployment of the Scriptures of Judaism by the adherents of the New Covenant, in order to express their understanding of it. *NTS* records the leadership of the group by Hanson and Wilcox from 1977 to 1982,[5] and one number contains a brief account of their first two meetings, when they studied James 1–3 and sought to isolate its Old Testament subtext.[6]

At some point it became clear that the British members of the SNTS Seminar group wanted to meet on another occasion in the year, in addition to the international meeting in the summer, and so in the middle 70s Hanson and Wilcox began to organize a national group, which came to include participants who either did not or could not attend the international gatherings.[7] In 1982 Hanson retired from his chair in Hull and in 1987 Wilcox from his in Bangor, returning to his native Australia.[8] Lionel North had joined the Theology Department in Hull as the Barmby Lecturer in New Testament Studies in 1980, and he succeeded Hanson as Chairman of the Seminar in 1982, a post he relinquished in 1999. Wendy Sproston North, also in Hull, was the Seminar's Secretary from 1979 to 1999.[9]

In the last 20 years the British Seminar has met annually in the spring, to avoid conflict with the international SNTS and the British New Testament Conference meetings later in the year. It has developed independently of parallel groups in the international and British conferences, so much so that it is doubtful whether non-British members of SNTS know of its existence. It would be interesting to learn if other specialist seminar groups, originating under the aegis of SNTS, have developed nationally and independently, or is it the only one, with this

4. See e.g. *Cumulative Index* (n. 2), p. 23.

5. 24 (1977–78), p. 548; 25 (1978–79), p. 528; 26 (1979–80), p. 422; 27 (1980–81), p. 415; 28 (1982), p. 264; 29 (1983), p. 267.

6. 25 (1978–79), pp. 526-27.

7. According to Wilcox, it was at one of these meetings, at Bristol in 1976, that the idea of *JSNT* was floated. Hanson and Wilcox were to become two of its first editors.

8. Anthony Hanson died on 28 May 1991 and Matthew Black on 2 October 1994.

9. Thanks are due to the Theology Department at Hull for the office assistance given to the Secretary.

pedigree, to survive? Once, it was suggested that the Seminar merge with the British New Testament Conference and become one of its seminar groups. The suggestion was not adopted because it became clear that for all our recognition of the topic's importance it would not be the first choice of several who also attended the larger conference which could offer a wide range of interest groups. We agreed to continue as we were.

Various venues have been used: Bristol, Cambridge, Hull and, for several years, Crowther Hall in Selly Oak, Birmingham. But throughout the 90s we have found St. Deiniol's Library, Hawarden, N. Wales, a perfect setting, with access to W.E. Gladstone's famous library made available to members of the Seminar.

There has been very considerable loyalty to the Seminar. One of the reasons has been the smallness and therefore the informality of the occasion. We have made a point of welcoming postgraduate students and encouraging them to participate, usually with a section from their thesis read at one of our five sessions. In this regard, Durham University's Theology Department has been particularly forthcoming.

There has also been a great deal of practical support from the British New Testament 'establishment' (Professors Birdsall, Grabbe, Hooker, O'Neill and Rowland and especially Ellingworth, Goulder and Lindars), but one of the delights has been for colleagues-become-friends to share each year the results of their own investigations. We regard ourselves as a working seminar, focusing on the central theme from a variety of angles and other interests. This variety and flexibility may be another reason why the Seminar has survived. Matthew's Gospel has attracted the attention of Peter Head, Ivor Jones and Maarten Menken; Mark, of Maurice Casey and Joel Marcus; Luke–Acts of Peter Doble and Crispin Fletcher-Louis, and the Johannine literature, of Anthony Hanson, June Higginson, Judith Lieu and Wendy Sproston North. But it is the Pauline corpus which has overwhelmingly been the main attraction: Gervais Angel, Bill Campbell, Colin Hickling, David Instone Brewer, Andrew Lincoln, Alan Lowe, Justin Meggitt, Brian Rosner, Margaret Thrall and John Ziesler have all contributed. Hebrews has been attended to by Paul Ellingworth and Barnabas Lindars; the Catholics by Richard Bauckham and Lionel North; the Revelation by Jan Fekkes and Steve Moyise. Time would fail to list the perspectives from which the theme has been approached, but I should mention the Dead Sea Scrolls, Apocrypha and Pseudepigrapha, Artapanus and

Jewish Proselytism; the *Testimonium Flavianum*, the Testimonia Book hypothesis and Sacred Tatooing! Christology, of course, including the Baptism, the Eucharist, the *Descensus ad Inferos*, the Suffering Servant and the Resurrection, has been central.

With retirement comes kairos for new thinking and development. From 2000 Dr Steve Moyise will be the Seminar's Secretary and from 2002 Professor George Brooke (Manchester) the Chairman, both accomplished scholars. We wish them well. For Wendy and Lionel North 'Hawarden' has been a high point in the year—a delightful setting, old friends, a great theme. We leave, formally at least, with many memories to cheer the passing moments; when a lecturer on Paul the Matchmaker referred to Jn 3.29 to show that the matchmaker's work was complete only when he was assured that conjugal relations had taken place, Barnabas, tongue in cheek, said, 'Oh, I thought the couple were repeating their marriage vows'. A delightful Korean lecturer amused us with 'guns under the blanket'. Michael, never one to pass up an allusion, was once invited to consider the influence of Ezekiel on Philemon. Maurice, always in trepidation about 'the bells', was asked for an example of conflation of Scripture in the Scrolls. Without a moment's hesitation he responded with a section from the Damascus Rule containing the phrase 'and chose the fair neck' (1.14). As quickly some wit retorted, 'From a Transylvanian Scripture, I presume'. Long may it continue![10]

---

10. Anyone interested in the Seminar may contact Dr Steve Moyise, 24 Chiltern Park Avenue, Berkhamsted, Herts, HP4 1EU (Tel: 01442 862285; Fax: 01442 863696; E-Mail: Stevemoyise@compuserve.com).

OLD TESTAMENT

16.14	152	2	136	7.47	181, 182,
16.21-22	156	2.14-36	44		191, 194,
16.22	236	2.30	193		195, 197,
16.23-26	173	2.31	193		205
16.23-24	172, 173,	2.32	44	7.48	137
	178	2.34-35	186	7.49	197, 198
16.26	173	2.34	193	7.50	191, 197,
16.33	158	2.35	198		201
17	168	2.36	205	7.51-53	182, 191,
17.1	180	2.42–6.15	129		199-201
17.6	163	3.11	182	7.51	181, 182,
17.8	163	3.13	73		191, 199-
17.12	149, 156-	3.18	190		201
	58	3.20-21	203	7.52	204
18.4	156	3.20	72, 204	7.53	202
18.8-9	157	3.22	72	7.55-58	199
18.9	149, 155,	4.1	50	7.55-56	202, 203
	158	4.2	50	7.55	203-205
18.31	160	4.6-7	50	7.56	203
18.32	149, 155,	4.11	128	7.57-60	182
	157, 158	4.24-30	73	7.58	182
19.7	55, 147,	4.25-28	190	8.1	182
	160	4.27	73	9.1-2	50
19.19	156	4.30	73	9.22	190
19.24	149, 151,	4.35-36	140	9.31	128
	155, 156	4.36	141	9.36-41	103
19.28-29	156	5.12	182	10.31	177
19.28	149, 150,	5.28	50	10.36	70
	156	6.1	102, 103	10.38	70
19.35	163	6.8–7.56	182	13.27-37	190
19.36-37	149	6.14	137	13.50	112
19.36	149, 150	7.2	205, 206	14.36	141
19.37	150	7.30-31	206	17.2-3	190
20.9	153	7.34	177	17.6-7	243
20.28	55	7.37	72	17.11	190
20.31	163, 170,	7.44-46	201	18.24-28	190
	175	7.44	215	20.32	128
21.24-25	163	7.45-50	236	23.3	81, 97
		7.46-56	192, 204,	24.1	50
Acts			205	26.22-23	190
1.2	203	7.46-50	182	26.22	205
1.8	182	7.46-47	182, 191,	26.27	190
1.9	202, 203		194-96		
1.10	203	7.46	181, 192,	*Romans*	
1.11	203		193, 195,	1–8	230
2–4	72		197, 205,	1–3	247
			206	1	19, 231

INDEX OF AUTHORS